Bootstrapping Microservices, Second Edition

WITH DOCKER, KUBERNETES, GITHUB ACTIONS, AND TERRAFORM

ASHLEY DAVIS

MANNING

SHELTER ISLAND

Manning Publications Co.
20 Baldwin Road
PO Box 761
Shelter Island, NY 11964

Development editor:	Elesha Hyde
Technical editor:	Scott Ling
Review editors:	Adriana Sabo and Dunja Nikitović
Production editor:	Andy Marinkovich
Copy editor:	Julie McNamee
Proofreader:	Katie Tennant
Technical proofreader:	Thorsten P. Weber
Typesetter:	Gordan Salinovic
Cover designer:	Marija Tudor

ISBN 9781633438569
Printed in the United States of America

brief contents

contents

2   *Creating your first microservice*   26

3   *Publishing your first microservice*   57

preface

I first tried building applications with microservices around 2013. That was the year Docker was initially released, but back then, I hadn't heard about it. At that time, we built an application with each microservice running on a separate virtual machine. As you might expect, that was an expensive way to run microservices.

Because of the high running costs, we then opted to create fewer rather than more microservices, pushing more and more functionality into the existing microservices to the point where we couldn't really call them microservices anymore. It was still a distributed application, of course, and it worked well enough, but the services weren't as *micro-sized* as we had hoped.

I already knew at that stage that microservices were a powerful idea, if only they were cheaper. I put microservices back on the shelf but made a note that I should look at them again later.

Over the years, I watched from the sidelines as the tools and technology around microservices developed, powered by the rise (*and rise*) of open source coding. And I looked on as the cost of cloud computing continued to drop, spurred on by competition between vendors. Over time, it was clear that building and running a distributed application with micro-sized components was becoming more cost effective.

After what seemed like a lifetime, in early 2018, I officially returned to the world of microservices. I had two opportunities for which I believed microservices were the right fit. Both were startups. The first was a contract job to bootstrap a new microservices application for a promising young company. The second was building a microservices application for my own startup.

To be successful, I knew that I needed new tools. I needed an effective way to package microservices. I needed a computing platform on which I could deploy microservices. Crucially, I needed to be able to automate deployments.

By then, Docker had already gained a big foothold in our industry, so I knew it was a safe bet as a way to package microservices. I also liked the look of Kubernetes as a computing platform for microservices, but, early on, I was extremely uncertain about it. Kubernetes, however, promised a future of freedom from the tyranny of cloud vendor lock-in—that was very appealing.

At this point, I'd read quite a few books on microservices. These were all interesting, providing good value on a theoretical level. I do enjoy reading the theory, but these books lacked the practical examples that would have helped me smash through my own learning curve. Even as an experienced developer, I was struggling to know where to start! I knew from past experience that bad technical decisions made at the beginning of a project would haunt me to the end.

Learning Kubernetes was especially hard. From the outside, it seemed incredibly difficult to penetrate. But I had a job to do, and I needed a way to deliver software, so I pushed on. The going was tough, and I almost gave up on Kubernetes a few times.

The situation changed when I discovered Terraform. This was the missing piece of the puzzle for me. It's what made Kubernetes understandable and usable to the point where I could do nothing else but commit to using it.

Terraform is the tool that allowed me to describe the infrastructure of my application. I began writing *infrastructure as code*, and it felt like I had moved to the big leagues.

I forced my way through the learning curve, bolstered by my longtime experience of evaluating technology and learning quickly on the job, with a splash of trial and error mixed in for good measure. My efforts delivered software that is performant, flexible, reliable, scalable, and extensible. Through this time, my desire to write this book sparked and grew to the point where I had to take action.

A new mission formed—*I wanted to make microservices more accessible.* I felt compelled to write this book; it's the book I wanted but didn't have. I knew I could help people, and the best way to do that was with a practical book—this book. A book that shows you, step-by-step, that microservices don't have to be difficult or complex; it all depends on your approach and the perspective you take. You now have in your hands the fruits of that labor. I learned the hard way so that you don't have to.

acknowledgments

In *Bootstrapping Microservices, Second Edition,* I share my years of hard-won experience with you. Such experience wouldn't be possible without being surrounded by people who supported and encouraged me.

Many people helped me get where I am today. I wouldn't be a developer without my parents, Garry and Jan, who bought me my first PC. My partner in life, Antonella, has tirelessly supported me through multiple books now. Thank you!

Of course, I thank Manning for the opportunity and Helen Stergius and Elesha Hyde, who edited the first and second editions of this book. Thanks also go to the entire team at Manning for their efforts.

A big thanks goes to Scott Ling and Thorsten Weber for making sure the tech and code were up to scratch. I also thank all the reviewers—Adam Wan, Alceu Rodrigues de Freitas Junior, Allan Makura, Antonio Bruno, Becky Huett, Christopher Forbes, Didier Garcia, Fernando Bernardino, Frankie Thomas-Hockey, John Zoetebier, Juan Jose Rubio Guillamon, Kent Spillner, Maqbool Patel, Mikael Dautrey, Prashant Dwivedi, Roland Andriese, Roman Zhuzha, Sachin Rastogi, Sebastian Zaba, Seungjin Kim, and Tan Wee—your suggestions helped make this book what it is.

Finally, I'd like to thank the first edition readers—your love for this book is what made me come back for a second edition. I wrote this book for you!

about this book

Building applications with microservices—building *distributed applications*—can be a complicated process and difficult to learn. If you're thrown into a modern, complex application, it can be difficult to see the forest for the trees. There's so much more to consider than simply coding, and this isn't an easy journey to take on your own.

To use microservices, we must understand how to build a distributed application. But, by itself, that's not enough. We also must learn the deep and complex tools that are necessary to develop, test, and deploy such an application. How do we assemble a robust toolkit for development? Where do we start?

Along the way are many more questions: How do we package and deploy a microservice? How do we configure our development environment for local testing? How do we get our microservices communicating with each other, and how do we manage the data? Most importantly, how do we deploy our microservices to production? Then, once in production, how do we manage, monitor, and fix problems with potentially hundreds of microservices?

This book, *Bootstrapping Microservices, Second Edition,* answers these questions and more! It's your guide to building an application with microservices, using the latest tools. We'll start from nothing and go all the way to a working microservices application running in production.

You won't find much theory in this book. *Bootstrapping Microservices, Second Edition,* is practical and project based. Together, we'll work through numerous examples of microservices, eventually getting to production, and covering everything you need to know to be a confident microservices developer.

Each example in this book comes with working code that is available on GitHub. You can try it out for yourself and make your own experimental changes.

Who should read this book?

This book is aimed at anyone who wants to learn more about the practical aspects of working with microservices: those who need a clear guide on how to assemble their toolkit and take their application all the way to production. This book doesn't teach coding, so basic coding skills are advised.

> **NOTE** If you have some basic or entry-level experience with modern programming languages such as C#, Java, Python, or JavaScript, you should be able to follow along with this book.

The code examples are as simple as they can be, but this book isn't about the code. It's more about teaching you how to assemble the toolkit you need for building a microservices application.

If you don't have coding experience, but you're a fast learner, you can learn basic JavaScript (through another book, tutorials, videos, etc.) while you read *Bootstrapping Microservices, Second Edition*. Like I said, the code examples are as simple as they can be, so you stand a good chance of being able to read the code and get the gist of it without much coding experience. Our coding adventure starts in chapter 2, where you learn how to build a simple microservice using JavaScript and Node.js.

How this book is organized: A road map

In the 12 chapters of this book, we go from building a single microservice all the way to running multiple microservices in a production-ready Kubernetes cluster. Here's what you'll find in each chapter:

- Chapter 1 is an introduction to microservices and explains why we want to use them.
- Chapter 2 works through building a simple microservice using Node.js and JavaScript. You learn how to use live reload for a more streamlined development process.
- Chapter 3 introduces Docker for packaging and publishing our microservice to get it ready for deployment.
- Chapter 4 scales up to multiple microservices and introduces Docker Compose for simulating our microservices application on our development computer during development. We then cover data management for microservices, including having a database and external file storage.
- Chapter 5 upgrades our development environment for whole application live reload. We then cover communications among microservices, including HTTP for direct messaging and RabbitMQ for indirect messaging.

- Chapter 6 introduces Kubernetes. We start by deploying our application to our local Kubernetes instance. Then, we create a Kubernetes cluster in the cloud and deploy our application to it.
- Chapter 7 uses Terraform to create our infrastructure (container registry and Kubernetes cluster) using infrastructure as code.
- Chapter 8 builds a continuous deployment (CD) pipeline for a microservice using GitHub Actions.
- Chapter 9 shows how we can apply multiple levels of automated testing to microservices.
- Chapter 10 is an overview of the example application and a review of the skills you learned so far while deploying the example application for yourself.
- Chapter 11 explores the ways we can build reliable and fault-tolerant microservices and then monitor them to help maintain a healthy application.
- Chapter 12 wraps up the book by showing practical ways your microservices application can be scaled to support your growing business and can be organized to manage your growing development team. It also touches on security, refactoring a monolith, and how to build with microservices on a budget.

Changes since the first edition

A lot has changed since the first edition! Here's a summary:

- There's an all-new chapter 6, with revised and improved coverage of Kubernetes, including deployment to the local Kubernetes instance that comes with Docker Desktop.
- I changed the deployment model for Kubernetes to use kubectl and Kubernetes YAML files instead of using Terraform for deployments (originally, I thought this was the simplest way to teach Kubernetes deployments, but since then, I've changed my mind).
- There's an all-new chapter 8 on continuous deployment (CD) with GitHub Actions, replacing the older chapter on BitBucket Pipelines.
- I converted from Cypress to Playwright in chapter 9 on automated testing.
- Observability, which has been gaining in popularity since the first edition, is mentioned in chapter 11.
- Mono-repos and the ability to have multiple CD pipelines per code repository with GitHub are now covered in chapter 12.
- You'll find expanded coverage of monoliths versus microservices and the spectrum of options in between these.
- All software has been updated to the latest versions.
- Much of the code has been simplified and streamlined for easier understanding.
- Many changes and improvements have been made based on reader feedback from the first edition.
- Many improvements have been made to the text and graphics.

About the code

This book contains many examples of source code both in numbered listings and in line with normal text. In both cases, source code is formatted in a `fixed-width font like this` to separate it from ordinary text.

In many cases, the original source code has been reformatted; we've added line breaks and reworked indentation to accommodate the available page space in the book. In some cases, even this was not enough, and listings include line-continuation markers (➥). Additionally, comments in the source code have often been removed from the listings when the code is described in the text. Code annotations accompany many of the listings, highlighting important concepts.

You can get executable snippets of code from the liveBook (online) version of this book at https://livebook.manning.com/book/bootstrapping-microservices-second-edition. The complete code for the examples in the book is available for download from the Manning website at www.manning.com, and from GitHub at https://github.com/bootstrapping-microservices-2nd-edition.

You can download a zip file to accompany each chapter (chapters 2–10), or you can use Git to clone the Git code repository for each chapter. Each example is designed to be as simple as possible, self-contained, and easy to run. As you progress through the book, you will run the code in different ways.

We start by running code for a single microservice directly under Node.js (chapter 2), then under Docker (chapter 3). We then run multiple microservices under Docker Compose (chapters 4 and 5).

Then, we do our first deployments to Kubernetes (chapter 6), followed up by creating our infrastructure using Terraform (chapter 7). Then we set up CD using GitHub Actions (chapter 8). Next, we get into some automated testing using Jest and Playwright (chapter 9). Finally, we review the entire application and deploy it to production (chapter 10).

Throughout the code examples, I aim to follow standard conventions and best practices. I ask that you provide feedback and report any issues through GitHub.

liveBook discussion forum

Purchase of *Bootstrapping Microservices, Second Edition*, includes free access to liveBook, Manning's online reading platform. Using liveBook's exclusive discussion features, you can attach comments to the book globally or to specific sections or paragraphs. It's a snap to make notes for yourself, ask and answer technical questions, and receive help from the author and other users. To access the forum, go to https://livebook .manning.com/book/bootstrapping-microservices-second-edition/discussion. You can also learn more about Manning's forums and the rules of conduct at https://livebook .manning.com/discussion.

Manning's commitment to our readers is to provide a venue where a meaningful dialogue between individual readers and between readers and the author can take place. It is not a commitment to any specific amount of participation on the part of the author, whose contribution to the forum remains voluntary (and unpaid). We suggest you try asking the author some challenging questions lest their interest stray! The forum and the archives of previous discussions will be accessible from the publisher's website for as long as the book is in print.

Staying up to date

For infrequent updates on *Bootstrapping Microservices, Second Edition,* and related content, please join the email list here: www.bootstrapping-microservices.com/.

about the author

 **ASHLEY DAVIS** is a software craftsman, entrepreneur, and author with more than 25 years of experience in software development, from coding to managing teams to founding companies. He has worked for a range of companies, from the tiniest startups to the largest internationals. Along the way, he has contributed back to the community through his writing and open source coding.

Ashley is the creator of Data-Forge Notebook, a notebook-style desktop application for exploratory coding and data visualization using JavaScript. He is now writing *Rapid Fullstack Development* (go to https://rapidfullstackdevelopment.com/ to learn more).

For updates on Ashley's writing, open source coding, and more, follow him on X @codecapers. For more on Ashley's background, see his web page (www.codecapers .com.au/about) or his LinkedIn page (www.linkedin.com/in/ashleydavis75).

ABOUT THE TECHNICAL EDITOR

Scott Ling is an executive technical consultant with more than 30 years of experience covering multiple programming languages, technologies, and business areas. Most recently he has focused on the Rust, Go, and Zig programming languages and various applications of APIs, microservices, AI, and ML across the enterprise.

about the cover illustration

The figure on the cover of *Bootstrapping Microservices, Second Edition,* is captioned "Catalan" or a man from Catalonia, in northeast Spain. The illustration is taken from a collection by Jacques Grasset de Saint-Sauveur, published in 1797. Each illustration is finely drawn and colored by hand.

In those days, it was easy to identify where people lived and what their trade or station in life was just by their dress. Manning celebrates the inventiveness and initiative of the computer business with book covers based on the rich diversity of regional culture centuries ago, brought back to life by pictures from collections such as this one.

Why microservices?

1

This chapter covers

- The learning approach of this book
- The what and why of microservices
- The benefits and drawbacks of using microservices
- What's wrong with the monolith?
- The basics of microservices design
- A quick overview of the application we build

As software continues to become larger and more complicated, we need improved methods of managing and mitigating its complexity. As it grows alongside our business, we need better ways of dividing up the software so that multiple teams can participate in the construction effort.

As our demanding customer base grows, we must also be able to expand our software. At the same time, our application should be fault tolerant and able to scale quickly to meet peak demand. How do we then meet the demands of modern business while evolving and developing our application?

The *microservices* architectural pattern plays a pivotal role in contemporary software development. A *distributed application* composed of microservices solves these problems and more, but typically it's more difficult, more complex, and more time consuming to architect than a traditional *monolithic application*. If these terms—microservices, distributed application, and monolithic application—are new to you, they will be explained soon.

Conventional wisdom says that microservices are too difficult. We're told to start "monolith-first" and later restructure to microservices when necessary to scale. But I argue that this attitude doesn't make the job of building an application any easier! Your application is always going to tend toward complexity, and, eventually, you'll need to scale it. When you do decide you need to change, you now have the extremely difficult job of safely converting your monolith to microservices when staff and customers already depend on it.

Now is also the perfect time to be building microservices. The confluence of various factors—accessible and cheap cloud infrastructure, ever-improving tools, and increasing opportunities for automation—is driving an industry-wide movement toward smaller and smaller services, aka *microservices*. Applications become more complex over time, but microservices offer us better ways to manage such complexity. There is no better time than now to go "microservices-first."

In this book, I'll show you that a microservices-first approach is no longer as daunting as it once was. I believe the balance is firmly tipping toward microservices. The remaining problem is that *learning* microservices is difficult. The learning curve is steep and holds back many developers in their quest to build microservices. Together, we'll break the learning curve. We'll say "Boo" to the monolith, and we'll build from the ground up a simple but complete video-streaming application using microservices.

> **The architecture spectrum**
>
> Not convinced that microservices are the way to go? Our reality is that we aren't just making a choice between monolith and microservices. There's actually a continuum of choices available to us. So, this book isn't really just about microservices; ultimately, it's about having a choice of where we position ourselves on that spectrum. For any given project, we might choose monolith, microservices, or somewhere in the middle. But if you don't know how to use the tools to build with microservices, then you won't have the choice—you'll be forced to create a monolith for every project. This book gives you the tools that open up the full monolith–microservices spectrum (more on that soon). It gives you the freedom to choose where you land on that spectrum. Where you go with that is up to you.

1.1   *This book is practical*

Why are you reading this book? You're reading this because you want or need to build a microservices application, which is an important skill set for modern developers, but it's a difficult skill set to obtain, and you need some guidance. You may have read other books on microservices and been left wondering, where do I begin? I understand your torment.

Microservices are tough to learn. Not only do you have to learn deep and complicated tools, you must also learn to build a distributed application. This requires new techniques, technologies, and protocols for communication. There's a lot to learn in anyone's book.

In this book though, we cut through the seemingly impenetrable learning curve of building microservices applications. We'll start as simple as possible, and, piece-by-piece, we'll build up to deploying a more complex microservices application to production.

This book is about busting through the learning curve and bootstrapping a working application that will last indefinitely and that we can continuously update and build on to satisfy the ongoing and changing needs of our customers and users. Figure 1.1 illustrates this idea of cutting through the learning curve. While our example application is small and simple, from the start, we'll build in pathways to scalability that will later allow it to be expanded out to a truly massive distributed application.

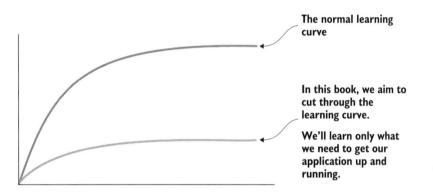

Figure 1.1   Cutting through the learning curve. In this book, we'll learn only the bare minimum—just enough to bootstrap our application.

How is this book different from all the other books on microservices? Other books are notably theoretical. That's a good approach for an experienced developer or architect looking to broaden their knowledge, but acquiring practical skills that way is challenging and doesn't help you navigate the minefield of bootstrapping a new application. The technical choices you make at project inception can haunt you for a long time.

This book is different; this book *is not* theoretical. We'll take a practical approach to learning. There is a small amount of theory interspersed throughout, and we'll actually build a substantial microservices application. We'll start from nothing and work through bringing our application into existence and getting it into production. We'll build and test the application on our development computer and, ultimately, deploy it to the cloud.

This book won't teach you everything; there's far too much to learn for any single book to do that. Instead, we'll take a different approach: we'll learn practically the minimum that is necessary to bootstrap a new application and get it in front of our customers.

Together, we'll get our microservices application off the ground without having to learn the deepest details of any of the tools or technologies. An example of this book's learning model is illustrated in figure 1.2.

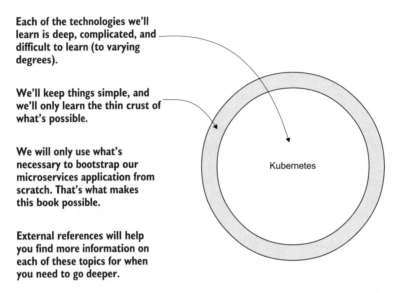

Each of the technologies we'll learn is deep, complicated, and difficult to learn (to varying degrees).

We'll keep things simple, and we'll only learn the thin crust of what's possible.

We will only use what's necessary to bootstrap our microservices application from scratch. That's what makes this book possible.

External references will help you find more information on each of these topics for when you need to go deeper.

Kubernetes

Figure 1.2   The learning model for this book. We'll skim the surface of these deep and complicated technologies to use only what's necessary to bootstrap our application.

This book is about building a microservices application, starting with nothing. But some people have already asked why I didn't write this book to show how to convert a monolith to a microservices application. This is something that many people would like to learn.

I wrote the book in this way because it's much easier to learn how to write an application from scratch than it is to learn how to refactor an existing application. I also believe these skills are useful because, in time, more and more applications will be written microservices-first.

In any case, refactoring an existing application is much more complicated than building a fresh application. It's a process with much complexity and depends heavily on the particulars of the legacy codebase. I make the presumption that it will be easier for you to figure out your own monolith conversion strategy once you know (once you've experienced) how to create a greenfield (new) microservices application.

I can assure you that when you can build an application microservices-first, you'll be much better equipped to clearly see a route from your existing monolith to microservices. That journey from monolith to microservices will no doubt still be demanding, so stay tuned. In chapter 12, we'll discuss more about converting from monolith to microservices.

Throughout this book, you'll learn concrete and practical techniques for getting a microservices application off the ground. Of course, there are many diverse ways to go about this and many different tools you could use. I'm teaching you one single recipe and one set of tools (albeit a popular toolset). You'll also get many opinions from me, and I'm sure you'll disagree with at least some of them. That's okay because this book isn't intended to be the gospel of microservices—it's simply a starting point. No doubt, you'll find many ways to improve on this recipe, add your own techniques to it, throw out the parts you don't like, and enhance those that you do for your own situation.

Other experienced developers will, of course, already have their own opinions and their own recipes. What I'm trying to say is that this is my way, and it's just one of a multitude of ways that can work; however, I can attest that I've tried every technique in this book in production on *real projects* and found these to be a set of techniques that generally work well. So, without further ado, let's commence our journey into microservices.

1.2 What will you learn?

You can't learn everything about building with microservices just from reading a book. But this book will take you a long way, especially if you try running the code examples and then experimenting with them.

Here is the journey we'll take together. Starting with nothing, we'll create a single microservice and run it on our local computer for development and testing. Next, we'll scale up to running multiple microservices on our local computer, still for development and testing. Eventually, we'll create a Kubernetes cluster and deploy our microservices to the cloud, thereby completing our journey and getting our application in front of our customers. Along the way, you'll learn about how to manage data, how our microservices can communicate with each other, how to do testing, and how to create an automated deployment pipeline.

There's a lot to cover, but we'll progress from easy to more difficult. Over 12 chapters, we'll work up to a more complex application and the infrastructure that supports it, but we'll do it in incremental steps so that you never get lost. After reading this book and practicing the skills taught, you should be able to

- Create individual microservices
- Package and publish microservices using Docker
- Develop a microservices application on your development computer using Docker Compose
- Test your code, microservices, and application using Jest and Playwright
- Integrate third-party servers into your application (e.g., MongoDB and RabbitMQ)
- Communicate between microservices using HTTP and RabbitMQ messages
- Store the data and files needed by your microservices
- Deploy your microservices to a production Kubernetes cluster
- Create a production infrastructure using Terraform
- Create a continuous deployment pipeline that automatically deploys your application as you push changes to your code repository on GitHub

1.3   *What do you need to know?*

You might be wondering what you need to know going into this book. I've written this book with as few assumptions as possible about what you already know. We're going on a journey that takes you from absolute basics all the way through to some very complicated concepts. I think there's something here for everyone, no matter how much experience you might have already as a developer.

It's best coming into this book if you have some entry-level understanding of computer programming. I don't think you'll need much, so long as you can read code and get the gist of what it's doing. But don't worry; I'll explain as much as possible about anything important that is happening in the code.

If you have a background in programming, you'll have no problem following along with the examples in this book. If you're learning programming while reading this book, you could find it challenging, but not impossible, and you might have to put in extra work.

This book uses Node.js for examples of microservices, but starting out, you don't need to know JavaScript or Node.js. You'll pick up enough along the way to follow along. This book also uses Microsoft Azure for examples of production deployment. Again, starting out, you don't need to know anything about Azure either.

Rest assured that this book *isn't* about Node.js or Azure; it's about building microservices applications using modern tooling such as Docker, Kubernetes, and Terraform. Most of the skills you'll take away from this book are transferable to other languages and other cloud providers, but I had to pick a programming language and cloud vendor that I could use to demonstrate the techniques in this book, so I chose Node.js and Azure. That's a combination I've used extensively in production for my own software products.

If Node.js and Azure aren't your thing, with some extra research and experimentation on your part, you'll be able to figure out how to replace Node.js and JavaScript with your favorite programming language and replace Azure with your preferred cloud vendor. In fact, the main reason I use Docker, Kubernetes, and Terraform in the first place is that these tools offer freedom—freedom of choice for programming language and freedom from cloud vendor lock-in.

1.4   *Managing complexity*

A microservice application, like any application, will become more complex over time—but it doesn't need to start that way! This book takes the approach that we can begin from a simple starting point and that each iteration of development can also be just as simple. In addition, each microservice is small and simple. Microservices are known to be more difficult than building a monolith, but I'm hoping this book will help you find an easier path through the difficulty.

Microservices give us a way to manage complexity at a granular level, and it's the level we work at almost every day—the level of a single microservice. At that level, microservices aren't complex. In fact, to earn the name *microservice*, they have to be small and simple. A single microservice is intended to be manageable by a single developer or a small team!

We'll use microservices to divide up our complex application into small and simple parts that have hard boundaries. We can divide up a monolith in the same way, but it's much harder to keep the parts distinct from each other—they tend to become tangled up over time. This difference between monolith and microservices is illustrated in figure 1.3.

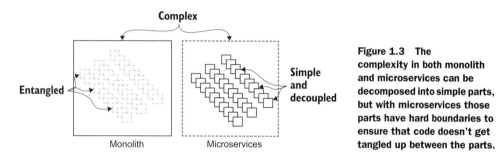

Figure 1.3 The complexity in both monolith and microservices can be decomposed into simple parts, but with microservices those parts have hard boundaries to ensure that code doesn't get tangled up between the parts.

It's true, though, that through continued development and evolution, a complex system will emerge. There's no denying that a microservices application will become complex. But such complexity doesn't evolve immediately; it takes time. Although our applications tend toward complexity, microservices themselves are the cure to, rather than the cause of, that complexity. Through development and operations, we can use the microservices architecture to manage the growing complexity of our application so that it doesn't become a burden.

It might seem that the infrastructure required for microservices can add significant complexity to our development process. Yes, to some extent this is the truth, but then again, all applications require infrastructure, and, in my experience, microservices don't add a whole lot more. In fact, you'll see that, by chapter 8, we'll build a continuous deployment pipeline that automates deployment of our application code to production. For any team that does this, they will find that the deployment and operational complexity of microservices tends to fade into the background and seems like magic.

Maybe it's just that we're noticing the complexity of our infrastructure more now because we have to deal with it more frequently. In the past, we had an operations team and possibly a build or testing team that would handle most of that work for us and hide the complexity. More and more, though, microservices are handing power back to the developers, allowing us to clearly see the complexity that was always there in our development, testing, and operational infrastructure.

Any complexity added by microservices must be offset by their benefits. Like all design or architectural patterns, to get value from microservices, we must be sure that their advantages outweigh the cost of using them. That's a tough call that we must make on a project-by-project basis, but for an increasing number of scenarios, microservices will more than pull their weight.

A microservices application is a form of *complex adaptive system*, where complexity emerges naturally from the interactions of its constituent parts. Even though the system as a whole can become far too complex for any mere mortal to understand, each of its components remains small, manageable, and easy to understand. That's how microservices help us deal with complexity: by breaking the complexity apart into small, simple, and manageable chunks. But don't worry—the example application we'll build in this book isn't very complex.

Development with microservices (with help from our tools and automation) allows us to build extremely large and scalable applications without being overwhelmed by the complexity. And, after reading this book, you'll be able to zoom in and look at any part of the most complex microservices application and find its components to be straightforward and understandable.

1.5   *What is a microservice?*

Before we can understand a microservices application, we must first understand what it means to be a microservice.

> **DEFINITION** A *microservice* is a small and independent software process (an instance of a computer program) that runs on its own deployment schedule and can be updated independently.

Let's break that definition down. A microservice is a small, independent software process that has its own separate deployment frequency, which means it must be possible to update each microservice independently from other microservices.

A microservice can be owned and operated either by a single developer or a team of developers. A developer or team might also manage multiple other microservices. Each developer/team is responsible for the microservice(s) they own. In the modern world, this often includes development, testing, deployment, and operations. We might find, however, that when we work for a small company or a startup (as I do) or when we're learning (as you are in this book), we must manage multiple microservices or, indeed, even an entire microservices application on our own.

An individual microservice might be exposed to the outside world so our customers can interact with it, or it might be purely an internal service and not externally accessible. The microservice typically has access to a database, file storage, or some other method of state persistence. Figure 1.4 illustrates these internal and external relationships.

By itself, a single microservice doesn't do much. A well-designed system, however, can be decomposed into such simple services. The services must collaborate with each other to provide the features and functionality of the greater application. This brings us to the microservices application.

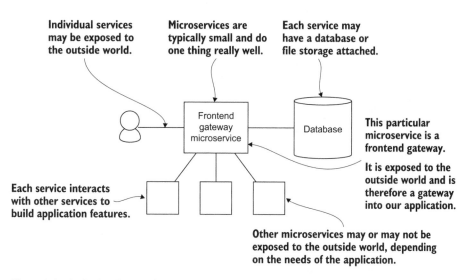

Figure 1.4   A single microservice can have connections to the outside world or other services, and it also can have a database and/or attached file storage.

1.6   What is a microservices application?

A microservices application is traditionally known as a *distributed application,* a system composed of components that live in separate processes and communicate via the network. Each service or component resides on a logically distinct (virtual) computer and sometimes even on a physically separate computer.

> **DEFINITION**   A *microservices application* is a distributed program composed of many small services that collaborate to achieve the features and functionality of the overall project.

Typically, a microservices application has one or more services that are externally exposed to allow users to interact with the system. Figure 1.5 shows two such services acting as gateways for web-based and mobile phone users. You can also see in figure 1.5 that many services are working together within the *cluster.* It's called a cluster because it's a group of computers that are represented to us (the developers) as a single cohesive slab of computing power to be directed however we like. Somewhere close by, we also have a database server. In figure 1.5, it's shown to be outside the cluster, but it could just as easily be hosted inside the cluster. We'll talk more about this in chapter 4.

The cluster is hosted on a cluster orchestration platform; in this book, we use Kubernetes for that purpose. *Orchestration* is the automated management of our services. This is what Kubernetes does for us—it helps us deploy and manage our services.

The cluster itself, our database, and other virtual infrastructure are all hosted on our chosen cloud vendor. We'll learn how to deploy this infrastructure on Microsoft Azure, but with some work on your own, you can change the examples in this book to deploy to Amazon Web Services (AWS) or Google Cloud Platform (GCP).

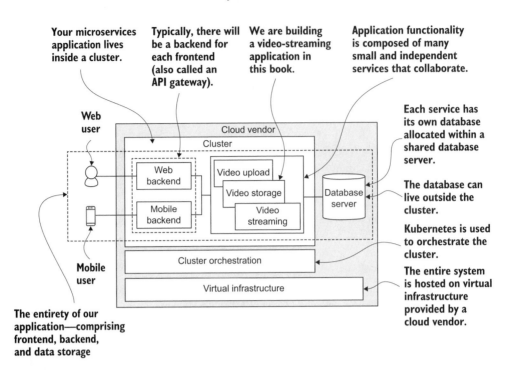

Your microservices application lives inside a cluster.

Typically, there will be a backend for each frontend (also called an API gateway).

We are building a video-streaming application in this book.

Application functionality is composed of many small and independent services that collaborate.

Each service has its own database allocated within a shared database server.

The database can live outside the cluster.

Kubernetes is used to orchestrate the cluster.

The entire system is hosted on virtual infrastructure provided by a cloud vendor.

The entirety of our application—comprising frontend, backend, and data storage

Figure 1.5   A microservices application is composed of multiple, small independent services running in a cluster.

A microservices application can take many forms, is very flexible, and can be arranged to suit many situations. Any particular application might have a familiar overall structure, but the services it contains will do different jobs, depending on the needs of our customers and the domain of our business.

1.7   *What's wrong with the monolith?*

What is a monolith and what is so wrong with it that we'd like to use microservices instead? Although distributed computing has been around for decades, applications were often built in the monolithic form. This is the way the majority of software was developed before the cloud revolution and microservices. Figure 1.6 shows what the services in a simple video-streaming application might look like and compares a monolithic version of the application with a microservices version.

> **DEFINITION**   A *monolith* is an entire application that runs in a single process.

It's much easier to build a monolith than a microservices application. You need fewer technical and architectural skills. It's a great starting point when building a new application, say, for an early-stage product, and you want to test the validity of the business model before you commit to the higher technical investment required by a microservices application.

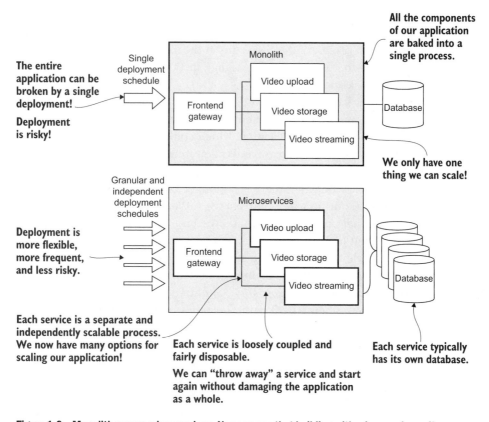

Figure 1.6 Monolith versus microservices. You can see that building with microservices offers many advantages over the traditional monolithic application.

A monolith is a great option for early throwaway prototyping. It also might be all that you need for an application that has a small scope or an application that stabilizes quickly and doesn't need to evolve or grow over its lifetime. If your application will always be this small, it makes sense for it to be a monolith.

Deciding whether to go monolith-first or microservices-first is a balancing act that has traditionally been won by the monolith. However, in this book, I'll show you, given the improvements in modern tooling and with cheap and convenient cloud infrastructure, that it's important to consider going microservices-first or at least push toward the microservices end of the spectrum (more on the spectrum of possibilities soon).

Most products generally need to grow and evolve, and as your monolith grows bigger and has more useful features, it becomes more difficult to justify throwing away the throwaway prototype. So, down the road, you might find yourself stuck with the monolith at a time when what you really need is the flexibility, security, and scalability of a microservices application.

Monoliths come with a host of potential problems. They always start out small, and we always have the best of intentions of keeping the code clean and well organized. A good team of developers can keep a monolith elegant and well organized for many years. But as time passes, the vision can be lost, or sometimes there wasn't a strong vision in the first place. All the code runs in the same process, so there are no barriers and nothing to stop us from writing a huge mess of spaghetti code that will be nearly impossible to pick apart later.

Staff turnover has a big effect. As developers leave the team, they take crucial knowledge with them, and they are replaced by new developers who will have to develop their own mental model of the application, which could easily be at odds with the original vision. Time passes, code changes hands many times, and these negative forces conspire to devolve the codebase into what is called a *big ball of mud*. This name denotes the messy state of the application when there is no longer a discernible architecture.

Updating the code for a monolith is a risky affair—it's all or nothing. When you push a code change that breaks the monolith, the entire application ceases operation, your customers are left high and dry, and your company bleeds money. We might only want to change a single line of code, but still, we must deploy the entire monolith and risk breaking it. This risk stokes deployment fear, and fear slows our pace of development.

In addition, as the structure of the monolith degenerates, our risk of breaking it in unanticipated ways increases. Testing becomes harder and breeds yet more deployment fear. Experimentation and innovation eventually grind to a halt. Have I convinced you that you should try microservices? Wait, there's more!

Due to the sheer size of an established monolith, testing is problematic, and because of its extremely low level of granularity, it's difficult to scale. Eventually, the monolith expands to consume the physical limits of the machine it runs on. As the aging monolith consumes more and more physical resources, it becomes very expensive to run. I've witnessed this! To be fair, this kind of eventuality might be a long way off for any monolith, but even after just a few years of growth, the monolith leads to a place that we would prefer not to be.

Despite the eventual difficulties with the monolith, it remains the simplest way to bootstrap a new application. Shouldn't we always start with a monolith and later restructure when we need to scale? My answer: it depends.

Many applications will always be small. There are plenty of small monoliths in the wild that do their job well and don't need to be scaled or evolved. They aren't growing, and they don't suffer the problems of growth. If you believe your application will remain small and simple and doesn't need to evolve, you should definitely build it as a monolith.

However, there are many applications that we can easily predict will benefit from a microservices-first approach. These are the kinds of applications we know will continually be evolved over many years. Other applications that can benefit are those that need to be flexible or scalable or that have security constraints from the start. Building these types of applications is much easier if you start with microservices because converting from an existing monolith is difficult and risky.

By all means, if you need to validate your business idea first, do so by initially building a monolith. However, even in this case, I would argue that with the right tooling, prototyping with microservices isn't much more difficult than prototyping with a monolith. After all, what is a monolith if not a single large service?

You might even consider using the techniques in this book to bootstrap your monolith as a single service within a Kubernetes cluster. When the time comes to decompose to microservices, you're already in the best possible position to do so, and, at your leisure, you can start chipping microservices off the monolith. With the ease of automated deployment that modern tooling offers, it's easy to tear down and recreate your application or create replica environments for development and testing. If you want or need to create a monolith first, you can still benefit from the techniques and technologies presented in this book.

If you do start with a monolith, for your own sanity and as early as possible, either throw it away and replace it or incrementally restructure it into microservices. We'll talk more about breaking up an existing monolith in chapter 12.

1.8 Why are microservices popular now?

Why does it seem that microservices are exploding in popularity right now? Is this just a passing fad? No, it's not a passing fad. Distributed computing has been around for a long time and has always had many advantages over monolithic applications. Traditionally, though, it has been more complex and more costly to build applications in this way. Developers only reached for these more powerful application architectures for the most demanding problems: those where the value of the solution would far outweigh the cost of the implementation.

In recent times, however, with the advent of cloud technology, virtualization, and the creation of automated tools for managing our virtual infrastructure, it has become much less expensive to build such distributed systems. As it became cheaper to replace monolithic applications with distributed applications, we naturally considered the ways this could improve the structure of our applications. In doing so, the components of our distributed systems have shrunk to the tiniest possible size so that now we call them microservices.

That's why microservices are popular now. Not only are they a good way to build complex modern applications, but they are also increasingly cost effective. Distributed computing has become more accessible than ever before, so naturally more developers are using it. Right now, it appears to be nearing critical mass, so it's reaching the mainstream.

But why are microservices so good? How do they improve the structure of our application? This question leads to the benefits of microservices.

1.9 Benefits of microservices

Building distributed applications provides many advantages. Each service can potentially have its own dedicated CPU, memory, and other resources. Typically, though, we share physical infrastructure between many services, and that's what makes microservices cost effective. But we're also able to separate these out when necessary so that the services with the heaviest workloads can be allocated dedicated resources. We can say that each small service is independently scalable, and this gives us a fine-grained ability to tune the performance of our application. Here are the benefits of microservices:

- *Allow for fine-grained control*—Microservices allow us to build an application with fine-grained control over scalability.
- *Minimize deployment risk*—Microservices help us minimize deployment risk while maximizing the pace of development.
- *Allow us to choose our own tech stack*—Microservices allow us to choose the right stack for the task at hand so that we aren't constrained to a single tech stack.

Having a distributed application offers us the potential for better reliability and reduced deployment risk. When we update a particular service, we can do so without the risk of breaking the entire application. Of course, we might still risk breaking a part of the application, but that is better and easier to recover from than bringing down the entire application. When problems occur, it's easier to roll back just a small part of the system rather than the whole. Reduced deployment risk has the knock-on effect of promoting frequent deployments, and this is essential to agility and sustaining a fast pace of development.

These benefits are nothing new. After all, we've been building distributed applications for a long time, but such systems are now cheaper to build, and the tools are now easier to use. It's easier than ever before to build applications this way and to reap the rewards. As costs decreased and deployment convenience increased, our services tended toward the micro level, and this brought its own complement of benefits.

Smaller services are quicker to boot than larger services. This helps make our system easier to scale because we can quickly replicate any service that becomes overloaded. Smaller services are also easier to test and troubleshoot. Even though testing an overall microservices system can still be difficult, we can more easily prove that each individual part of it is working as expected.

Building applications with many small and independently upgradeable parts means we can have an application that is more amenable to being extended, evolved, and rearranged over its lifetime. This combination of flexibility and safety encourages experimentation and innovation that can really benefit the business. The fact that we've enforced process boundaries between our components means that we'll never be tempted to write spaghetti code. However, if we do write terrible code (we all have bad days, right?), the effect of bad code is controlled and isolated because every microservice (to earn the name) should be small enough that it can be thrown away and rewritten within a matter of weeks, if not days. In this sense, we're *designing our code for disposability*. We're designing it to be replaced over time. The ongoing and iterative replacement of our application is not only made possible but also actively encouraged, and this is what we need for our application architecture to survive the continuously evolving needs of the modern business.

Another benefit that really excites developers using microservices is that we're no longer constrained to a single technology stack for our application. Each service in our application can potentially contain any tech stack. For larger companies, this means that different teams can choose their own tech stack based on their experience or based on the stack that is best for the job at hand. Various tech stacks can coexist within our cluster and work together using shared protocols and communication mechanisms.

Being able to change between tech stacks is important for the long-term health of the application. As the tech landscape evolves, and it always does, older tech stacks fall out of favor and must eventually be replaced by new ones. Microservices create a structure that can be progressively converted to newer tech stacks. As developers, we no longer need to languish on out-of-date technologies.

Technology (tech) stack

Your technology stack is the combination of tools, software, and frameworks on which you build each microservice. You can think of it as the fundamental underlying elements needed by your application.

Some stacks have names, for example, MEAN (MongoDB, Express, Angular, Node.js) or LAMP (Linux, Apache, MySQL, PHP). But your stack is just the combination of tools you use, and it doesn't need a name to be valid.

When building a monolith, we have to choose a single tech stack, and we have to stay with that stack for as long as the monolith remains in operation. The microservices architecture is appealing because it gives us the potential to use multiple tech stacks within one application. This allows us to change our tech stack over time as we evolve our application.

1.10   Drawbacks of microservices

This chapter would not be complete without addressing the main problems that people have with microservices:

- Microservices require a higher level of technical skills.
- Building distributed applications is hard.
- Microservices have scalable difficulty.
- People often fear complexity.

1.10.1   Higher-level technical skills

The first problem is the steep learning curve. Learning how to build microservices requires that we learn a complicated and deep set of technologies. Although learning how to build microservices will still be difficult, this book will help you shortcut the learning curve.

> **NOTE** I can understand if you feel daunted by what's in front of you. But recently, huge progress has been made in the development of tooling for building distributed applications. Our tools are now more sophisticated, easier to use, and most importantly, more automatable than ever before.

Ordinarily, it might take months or longer to conquer the learning curve on your own—mastering any of these tools takes significant time! But this book takes a different approach. Together, we'll only learn the bare minimum necessary to bootstrap our application and get it running in production. Then, we'll produce a simple but working microservices application.

1.10.2 *Building distributed applications is hard*

Not only must we learn new technologies to build with microservices, we must also learn the new techniques, principles, patterns, and tradeoffs required for building distributed applications. Building distributed applications is hard. Running them is also hard! Understanding them in their entirety is even more difficult. To consider any new sort of technology, we must understand the costs versus the benefits. Microservices are no different. Microservices come with important benefits, but we still have to ask ourselves, are the benefits worth how much it will cost us?

To better understand how hard it is to build software this way, read this summary of the "Eight Fallacies of Distributed Computing" to see the kinds of false assumptions we make when building these kinds of applications: https://nighthacks.com/jag/res/Fallacies.html.

In this book, you'll learn the basics of structuring distributed applications. We'll cut through the confusion and just focus on the practical concerns of getting our application to our customers.

1.10.3 *Microservices have scalable difficulty*

I hate to break it to you, but microservices aren't silver bullets. Microservices can't solve all our problems, and, in fact, they can even make our problems significantly worse. Microservices are scalable not only for performance and development but also for difficulty! Microservices can scale up whatever problems you're already having with your monolith.

It's more difficult to build a microservices application than to build a monolith. We need the skills (see section 1.10.1), and, above all, we need to have invested in good automation. We also need good tools to help us manage the system. Just understanding how microservices communicate with each other is a problem that grows exponentially with the number of services in our application.

Having the right skillset combined with good automation and good tooling makes all the difference and can make microservices seem easy. But you're in for a big shock if you can't or won't invest in skills, automation, and tooling. Even though you can survive in the early days of your microservices application without much, managing a growing fleet of microservices will become increasingly overwhelming, and you'll need all the help you can get to be successful in managing it.

1.10.4 *People often fear complexity*

Building a microservices application, or any distributed application, is going to be more complicated than building the equivalent monolith. It's hard to argue with this.

The first thing I would say is that, yes, building a monolith is simpler in the beginning, and, in many cases, it's the right decision. If your application is one of those that must later be converted or restructured to microservices, however, then you should consider the eventual cost of unraveling your big ball of mud.

My main advice is not to be frightened by complexity; it happens whether we like it or not. Fortunately, microservices offer us tangible ways of managing complexity.

If you've thought through the benefits versus the costs, you might concede that building with microservices, at least in certain situations, is actually less complicated than building a monolith. Consider this: *any* significant application is going to become complex. If not at the start, it *will* grow more complex over time. You can't hide from complexity in modern software development; it *always* catches up with you eventually. Instead, let's take control of this situation and meet the complexity head-on. What we want are better tools to help manage complexity. Microservices as an architectural pattern is one such tool.

1.10.5 *Bringing the pain forward*

Think of microservices as a way to *bring the pain forward* to a place where it's more economical to deal with. Yes, it can be more difficult working with microservices than working with a monolith, but sometimes dealing with problems (e.g., complexity) earlier can pay dividends throughout the life of the project.

What do we get in return for the effort we invest? Microservices help us deal with complexity in our application. They provide hard boundaries that prevent us from writing spaghetti code. Microservices allow us to more easily rewire, scale, upgrade, and replace our application over time. Microservices also force us to apply better design. We can't prevent complexity, but we can manage it, and modern tooling for distributed applications is already here to help us.

1.11 *Modern tooling for microservices*

This book is all about the tooling. Together, we'll learn the basics of a number of different tools. To start with, we must be able to create a microservice. We'll use Java-Script and Node.js to do this, and we'll cover the basics of that in the next chapter.

We're using Node.js because that's my weapon of choice. However, as far as microservices are concerned, the tech stack within the service isn't particularly important. We could just as easily build our microservices with Python, Ruby, Java, Go, or virtually any other language.

We'll encounter numerous tools along our journey, but these are the most important ones:

- *Docker*—To package and publish our services
- *Docker Compose*—To test our microservices application on our development computer
- *Kubernetes*—To host our application in the cloud
- *Terraform*—To build our production infrastructure in the cloud
- *GitHub Actions*—To build a continuous deployment pipeline

The technological landscape is always changing, and so are the tools. So why should we learn any particular toolset when the tools are constantly outdated and replaced? Well, it's because we'll always need good tools to work effectively. And with better tools, we can do a better job, or maybe we just get to do the same job but more effectively. Either way, our tools help us be more productive.

I selected the tools for this book because they make the job of building microservices applications significantly easier and quicker. All technologies change over time, but I don't think these particular tools are going anywhere soon. They are popular, are currently the best we have, and all fill useful positions in our toolkit.

Of course, these tools will eventually be replaced, but hopefully, in the meantime, we'll have extracted significant value and built many good applications. When the tools do change, they will certainly be replaced by better tools (if they aren't better, we won't migrate) that lift the bar of abstraction even higher, making our jobs easier and less frustrating.

Docker is the one tool of them all that is ubiquitous. It seems to have come from nowhere and taken over our industry. Kubernetes isn't quite as ubiquitous as Docker, although it does have a strong future and seems on track to be the computing platform of choice for microservices.

Kubernetes allows us to transcend the boundaries of cloud vendors. This is good news if you have ever felt trapped with any cloud provider. We can run our Kubernetes-based application on pretty much any cloud platform, and we have freedom of movement when needed.

Terraform is a relative newcomer, but I think it's a game changer. It's a declarative configuration language that allows us to script the creation of infrastructure in the cloud. The important thing about Terraform is that it's one language that can work with potentially any cloud vendor. No matter which cloud vendor you choose, now or in the future, chances are that Terraform will support it, and you won't have to learn something new.

Think about this for a moment: Terraform means we can easily code the creation of cloud infrastructure. This is something! In the past, we would laboriously and physically piece together infrastructure, but now we're able to create it with code, a concept that is called *infrastructure as code*, which we'll look at in chapter 7.

1.12 *Not just microservices*

You might already know this, but the tools we use in this book weren't actually designed for building microservices—we can also use Docker, Kubernetes, Terraform, and GitHub Actions for building monolithic applications! Although, it might be overkill to create a Kubernetes cluster to host just a single process.

As I've mentioned before, microservices have become popular, in part, because these tools have helped make microservices and the underlying infrastructure easier to build, but you really can use these tools to build distributed applications with services of any size, not just microservices. I don't want you to think that I'm particularly dogmatic about microservices. In fact, I'd rather we replace the term *microservices* with *right-sized services* to indicate that the size doesn't really matter—different situations demand different sizes of services. However, for the purpose of this book, microservices make up the compelling vehicle through which we can learn this toolset—but the skills you learn here can take you far beyond microservices.

How you use these tools in the future—be it for monolith, for microservices, or, more likely, somewhere in between—is entirely up to you. Let's be pragmatic and acknowledge that real-world solutions are never as clean as the phrase *monolith versus microservices* wants you to believe.

Many developers don't care either way, so long as they are building useful software and have a reasonably good development experience. Your customers definitely don't care: they want a good user experience, but they really don't know or care about how the developers structure the software they are using.

1.13 The spectrum of possibilities

The truth of the matter is that it's not just a black-and-white choice between monolith and microservices. There's actually a spectrum of possibilities, as shown in figure 1.7.

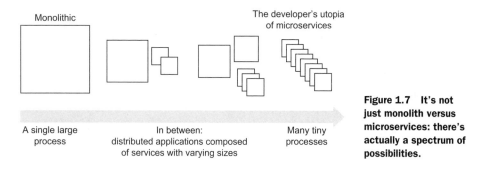

Figure 1.7 It's not just monolith versus microservices: there's actually a spectrum of possibilities.

Despite this being a book about microservices, I don't advocate that we adopt any specific position on this continuum. Do you want a monolith? That's great; it's totally okay to have a monolith. Do you need microservices? Awesome, microservices can bring many benefits.

Most likely, you'll be somewhere in the middle of the spectrum. In fact, *somewhere in between* is what the real world often looks like! Maybe toward the left with a monolith and some helper services, or maybe toward the right with many small services and a few bigger services. There's no right answer to this question. You must take an appropriate position to improve things for yourself, your team, your company, and ultimately who you really should care about—your customers.

In this book, I promote an idealized version of microservices development, what I like to call "the developer's utopia of microservices." It's a form of development that's most achievable when starting a greenfield (new) application and, even then, only when you can stay true to that path going into the future. I believe this is an amazing way to work, assuming we can maintain the discipline. But please don't stress when you see that real-world development is never quite this perfect.

The nature of development is that it's complicated and messy. The techniques in this book can help you bring back some level of control, but it can be difficult to apply them in practice, especially when you're up against a legacy codebase and constantly changing requirements from the business.

The good news is that we don't need a perfect implementation of microservices for them to start providing benefits to our application and development process. We can simply push toward the microservices end of the spectrum, and any kind of movement in that direction will be beneficial. We'll return to the spectrum of possibilities in chapter 12.

1.14 Designing a microservices application

This isn't a book about theory, and it's not about software design either. But there are some things I'd like to say about software design before we get into the practical parts of this book.

1.14.1 Software design

Designing a microservices application isn't particularly different from designing any software. You can read any good book on software design and apply those same principles and techniques to microservices. There aren't many hard and fast rules that I follow, but I feel these few are especially important:

- Don't overdesign or try to future proof your architecture. Start with a simple design for your application.
- Apply continuous refactoring during development to keep it as simple as it can be.
- Let a good design emerge naturally.

I feel that the last rule is especially encouraged by microservices. You can't conclusively preplan a big microservices application. The architecture has to emerge during development and over the lifetime of the application.

I'm not saying that you shouldn't do any planning. You definitely should be planning at each and every iteration of development. What I'm saying is that you should be planning for your plan to change! You should be able to respond quickly to changing circumstances, and that's something also well supported by microservices.

1.14.2 Design principles

Let's briefly discuss some design principles that seem particularly relevant to microservices:

- Single responsibility principle
- Separation of concerns
- Loose coupling
- High cohesion

Generally, we'd like to have each microservice be as small and simple as possible. One individual service should cover only a single conceptual area of the business; that is, each service should have a single, well-defined area of responsibility. This is known as the *single responsibility principle*. Each microservice having its own area of concern naturally leads to *separation of concerns*, that is, clear separation of responsibilities rather than intermingled responsibilities, which helps make each microservice simpler and easier to understand.

Microservices should be *loosely coupled* and have *high cohesion*. Loosely coupled means that the connections between services are minimal and that they don't share information unless necessary. When we reduce the connections and dependencies between microservices, we make it easier to upgrade individual services without having problems ripple through our application. Loose coupling helps us pull apart and rewire our application into new configurations. This makes our application more flexible and responsive to the changing needs of the business.

The code contained within a microservice should be highly cohesive. This means that all the code in a microservice belongs together and contributes to solving the problem that is the service's area of responsibility. If a microservice solves more than one problem or has a larger area of responsibility, then this is an indication that it's not highly cohesive.

1.14.3 Domain-driven design

One design paradigm that works well for microservices is called *domain-driven design* (DDD). Using DDD is a great way to understand the domain of a business and to model the business as software. The technique comes from the book, *Domain-Driven Design*, by Eric Evans (Addison-Wesley Professional, 2003). I've used it multiple times myself and find that it maps well to designing distributed applications. Specifically, the concept of the *bounded context* fits well with the boundary of a microservice, as illustrated in figure 1.8.

Figure 1.8 shows how the boundaries of concepts in our video-streaming domain might fit into microservices. Concepts such as *User*, *Like*, and *Video* live within our microservices, and some concepts (e.g., Video) create the relationships between microservices. For example, in figure 1.8, the idea of a video is almost the same (but there can be differences) between the recommendations and the video-storage microservices.

A bounded context is a conceptual bubble within the domain model in which all the terms, entities, and logic within the bubble make sense together, belong together, and are consistent with each other. Creating bounded contexts is a way to carve up our domain models into logical and self-contained parts. The process of DDD can help us figure out the answer to this question: What goes into each microservice?

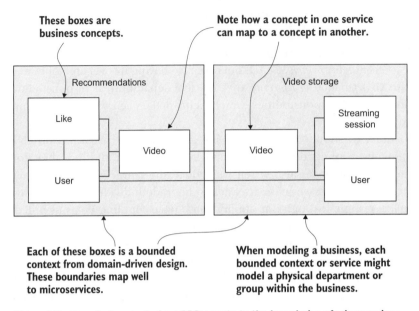

These boxes are business concepts.

Note how a concept in one service can map to a concept in another.

Each of these boxes is a bounded context from domain-driven design. These boundaries map well to microservices.

When modeling a business, each bounded context or service might model a physical department or group within the business.

Figure 1.8   Bounded contexts from DDD equate to the boundaries of microservices.

1.14.4 *Don't repeat yourself*

There is a coding principle that seems like it might be under attack by microservices. Many developers live by the motto *Don't repeat yourself* (DRY). But in the world of microservices, we're developing a higher tolerance for duplicated code than what was previously considered acceptable. This is partly because the cost of duplicated code is usually less than the cost of the bad abstraction we might create to share the code. But also, it's because sharing code is just hard and can even be harder with microservices.

The hard process boundaries in a microservices application certainly make it more difficult to share code, and the practice of DDD seems to encourage duplicating concepts, if not replicating code. In addition, when microservices are owned by separate teams, we then encounter all the usual barriers to sharing code that already exist between teams.

Be assured there are good ways to share code between microservices, and we aren't simply going to throw out DRY. We'd still like to share code between microservices when it makes sense to do so.

1.14.5 *How much to put in each microservice*

Here is an aspect of design that causes much argument: Exactly how much code should we put in each microservice? There is no right answer to this question. But the "micro" part of the name *microservices* has unfortunately pushed some people to think that the smaller their services are, the better. This isn't true. In fact, I don't even like the term "microservices" because I think it implicitly pushes people to make their services too small. Is it too late to rename "microservices" to "right-sized services"? Your services should be whatever size works best for your circumstances, and we shouldn't be competing to create the smallest services.

Services that are too small need to communicate more with the system to get work done. The smaller we make our services, the higher we make the overall complexity of our system. So instead of building services around the goal of making them as small as possible, we should be building them around the concepts in our domain and to whatever size feels natural for that domain (hence, section 1.14.3 on DDD).

The problem of how much to put in each microservice is the same kind of problem we encounter in every other part of software development. How much code should I put in each function? How much code should I put in each class or module? These questions have no right answers, except to say that design principles like those from section 1.14.2 can help guide us in the right direction.

1.14.6 *Learning more about design*

This book is about the practical aspects of building microservices, not about designing them. So, what's coming up is much more practical than theoretical. Whatever your preferred flavor of development (e.g., object-oriented versus functional), there are many good books about software design available. Pick one that appeals to you and read it.

Specifically, to learn about designing microservices, I recommend you read *Designing Microservices* (Manning, in press) by S. Ramesh. Another book with some great information on designing distributed applications that goes really well with this book is *Micro Frontends in Action* by Michael Geers (Manning, 2020). To keep up to date with new content relating to this book, join the mailing list at www.bootstrapping-microservices.com.

1.15 *An example application*

By the end of this book, we'll have built a simple but complete microservices application. In this section, we'll develop an idea of what the final product looks like.

The example product we'll build is a video-streaming application. Every good product deserves a name, so after much brainstorming and throwing around various ideas, I've landed on the name *FlixTube*, the future king of the video-streaming world. Got to start somewhere, right?

Why choose video streaming as the example? Simply because it's a fun example and is surprisingly easy to create (at least in a simple form). It's also a well-known use case for microservices, being the approach successfully taken to the extreme by Netflix. (Reports vary, but we know they run hundreds, if not thousands, of microservices.)

We'll use the FlixTube example application to demonstrate the process of constructing a microservices application. It will only have a small number of microservices, but we'll build in the pathways we need for future scalability, including adding more virtual machines to the cluster, replicating services for scale and redundancy, and having separate deployment schedules for our services.

Our application will have a browser-based frontend so our users can view a list of videos. From there, they can select a video, and it will begin playing. We'll build and publish Docker images for our microservices in chapter 3. During development, we'll boot our application using Docker Compose, which we'll cover in chapters 4 and 5. In chapters 6, 7, and 8, we'll deploy our application to production and set up continuous deployment. In chapter 9, we'll swing back to development for some automated testing.

Our application will contain services for video streaming, storage, and upload, plus a gateway for the customer-facing frontend. We'll work up to deploying the full application (see figure 1.9) in chapter 10. In chapters 11 and 12, we'll look at all the ways this architecture can help us scale in the future as our application grows. Are you ready to start building with microservices?

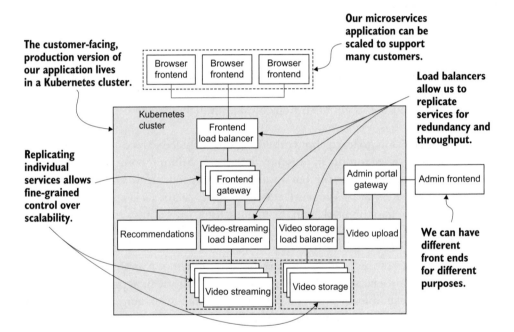

Figure 1.9   Our example application running in production on Kubernetes

Summary

- We take a practical rather than a theoretical approach to learning how to build a microservices application.
- Microservices are small and independent processes that each do one thing well.
- A microservices application is composed of numerous small processes working together to create the application's features.
- A monolith is an application composed of a single massive service.
- Although building a microservices application is more complicated than building a monolith, it's not as difficult as you might think.

- Applications built from microservices are more flexible, scalable, reliable, and fault tolerant than monolithic applications.
- All applications, monolith or microservices, grow complex—using microservices is an architecture that can help us manage complexity instead of being overwhelmed by it.
- Modern tools such as Docker, Kubernetes, Terraform, and GitHub Actions make building a microservices application much easier than it used to be.
- Domain-driven design (DDD) is an effective way to design a microservices application.
- Bounded contexts from DDD map well to the boundaries of microservices.
- The single responsibility principle, loose coupling, and high cohesion design principles are particularly relevant to microservices.
- FlixTube, the example application we're building in this book, is a video-streaming platform based on microservices.

Creating
your first microservice

2

This chapter covers

- Our philosophy of development
- Establishing a single-service development environment
- Building a microservice for video streaming
- Setting up for production and development
- Using Node.js to run our microservice

Our goal for this book is to assemble an application that consists of multiple microservices. But before we can build multiple microservices, we must first learn how to build a single microservice. In this chapter, we'll create our first microservice. This simple microservice does very little, but it illustrates the process so that you can understand it and repeat it. Indeed, this is the process we'll use to create multiple microservices through the course of this book.

This first microservice is a simple HTTP server that delivers streaming video to a user watching in a web browser. This is the first step on our road to building FlixTube, our video-streaming application. Video streaming might sound difficult, but the simple code we examine at this stage shouldn't present much trouble.

In this book, our microservices are programmed with JavaScript and run on Node.js, but note that we could use any tech stack for our microservices. Building applications with microservices gives us a lot of freedom in the tech stack we use.

You don't have to use JavaScript to build microservices. You can just as easily build your microservices using Python, C#, Ruby, Java, Go, or whatever language is in vogue by the time you read this book. I had to make a choice, however, because this is a practical book, and we need to get down to the nitty-gritty of actual coding. But, keep in mind that you can just as easily use your own favorite programming language to build your microservices.

We're about to embark on a whirlwind tour of Node.js. Of course, we can't cover the full details, and as is the theme in this book, we're only going to skim the surface of what's possible. At the end of the chapter, you'll find references to other books on Node.js to drill down for deeper knowledge.

If you already know Node.js, then you'll find much of this chapter to be familiar, and you might be tempted to skip it. But please skim through it because there are some important notes on setting up your development environment, preparing for production deployment, and getting ready for fast, iterative development that we'll rely on throughout the book.

Hold onto your hats! This book starts out simple, but in no time at all, it turns into a pretty wild ride.

2.1 New tools

Because this book is all about the tools, in most chapters, we'll start with the new tools you need to install to follow along with the examples in the chapter. Starting with our first microservice, table 2.1 shows the tools we need: Git, Node.js, and Visual Studio Code (VS Code). We'll use Git to get the code. We'll use Node.js to run and test our first microservice, and we'll use VS Code to edit our code and work on our Node.js project.

Throughout the book, I'll tell you the version numbers for each tool used to develop the examples in this book. This gives you a version number that you can use to follow along with the examples.

Later versions of these tools should also work because good tools are usually backward compatible, but occasional major increments to versions can break old examples. If that happens, let me know by logging an issue on GitHub (see the next section).

Table 2.1 Tools introduced in chapter 2

Tool	Version	Purpose
Git	2.36.1	Version control is an essential part of day-to-day development; in this chapter, we use Git to get a copy of the chapter 2 code.
Node.js	18.17.1	We use Node.js to run our microservices.
Visual Studio Code (VS Code)	1.81.1	We use VS Code for editing our code and other assets.

Of course, you can use some other integrated development environment (IDE) or text editor for editing your code. I recommend VS Code because it's very good and widely used.

2.2 Getting the code

Numerous working example projects accompany this book. The code for each project is available on GitHub. You can clone or download the code repositories there to follow along with the examples in the book. I strongly recommend that you run these examples as you work through the book. That's the best way for you to get practical experience and the most out of your learning.

Following standard conventions, these examples are easy to run and all have a similar setup. Once you understand the fundamentals (which we'll cover), you'll find it easy to run the examples. The examples become more complex as we progress, but still, I'll keep these as accessible as possible, explain how they work, and help you get them up and running.

To find the *Bootstrapping Microservices,* 2nd ed., organization on GitHub, point your web browser to http://mng.bz/vPVr. Each chapter has its own code repository, starting with the chapter-2 repository at http://mng.bz/46Yv. Under each repository, you can find the code organized by the example project that is listed throughout that chapter. If you find any problems with the code, or you're having trouble getting it working, log an issue in the appropriate code repository on GitHub so that I can help you get it working.

2.3 Why Node.js?

In this book, we use Node.js to build our microservices. Why is that? One of the advantages of building microservices is that we can choose the tech stack that we like. I happen to like Node.js, and I use it in my day-to-day work, but I also have other reasons for choosing it.

Building our microservices with Docker (which we look at in chapter 3) means we can compose applications from multiple tech stacks. That might sound like it just makes things more confusing, which is probably true, but it gives us the ability to mix and match technologies. We can use this freedom to ensure we're choosing the most appropriate stack that each situation demands.

> **NOTE** Node.js is network orientated and high performance, making it well suited to building microservices. We plan to build many services, so let's be kind to ourselves and choose a platform that makes our work easier.

Node.js is also popular and well known. That might not sound like much, but it's important because there's an ecosystem of people, tools, and resources around Node.js. Having a big community to fall back on when you need help is important. That makes it easier to find assistance while learning, and it's also good to have the support during ongoing software development.

Node.js is made for microservices. It's all there in the name. *Node* implies its use for building nodes in distributed, network-based applications. (JavaScript moved from the browser to the server in 2009 and has since established itself as an extremely competent server-side programming language.)

Node.js is made for creating small, high-performance, and lightweight services, and it avoids the unnecessary baggage that comes with many other platforms. Building an HTTP server in Node.js is trivial, which makes it easy for us to bootstrap new microservices quickly. That's a good motivator because we're planning to create many small services. Node.js is also convenient for this book because you don't need to spend a lot of time learning how to code a basic microservice, and, as you'll soon see, you can build a microservice with only a small amount of code using Node.js.

Using JavaScript promotes full-stack coding. These days there aren't many places JavaScript doesn't go. We can use it in our application's backend to build microservices. We can use it in our web-based frontend (that's where JavaScript was born, of course). Not only that, but we can also use JavaScript for desktop development (Electron and Tauri), mobile development (Ionic/Capacitor), embedded development (Internet of Things [IoT] devices), and—as I showed in my previous book, *Data Wrangling with JavaScript* (Manning, 2018)—when working with data, a domain normally dominated by Python. Using JavaScript as much as possible means we can go anywhere in our application without triggering a mental context switch.

These days, many developers (including myself) use TypeScript, which is a language on top of JavaScript that brings static typing to JavaScript. The beauty of TypeScript is that it's flexible enough that we can mix and match static and dynamic typing to get the best of both worlds.

The other big thing we get with Node.js is npm, the Node Package Manager, which is a command-line tool used to install Node.js packages (code libraries and command-line tools). This isn't specifically related to building microservices, but it's extraordinarily useful to have a fantastic package manager and a vast number of open source packages at our fingertips. My superpower as a developer is that I have more than 2,625,124 code libraries within easy access. Whatever I need to do is often just a quick npm search away!

> **NOTE**   Node.js is open source, and you can find the code for it on GitHub at https://github.com/nodejs/node.

What is npm?

As mentioned earlier, npm is the Node Package Manager. It's a command-line application that talks to the npm repository online and allows you to manage third-party packages in your Node.js project. Installing a readily available package is a fast way to solve a problem you'd otherwise have to write more code to achieve! You can search for packages on the npm website at www.npmjs.com.

2.4   *Our philosophy of development*

Before we get into the coding, I want to brief you on my philosophy of development, which we'll use throughout this book. You'll see this manifested time and again, so a quick explanation is in order. I'll sum up my philosophy of development with the following three points:

- Iterate
- Keep it working
- Move from simple to complex

Iteration is a key ingredient. I'm talking about small, personal iterations of coding and not the larger iterations in agile that are commonly known as *sprints* (although larger iterations are also useful). I write code through a series of personal work iterations. I add and edit code, iteration by iteration, as shown in figure 2.1. When working this way, each iteration gives us feedback. Feedback allows us to discover when we're veering off track and make immediate course corrections. Fast iteration allows us to align our work closely with our evolving goals.

> **NOTE** Small, fast-paced increments of coding are essential to the software development journey.

At each iteration, we do only a small amount of coding. How small depends on what we're doing and how difficult it is. But the key is that it should be small enough so that we can easily understand and test the code we just wrote.

Each iteration must produce working and tested code. This is the most important factor. Have you ever typed in a whole page of code and then struggled for hours to get it working? When we work in small and well-tested iterations of code, the sum total at the end of a day's coding is a large body of working code. You can see how this works in figure 2.1.

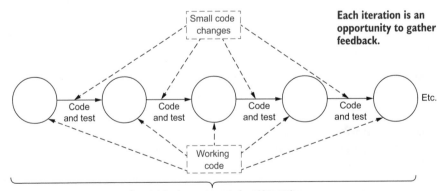

Figure 2.1   A series of small and well-tested code changes results in a large body of working code.

This notion of producing a large body of working code satisfies my second point: *keep it working*. We'll rarely get into trouble if we work in small, easily tested increments. When typing large amounts of code, we face many difficulties getting that code to work. Most likely we'll have a large amount of broken (nonworking) code. But even if the code does appear to work, it probably still harbors many "nasties" that are yet to be found. When we keep it working and it gets into trouble, we can easily wind our code back to the previous iteration to restore it to working order. Because each iteration of our code is small, we don't give up much progress when we need to revert back. Getting into trouble really isn't any trouble at all!

Of course, restoration of the previous iteration implies that you're staging or committing your code to Git or some other form of version control. That should go without saying. Even if you aren't using version control (you really should be), then it's up to you to find another way to preserve the results of your iterations.

The third and final point in my philosophy of coding is to *start simple*. We should start coding at the simplest possible starting point and iterate our application toward greater complexity. All applications become complex over time; that's unavoidable in the long run, but we shouldn't start with complexity. Don't try to lay down a complex system all at once in the "big bang" style—that probably won't work out well for you.

> **NOTE** Complexity is where applications always end up, but it doesn't mean that's where they have to start. Each code change should also be simple, avoiding too much complexity in any single iteration.

Start with the simplest possible code, and then, iteration by iteration, you can build it up to something more complex, as illustrated in figure 2.2. Don't be too eager to take on complexity. Keep it simple for as long as you can. As our application becomes more and more complex, we need to bring in tools, techniques, processes, and patterns to help us manage that complexity.

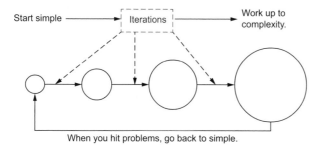

Figure 2.2 Start simple and work up to complexity through a series of small iterations.

Microservices are tools for managing complexity. Again, any given microservice should be simple. It should be small. Making a small update to an existing microservice should be easy, and adding a new microservice to an existing application should be effortless. These statements are true, even when the application itself has become extremely complex.

Just because our code becomes more complex doesn't mean our iterations need to do the same. We should strive to keep every modification to the code as simple as possible. Simple changes are easier to understand and simpler to test and integrate into the application. All of this increases the probability that the evolving system continues to behave as expected.

> **TIP** When solving problems in complex applications, don't be afraid to extract the problem from the application and reproduce it in a simpler environment. If you can isolate a problem with a smaller amount of code, that problem has less space in which to hide!

If we encounter problems in a complex application that we can't easily solve, we have a new option now. As indicated previously in figure 2.2, where the arrow cycles back to the simple beginning, we can extract our problematic code at any time from the complex application and reproduce it in a simpler environment.

Thankfully, this is easy to do when coding in JavaScript. We might load our code in an automated test where we can repeatedly run the code to troubleshoot and fix it. If that's not possible, we might extract the code to a separate Node.js project to isolate the problem and make it easier to solve. I often start up Data-Forge Notebook (an application that I built and have released to the public; www.data-forge-notebook.com) for this purpose.

But what can we do if the code isn't so easy to extract? In that situation, I like to tear down the application around the problematic code and pull code out of the application (as much as possible) until the problem is isolated. We do this because when you've isolated a problem, it has nowhere to hide. Finding problems is usually much more time consuming than fixing them once they are found. So having faster ways to triangulate the location of problems in our code is one of the best ways for us to enhance our productivity. We'll talk more about the art of debugging in chapter 11.

This is another thing to love about microservices. Our application is already compartmentalized, so it should be easy for us to tear out nonessential microservices. Having said that, eliminating code from our application in this way is an advanced technique and can easily result in a broken application!

I've covered my philosophy of development here because I think it can help you be a better and more productive developer. The evolution of our software in small and well-tested increments is the main goal. We're taking our code on a journey of iterations from working state to working state. At no time should our code ever be fundamentally broken.

You'll see this philosophy in action in this chapter and throughout the book. Start simple. Start small. Iterate with small changes. Keep it working. Before you know it, you'll have built something big and complex! But that doesn't happen all at once. It happens through a series of small changes that, taken together, add up to something huge.

> **NOTE** To learn more about implementing this philosophy of development for yourself, please see the web page for my upcoming book *Rapid Fullstack Development* (https://rapidfullstackdevelopment.com/), where I present the full version.

2.5 *Establishing our single-service development environment*

To create and work on a microservice, we need to set up our development environment. This provides a way for us to create and edit code and then run it locally to make sure the code works. In this chapter, we'll build a single microservice and run it using Node.js directly on our development computer. We'll edit our code using VS Code or some other IDE or text editor of your choice.

Node.js is easy to install and run on any of the main operating systems, so you can choose Linux, Windows, or macOS for the development of your microservice. (Your choices are summarized in table 2.2.)

Running a single service under Node.js directly is easy, as you'll see in the coming sections of this chapter. But when it comes to developing and testing multiple microservices, which we'll cover in chapter 4, things become more complicated. That's when we'll need to enlist the help of Docker (from chapter 3 forward). For now, let's focus on running our first microservice directly under Node.js in our chosen operating system.

Even after we start developing and testing multiple microservices, there will be times during development, testing, and troubleshooting when we'll want to pull a single microservice out of the application and run it individually so that we can focus on just that isolated part without having to worry about the application and all the baggage that it brings. Having a single-service development environment is more than just a convenient stepping stone in the early stages—it's useful to have on standby, ready to be called into action at any time during ongoing development.

Table 2.2 Options for running Node.js

Platform	Notes
Linux	Node.js was built for Linux, so it works pretty well there!
	For this book, I demonstrate most commands under Ubuntu Linux. If you also run Ubuntu or another variant of Linux, you're well placed to follow along with the examples in the book.
Windows	Node.js also works well under Windows. In fact, I do most of my day-to-day development, testing, and troubleshooting with Windows.
macOS	Node.js also works well under macOS.

NOTE When working with just Node.js, you can use it on any platform, and there really isn't one that is better than any other.

Figure 2.3 gives you an indication of what our single-microservice development environment looks like. We'll edit our code in VS Code or an alternative editor. Our microservice project is a Node.js project with JavaScript code. (I'll show you how to create this soon.) Executing our project under Node.js produces a running instance of our microservice. All of this is running on our development computer on our host operating system of choice: Linux, Windows, or macOS.

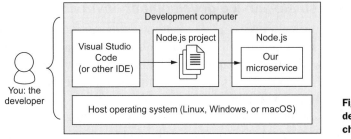

Figure 2.3   Our single-service development environment for chapter 2

2.5.1   *Installing Git*

The example projects and code for this book are in GitHub under the Bootstrapping Microservices organization (see the links in section 2.2). Figure 2.4 shows how each code repository is structured. Each subdirectory (example-1, example-2, etc.) is a working project that you can run yourself to follow along with the book (assuming you don't want to type in all the code yourself).

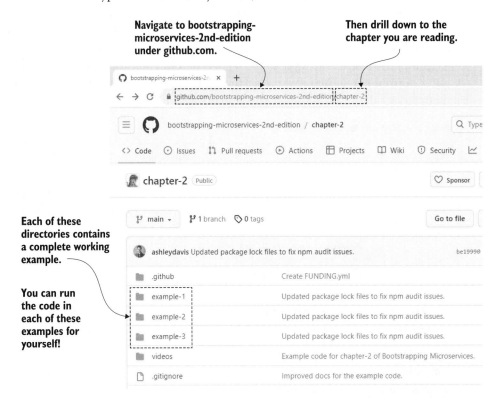

Figure 2.4   Each example project in the GitHub repository is a complete working project that you can run for yourself.

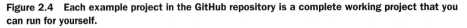

The simplest way to get the code is to download it as a zip file from GitHub. To do this, go to the code repository (e.g., repository chapter-2 that accompanies this chapter), and look for the Clone or Download button. Click the button, and then choose Download ZIP.

The best way to get the code, of course, is to use Git to clone the code repository. To do this, you first need to install Git. You might already have it installed, for instance, if you (like me) use it for everyday work. Or you might be running a variant of Linux that comes with Git preinstalled. On macOS, you might have Xcode installed, which comes with Git.

How do you know if you have Git installed? To find out which version of Git you have (if any), open a terminal (on Windows, open the Command Prompt, or—even better— install Windows Terminal from the Microsoft Store), and run the following command:

```
git --version
```

If Git is already installed, you'll see its version number, which is something like this:

```
git version 2.36.1
```

If you don't already have Git, installing it isn't difficult. Follow the instructions at the Git website (https://git-scm.com) to download and install the version for your platform.

> **New to using the command line?**
> Using the command line is one of the best and most productive ways to work as a software developer. Using UIs and visual editors is great for doing the most common, everyday tasks, but for more complex or customized tasks, you need to be comfortable using the command line. If you're new to it, consider first doing a tutorial to get the basics of working in the command line of your operating system.

2.5.2 Cloning the code repository

With Git installed, you can now clone the code repository for each chapter of this book. For example, at this point, you should clone the repository for chapter 2 so you can follow along with this chapter:

```
git clone
  https://github.com/bootstrapping-microservices-2nd-edition/chapter-2
```

This command gets a copy of the code repository from GitHub and places it on your local hard drive (in the current working directory) under a directory named chapter-2. I won't explain how to clone a repository again in future chapters. But at the start of each new chapter, I'll show you where to get the code for that chapter; then you can use Git to get your own copy. Feel free to return here at any time for a reminder of how to clone a code repository with Git.

2.5.3   *Getting VS Code*

I use VS Code for all my coding and recommend it to you because I think it's a great environment for editing code. You can find the download and installation instructions for Windows, Linux, and macOS on the VS Code website at https://code.visualstudio.com.

I like VS Code because it's lightweight, has great performance, and is configurable. It's also commonly used for Node.js and JavaScript projects. You don't need any extra plugins for this book, but it's worth noting that there is a vast range of easily installable plugins for different programming languages and tasks. You can also customize VS Code for all of your development needs.

Of course, if you already have your own favorite IDE or text editor, feel free to use it, as it doesn't really make any difference. When I mention VS Code throughout the book, just pretend it's your preferred text editor instead!

2.5.4   *Installing Node.js*

To run our microservice, we need Node.js. That's something we can't do without because the example microservices in this book are Node.js projects. All the code examples are written in JavaScript, which runs on Node.js. If you already have Node.js installed, you can open a terminal and check the version with the following commands:

```
node --version
v18.17.1

npm --version
9.6.7
```

These are the versions I currently use for Node.js and npm. You can use these versions or later ones.

> **NOTE** We use the `npm` command for installing third-party packages. When you install Node.js, you get npm at the same time.

Installing Node.js for any platform is straightforward, and you can get the download and installation instructions at the Node.js website (https://nodejs.org). It's not difficult, and you shouldn't have any problems.

If you already have Node.js installed and want to get a newer version, or if you'd like to manage multiple versions of Node.js, it's worth looking at nvm (Node Version Manager), described in the second sidebar that follows.

After installing Node.js, open a terminal, and double-check that it installed okay. To do this, print the version numbers:

```
node --version
npm --version
```

Now that we have Node.js installed, we're ready to build and run our first microservice.

It's important to know what version you're using!

Using the `--version` argument is a good way to check if you have something installed, but it's also important to know what version you have. When you're working on a real product, it's crucial that you use the same version in development as you use in production. That's the best way to know that your code will run in production.

Need to run different versions of Node.js?

Running multiple versions of Node.js is easy. Say you're maintaining or have to work on multiple production applications that are built with different versions of Node.js. Or, maybe you're just working on a single application, but it has been in development for quite some time, and different microservices are on different versions of Node.js. In these cases, I highly recommend you use nvm (the Node Version Manager) to install different versions of Node.js and switch between them.

There are actually two different applications called nvm, and which one you choose depends on your operating system. See the following links for setup instructions:

- For Linux and macOS: https://github.com/nvm-sh/nvm
- For Windows: https://github.com/coreybutler/nvm-windows

This isn't for the faint of heart! You must be proficient at using the command line to install this software.

2.6 Building an HTTP server for video streaming

Now that we have our development environment, we can build our first microservice. This isn't a difficult project, and we're just building it to illustrate the process of creating a basic microservice. It's the first step in creating FlixTube, our example microservices application. You can follow along with the code while reading this chapter, typing in the code as you see it, or you can read it first and then try out the example projects that are available in the chapter-2 repository on GitHub.

The microservice we're building is a simple video-streaming service. Streaming video might sound difficult—and it can become complicated in a real production application—but we're starting with something that's much simpler. You might be surprised at just how little code we need to create this.

Figure 2.5 shows the output for the end result of this chapter's project. Our microservice delivers streaming video to the web browser via port 3000 and the route `/video`. We can watch the video directly through our browser by pointing it at http://localhost :3000/video.

In figure 2.5, you can see we use Chrome to watch the video. The sample video we're using was downloaded from https://sample-videos.com. Here, we use the shortest possible video, but feel free to download one of the larger sample videos for your own testing. The chapter-2 code repository includes the short example video under the videos subdirectory. If you download other videos for testing, you might like to copy them to this same directory.

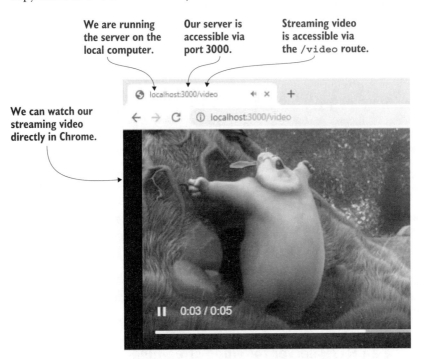

Figure 2.5   Watching the streaming video from our microservice directly in Chrome

To create our microservice, we must follow these steps:

1 Create a Node.js project for our microservice.
2 Install Express, and create a simple HTTP server.
3 Add a handler for an HTTP GET route /video that retrieves the streaming video.

After creating this basic first microservice, we'll talk briefly about how we can configure our microservices. Then, we'll cover some fundamentals for production and development setup.

2.6.1   *Creating a Node.js project*

Before we can start writing code, we need a Node.js project where our code can live. The project we'll soon create is shown in figure 2.6. This is a basic Node.js project with a single entry point: the script file index.js. You can also see package.json and package-lock.json, which are the files that track the dependencies and metadata for our project. The dependencies themselves, which are code libraries we can download and use, are installed under the node_modules directory. Let's create this project!

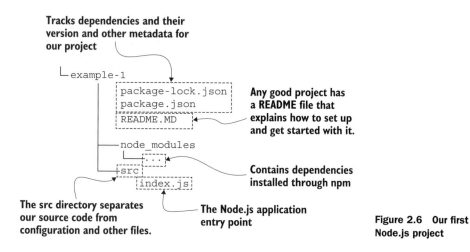

Figure 2.6   Our first Node.js project

DEFINITION   A *Node.js project* contains the source code and configuration for our Node.js application. It's where we edit the code that creates the features of our microservice.

If you're creating a project from scratch (and not just running the code from GitHub), you must first create a directory for the project. You can do this from the terminal on Linux and macOS using the `mkdir` command:

```
mkdir my-new-project
```

If you're working on Windows, you can instead use the `md` command:

```
md my-new-project
```

Now change into your new directory using the `cd` command:

```
cd my-new-project
```

We're now ready to create an empty Node.js project. This means we're creating our package.json file. We can do this using the npm `init` command:

```
npm init -y
```

The `-y` argument means that we don't have to answer any interactive questions while initializing our project. That makes it a little simpler and faster to create our project.

After running `npm init`, we now have a package.json file with all of its fields set to defaults. You can see an example of this in listing 2.1. Because the fields in this file have default values, you might want to come back later and set these to values that are more appropriate for your project. For the moment though, we'll leave these as they are.

Listing 2.1   The empty Node.js package file we just generated

The package name. It defaults to the name of the directory that contains the package; in this case, my-new-project because we initialized it in the my-new-project directory we just created.

```
{
  "name": "my-new-project"          ◁─┐    These fields are important if you publish
  "version": "1.0.0",                  │    this package to www.npmjs.com.
  "description": "",
  "main": "index.js",         ◁─┐    This code file is the default entry point for a Node.js
  "scripts": {                   │    project. We haven't created this file yet!
    "test": "..."
  },
  "keywords": [],                    npm scripts go here. We'll talk more
  "author": "",                      about this later in the chapter.
  "license": "ISC"
}
```

These fields are important if you publish this package to www.npmjs.com.

After creating your Node.js project, I encourage you to open the folder in VS Code and explore your new project by opening the package.json file and examining it. With the project opened in VS Code, you're now ready to start adding some code to your project.

Package.json vs. package-lock.json

Although package.json is automatically generated and updated by npm, it can also be edited by hand. That way, you can manually change the metadata and npm module dependencies for your Node.js project.

Usually, package.json doesn't specify exact version numbers for dependencies (although it can if you want it to). Instead, package.json generally sets the minimum version for each dependency and can also set a range of versions. In addition, package.json only tracks top-level dependencies for the project. You don't need to specify dependencies of dependencies; that's handled automatically for you. This makes package.json smaller, more concise, and therefore more human readable.

The problem with package.json is that you and your colleagues can end up running different versions of dependencies. Even worse, you could be running different versions compared to what's in production.

That's because package.json usually doesn't specify exact versions, so depending on when you invoke `npm install`, you can get a set of versions different from everyone else. This is a recipe for chaos and makes it difficult to replicate production problems because you may not be able to reproduce the exact configuration that is running in production.

Package-lock.json was introduced in npm version 5 to solve this problem. It's a generated file and isn't designed to be hand edited. Its purpose is to track the *entire* tree of dependencies (including dependencies of dependencies) and the *exact* version of each dependency.

You should commit package-lock.json to your code repository. Sharing this file with teammates and the production environment is the best way to ensure that everyone has the same configuration for their copy of the project.

2.6.2 Installing Express

To stream video from our microservice, we'll make it an HTTP server (also known as a *web server*). In other words, it will respond to HTTP requests from a browser, in this case, a browser's request to play streaming video. To implement our HTTP server, we'll use Express.

> **NOTE** Express is the de facto standard framework for building HTTP servers on Node.js. It's easier for us to create a web server with Express than if we only used the low-level Node.js API.

Express is the most popular code library for building HTTP servers on Node.js. You can find documentation and examples on the Express website at http://expressjs.com/. While there, I'd encourage you to explore the many other features of Express as well. Of course, we could build an HTTP server directly on Node.js without Express, but Express allows us to do this at a higher level of abstraction, with less code, and without the nuts-and-bolts code we'd otherwise need using the low-level Node.js API.

Using Express is also a good excuse for us to learn how to install an npm package for use in our microservice. npm is the package manager for Node.js, and it puts a whole world of packages at our fingertips. This includes many libraries and frameworks, such as Express, that we can use to quickly and easily do a whole range of jobs when coding. Otherwise, we'd have to write a lot more code (and probably cause a load of bugs in the process) to achieve the same effect. We can install the latest version of Express from the terminal using the command `npm install` as follows:

```
npm install --save express
```

Running this command installs the Express package into our project. For the purposes of this book, I decided to use the Express v5 beta:

```
npm install --save express@5.0.0-beta.1
```

Express v5 beta supports asynchronous route handlers that will simplify later coding. I hope by the time you're reading this that v5 is out of beta and is the latest version. Don't worry too much about the differences between Express v4 and v5; besides the support for async route handlers, I haven't noticed any other significant differences that are worth pointing out, and all the code examples in this book should run in both versions (except Express v4 and earlier will handle asynchronous errors a little differently).

The `--save` argument causes the dependency to be added to and tracked in the package.json file. Note that `--save` isn't necessary anymore. In older versions of Node.js, this was required; these days, it's the default. I've included `--save` explicitly so that I can highlight what it does, but you don't need to use it anymore.

You can see the result of our package install in figure 2.7, which shows the express subdirectory created in the node_modules directory of our Node.js project. You'll also note that many other packages have been installed alongside Express. These other packages are the dependencies needed by Express, and npm has automatically installed them for us.

Listing 2.2 (chapter-2/example-1/package .json) shows our updated package.json file after installing Express. The difference from listing 2.1 is that we now have a `dependencies` field that includes the particular version of Express we installed.

Listing 2.2 refers to an actual file in the chapter-2 code repository on GitHub (chapter-2/ example-1/package.json). Each time a code listing shows a actual file, you'll find the path of that file in the text so you can navigate the code repository and find the file for yourself. If you go to the chapter-2 repository and look in the example-1 subdirectory, you'll see the package.json file. It's the same file shown in this code listing. You can find this file directly via http://mng.bz/QRzQ.

Most of the listings in this book follow this

Express is now installed in our node_modules directory.

Figure 2.7 Note where the express subdirectory is installed into the node_modules directory.

convention. They show a snippet of a file (or in this case, a complete version) that is part of a working example project on GitHub. To see this file in context, you can follow the reference to its location in GitHub or in the copy of the code repository that you cloned to your computer. From there, you can either just inspect the code as it exists within its project, or you can (and should) run the code on your own computer because every example in this book (in this case, example-1 in chapter-2) is a working project that you can try out for yourself to help cement into place what you're learning.

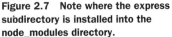
Listing 2.2 The package file with Express installed

```
{
  "name": "example-1",
  "version": "1.0.0",
  "description": "",
  "main": "index.js",
  "scripts": {
    --snip--
  },
  "keywords": [],
  "author": "",
  "license": "ISC",
  "dependencies": {
    "express": "^5.0.0-beta.1"      ◁── We're using Express v5 beta because it
  }                                        supports asynchronous route handlers.
}
```

Having the dependencies tracked through the package.json file means you can pass your project and code to other programmers (e.g., teammates) so that they can replicate your work. It also means I can make this code available to you and you can easily get it working.

For example, say you want to get example-1 working. First, you need to clone the chapter-2 code repository as shown earlier in section 2.5.2, and then, from the terminal, change the directory to the code repository:

```
cd chapter-2
```

Now, change the directory into the particular example that you want to get running. In this case, it's example-1:

```
cd example-1
```

Then, you can use npm to install all the dependencies:

```
npm install
```

The command `npm install` by itself (not specifying any particular package) installs all the dependencies listed in package.json. In this case, only Express is listed, so only Express is installed (plus its dependencies). For other examples in this book, there will be more dependencies. But we still only need to invoke `npm install` once per example, and that's enough to install everything you need to run each Node.js example project.

2.6.3 Creating the Express boilerplate

Before we add video streaming to our microservice, we must first create the standard Express boilerplate HTTP server. Listing 2.3 (chapter-2/example-1/src/index.js) is the customary Hello World example that you get by following the official Express getting started guide (available at https://expressjs.com/).

This is only a small amount of code, but it's the simple starting point we need for this project. You should now create an index.js file under a src directory in your Node.js project, and type in the code. If that's too much work, just open example-1 from the chapter-2 repository, and find the version I prepared for you.

The code in listing 2.3 starts a web server, albeit the simplest possible web server. It uses the Express `get` function to define a route handler that returns the string `Hello World!`. The `listen` function is then called to start this HTTP server, listening for HTTP requests on port 3000.

Listing 2.3 A minimal Express web server

```
const express = require('express');     ⟵── Loads the Express library for use in our code

const app = express();                  ⟵── Creates an instance of an Express "app"
```

```
const port = 3000;            ⟵—— Our HTTP server will listen on port 3000.

app.get('/', (req, res) => {  ⟵—— Creates a route handler for the main HTTP GET route
  res.send('Hello World!');   ⟵
});                                 The handler prints Hello World! in the web browser.

app.listen(port);            ⟵—— Initiates the HTTP server
```

We called the file index.js because that's one of the standard names for the main entry point of a Node.js application. We could just as easily have called it something else, such as main.js or server.js. The choice is up to you. By calling it index.js, we're giving it a name that many other Node.js developers will immediately recognize as being the *main* file.

We placed the file index.js under the src directory as a convenient way to keep our source code files (src is short for "source") separated and easily distinguished from our configuration and other files. We don't really need this yet, but it's worthwhile getting it in place now because we'll need to make use of this distinction in the next chapter. This directory doesn't have to be called src—you can call it anything you like—but src is a common name for it. Don't forget to update your package.json file to include the location of index.js within the src directory.

The port number allows us to run multiple HTTP servers on the same computer. The servers can each have their own port number so they won't conflict with each other. The choice of port 3000 is another convention. It's customary during development to set your Node.js application to listen on port 3000, but we'll often want to set this to the standard HTTP port 80 in production. Later, we'll see how to set the port number as a configuration option supplied to the microservice when it's booted up.

We could have chosen another port, and, if you're already running something else on port 3000, you might have to. For example, if port 3000 doesn't work for you, try changing it to something different, for example, port 4000 or 5000.

Later, when we're running multiple microservices at the same time, instead of just one port, we'll use a series of port numbers starting at 4000 (4000, 4001, and so forth). Right now, though, we're ready to try running our ultrasimple web server.

What is index.js?

By convention, index.js is the JavaScript file that serves as the entry point for the Node.js application. When trying to understand an existing Node.js project, you should start with index.js.

2.6.4   *Running our simple web server*

To test our fledgling HTTP server, we'll run it from the terminal. First, we need to make sure we're in the same directory as our Node.js project. If you built the project yourself from scratch, you'll have to change to the directory that you created. For example:

```
cd my-new-project
```

Otherwise, if you're using the code from the chapter-2 GitHub repository, you should change to the example-1 directory:

```
cd chapter-2
cd example-1
```

Now, you can use Node.js to run the JavaScript code and start the HTTP server:

```
node src/index.js
```

If you're running on Windows, you may need to change the forward slash to a backslash. I'm using Windows 11 as I write the second edition of this book, and the forward slash works for me, but it may not work on older versions of Windows.

What we're doing here is running Node.js with `src/index.js` as the argument. We're telling Node.js to run our script file. Node.js executes the JavaScript code in this file, and, if successful, we'll see the following output in our terminal:

```
Example app listening on port 3000!
```

We can now test that this has worked. Open your web browser and point it at http://localhost:3000. You should see the `Hello World` message displayed.

We now have a basic HTTP server running, and it's time to add streaming video to it. When you're ready to stop your HTTP server, go back to the terminal where it's running, and press Ctrl-C to quit the Node.js application.

2.6.5 *Adding streaming video*

In listing 2.3, we only had a single HTTP route handler that returned Hello World. Now we'll change this and create a REST API for streaming video to the browser. A Representational State Transfer (REST) application programming interface (often just called an API) sounds complicated, but it really isn't. A REST API in its simplest sense is just a collection of HTTP route handlers that interface with systems and logic running in the backend.

Often, routes in REST APIs return JSON data, but we'll add a new route that returns streaming video. You can see what it looks like in figure 2.8. The diagram shows how our HTTP server will read the video from the filesystem and deliver it to the web browser via port 3000 and the video route.

We define the new video route as shown in listing 2.4 (chapter-2/example-2/src/index.js). If you're following along with the code, you can update the Express boilerplate HTTP server that you created earlier. Otherwise, you can open example-2 from the chapter-2 repository in VS Code to see the updated index.js.

Listing 2.4 reads a video from the local filesystem and streams it to the browser. This is a simple starting point that does just what we need, which is streaming video, the core feature for our microservices application FlixTube. The video itself can be found in the videos subdirectory under example-2 (found at chapter-2/example-2/src/index.js). Feel free to open Finder in macOS or Explorer in Windows and inspect

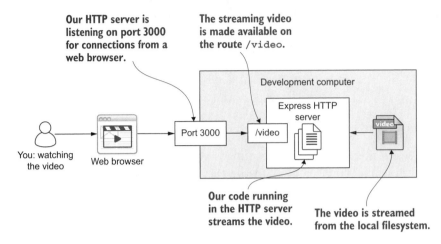

Figure 2.8 How the web browser interacts with our microservice through the video route

the video yourself before running the code. We'll use this example video throughout the book for testing, so you'll come to know it very well!

Listing 2.4   Simple streaming video server with Node.js

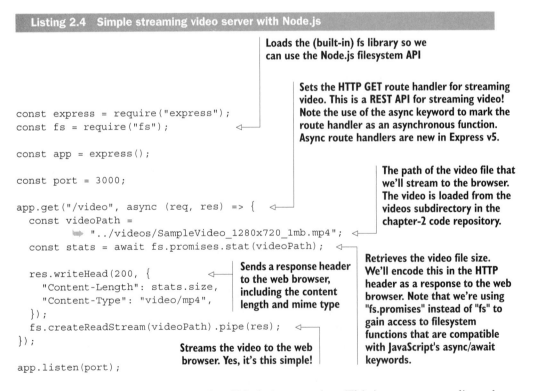

The code in listing 2.4 is an example of Node.js streaming. This is a more complicated topic than we have time to get into here, but, in short, we're opening a readable stream from the video file. Then, we're piping the stream to our HTTP response (look for the call to the `pipe` function).

We've created a conduit through which to stream the video byte by byte to the browser. We set up this pipeline for video streaming and then let Node.js and Express take care of the rest. Node.js and Express make this easy! To run this code, first change to the example-2 subdirectory:

```
cd chapter-2/example-2
```

Then, install the dependencies:

```
npm install
```

Start our fledgling video-streaming microservice like this:

```
node src/index.js
```

We can now point our browser to http://localhost:3000/video to watch the video. It's going to look similar to what was shown earlier in figure 2.5.

To test the code for this book, I've used the Chrome web browser. I discovered that such simple video streaming doesn't work under older versions of the Safari web browser. For details on how to make video streaming work for Safari, see my blog post at www.codecapers.com.au/video-streaming-in-safari. We'll talk more about ways we can test our microservices in chapter 9.

2.6.6   *Configuring our microservice*

At this point, it's worthwhile to spend a moment thinking about how we can configure our microservice. This is an important concern and will help us make better use of the microservices that we create. In future chapters, we'll see examples of how we can wire together microservices using their configurations. For now, though, let's look at a simple example of configuring a microservice.

We need a way to configure our microservice so it knows the port number to use when starting the HTTP server. There are several techniques we might use to configure our microservice, such as configuration files or command-line arguments. These techniques work, but another has emerged as the standard way to configure a microservice, and it's well supported by all the tools we'll be using.

We'll configure our microservices using *environment variables*. Specifically, in this case, we need a single environment variable to set the port number for the HTTP server. Figure 2.9 shows how we'll wire the PORT environment variable into our microservice.

Using environment variables to configure our code in Node.js is easy. We simply access the appropriately named field of `process.env`. You can see how this works in listing 2.5 (extract from chapter-2/example-3/src/index.js), where our code uses `process.env.PORT` to get the value for the port number. The code throws an error if the PORT environment variable isn't supplied. I like to add this error checking so that the

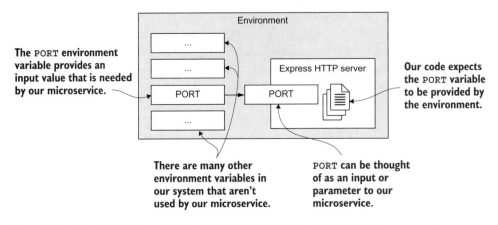

Figure 2.9   Using the PORT environment variable to configure our microservice

microservice clearly states the configuration it's expecting. This means we can't accidentally start our microservice in production without configuring it. If we try that, the microservice will refuse to start, and it's going to tell us the reason why.

I think it's better that the microservice refuses to start rather than operate on potentially the wrong configuration simply because we forgot to configure it. The microservice then shows us how to fix the problem. This means we don't have to waste time debugging the code to figure out what the problem is.

Listing 2.5   Configuring a microservice

```
const express = require("express");
const fs = require("fs");

const app = express();

if (!process.env.PORT) {
  throw new Error(--snip--);
}
```
Throws an error that tells us when the required environment variable isn't supplied

```
const PORT = process.env.PORT;
```
Copies the environment variable to a global variable for easy access

```
--snip--

app.listen(PORT)
```
Starts the HTTP server using the port number that was input to the microservice

Now, let's run this code:

```
cd chpater-2/example-3
npm install
node src/index.js
```

Oops. We forgot to configure the required environment variable, and our microservice has thrown the error! How did we forget so soon about the environment variable we were supposed to configure? It's important that we don't waste time debugging configuration errors; we have enough to worry about without making more problems for ourselves. But it's okay because the error log conveniently gives us a helpful message telling us how to fix the problem:

```
Error: Please specify the port number for the HTTP server
 ➥ with the environment variable PORT.
    at Object.<anonymous> (chapter-2\example-3\index.js:7:11)
```

Now we must set the PORT environment variable before trying to run the code again. On Linux and macOS, we set it using this command:

```
export PORT=3000
```

On Windows, do this instead:

```
set PORT=3000
```

Start the microservice again:

```
node src/index.js
```

It should work correctly now. We set the PORT environment variable so the microservice knows which port number to use for its HTTP server. To test this, we can point our browser at http://localhost:3000/video. We should see our video playing the same as before.

Now that we can configure the port for the HTTP server, we could easily start multiple separate instances of this microservice directly on our development computer. We can only do that if they have different port numbers. Because we can set the port number, we can easily start each microservice using a different port. This doesn't make a lot of sense with a single microservice, but soon we'll have multiple different microservices, and to run them at the same time, we'll have to start them on separate port numbers.

Configuring our microservices through environment variables is important and is something we'll use again in future chapters. For example, we're going to need it when we add the database to our application (chapter 4) and when we connect our microservices to a message queue server (chapter 5).

We can also use environment variables to pass secret and sensitive data into a microservice (e.g., the password for our database). We need to treat this information carefully, and we shouldn't store it in the code where everyone in the company can see it. In chapter 12, we'll touch on the important topic of managing sensitive configuration such as passwords and API keys.

2.6.7   *Setting up for production*

So far, we set up our microservice to run on our development computer. That's all well and good—we need that for ongoing development and testing—but before we get to the fun stuff (Docker, Kubernetes, Terraform, etc.), we need to know how to set up our microservice to run in the production environment.

When I say *production environment*, what I mean is our *customer-facing* environment. That's where our application is hosted so it can be accessed by our customers. For this book, our production environment is Kubernetes, and we're gearing up to run our application in a Kubernetes cluster to make it publicly accessible.

I've already said that to get an existing Node.js project ready to run, you must first install dependencies like this:

```
npm install
```

Well, to get our microservice ready to run in production, we'll use a slightly different version of this command:

```
npm install --omit=dev
```

We added the argument `--omit=dev` to omit development dependencies and only install those dependencies that are required in production. This is important because when creating a Node.js project, we'll usually have a bunch of these so-called *dev dependencies* that we only need to support our development efforts—we don't want to install these into our production environment. You haven't seen an example of dev dependencies yet, but you'll see it coming up in the next section.

Up until now, we've run our HTTP server on our dev computer like this:

```
node src/index.js
```

That's OK, but now we'll start running our microservice using the following standard convention for Node.js:

```
npm start
```

Invoking the command `npm start` is the conventional way to start a Node.js application. This is a special case of an *npm script*, and soon you'll see more examples of different types of npm scripts. In listing 2.6 (chapter-2/example-3/package.json), you can see that we've updated the package.json file to include a `start` script under the `scripts` field. This simply runs Node.js with index.js as the argument.

There are no surprises here, but the nice thing about this convention is that for almost any Node.js project (at least those that follow this convention), we can run `npm start` without actually knowing if the main file is called index.js or if it has some other name. We also don't need to know if the application takes any special command-line arguments or configuration because those details can be recorded here as well.

This gives us a single command to remember regardless of whatever project we're looking at and however the particular application is started. This makes understanding how to use any Node.js project much easier, even those created by other people.

Listing 2.6   Adding a `start` script to package.json

```
{
  "name": "example-1",
  "version": "1.0.0",
  "description": "",
  "main": "src/index.js",
  "scripts": {
    "start": "node src/index.js"          ⊲──── Adding the npm start script to
  },                                              package.json lets us run this
  "keywords": [],                                 project with "npm start."
  "author": "",
  "license": "ISC",
  "dependencies": {
    "express": "^5.0.0-beta.1"
  }
}
```

You'll note in listing 2.6 that I updated the example-3 package.json to include an npm start script. To try it out:

```
cd chapter-2/example-3
npm install
npm start
```

Make sure you run `npm install` to get the dependencies first or execute `npm install --omit=dev` if you want just the production dependencies.

From now on in this book, we'll use `npm start` to run each of our microservices in production. In the future, I'll refer to this as running our microservice in *production mode*. It's worth remembering this command because so many other Node.js applications you'll encounter in the wild conform to this convention, and it's a shortcut you can remember that will help you get other people's code working.

The commands you've just learned are enough for getting our microservice working in production. They are the commands we'll use to get our microservice running in Docker in chapter 3, so we'll return to them soon.

Another useful command you might have heard of is `npm test`. This is the command that is conventionally used to run automated tests for a Node.js project. That's something we'll come back to and investigate in chapter 9.

2.6.8   *Live reloading for fast iteration*

Now that we have a convenient way to set up and run our microservice in production, we can also look for a better way to run it in development. Live reloading our code as we're editing it gets us fast feedback, streamlines our development workflow, and helps us create a rapid pace of development. As we change code, we can immediately see the results of executing the code. Whether the result is an error or output from a successful run doesn't matter; what matters is that we minimize the distance between changing our code and being able to test the result.

In this section, we'll get set up for live reload, as illustrated in figure 2.10. This way of working is important because it automates the restarting of our microservice (but only during development and testing), which helps us cycle more quickly through our personal coding iterations, see instant results, and be more productive. Iteration and fast feedback are crucial in my philosophy of development, as I pointed out in section 2.4. (Live reload also works well with test-driven development, which we'll talk about in chapter 9.)

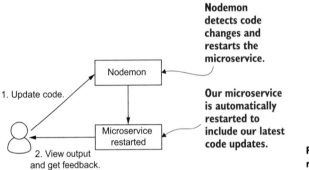

Nodemon detects code changes and restarts the microservice.

Our microservice is automatically restarted to include our latest code updates.

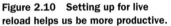

Figure 2.10   Setting up for live reload helps us be more productive.

To create our live reload pipeline, we'll install a package called nodemon. Figure 2.10 shows how it works. We use nodemon to run our microservice, and it automatically watches for code changes in our project. When a code change is detected, nodemon automatically restarts our microservice for us, saving us the effort of doing so manually.

This might not sound like it does much at all, but I've found that it makes for a fast and fluid development cycle. Once you've tried it, you might wonder how you ever did without it. We can install nodemon in our Node.js project as follows:

```
npm install --save-dev nodemon
```

Note that now we're using the --save-dev argument. This installs the package as a *dev dependency* rather than a *production dependency*. I mentioned this in the previous section when talking about installing production-only dependencies for running our microservice in a production environment. Here you can see why it's useful for installing a dependency that you want to have in development while excluding it from production.

We use nodemon during development, but there's no need to have it installed in production where, at best, it's just useless bloat, and, at worst, it might be a security concern. Not that I have any reason to believe nodemon in particular has any security problems. But, generally, the less we install in our production environment, the better. This is a topic we'll return to in chapter 12 when we talk about security.

So, when we run `npm install --omit=dev`, the packages we install to help with development, such as nodemon, will be excluded. Normally, when we run our Node.js code, we do it like this:

```
node src/index.js
```

Now that we're going to be using nodemon instead, we'll replace `node` with `nodemon` and run it like this:

```
npx nodemon src/index.js
```

The `npx` command that's suddenly appeared is a useful command that comes with Node.js and allows us to run locally installed packages directly from the command line. Before `npx` was added to Node.js, we used to install modules such as nodemon globally. Now we can run tools like this directly from the current project's dependencies. This really helps us use the right versions of modules for each project and prevents our computer from being cluttered up with globally installed modules.

Stopping the microservice running under nodemon is the same as when it's running under Node.js. Just press Ctrl-C at the terminal where it's running, and the microservice stops.

I usually like to wrap nodemon in an npm script called `start:dev`. This is a personal convention of mine, but I find that many other developers have something similar, often with a different name. You can see how our updated project setup looks in listing 2.7 (chapter-2/example-3/package.json). At the bottom of the package.json, nodemon has been added as a `devDependency`, and you can see our new script, `start:dev`, in the `scripts` section.

Listing 2.7 Adding a `start` script for development

```
{
  "name": "example-3",
  "version": "1.0.0",
  "description": "",
  "main": "src/index.js",
  "scripts": {
    "start": "node src/index.js",
    "start:dev": "nodemon src/index.js"
  },
  "keywords": [],
  "author": "",
  "license": "ISC",
  "dependencies": {
    "express": "^5.0.0-beta.1"
  },
  "devDependencies": {
    "nodemon": "^2.0.18"
  }
}
```

The normal start script starts this microservice in production mode.

Our new start:dev script starts this microservice in development mode.

Development dependencies go here; these are dependencies that aren't installed in production.

The new dependency on the nodemon package that we just added

In the previous section, you learned about the convention of using `npm start`. We configured our project so that we could run our code in production mode like this:

```
npm start
```

Now that we've defined the `start:dev` command, we can run our microservice in development mode like this:

```
npm run start:dev
```

Notice the use of `npm run` to run our new script. We can use `npm run` to run any npm script that we add to our package.json file. This is a great way to add build scripts and other utility scripts to our project. We can omit the `run` part for `npm start` and `npm test` (which you'll learn about in chapter 9) because npm has special support for these particular conventions.

This should tell you that this `start:dev` script isn't a Node.js convention the way `start` and `test` are. That's why we have to specifically use the `npm run` command to invoke it. Using `start:dev` to run in development is simply my own personal convention. We'll use it throughout this book though, and I'm sure you'll also find it useful in your own development process.

With these commands in place, we can run our microservice in either production mode or development mode. It's important to make this distinction so that we can cater separately to the differing needs of each mode.

In development mode, we'd like to optimize for fast iterations and rapid development. Alternatively, in production mode, we'd like to optimize for performance and security. These requirements are at odds with each other; so, we must treat them separately. You'll see this become important again in chapters 6, 7, and 8, as we approach production deployment of our microservices application.

> **NOTE** All the microservices that are forthcoming in this book follow the conventions that we've laid down in the previous two sections.

2.6.9 *Running the finished code from this chapter*

If you get to this point and you haven't yet tried out the code in this chapter, now is the time to do so. Here's a quick summary to show you how easy it is to get the examples in this chapter running. Get a local copy of the chapter-2 code, either by downloading it or cloning the chapter-2 repository from GitHub:

- To look at the streaming video, try out example-2.
- To see the example of configuring a microservice using environment variables, try example-3.

As an example, let's say you want to try out example-3. Open a terminal, and change to the appropriate subdirectory:

```
cd chapter-2/example-3
```

Now, install the dependencies:

```
npm install
```

If you wanted to simulate a production deployment, you'd do this instead:

```
npm install --omit=dev
```

To run it like you would in production, invoke

```
npm start
```

To run it with live reload for fast development, invoke

```
npm run start:dev
```

These are the main commands you need to remember to run any Node.js example in this book. Put a bookmark on this page, and jump back here whenever you need to remember how to do this.

2.7 Node.js review

Before we move on, we have time for a quick review of all the Node.js commands you've learned in this chapter, as listed in table 2.3.

Table 2.3 Review of Node.js commands

Command	Description
`node --version`	Checks that Node.js is installed; prints the version number
`npm init -y`	Creates a default Node.js project with a stub for our package.json, the file that tracks metadata and dependencies for our Node.js project
`npm install --save <package-name>`	Installs an npm package. There are many other packages available on npm, and you can install any by inserting a specific package name.
`npm install`	Installs all dependencies for a Node.js project that have been recorded in package.json
`node <script-file>`	Runs a Node.js script file. We invoke the `node` command and give it the name of our script file as an argument. You can call your script main.js or server.js if you want, but it's probably best to stick to the convention and just call it index.js.
`npm start`	The conventional npm script for starting a Node.js application regardless of what name the main script file has or what command-line parameters it expects. Typically, this translates into `node index.js` in the package.json file, but it depends on the author of the project and how they have set it up. The nice thing is that no matter how a particular project is structured, you only have to remember `npm start`.
`npm run start:dev`	My personal convention for starting a Node.js project in development. I add this to the scripts in package.json. Typically, it runs something like nodemon to enable live reload of your code as you work on it.

2.8   *Continue your learning*

This chapter has been a fast-paced introduction to building a barebones HTTP server with Node.js. Unfortunately, we've barely scratched the surface. But this book isn't about Node.js; that is simply the vehicle we're using to travel to the land of microservices. I do, however, have some references for you to learn more should you wish to drill deeper and gain more expertise in Node.js and Git:

- *Get Programming with Node.js* by Jonathan Wexler (Manning, 2019)
- *Node.js in Action*, 2nd ed., by Alex R. Young, Bradley Meck, and Mike Cantelon (Manning, 2017)
- *Git in Practice* by Mike McQuaid (Manning, 2014)

In addition, see the extensive Node.js documentation that you can find online at https://nodejs.org/en/docs/.

Next, we'll move on to packaging and publishing our microservice so that it's ready for deployment to the cloud. For this, we'll use Docker, a tool that has become ubiquitous and indispensable in our industry. Docker has made microservices more accessible and has done nothing less than revolutionize the way we build and deploy our software.

Summary

- Our philosophy of development for this project is *iterate, keep it working, start simple.*
- To create and work on individual microservices, we need a development environment on our local development computer.
- To edit code, we need an editor such as VS Code.
- Git is used to clone the example code repository. You'll also use Git as you're working to record your code changes.
- Node.js is made for developing network-oriented distributed applications and makes it particularly easy to create individual microservices.
- Using JavaScript promotes fullstack coding and makes it easier to switch between working on the backend and the frontend of our application.
- Express.js is the de facto standard web server framework for Node.js and allows our microservices to handle incoming HTTP requests from the network.
- Streaming video is a simple example to use in our first microservice and is the core feature of the FlixTube application.
- Our first microservice supports running in either development or production mode, which is important because these modes have different needs.
- Using nodemon to run our microservice enables live reload in development for fast feedback to help create a rapid pace of development.
- Environment variables are the way we configure microservices throughout this book.

Publishing
your first microservice

3

This chapter covers

- Differences between images and containers
- Using Docker in the development environment
- Packaging and publishing your microservice as a Docker image
- Creating a private container registry
- Instantiating your microservice in a container

By the end of this book, we'll have deployed multiple microservices to our production environment: a Kubernetes cluster. But before we can deploy an entire microservices application, we must first be able to package and publish a single microservice! In this chapter, we'll take the video-streaming microservice we created in chapter 2 and publish it so that it's ready for deployment to our cluster.

To deploy a microservice to a cluster running in the cloud, we have to publish it somewhere that's accessible by the cluster. To achieve this, we must first package our code, assets, and dependencies into a single bundle. We'll then need a location in the cloud to host this package. For that, we'll create a container registry. If you haven't heard of containers yet, this will be explained soon.

In this book, we want to emulate the building of a proprietary application for a private company. Security and privacy are important, and that's why we'll create a private container registry as opposed to a public one. We'll create this container registry manually on Microsoft Azure, but later, in chapter 7, you'll learn how you can build your registry with code. At the end of this chapter, we'll test that we can instantiate our published microservice directly from the remote container registry onto our development computer.

3.1   New tool: Docker

This chapter introduces an important new tool: Docker (see table 3.1). We lay some necessary groundwork in this chapter because from here on in, we'll use Docker extensively. You'll also need some basic skills in place to understand how it works, which will help you troubleshoot when things go wrong.

Table 3.1   Tool introduced in chapter 3

Tool	Version	Purpose
Docker	24.0.5	We use Docker to package, publish, and test our microservices.

Docker works on Linux, macOS, and Windows 10+. If you're working on Windows, you'll first need to install WSL2 (the Windows integrated Linux kernel); see section 3.7.1 for a link to download and install WSL2 for Windows.

3.2   Getting the code

This chapter has only one example project, which is based on example-2 from chapter 2. It's the video-streaming microservice we created in that chapter. To follow along in this chapter, you need to download the code or clone the repository.

You can download a zip file of the code from here: http://mng.bz/XqEp. You can clone the code using Git like this:

```
git clone
➥ https://github.com/bootstrapping-microservices-2nd-edition/chapter-3
```

For help on installing and using Git, see chapter 2. If you have problems with the code, log an issue in the repository in GitHub.

3.3   What is a container?

Simply put, a container (as the name implies) is something that contains something else. What does it contain? In this situation, we'll use it to contain (or host) a microservice.

DEFINITION   A *container* is a way of virtualizing a server.

More formally, a container provides a way of virtualizing both the operating system and the hardware. This allows us to abstract (or *virtualize*) the resources required by our microservice. Containers provide a way to divide up the resources on one computer so that we can share these among many such services. Containers are one of the modern technologies that help make it cost effective to run microservices.

Containers are often compared to virtual machines (VMs). Both VMs and containers allow us to isolate our microservices to prevent them from interfering with each other. Before containers were invented, we ran our services in VMs, and we can still choose to do that when appropriate today. Figure 3.1 compares VMs to containers so you can visualize the differences.

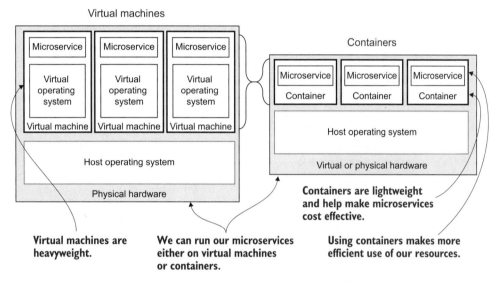

Figure 3.1   Comparing virtual machines to containers

As you can see in figure 3.1, VMs are more heavyweight than containers. A VM contains a complete copy of its operating system that's running on fully virtualized hardware. A container, on the other hand, virtualizes the operating system as well as the hardware. A container is therefore smaller and does less work, which makes for more efficient use of our computing resources.

Ultimately, we'll have many containers running on our Kubernetes cluster. But for now, we're aiming to instantiate just a single container to host the video-streaming microservice we created in the previous chapter.

3.4   What is an image?

As you know, an image is a snapshot of something, but the word *image* is used in many different scenarios. We could be talking about an image that's a photograph, or we could be talking about an image that's a snapshot of the hard drive for a VM. In this book, we're talking about Docker images.

> **DEFINITION**   An *image* is a bootable snapshot of a server (in our case, a microservice), including all the code, dependencies, and assets that it needs to run.

In the example for this chapter, we create a snapshot of our video-streaming microservice. Images are *immutable*, which means an image that has been produced can't be modified. Containers, on the other hand, aren't immutable. Once an image has been instantiated to a container, the contents of its filesystem can be modified. We'll make use of this in chapter 5 for an improved development experience.

Knowing images are immutable is important. We might have applied tests or security checks to an image, and because we know the image can't be tampered with, we know that our tests and security checks will remain valid.

You can think of an image as being a dormant version of a microservice, a way of storing it prior to running it. It's in a state just waiting to be booted as a container, ready for when we need to instantiate it into our application.

Figure 3.2 shows how a container is booted from an image. The image itself contains everything needed to instantiate a container: the code for the microservice, its dependencies, and any other assets and resources that our microservice needs to do its job.

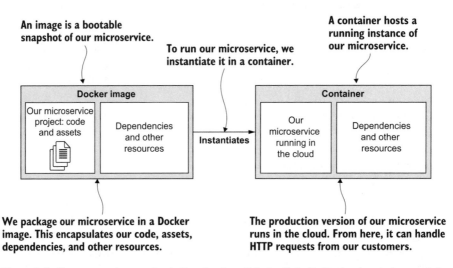

Figure 3.2   To run our microservice in the cloud, we'll instantiate its Docker image in a container.

Soon, we'll build an image for our microservice and run it as a container. Before that, let's learn more about Docker.

3.5   *Why Docker?*

I'm sure you've already heard about Docker. It's probably one of the reasons you bought this book. Almost everyone building cloud-based applications is using Docker or wanting to use it. Let's look at why this is.

Docker is quasi-ubiquitous in the software industry. There are alternatives to Docker, but Docker as a technology for packaging and deploying containers has captured mainstream attention. It's well known and well supported.

Docker is even making inroads in other areas. For example, I've heard of people using Docker to deploy applications to Internet of Things (IoT) devices. What exactly is the job it's doing for us? Docker is the tool we'll use to package and publish our microservices. Although there is a lot you can learn about Docker, we'll learn the minimum we need to get this show on the road. At the end of this chapter, I'll provide references for you to dig deeper to understand Docker more broadly.

I like to think of Docker as the *universal package manager*: the one package manager to rule them all! Normally, you wouldn't think of Docker in this way, but if you think it through, it kind of makes sense. The *package manager* part is obvious; we use Docker to package and publish our work. I say that it's *universal* because it supports many different technology stacks. Docker is open source, and you can find the code for the command-line interface (CLI) tool here: https://github.com/docker/cli. You can see other open source projects from the makers of Docker here: www.docker.com/community/open source.

> **Standardize your environment**
>
> Docker is also really good for standardizing your environments, ensuring that all of your developers run the same development environment. This, in turn, is the same as the production environment. It maximizes the probability that code that works in development also works in production, giving developers a better chance to find problems before the code gets to the customer.

3.6   Why do we need Docker?

Let's break this question down. We'll use Docker for these tasks:

- Package our microservice into a Docker image
- Publish our image to our private container registry
- Run our microservice in a container

The last bullet point is most important. We want to have our microservice running in our production environment, but we can only do that if we first package and publish it.

We aren't ready to deploy our microservice to production just yet, so instead, we'll focus on learning the Docker commands that we need to package, publish, and test our image on our development computer.

Figure 3.3 gives you the general picture of what we need to do here. We'll take the Node.js project for our video-streaming microservice (on the left of figure 3.3), package it as a Docker image, and then publish it to our private container registry. From there, we can deploy the microservice to our Kubernetes cluster (that's a job we'll save for chapter 6).

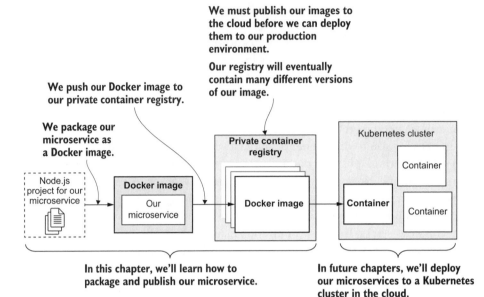

We package our
microservice as
a Docker image.

We push our Docker image to
our private container registry.

We must publish our images to
the cloud before we can deploy
them to our production
environment.

Our registry will eventually
contain many different versions
of our image.

In this chapter, we'll learn how to
package and publish our microservice.

In future chapters, we'll deploy
our microservices to a Kubernetes
cluster in the cloud.

Figure 3.3   Publishing Docker images to our private container registry in the cloud

3.7   *Adding Docker to our development environment*

Before we can use Docker, we must upgrade our development environment. To follow along with this chapter, you'll need to have Docker installed on your own computer. In this section, we install Docker and make sure it's ready to go.

Figure 3.4 shows what our development environment will look like with Docker installed. Even though you can see that we'll run our Node.js microservice under Docker, we won't always have to run our microservices this way. When we're testing an individual microservice, we can still choose to run it directly on our host operating system (without using Docker), just like we did in chapter 2.

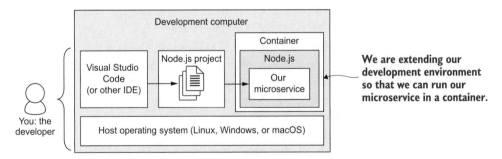

Figure 3.4   Extending our development to run our microservice in a container

Because we need to package our microservice using Docker, it's useful to be able to test it locally, both before and after we publish it. The ability to test will be useful later for any microservice that is misbehaving on Kubernetes. We'll talk more about that in chapter 11.

3.7.1 Installing Docker

To install Docker, go to the Docker website at https://docs.docker.com. Once there, find the download/install link, and follow the instructions to install Docker Desktop for your platform. Table 3.2 provides the details for installing Docker for your particular platform.

On Windows, you need WSL2 (the Windows integrated Linux kernel) installed before you install Docker. Follow the instructions in table 3.2 to do that.

Table 3.2 Platforms supported by Docker

Platform	Description
Linux/macOS	Go to the Docker website at https://docs.docker.com. Click the download/install link, and follow the instructions to install Docker Desktop on your system.
Windows	WSL2 must be installed before you can install and use Docker.
	To install WSL2, follow the instructions here:
	https://docs.microsoft.com/en-us/windows/wsl/install.
	After installing WSL2, you can install Docker with the instructions here:
	https://docs.docker.com/desktop/windows/install/.

Windows users: Linux terminal or Windows Terminal?

If you're a Windows user, you need WSL2 and a virtual installation of Linux to be able to use Docker. After installing WSL2 and Docker, you'll be able to use Docker from the Windows Terminal. In fact, I do most of my day-to-day work on Windows using Windows Terminal. (You can install Windows Terminal for free from the Microsoft Store.)

Many of the commands we'll cover in this book will work from the Windows Terminal; however, some of the later examples of commands in this book will only run from a Unix-style terminal. For example, in chapter 8, we'll be running various shell scripts that won't work from Windows Terminal. These will work under Windows, but you have to be running them under your virtual Linux terminal (powered by WSL2).

Don't worry about it too much for now. If you're happier using Windows Terminal, please continue to use that. If you'd like to get more into using virtual Linux under WSL2, that's also okay. I'll let you know later in the book which examples require Linux.

3.7.2 Checking your Docker installation

Once you have Docker installed, you can use the terminal to check that it's okay by printing the version:

```
docker --version
```

If you have the same version installed as I do (as of this writing), the output will look like this:

```
Docker version 24.0.5, build ced0996
```

But don't worry if you're using a later version of Docker. Most likely, it will be backward compatible.

3.8   *Packaging our microservice*

With Docker installed, we can start to think about using it to package our microservice for deployment. Ultimately, we want to deploy our microservice to production. But first, we need everything bundled and ready to ship. We'll package our microservice with the following steps:

  1 Create a Dockerfile for our microservice.
  2 Package our microservice as a Docker image.
  3 Test the published image by booting it as a container.

3.8.1   *Creating a Dockerfile*

For every Docker image we want to create, we must create a Dockerfile. You can see the location of this file within the example-1 project in figure 3.5.

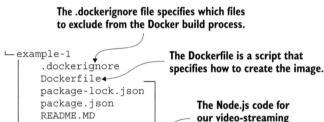

Figure 3.5   The layout of the example-1 project showing the location of the Dockerfile

The *Dockerfile* is a specification for an image created by Docker. I like to think of the Dockerfile as a script file with instructions on how to construct the image. You can see this illustrated in figure 3.6.

The lines in the Dockerfile define our microservice, its dependencies, and any supporting assets. Different lines in the Dockerfile cause different files to be copied across to the image. To the Dockerfile, we'll add instructions for copying across our Node.js project and for installing our npm dependencies.

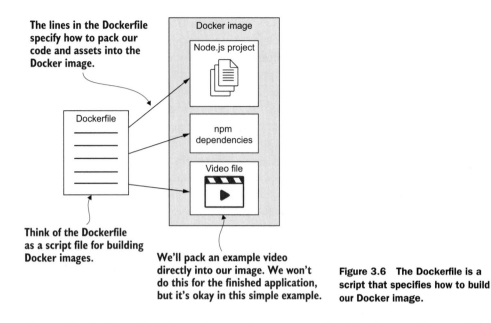

The lines in the Dockerfile specify how to pack our code and assets into the Docker image.

Think of the Dockerfile as a script file for building Docker images.

We'll pack an example video directly into our image. We won't do this for the finished application, but it's okay in this simple example.

Figure 3.6 The Dockerfile is a script that specifies how to build our Docker image.

Also notice in figure 3.6 that we're copying an example video into our image. Baking the video into the image isn't something we'll want to do in the final production version, but it's useful in this example—we don't yet have any other way of storing this video.

Having only a single video would make for a pretty boring video-streaming application, but fixing that will have to wait until chapter 4. For now, this serves as a good example to show that it's not just code we can include in our image. Copying other types of assets into an image presents no problem for Docker!

Listing 3.1 (chapter-3/example-1/Dockerfile) shows the Dockerfile for our video-streaming microservice. There's not much to it, but it's a good example of a Dockerfile for a Node.js application. Have a read, and try to visualize how each line copies files to the resulting image.

Listing 3.1 A Dockerfile for our video-streaming microservice

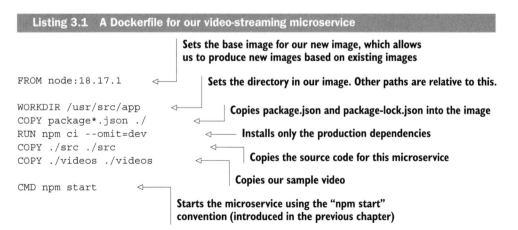

Sets the base image for our new image, which allows us to produce new images based on existing images

```
FROM node:18.17.1
```
Sets the directory in our image. Other paths are relative to this.

```
WORKDIR /usr/src/app
COPY package*.json ./
RUN npm ci --omit=dev
COPY ./src ./src
COPY ./videos ./videos

CMD npm start
```

Copies package.json and package-lock.json into the image

Installs only the production dependencies

Copies the source code for this microservice

Copies our sample video

Starts the microservice using the "npm start" convention (introduced in the previous chapter)

In listing 3.1, the first line includes the FROM instruction. This specifies the *base image* from which we derive our new image. By saying our base image is node:18.17.1, we're stating that our derived image should include Node.js version 18.17.1.

If you're working with languages or frameworks other than JavaScript and Node.js, then you'll choose a different base image. Choose one that is appropriate to your own tech stack.

Being able to choose the base image is extremely useful. We might choose to use any of the many public images available on Docker Hub (https://hub.docker.com), or we can even create our own custom base image. This means we can reuse existing images, and by the end of this book, we'll also have seen several examples of reusing third-party images.

Also in listing 3.1 are various lines with the COPY instruction. These lines copy files into our image. You can see that package.json, package-lock.json, our code, and the example video are all copied into the image.

The RUN instruction is worth noting too. You can run software within the image during the build process to make changes to the image, install dependencies, and perform other setup tasks. In this example, we use RUN to install our npm dependencies to bake them into the image.

The last and most important line in listing 3.1 is the CMD instruction. This sets the command that is invoked when our container is instantiated. This is how we tell it to run our Node.js application using the npm start script we added to our package.json file in chapter 2 (section 2.6.7).

The .dockerignore file

You're probably wondering about the .dockerignore file from the example-1 project that is depicted in figure 3.5. It's completely optional, but very useful, to include this file in your Docker project because here you can list the files and directories that Docker should ignore during the build process. If you ever find your Docker builds are slower than you think they should be, it might be because they're dealing with too many files.

Typically, we should add directories such as .git, .github, and node_modules to the .dockerignore file. These directories can grow very large and aren't needed for the build process (node_modules is usually created within the image during the build process). If you forget to make Docker ignore directories like these, the Docker build process will get slower and slower as your project grows larger.

3.8.2   *Packaging and checking our Docker image*

Now that we've created our Dockerfile, we can package our microservice as a *ready-to-run* image. We'll build the image using the docker build command, which takes as input our Docker file containing the instructions to build the image. Figure 3.7 shows this process in action.

> **NOTE**   Before we can deploy our microservice to production, we must be able to package it in a Docker image.

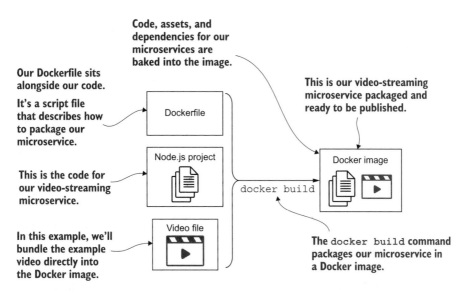

Figure 3.7 The `docker build` command produces a Docker image as specified by our Dockerfile.

Now comes the fun part. It's time to create an image from our microservice. To follow along, you'll need a Dockerfile like the one shown earlier in listing 3.1 and a Node.js project. You can create your own or use example-1 from the chapter-3 code repository on GitHub (see section 3.2).

When you're ready, open a terminal, and change the directory to chapter-3/example-1 (or whichever directory contains your code and Dockerfile). Now invoke `docker build` as follows:

```
cd chapter-3/example-1
docker build -t video-streaming --file Dockerfile .
```

Don't forget to add the period (full stop) at the end of that command! It's easy to miss, but that's what tells the command to operate on the current directory.

Let's understand the various parts of this command:

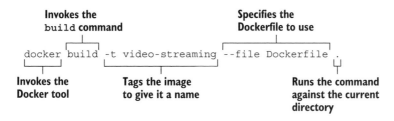

When you invoke `docker build`, you'll see the various pieces of the base image being downloaded. This download only happens the first time; subsequently, you'll already have the base image cached on your computer, so it won't be downloaded again (at least not until you delete all of your local images later in section 3.9.3). Once it completes, you should see something like this at the end of the output:

```
[+] Building 2.0s (11/11) FINISHED

--snip--

 => => writing image sha256:2c68c7c4e2989f9aaeacb30abaedf...
 => => naming to docker.io/library/video-streaming
```

This tells you that the image was successfully built. The output shows the unique ID for your image and displays the tag that you set for it.

> **NOTE** When you invoke this command for yourself, you'll see a different output because the ID allocated to your image will be different from the ID that was allocated to my image.

Because it's a unique ID, it's going to be different for every new image that you create. You can take note of this ID if you want and use it to reference the image in future Docker commands. You don't really need to do that, however, because we tagged it with a meaningful name (video-streaming) that we can use instead of the ID.

Note also in the output that the version was automatically set to latest because we didn't specify anything for it. In chapter 8, we'll set this version automatically as part of our continuous deployment pipeline. This will distinguish each new version of the image we produce as we iteratively update our code and build new images.

Some other points to note are as follows:

- *The -t argument allows us to tag or name our image.* You'll want to do this; otherwise, you'll have to reference your image by its unique ID, the big ugly string of numbers you saw in the previous output. Having a tag that we can more easily remember is better than relying on the ID.
- *The --file argument specifies the name of the Dockerfile to use.* Technically, this is unnecessary because it defaults to the file named Dockerfile anyway. I'm including this explicitly so that you know about it, and it's something we'll make use of later in chapter 5. In that chapter, we'll separate our Dockerfiles to have different versions for development and production.
- *Don't forget the period at the end!* It's easy to miss. The period tells the build command to operate against the current directory. This means that any instructions in the Dockerfile are relative to the current working directory. Changing this directory makes it possible to store our Dockerfile in a directory different from our project's assets. This can be useful at times, but it's not a feature we need right now.

Here's the general format for the docker build command:

```
docker build -t <your-name-for-the-image> --file <path-to-your-Dockerfile>
➥ <path-to-project>
```

We can plug in the particular name of our microservice as the image name, the path to its Dockerfile, and the path to its project folder. After building our image, we should now check it to make sure it's okay. We can list our local images using this command:

```
docker image list
```

This lists the images on our local computer. If our `docker build` command from the previous section completed successfully, we should see the image we just built:

```
REPOSITORY          TAG      IMAGE ID       CREATED         SIZE
video-streaming     latest   bffcbcc3f39c   6 seconds ago   1.1GB
```

You might see other images in this list if you've already been using Docker to create other images locally or if you've been exploring the many publicly available images on Docker Hub (see the sidebar, "Exploring other containers," later in this chapter).

Note the columns in the preceding output. Under the REPOSITORY column, you can see `video-streaming`, where `video-streaming` is the image for our microservice that we just created.

TAG is the next column, and it usually shows the image's version number. Because we didn't specifically choose a version for our video-streaming image, it was automatically allocated the version `latest`.

The next column is IMAGE ID, which shows the unique ID for each image. Note here that the ID for our video-streaming image is a shortened version of the same from the earlier output of the `build` command. Again, expect the unique ID for your image to be different to what you see here. Other columns in this output include CREATED, which tells you when the image was created, and SIZE, which shows you the size of the image.

3.8.3 *Booting our microservice in a container*

Before we publish our newly created Docker image, we should do a test run on our development computer to make sure everything is in working order. Once we've packaged our microservice as a Docker image, we can use the `docker run` command to instantiate it as a container, as shown in figure 3.8. This creates a local instance of our video-streaming microservice that we can then test using a web browser.

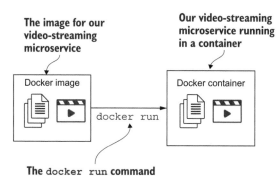

The image for our video-streaming microservice

Our video-streaming microservice running in a container

Docker image

docker run

Docker container

The `docker run` command instantiates our Docker image in a container.

Figure 3.8   The `docker run` command produces an instance of our microservice running in a container.

When you're ready, invoke the following command to instantiate your microservice from the image:

```
cd chapter-3/example-1
docker run -d -p 3000:3000 -e PORT=3000 video-streaming
```

There's a lot going on there, so let's understand the parts of that command:

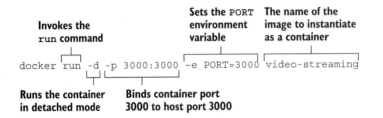

On running the command, you should see the unique ID for the container printed as output. Here is the output from when I invoked the command:

```
460a199466896e02dd1ed601f9f6b132dd9ad9b42bbd3df351460e5eeacbe6ce
```

Seeing such output means your microservice started successfully. When you run this command, you'll see different output because your container will have a unique ID different from mine. You'll still see a big, long string of numbers like that shown, just different. You'll need this ID to invoke future Docker commands that relate to the container.

Don't worry about trying to remember it (unless you have a photographic memory) because you can easily recall this and other details of the container on demand, as you'll soon see. Following are some points to note:

- *The -d argument causes our container to run in detached mode.* This means it runs in the background so we can't directly see its logs. If we omitted this, our container would run in the foreground, and we'd see its output directly, which can be useful sometimes but also ties up our terminal.
- *The -p argument binds the port between the host operating system and our container.* This is like port forwarding; network traffic sent to port 3000 on our development computer is forwarded to port 3000 inside our container. We set it up this way because we configure our microservice to listen on port 3000 (see the next bullet point).
- *The -e argument sets the PORT environment variable to 3000.* This configures this microservice to run on that port. The number 3000 itself isn't important here. We could have used almost any number for this, but 3000 is often used by convention when developing/testing individual HTTP servers.

- *The last argument,* video-streaming, *is the name we gave our image.* This is how we specify which image (we could have many) will be instantiated. This relates to the name we gave the image using docker build and the -t argument back in section 3.8.2.

A common error at this point is when the port we're using (e.g., port 3000) is already allocated to another application. If this happens, you'll need to either shut down the other application, or, if you can't do that, you'll have to choose a port other than 3000. You can do this by using a PORT environment variable as we did in section 2.6.6 in chapter 2.

Here is the general format for the docker run command:

```
docker run -d p <host-port>:<container-port> -e <name>=<value> <image-name>
```

You can use this to boot other microservices by plugging in the particular name for each image that you create.

CHECKING THE CONTAINER

We have a running container now, but let's check to make sure it's in working order. To show the containers you have, invoke this command:

```
docker container list
```

Here's a cut-down version of the output:

```
CONTAINER ID   IMAGE            STATUS          PORTS
460a19946689   video-streaming  Up 20 seconds   0.0.0.0:3000->3000/tcp
```

Your output will look different from that shown because I removed the columns COMMAND, CREATED, and NAMES to make it fit. But you can invoke the command yourself to see those.

Note the CONTAINER ID column. This shows you the unique ID of the container. It's a reduced version of the longer ID that was output from the docker run command in the previous section. Both are the unique IDs of your container, and, as you'll see in a moment, we'll use the ID to identify the container when we run Docker commands against it.

CHECKING OUR MICROSERVICE

We've successfully instantiated a container from our image and checked that it's running. But how do we know if our microservice inside the container is functional? It could be throwing all sorts of errors, and, as yet, we wouldn't know about it. Let's check the output of the microservice and see what it tells us:

```
docker logs 460a19946689
```

Whoa, hold up! You can't just invoke that command and use the unique ID for my container. Remember, the ID will be different for the container created on your computer. You'll get an error if you invoke it exactly like this. So, note the ID of *your* container as demonstrated in the previous section, and invoke the command like this, plugging in your own container ID:

```
docker logs <container-id>
```

Now you should see the output from your microservice. If you run the code from example-1 in the chapter-3 code repository, you should see something like this:

```
Microservice listening on port 3000, point your browser at
➡ http://localhost:3000/video
```

Success! We built an image. We instantiated it as a container, and we confirmed that our microservice is operational.

Now, let's test this in the web browser. Point your browser at http://localhost :3000/video. You should see the streaming video, and the result should look the same as what we tested earlier in chapter 2.

This works because we used the -p argument with the docker run command to forward port 3000 on our development computer (assuming that this port wasn't already allocated) to port 3000 in the container. Our microservice was listening on port 3000, and it responded!

There's obviously more we could do to test our code, but we'll save that for later. In chapter 9, we'll look at how we can apply automated, code-driven testing to our microservices. Then, in chapter 11, we'll see how to monitor our microservices, how to debug them when problems are found, and what techniques we can use for building fault-tolerant systems. But now, we're ready to publish our image!

Exploring other containers

Did you know that you can easily run any public image using the docker run command? Two images we'll use later in the book are mongodb and rabbitmq. Try running the following command for yourself to get an *instant database* available on localhost:27017. For example:

```
docker run -p 27017:27107 mongo:latest
```

There are many public images available online, and you don't need an account to access these. Search Docker Hub to find more at https://hub.docker.com.

3.8.4 *Debugging the container*

When we're running a container locally, especially one that is having problems, it can be useful to shell into it and inspect it from the inside. This can help us understand what's happening inside our container. We can open a shell into our container like this:

```
docker exec -it <container-id> bash
```

Just make sure you use the *container* ID for your own container (the output from when we started it in section 3.8.3). From here, you can use common Linux commands such as `cd`, `ls`, and `ps` to inspect the filesystem and process inside the container. This is a valuable technique for debugging and understanding what is going on in your container, so please spend some time exploring inside your container.

3.8.5 Stopping the container

Starting our container in detached mode (using the `-d` argument) means that the container is running in the background and will continue running until we explicitly tell it to stop. To stop our container, we must know its ID, which was printed in the terminal earlier when we started the container (see section 3.8.3). If we need to find the container ID again later, we can invoke `docker container list` and pick out our container ID from the list.

To stop the container without deleting it, invoke

```
docker stop <container-id>
```

With the container stopped but not deleted, we can still shell into it, as described in the previous section, to inspect and debug it.

Note that after stopping our container, it no longer appears in the output of `docker container list` because stopped containers aren't shown normally. However, if you add the `--all` argument, that is, `docker container list --all`, the output will also show any stopped containers. After stopping our container, we can delete it like this:

```
docker rm <container-id>
```

3.9 Publishing our microservice

We're close now to having our first microservice ready for production deployment. We've packaged it in a Docker image, but that image currently resides locally on our development computer. That's great for our own testing and experimentation, but we still need to have our image published somewhere so that we can later deploy it to our Kubernetes cluster. Figure 3.9 illustrates how we'll now publish our image to a private container registry hosted in the cloud.

We publish our microservice with the following steps:

1. We create our own private container registry on Azure. We only need to do this the first time we publish an image. Later, when we publish new versions of the image and images for other microservices, we'll simply reuse this same registry.
2. Before publishing, we must authenticate with the registry using the `docker login` command.
3. We use the `docker push` command to upload our image to the registry. (This is the step that publishes our microservice.)
4. We use `docker run` again to check that we can boot our microservice from the published image.

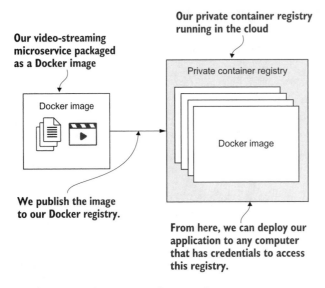

Our private container registry running in the cloud

Our video-streaming microservice packaged as a Docker image

Docker image

Private container registry

Docker image

We publish the image to our Docker registry.

From here, we can deploy our application to any computer that has credentials to access this registry.

Figure 3.9   Publishing our Docker image to a private container registry in the cloud

3.9.1   Creating a private container registry

Creating a private container registry turns out to be pretty simple. We'll create our registry on Azure, but all the major cloud vendors have support for this, so you can easily create your container register on Amazon Web Services (AWS; using Elastic Container Registry [ECR]), Google Cloud Platform (GCP), or another cloud platform. Why publish to a private registry? In this book, we're focused on how to build proprietary applications for a private company, so it makes sense to publish our images privately instead of using a public registry such as Docker Hub.

I'm using Azure for this book because it's the simplest cloud platform to use and a great starting point for learning how to build cloud-native applications. Azure provides a good deal for new signups, with free credit for your first month. That gives you some time to try out the cloud infrastructure demonstrated in this book for free.

Make sure you destroy all of your resources later, though, so you don't end up accidentally continuing to pay for them after your credit has run out. Incidentally, this is another reason to use Azure: Microsoft has made it easy to find and destroy cloud resources so that we don't forget about something and end up paying for unused infrastructure (you won't believe how difficult they make this on AWS). For now, we'll create our container registry manually through the Azure portal UI. But in chapter 7, we'll return to this and instead learn how to create our container registry through code using Terraform.

Load the Azure website (https://azure.microsoft.com) in your browser. Go through the steps to sign up, and then you should be able to sign in to the Azure portal at https://portal.azure.com.

Once in the Azure portal, click the Create a Resource option in the menu on the left. In the Search input box, enter `container registry`, and press Enter. You'll see matching options, as shown in figure 3.10. Find Container Registry by Microsoft. Click Create > Container Registry.

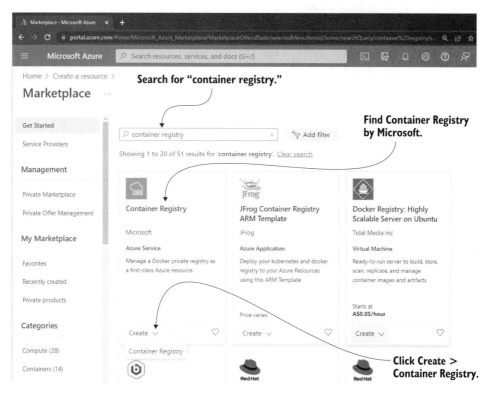

Figure 3.10   Creating a new private container registry in the Azure portal

You should now see a page that explains more about the Microsoft Container Registry. Have a read if you like before clicking the Create button.

Next, we fill in some details about the registry we're creating. Figure 3.11 shows that we first need to provide a name. The name is important because that creates a URL that we'll use later to communicate with the registry. The name I chose for my registry is bmdk1, and this results in having a URL like this: bmdk1.azurecr.io.

Because the name chosen for the registry generates the URL, it must be globally unique. In other words, you can't choose a name that someone else has already taken—you must choose your own unique name. You should take note of the URL because you'll need that soon when you invoke Docker commands for your registry.

Before clicking the Review + Create button, we need to select or create a *resource group*. As its name implies, resource groups in Azure allow cloud resources to be collected into groups for easier management.

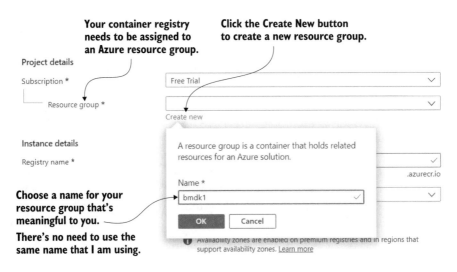

Figure 3.11   Filling out the details for our new private container registry

Figure 3.12 shows that I'm creating a new resource group to contain the new registry that I call bmdk1. To create a new resource group, click Create New, enter a name, and click OK.

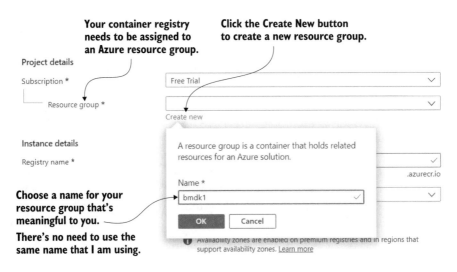

Figure 3.12   Creating a new resource group to contain the private container registry

This name doesn't matter. We can use the same name as before or we can use any other name we like. It doesn't need the same name as the container registry, and this time it doesn't have to be globally unique. Just make sure you give it a name that's meaningful to you so that when you see it again later, you're reminded of its purpose.

Now click the Review + Create button. On the next page, click Create to create your registry.

To follow up on the creation of our registry, we'll need to watch the notifications in the Azure portal. Click the Notification icon to open the Notifications sidebar and watch the progress of our deployment. This might take some time, but when completed, we'll see a Deployment Succeeded notification in the sidebar, as figure 3.13 shows.

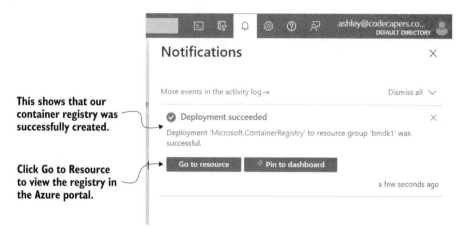

This shows that our container registry was successfully created.

Click Go to Resource to view the registry in the Azure portal.

Figure 3.13 The deployment of our new container registry was successful!

From the Deployment Succeeded notification, we can click Go to Resource to view details of the new registry. Otherwise, if we need to find our registry again later, click All Resources on the left-hand menu. Figure 3.14 shows that this lists all of our resources (if others have been created), along with our new container registry.

Next, click your container registry in the list to drill down to its details, and then click Access Keys in the menu on the left (see figure 3.15). You can see the registry's URL here.

> **NOTE** It's important to enable the Admin User option here to authenticate with our registry when pushing and pulling our images.

Now take note of your registry's username and password (you only need the first password). Don't bother noting the ones you see in figure 3.15. These are the details for my registry, and it won't exist by the time you read this. Be sure to use the details for your own registry!

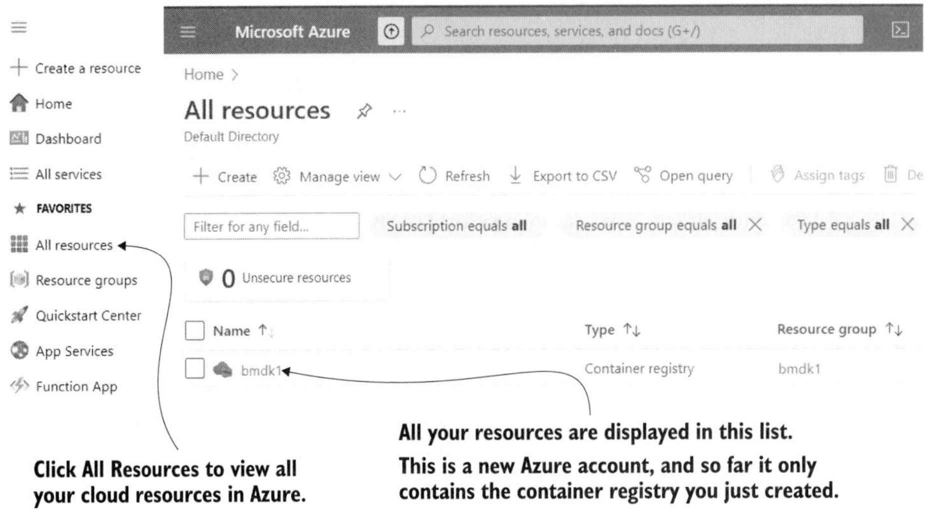

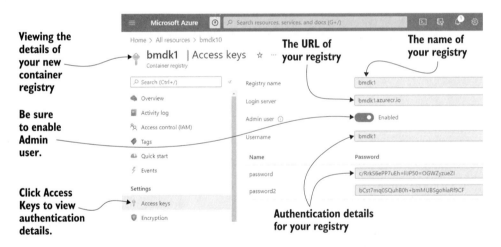

Figure 3.14   You can find your container registry in the All Resources list. At this stage, you only have a single resource, the registry itself.

Figure 3.15   Viewing the authentication details of your new private container registry

That's all there is to it! If you followed these instructions, you now have your own private container registry. You can push your images to the registry, and from there, you can deploy these to production. So, let's get our first image published!

> **Public vs. private**
>
> For this book, we're only interested in publishing private Docker images. But you might be interested to know that you can also publish public images. For example, let's say you create an open source microservice. Create a Docker image for it, and then publish it publicly to Docker Hub. That can help your users get it running quickly!
>
> To publish to Docker Hub, you'll have to sign up at https://hub.docker.com. Then you can use the `docker push` command to push your image to Docker Hub.
>
> Docker Hub also allows you to publish private images, although, to publish more than one of those, you'll need to upgrade to a paid account.

3.9.2 *Pushing our microservice to the registry*

Now that we have a private container registry, we have a place to publish our first microservice. We'll publish our image by invoking the `docker push` command, as shown in figure 3.16.

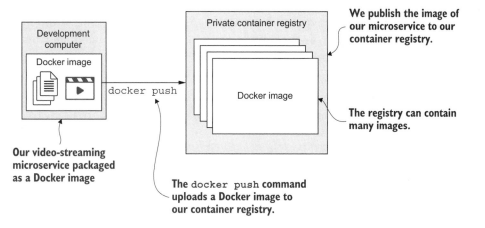

Figure 3.16 The `docker push` command uploads our Docker image to our private container registry.

AUTHENTICATING WITH THE REGISTRY

Before we can push to our registry, we must first log in. We have authentication enabled because we don't want just anyone to be able to publish images to our registry.

In the previous section, you created your private container registry and took note of its details. To communicate with the registry, you must know its URL. To push and pull images, you need the username and password. If you can't remember those, refer to section 3.9.1 to find your registry in the Azure portal and recall these details. To authenticate, we'll invoke the `docker login` command displayed in the next diagram.

I could have shown you the full command I used complete with the URL, username, and password of my own registry. But that won't fit on the page! In addition, it wouldn't help you because, at this point, you have to use the details of your own registry. When you invoke docker login, be sure to use your own URL, username, and password. After authenticating with docker login, you can now invoke other Docker commands against your registry.

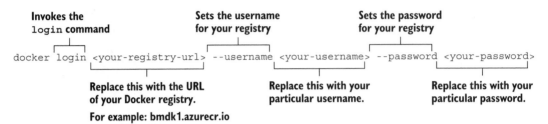

Assuming you got your login details correct, you should see a warning and a success message:

```
WARNING! Using --password via the CLI is insecure. Use --password-stdin.
Login Succeeded
```

Don't worry too much about that warning. You're only learning at the moment, so security problems aren't concerning just yet. But later, in chapter 8, we'll deal with this properly so that we don't get that warning.

TAGGING OUR IMAGE

Before we can publish our image to the registry, we must tell Docker where the image is being pushed. We do this by tagging the image with the URL of the registry with the command docker tag, as follows:

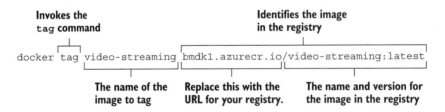

Of course, you can't just type that command verbatim. You have to use the URL for your own registry!

The docker tag command has the following general format:

```
docker tag <existing-image> <registry-url>/<image-name>:<version>
```

We set the name of an existing image to be tagged and then the new tag to apply to it. We're tagging in this case only because we want to push this image to our registry. For this reason, we're including the registry's URL in the tag.

We can check that our new tag was applied by invoking docker image list. Try doing that after applying the new tag. You should see a new entry in the table for the new tag. Note that Docker hasn't created a new image; it has simply applied a new tag to the existing image. We can check that this is the case by inspecting the image's unique ID, and we see that it's the same for both tagged versions.

PUSHING OUR IMAGE TO THE REGISTRY

Finally, we're ready to publish our image to the registry. To do that, we'll invoke the `docker push` command:

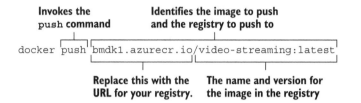

Again, make sure that you use the URL of your own registry here; otherwise, this command won't work for you.

Here is the general format for `docker push`:

```
docker push <registry-url>/<image-name>:<version>
```

The part of the command after the `docker push` identifies the image to push and the registry to push to.

If you're thinking this is a bit awkward, I agree. I believe there should be a one-step process for pushing an existing image to a registry without having to go through the malarky of tagging it first, but this is the way it's done. After starting the image uploading, sit tight and wait for it to complete.

CHECKING THAT OUR IMAGE MADE IT TO THE REGISTRY

After we've pushed our image to the registry, we now want to check that it made it there okay. How do we know that it was successful? The first clue was in the output. It should have said that the push was successful, and we can trust that's correct. But just because we're curious, let's go back to the registry in the Azure portal anyway and see what it looks like now.

In the Azure portal, navigate to All Resources, find your registry, and click it. Click Repositories from the menu on the left. As shown in figure 3.17, you should be able to see your video-streaming image in the list of repositories. If you look inside the repository (on the right of figure 3.17), you can see a list of versions here. There's only a single version currently (tagged as "latest"), but in the future, after you've pushed updates to this image, you can return here and see the other versions that are listed as well.

You can drill down even further through the latest tag to see the details about the image, including a manifest of its files. I encourage you to explore this interface more to see what you can find out about the image you just published.

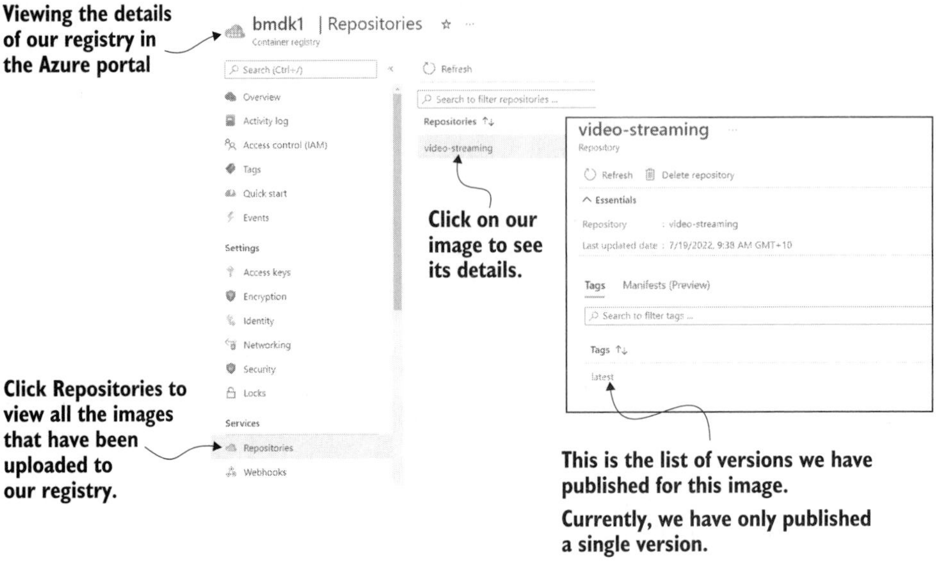

Viewing the details of our registry in the Azure portal

Click on our image to see its details.

Click Repositories to view all the images that have been uploaded to our registry.

This is the list of versions we have published for this image.

Currently, we have only published a single version.

Figure 3.17   Viewing the image pushed to the container registry via the Azure portal

UPLOADING NEW VERSIONS

We now have a manual pipeline that we can use to publish images. Normally, instead of tagging the word "latest," we'd instead tag it with an actual version number. Every time we change code in our microservices, we'll build, tag, and push it again.

You can try that as well if you like. Try making a small code change, invoke `docker build` again (section 3.8.2), and then tag with version "1" like this:

```
docker tag video-streaming bmdk1.azurecr.io/video-streaming:1
```

Now push version 1 to your container registry:

```
docker push bmdk1.azurecr.io/video-streaming:1
```

Please remember to replace the registry URL in those commands with the URL for your container registry.

Now try changing the code again, bumping the version to 2, and pushing it again. This exercise illustrates how we'd publish newer versions of our microservice as we evolve its code. This is just to see how it works; ultimately, we don't want to go through this process of manually building and publishing the image for our microservices (if this is tedious for you already, imagine how annoying it would be to manually build and publish, not to mention deploy, more than one microservice). In chapter 8, you'll learn how to automate this process for your microservices.

3.9.3 *Booting our microservice from the registry*

Congratulations, you just published your first image to your very own private registry. You could now deploy this image to your production environment, but we'll save that for chapter 6, where you'll learn how to deploy microservices to Kubernetes. Before then, you still have work to do and things to learn.

Before moving on, we should confirm that our published image works. What I mean is that we should be able to instantiate the image as a container directly from the registry in the cloud. Just because we don't have a production environment yet doesn't mean we can't simulate a deployment on our development computer. This isn't difficult, and it isn't anything different from what you've already learned in this chapter.

Running a container from an image is more or less the same regardless of whether the image is one we built locally or one that is available in a remote registry. So, let's return to the `docker run` command to test our published image, as shown in figure 3.18.

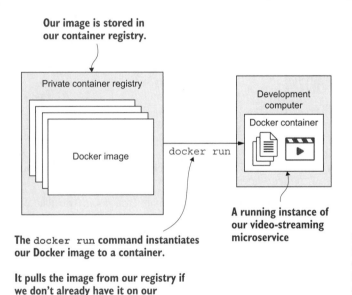
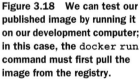

Figure 3.18 We can test our published image by running it on our development computer; in this case, the `docker run` command must first pull the image from the registry.

CLEANING UP OUR MESS

Before we can test our image from the registry, there's one thing left to do: we must first remove the local versions of our image. If we don't, when we invoke `docker run`, it will boot the container from the local version of the image that we already have, and unless we delete that local version, we won't be able to test the published image!

Instead, we'd like to test that we can pull the image from the remote registry. If we have a version of the image already cached locally, it doesn't need to pull the remote version. So, at this point, let's make sure we've removed local containers and images.

Containers don't go away by themselves. When we create containers for long-lived servers, the containers usually hang around! We need to shut them down when we're done so they don't continue to consume our system resources. If you didn't remove your containers already (in section 3.8.5), you'll have to do that now before you can remove the images.

> **NOTE** Before we can remove images, we must first remove any containers instantiated from them. Attempting to remove images that have running containers will result in an error.

We'll invoke `docker container list --all` from our terminal. The `--all` argument makes it show both running and stopped containers. If you see your video-streaming microservice in the list of containers, that's the one you want to remove. Take note of its container ID. You'll remember from earlier that the ID for my own container was 460a19946689. Yours will be different, of course, so don't expect to see that particular ID in your list of containers. I removed my container with the following commands:

```
docker stop 460a19946689
docker rm 460a19946689
```

Just remember to use the container ID for your container.

Here's the general format:

```
docker stop <your-container-id>
docker rm <your-container-id>
```

After removing the container, we can invoke `docker ps` again and check that the container is no longer in the list. After removing any container(s), we can now proceed with removing the image(s).

Invoke `docker image list`. We can see at least three images in the list. You should see the two tagged versions of our video-streaming microservice. We only need to remove the image for our microservice.

Note that both tagged versions of our image have the same image ID, and these are just the same image referenced multiple times. We can remove both by invoking the `docker rmi` command with the `--force` argument as follows:

```
docker rmi 9c475d6b1dc8 --force
```

Of course, you need to run this with your particular image ID (which you can find from the output of `docker image list`). The general format is

```
docker rmi <your-image-id> --force
```

We use `--force` here because, otherwise, we'd be stopped with an error message such as `Image is referenced in multiple repositories`. That's because we have multiple tagged versions of our image. We can use `--force` to make sure these are all removed. After removing the image, invoke `docker image list` again to check that this worked properly and that our video-streaming image is no longer in the list.

> **Cleaning up everything all at once**
>
> Need a way to nuke all Docker containers and images at once? A few steps are involved in doing this. The following commands work on macOS, Linux, and the WSL2 Linux terminal under Windows (but not under Windows Terminal).
>
> First, stop and remove all containers:
>
> ```
> docker stop $(docker ps -a -q)
> docker rm $(docker ps -a -q)
> ```
>
> Then, run the `prune` command with the following options to remove everything else:
>
> ```
> docker system prune --volumes --all
> ```
>
> This will remove all cached images on your computer. Be prepared to wait a lot longer for all subsequent Docker builds because it will download all the base images into your local cache again.

RUNNING A CONTAINER DIRECTLY FROM THE REGISTRY

With local containers and images cleaned up, we can now instantiate a new container directly from the image in the remote registry. We'll use `docker run` again like this:

```
docker run -d -p 3000:3000 -e PORT=3000
➥ bmdk1.azurecr.io/video-streaming:latest
```

As always, you must use the URL for your own registry. Here's the general format:

```
docker run -d -p <host-port>:<container-port> -e <name>=<value>
➥ <registry-url>/<image-name>:<version>
```

This time, when we invoke `docker run`, we use all the same arguments that we did back in section 3.8.3. There's `-d` for detached mode, `-p` to bind the port, and `-e` to set the port. The only thing we've changed here is the tag that we use to identify the image. In this case, the tag also identifies the remote registry from which to pull the image.

When you invoke `docker run` in your terminal, give it some time to download. It first must pull your image from your private container registry.

When this process has completed, you should have a running container. But this time, the image for it has been pulled *on-demand* from your private container registry in the cloud. When the `docker run` command has completed, you should see the container ID printed. We can also check that the container is running using the steps outlined earlier in section 3.8.3, or we can test it directly by pointing our web browser at http://localhost:3000/video to see the video. When you're finished testing, don't forget to stop the container running like we did in the previous subsection.

3.9.4 *Deleting your container registry*

At the end of this chapter, you have a choice. You can delete your container registry through the Azure portal, or you can leave it running there because you'll need it again for chapter 6.

Chapter 6 is a long way off though, and you might not want the container registry consuming your credits on Azure in the meantime. If that's the case, open your browser to the Azure portal (https://portal.azure.com/), and find your registry through the All Resources page. Then, click the Delete button in the toolbar.

3.10 Docker review

Wow! What a trip. Docker seems simple until you try and explain it in a single chapter! Here's what we just did:

- We created a Dockerfile for our microservice that instructs Docker how to build an image for it.
- We invoked `docker build` to package our microservice as an image.
- After creating our private container registry on Azure, we then invoked `docker tag`, `docker login`, and `docker push` to publish our image.
- We finished with a test run of our published image using `docker run`.

The complete pipeline we pieced together is shown in figure 3.19. Peruse this diagram with care and revel in what you've learned so far.

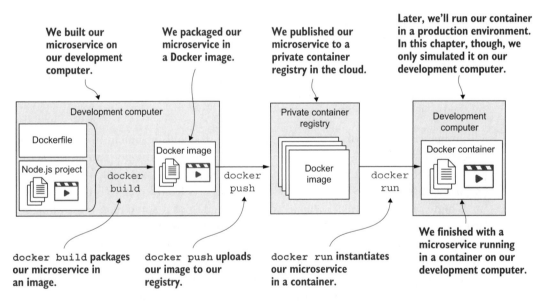

Figure 3.19 A complete Docker build pipeline showing where `build`, `push`, and `run` fit within the process

Before moving on, let's do a quick review of the commands we added to our toolbelt in this chapter, as listed in table 3.3.

Table 3.3   Review of Docker commands

Command	Description
`docker --version`	Checks that Docker is installed and prints the version number
`docker container list`	Lists running containers
`docker container list -a`	Lists all containers (running and stopped)
`docker image list`	Lists local images
`docker build -t <tag> --file` ➡ `<docker-file> .`	Builds an image from assets in the current directory according to the instructions in `docker-file`. The `-t` argument tags the image with a name you specify.

`docker run -d -p <host-port>:`
 `<container-port> -e <name>=<value>`
 `<tag>`
	Instantiates a container from an image. If the image isn't available locally, it can be pulled from a remote registry (assuming the tag specifies the URL of the registry).
	
	 The `-d` argument runs the container in detached mode, so it won't be bound to the terminal and you won't see the output. Omit this argument to see output directly, but this also locks your terminal.
	
	 The `-p` argument allows you to bind a port on the host to a port in the container.
	
	 The `-e` argument allows you to set environment variables.

`docker logs <container-id>`	Retrieves output from a particular container. You need this to see the output when running a container in detached mode.
`docker login <url>` ➡ `--username <username>` ➡ `--password <password>`	Authenticates with your private Docker registry so that you can run other commands against it
`docker tag <existing-tag>` ➡ `<new-tag>`	Adds a new tag to an existing image. To push an image to your private container registry, you must first tag it with the URL of your registry.
`docker push <tag>`	Pushes an appropriately tagged image to your private Docker registry. The image should be tagged with the URL of your registry.
`docker exec -it <container-id> sh`	Shells into a particular container to inspect and debug it from the inside
`docker stop <container-id>`	Stops a particular container locally
`docker rm <container-id>`	Removes a particular container locally (it must be stopped first)
`docker rmi <image-id>` ➡ `--force`	Removes a particular image locally (any containers must be removed first). The `--force` argument removes images even when they have been tagged multiple times.

3.11 Continue your learning

This chapter moved quickly. The aim is to give you the minimum you need to bootstrap your application, but there's so much more you could learn about Docker. Here are some references to other books that will help you go deeper into Docker:

- *Learn Docker in a Month of Lunches* by Elton Stoneman (Manning, 2020)
- *Docker in Practice, Second Edition,* by Aidan Hobson Sayers and Ian Miell (Manning, 2019)
- *Docker in Action, Second Edition,* by Jeff Nickoloff and Stephen Kuenzli (Manning, 2019)

Docker also has good online documentation. It's worth having a browse at http://mng.bz/yZVy.

In this chapter, we explored how to use Docker to build and publish a single microservice. We'll build on these skills in future chapters as we roll out more microservices and create our application. In the next chapter, we'll scale up to multiple microservices, and you'll learn how to easily run multiple Docker-based microservices on your development computer.

Summary

- Docker is the ubiquitous tool used to package, publish, and run containers.
- A container is a virtualized server, such as a microservice.
- An image is a snapshot of a container that is ready to instantiate as a server.
- A container registry is a place (private in our case) where we can publish images for our microservices so they are ready for deployment to our Kubernetes cluster.
- A Dockerfile is the script that is used to create an image. It specifies the code and assets to be included in a microservice.
- Docker Hub provides many free images that we can easily boot to host our own servers. In the sidebar, "Exploring other containers," we tried out MongoDB, which we'll use again in future chapters, but there are many other software packages available.
- The command `docker build` creates an image from a Dockerfile.
- The command `docker run` instantiates a container, and hence a microservice, from an image.
- The command `docker push` publishes an image to a container registry.
- The `docker tag` command is used to tag an image with the name of a container registry so that the image can be pushed to it.

Data management for microservices

This chapter covers

- Using Docker Compose to build and run our microservices application for development and testing
- Adding file storage to our application
- Adding a database to our application

When building any application, we'll typically need to deal with data, files, and sometimes both. Microservices are no different. We need a database to store dynamic data that's generated and updated by the application, and we need a place to store assets that are served by the application or uploaded to it.

In this chapter, we add both file storage and a database to our FlixTube example application. First, we'll add file storage so FlixTube has a location to store its videos. We want to have distinct areas of responsibility in our application for streaming and video storage. That implies that we'll need to add another microservice to our application, and, in this chapter, we'll create our second microservice.

Then, we'll add a database to record the metadata for each video. Currently, that's only the path to video, but this is just an excuse to get a database in place because, once we have it, we can continue to use it for the ongoing data storage for all of our microservices.

By adding a database server and a second microservice to our application, we're taking an important step. In chapter 2, we built our first microservice; in chapter 3, we used Docker to instantiate our first microservice in a container. In this chapter, we scale up our application to host multiple containers, which means we need a new tool!

4.1   New tools

This chapter introduces two ways of storing data for microservices: file storage and database. Typically, there are many ways of doing this and many tools we could choose for the job. The tools you choose for each project will be the ones that work best for the particular project, your team, your company, and your customer.

As for any example in the book, I need to make a choice, so starting in this chapter, we'll use MongoDB for our database and Azure Storage for our file storage. We'll also upgrade our development environment to run multiple containers at the same time. We could do this with Docker's `build` and `run` commands as you learned in the previous chapter, but we'd end up having to run those commands repeatedly for each container.

This isn't a big problem when only working with a few containers, but it doesn't scale to a larger application. Imagine how much effort it would be to run just 10 microservices this way! So, we need a better way to manage multiple microservices during development. For that, this chapter introduces Docker Compose. Table 4.1 lists the new tools you'll learn about in this chapter.

Table 4.1   Tools introduced in chapter 4

Tool	Version	Purpose
Docker Compose	Included with Docker 24.0.5	Docker Compose is included with Docker (installed in chapter 3) and allows us to configure, build, run, and manage multiple containers at the same time. It's useful for development, but we won't use it in production.
Azure Storage		Azure Storage is a service to store files in the cloud. We can manage the assets through the Azure portal, through the APIs, or from the command line. We upload a video through the Azure portal and then use the Node.js Azure Storage SDK to read it back.
@azure/storage-blob	12.15.0	We use this npm package to retrieve files from Azure Storage using JavaScript.
MongoDB	7.0.0	MongoDB is a popular NoSQL type of database. It's lightweight, easy to set up and use, and convenient for microservices.
mongodb	6.0.0	The Node.js "driver" for MongoDB is an npm package we use to interact with the database from JavaScript.

4.2 Getting the code

To follow along with this chapter, you need to download the code or clone the repository. You can download a zip file of the code at http://mng.bz/n16e. You can clone the code using Git like this:

```
git clone
➥ https://github.com/bootstrapping-microservices-2nd-edition/chapter-4
```

For help on installing and using Git, see chapter 2. If you have problems with the code, log an issue against the repository in GitHub.

4.3 Developing microservices with Docker Compose

At the end of the previous chapter, we created a single microservice running in a container on our development computer. We were able to test it using our web browser. Figure 4.1 illustrates our current situation.

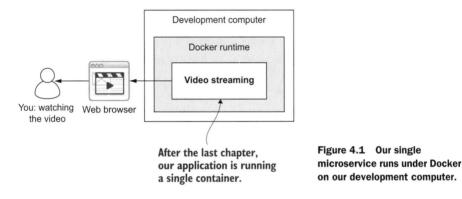

After the last chapter, our application is running a single container.

Figure 4.1 Our single microservice runs under Docker on our development computer.

A microservices application, however, isn't a microservices application if it only consists of a single microservice! The time has come to scale up our application, adding more containers to it, thus making the move to multiple microservices. To develop and test our microservices application, we'll now start using Docker Compose.

We're scaling up to multiple containers in this chapter because we'd like to add a database (that's one container, but it's not something we consider as a microservice), and we'd also like to add a new microservice to handle our file storage (that's another container). Given that we started with one container (our video-streaming microservice), by the end of this chapter, we'll have three containers, as depicted in figure 4.2.

To build, run, and manage our growing application, we could get by with running the various Docker commands multiple times (repeated for each image or container). This quickly becomes tedious during development, however, because we'll need to stop and restart our application many times during our working day. This only gets worse as our application continues to grow because we'll continue adding containers to it as we expand our application. We need a better tool.

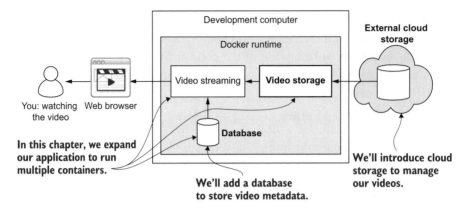

Figure 4.2   We expand our application to multiple containers.

4.3.1   *Why Docker Compose?*

Managing multiple containers in development can be painstaking; in chapters 6 and 7, you'll learn to use Kubernetes to manage containers in production. However, Kubernetes is a big and complex system designed to run on a cluster of multiple computers. We could use the local version of Kubernetes that is included with Docker Desktop (this is new since the first edition of this book!), but it's kind of resource hungry (try running it on a laptop if you want to see poor performance) and just not that convenient to use when we're working on multiple projects.

We'll come to Kubernetes in chapter 6, where you'll learn how to use it both for development and for production. So don't worry—you aren't missing out on anything, and we'll get to Kubernetes soon. For now, we can "simulate" Kubernetes on our development computer using Docker Compose, which is much easier and more straightforward than trying to dive straight into Kubernetes. Besides that, we already have Docker Compose installed! Docker Compose is now included with Docker instead of being separately installed (this is new since the first edition).

Why Docker Compose? In the same way that Docker allows us to build, run, and manage a single microservice, Docker Compose gives us a convenient way to build, run, and manage multiple microservices in development. During development and testing, we must frequently boot and reboot our entire application, which will eventually contain many microservices. After each small increment of development, we also must test the changes to our code. We can do this through the methods already covered in earlier chapters:

- Opening multiple terminals (one for each microservice) and then running each microservice separately using Node.js or whatever our tech stack is (as covered in chapter 2)
- Using Docker to build and run each container separately (as covered in chapter 3)

Each of these methods has been an important stepping stone for us in our quest to build a microservices application, and we'll often return to these when working with individual microservices. But when it comes to working with a whole microservices application, they are less effective.

If we only use these methods to run individual microservices, we'll spend more and more time, as our application grows, just on managing that process, at the expense of time spent doing development. This slows down our iterative progress, saps our productivity, and, ultimately, drains our motivation.

We need a more effective way of managing our application during development, and that's where Docker Compose comes in. Docker Compose v2 is an open source tool written in Go (v1 was Python); you can find the code here: https://github.com/docker/compose.

4.3.2   *Creating our Docker Compose file*

Docker Compose revolves around the Docker Compose file. I like to think of this as a script file that builds a local instance of a microservices application.

> **DEFINITION**   The *Docker Compose file* is a script that specifies how to compose an application from multiple Docker containers.

Recall the Dockerfile we created in chapter 3, section 3.8, which was a script for building a single image. The Docker Compose file scales this up and allows us to orchestrate the creation of a whole application from a collection of Dockerfiles. Docker Compose reads the Docker Compose file and produces a running application, as figure 4.3 shows.

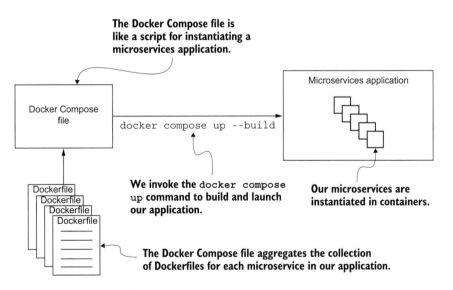

Figure 4.3   The Docker Compose file is like a script for building and launching a microservices application.

Before you learn how to use Docker Compose to create an application composed of multiple containers, let's keep it simple and create an application with just a single container. We'll do some experiments to get comfortable with Docker Compose. After that, we'll add more containers into the mix.

Example-1 for this chapter shows how to use Docker Compose to instantiate the video-streaming microservice we created in chapter 2's example-3. Example-2 follows on from chapter 3's example-1. You can start with the earlier examples if you like and make updates to them, or try out the code in the premade examples in the chapter-4 code repository. You can see the layout of the example-1 project in figure 4.4.

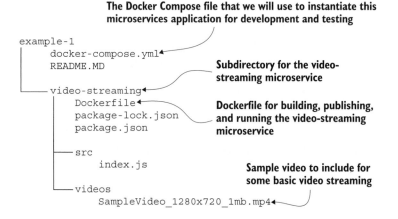

Figure 4.4   The layout of the example-1 project for chapter 4

The first thing we need to do is move the Dockerfile and code for our microservice into a new subdirectory. In this case, we call it video-streaming to match the name of the microservice. We do this because we're now building an application that will soon have more than one microservice. We must therefore put each microservice into its own separate subdirectory. Our convention is that each subdirectory will be named after its microservice.

Now let's create our Docker Compose file, which is called docker-compose.yaml. Because it doesn't belong to any single microservice, it lives in the root directory of our microservices application. Listing 4.1 shows our first Docker Compose file. You can type this code in yourself or just load it into Visual Studio Code (VS Code) from the example-1 directory in the chapter-4 code repository (chapter-4/example-1/docker-compose.yml).

Listing 4.1   Docker Compose file for our microservice

```
version: '3'          ⟵┐   Uses version 3 of the Docker Compose file format
services:                ⟵── Nests our containers under the "services" field

    video-streaming:        ⟵── Configures our video-streaming microservice
```

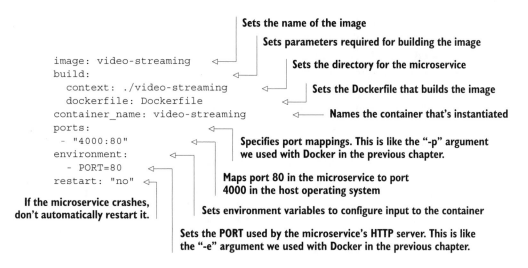

Listing 4.1 is a Docker Compose file that creates a single container: our video-streaming microservice. Note the `build` section. The fields here set the subdirectory that contains the microservice's project and the name of its Dockerfile. This is how Docker Compose finds the information to build the image for our video-streaming microservice.

Also note that Dockerfile is the default name of this file. We could have omitted this, but I've specified this explicitly because we'll separate out our Dockerfiles in the next chapter. That way, we can have separate versions for use in development and production. Various options (see the code annotations) are also configured that you might remember from chapter 2:

- Setting the image name to video-streaming
- Binding the port
- Setting environment variables to configure the microservice

In listing 4.1, we're starting the port numbers for our containers from 4000. Once we have multiple containers, they'll be numbered 4000, 4001, 4002, and so on. This is just so that port numbers for multiple microservices don't conflict with each other. If you're already running any web servers or services on your development computer that are using this range of ports, you'll need to either shut those down while you run these examples or change the port numbers used in these examples.

NOTE The choice of port numbers is arbitrary; for your own application, you can use a different set of numbers if you like.

You might be wondering why we set the `restart` option to `no` in listing 4.1. When working in development, we don't want our microservices to automatically restart when they crash. If they did that, we could easily miss problems! Instead, if these crash, we want them to stay that way so that we'll notice the problem. This is the opposite of how we'd usually like our microservices to work in production. We'll see later in chapter 11 how we can have Kubernetes automatically restart our production microservices that crash.

Even though our first Docker Compose file is simple, it's already pretty useful. This Docker Compose file only creates a single container, but it encodes all the information we need to build and run our microservice. Recording these configuration details already makes things a bit easier. Otherwise, we would have to type this configuration into the terminal every time we invoke the Docker `build` and `run` commands. Even at this early stage, you can see how Docker Compose can improve our development process.

> **YAML**
>
> You might have noticed that the Docker Compose file is a YAML format file (YAML is a recursive acronym for YAML Ain't Markup Language). YAML isn't a markup language; instead, it's probably best described as a data format or a configuration language. YAML's purpose is similar to JSON, but the language itself is structured to be more human readable. That's why you see YAML being used by tools such as Docker Compose and Kubernetes. These are configuration files designed to be edited by humans, while still being easily machine readable.

4.3.3   *Booting our microservices application*

So far, we've created a Docker Compose file to build and run our video-streaming microservice from chapter 2. We reused the entire project for this microservice, including the Dockerfile we added in chapter 3. We'll now test our work.

In this section, we use Docker Compose to boot a single service. This doesn't yet give us much advantage over just using Docker, but sit tight. This is just a starting point, and soon we'll extend our Docker Compose file to include multiple containers. Then, we'll use the Docker Compose file we just created to boot up our increasingly larger application with Docker Compose.

Open a terminal, and change to the directory that contains your Docker Compose file. If you're following along with the code from the chapter-4 code repository on GitHub, then you should change to the directory chapter-4/example-1. Now, invoke the Docker Compose `up` command:

```
cd chapter-4/example-1
docker compose up --build
```

The `up` command causes Docker Compose to boot our microservices application. The `--build` argument makes Docker Compose build each of our images before instantiating containers from these.

Technically, at this point, the `--build` argument isn't necessary because the first time we invoke the `up` command, it builds our images anyway. At other times (without the `--build` argument), the `up` command just starts our container from the image that was previously built (this can be a quick way to restart if we don't want to rebuild). This means that if we change some code in our microservice and invoke the `up` command again, it won't include our changes unless we use the `--build` argument. Unfortunately, this makes it all too easy to rerun the application while accidentally omitting the code changes we were trying to test.

When this happens, and you don't realize it, you end up wasting time testing changes that aren't even there. I don't like wasting my time, so I make a point to always use the `--build` argument every time I run the `up` command. That way, I just know, without having to think about it, that my code changes will always get propagated through to the running application.

When you invoke the `up` command, you'll see the various layers of your base image being downloaded. After that, you'll start to see the (by now familiar) output from your video-streaming microservice. It should look something like the following:

```
video-streaming    |
video-streaming    | > example-1@1.0.0 start /usr/src/app
video-streaming    | > node ./src/index.js
video-streaming    |
video-streaming    | Microservice online
```

You can see on the left of the output that it shows the name of the container. This is what identifies the output as coming from our video-streaming microservice. The name of the container isn't really important at the moment because, at this point, we're only running a single container in our application—all the output is coming from just that one container. But when we have multiple containers, this will be essential so that we can know what container each line of output is coming from.

Now that we have our microservice running, we can test that everything is okay Point your browser to http://localhost:4000/video to watch the video that you should know well from earlier chapters.

With just a single microservice, this isn't much of a microservices application. But now that we're set up to use Docker Compose, we can easily add new containers, and hence more microservices, to our application. But before we do that, let's take some time to learn some more about managing our application with Docker Compose.

Although we haven't yet scaled up to multiple containers, you might already recognize that Docker Compose has given us a more efficient process for working with even just a single container. Using the `up` command saves us from invoking separate Docker `build` and `run` commands.

That's a small savings in time right now, but as you'll soon see, the Docker Compose `up` command is scalable to many containers. You can imagine how much time it's going to save when you have, say, 10 microservices, and you can use a single `up` command to build and run all of these at once! That's 1 command (the `up` command) instead of 20 commands (10 `build` commands and 10 `run` commands).

> **TIP** The Docker Compose `up` command is probably the most important command you'll learn in this book. You'll invoke it time after time as you develop and test your application, and I'm going to make sure you don't forget about it!

4.3.4 *Working with the application*

After starting our application, Docker Compose continues to print output to the terminal while it's running. This locks up the terminal, so we can't do anything with it now except watch the output. We could use the -d argument with the up command to run in detached mode—just like we did with the Docker run command in chapter 3—but using the -d argument hides the application's output. We don't want that because being able to view the live output is very useful for understanding what's going on in there.

> **NOTE** The output can be recovered, of course, with the Docker Compose logs command. Still, I tend not to use the -d argument because I like the output to be visible front and center to see what's happening in real time.

Even though our terminal is locked up with Docker Compose, we can always open a new terminal and use it to invoke other commands. Let's try that now. Open a new terminal, change the directory to where the Docker Compose file is located, and invoke the following command:

```
docker compose ps
```

The ps command shows a list of our running containers. Because we only have one microservice running in our application, you should see output similar to this (I removed various columns to make it fit the page):

```
NAME              COMMAND       STATUS     PORTS
video-streaming   "docker-e…"   running    0.0.0.0:4000->80/tcp
```

At this point, note that Docker Compose is a subcommand of the regular Docker command, which means that all of our regular Docker commands work as well. As an example, you can try docker ps to get a list of containers or docker push to upload an image to the private container registry you created in chapter 3.

The output of Docker commands such as docker ps can be different from the output of docker compose ps. That's because Docker commands relate to all images and containers on our development computer, whereas Docker Compose commands only relate to the images and containers specified in our Docker Compose file.

In this sense, we're using Docker Compose like a scoping mechanism. It constrains the commands to apply only to images and containers in our current project. Essentially, it restricts the scope of these commands to the current working directory, which is another useful aspect of Docker Compose.

Put another way, docker compose ps shows us only the containers that are listed in our Docker Compose file, whereas, docker ps shows us all containers on our development computer. If you invoke the docker ps command and find that it shows more containers than docker compose ps, that's because you've previously created other containers on your computer, possibly when you were following along with chapter 3.

There are many other Docker Compose commands for you to explore in the official documentation. See the end of this chapter for a link.

4.3.5 *Shutting down the application*

You can stop your application in two ways. If you opened a second terminal in the previous section, you can use that to invoke the `stop` command:

```
docker compose stop
```

The other way to stop your application is by pressing Ctrl-C at the terminal where you invoked the `up` command in the first place. However, there are some problems with this approach.

The first problem is that you have to be careful to press Ctrl-C only once. If you press it just a single time, then the application will stop gracefully and patiently wait for all of your containers to stop. But if you're like me (impatient), then you'll tend to press Ctrl-C repeatedly until the process completes and gives you back your terminal. Unlike furiously pounding the walk button at a traffic intersection, this actually works. Unfortunately, it aborts the shutdown and can leave some or all of your containers in a running state.

The second problem is that stopping the application doesn't remove the containers. Instead, it leaves these in place in the stopped state so we can inspect them. That's a handy way to debug a crashed container! We'll talk more about debugging containers in chapter 11. Right now, though, it's more useful that we can remove our containers and return our development computer to a clean state. For that, we can use the `down` command:

```
docker compose down
```

I also usually add the `--volumes` argument like this:

```
docker compose down --volumes
```

The `--volumes` argument causes the volumes for each of the microservices to be deleted. If you don't use this, each container might get its old filesystem restored when you reboot the application. If you want to make sure you have a clean restart of your entire application, always use the `--volumes` argument.

I think we're better off always using the `down` command to shut down our application. Although Ctrl-C is needed to unlock our terminal, it's unreliable, and the `down` command makes the `stop` command redundant.

> **TIP** Get into the habit of using the `down` command after pressing Ctrl-C.

We can use both the `up` and `down` commands in combination to easily reboot our application when we want to get updated code or dependencies into it. We can chain these commands as follows:

```
docker compose down --volumes && docker compose up --build
```

Shell scripts

Tiring of all of these complicated commands? You might want to invest some time in creating shell scripts for the commands you use most often as you might find typing some of these commands onerous during the daily development grind. For example, typing `docker compose up --build` gets old quickly, so I usually wrap it up in a shell script called up.sh.

Typically, when I write such long commands, I'll create shell scripts that are easier to run; at least I do this when I have to run a command many times per day. Other shell scripts I use are listed here:

- down.sh for `docker compose down --volumes`
- reboot.sh for `docker compose down --volumes && docker compose up --build`

We'll talk more about how valuable shell scripts can be in chapter 8.

NOTE Shell scripts don't normally work on Windows. However, you can use shell scripts under your WSL2 Linux terminal. Otherwise, you could convert the suggested shell scripts to batch files (.bat files) that are like the Windows version of shell scripts.

We now have some good fundamentals in place for Docker Compose that will serve us well for development and testing of our microservices application. You'll learn more about using Docker Compose in chapter 5 and chapter 9.

4.3.6   *Why Docker Compose for development, but not production?*

Let's pause to consider why we're using Docker Compose for development but not for production. Docker Compose seems like a great way to define a microservices application, so shouldn't we use it in production? Why do we choose to use Kubernetes only in production instead of for both development and production, especially as a local Kubernetes installation is now bundled with Docker Desktop?

We don't use Kubernetes in development because it's simply easier to boot up a many-microservices application for development and testing using Docker Compose: just a single configuration file and a single command bring up the entire application. To do this with a local Kubernetes installation, we'd invoke numerous commands to deploy numerous configurations. Of course, there are developers who prefer developing against a local Kubernetes instance instead of using Docker Compose, which we'll explore in chapter 6. Then, you'll have multiple techniques for development and testing of microservices at your disposal. Developing directly on Kubernetes is possible, but it's not usually my preference to work that way. After chapter 6, you can decide for yourself which way you would like to work.

Using Docker Compose also makes it easier to change projects—I find this useful because I'm regularly switching between projects when I'm contracting for different companies or even when I'm just switching between projects at the same company. If we need to quickly drop one project and start another, it's as simple as invoking the down command on one project and then invoking the up command on the next. You might even like to create multiple subconfigurations for a single project (e.g., different setups for focusing on different collections of microservices), and then you can easily change between different configurations of your application using up and down.

We can't use Docker Compose in production because there are problems with doing that. We'd have to create a virtual machine (VM) in the cloud, install Docker on it, copy our application code there, and then boot our application under Docker Compose. That's certainly possible, but it's clunky, complicated, difficult to automate, and ultimately not very scalable (we'll talk about scaling Kubernetes in chapter 12).

You'll learn more about Kubernetes in chapters 6 and 7, but here I just wanted to explain why Docker Compose is the best option for development but probably not the best option for production. Of course, the strategy you choose depends on your situation, your project, and your company. You should never take my word as gospel!

4.4 Adding file storage to our application

Now that we're using Docker Compose, we can easily run multiple containers. This gives us the tools we need to move on to the real topic of this chapter—data management.

We'd like to add file storage and a database to our application. We're adding file storage so that we have a location to store the videos used by our application. A common approach is to use a storage solution provided by one of the big cloud vendors. Because we're using Azure in this book, we'll use Azure Storage as our storage provider.

> **NOTE** Many applications, including our example application, FlixTube, need to store files. There are various ways to do this, but one of the most common is to use external cloud storage such as Azure Storage, AWS S3, or Google Cloud Storage.

We could add cloud storage by directly connecting our video-streaming microservice to the storage provider, but we won't do that. Instead, we'll employ good design principles, namely, *separation of concerns* and the *single responsibility principle*, and we'll create a new microservice whose purpose is to be an abstraction of our file storage provider. Figure 4.5 illustrates what our application will look like once we've added the new video-storage microservice to it.

Figure 4.5 shows how the video-storage microservice will be an intermediary between the video-streaming microservice and the external cloud storage. At the end of this section, we'll talk more about the reasoning behind the separation of these microservices. For now, accept the excuse that this is as good a reason as any to introduce our second microservice and officially be running a microservices application (albeit a small one).

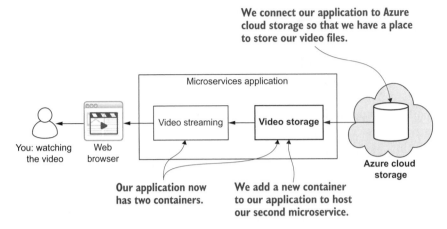

Figure 4.5   We add a second microservice and external cloud storage to our application.

4.4.1   Using Azure Storage

Azure Storage is a cloud storage service provided by Microsoft. We'll use it to add storage capability to our application. You should already have an Azure account from the work we did in chapter 3, and, in this section, we'll go back into Azure, create a storage account, and upload our test video. We'll then create a new microservice whose purpose is to retrieve the video from storage.

> **DEFINITION** *Azure Storage* is a Microsoft Azure service for hosting private or public files in the cloud. You upload your files to Azure Storage and can then access them through the Azure Storage API.

Although we can host both private and public files on Azure Storage, we'll use the private option. We don't want just anyone to be able to download our videos from storage. Instead, we want them to be available only to our customers through our frontend. The code we write for our new microservice will authenticate with Azure and retrieve videos using the package @azure/storage-blob, which is available via npm.

WHY AZURE STORAGE?

We have plenty of options for file storage, so why choose Azure Storage? The truth is we could just as easily use AWS S3 or Google Cloud Storage. For our purposes in this book, it doesn't make much difference. The code we write for the video-storage microservice would of course be different because if we used a different cloud vendor, we'd have to use a different storage API.

> **NOTE** The example for this chapter demonstrates external cloud storage using Azure. There's nothing particularly special about Azure in this case. The code will look different using a different API, but the structure of these microservices will be essentially the same.

It's convenient for us to use Azure because you've already signed up for it from the previous chapter. However, there's no need to be locked into Azure.

One of the advantages of the architecture we're putting into place is that we could easily swap out our azure-storage microservice and replace it with an alternative. We can even do this while our application is running in production! In this sense, you can think of this video-storage microservice as *hot-swappable.*

CREATING AN AZURE STORAGE ACCOUNT

Before we get our test video into storage, we must create an Azure Storage account. To do this, you'll need to log in to the Azure portal at https://portal.azure.com/ as you did in chapter 3. In the left-hand menu, click Create a Resource, and search for "storage account," as shown in figure 4.6.

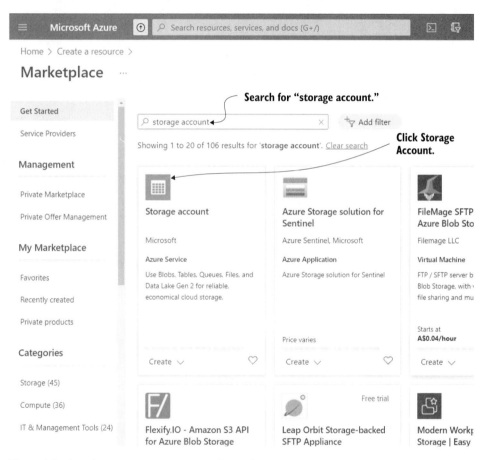

Figure 4.6   Creating a new storage account in the Azure portal

Click Microsoft's Storage Account option, and then click Create. You can now fill out the details of your new storage account, as shown in figure 4.7.

You'll need to choose a resource group. For that, you can use the resource group you created in chapter 3, or you can click Create New to create a new resource group. Then, you need to choose a name for your storage account.

The other settings can be left at their defaults. After filling out the details, click Review + Create. If the details pass validation, you can then click Create to create the storage account. If they don't validate, then you'll need to follow the instructions to fix the problem.

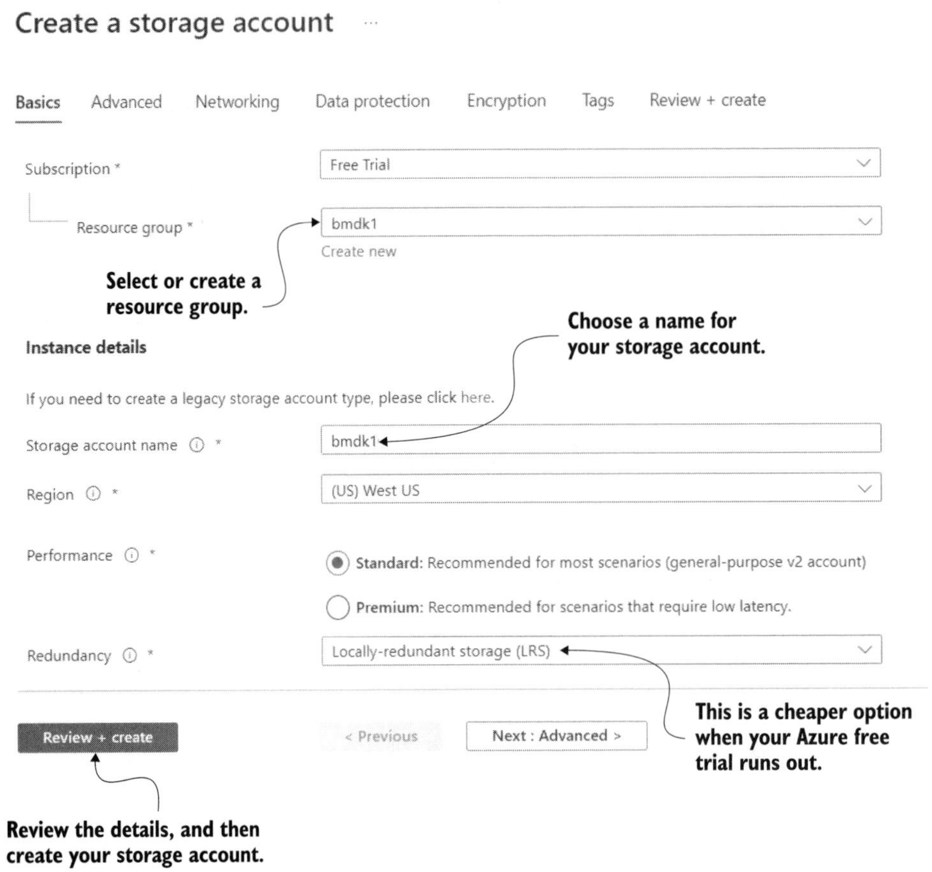

Figure 4.7   Filling out details for the new storage account

Now, wait until you get the notification saying your storage account has been deployed. At that point, you can click Go to Resource in the notification, or you can find your resource in the global list like you did in chapter 3.

Once you open the storage account in the Azure portal, click Access Keys in the left-hand menu. Here you'll see the access keys for your storage account, as shown in figure 4.8. These are the details you need to authenticate with your storage account. Make a note of your storage account name and one of the keys. You only need the value for one of the keys. You don't need the connection string.

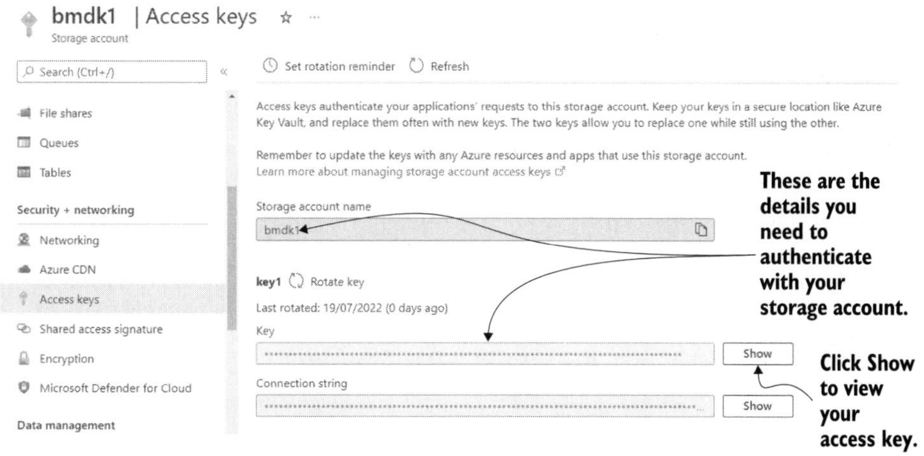

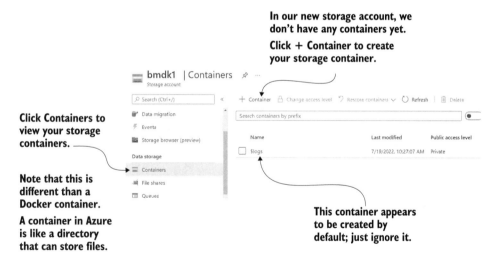

Figure 4.8   Viewing the authentication details of our new storage account

UPLOADING YOUR VIDEO TO AZURE STORAGE

With our storage account created, we can now upload our test video. In the Azure portal, with your storage account open, click Containers in the menu on the left. You should see an empty list of containers, like what is shown in figure 4.9.

Figure 4.9   Navigating to the Containers option and creating our videos container

By the way, just to avoid confusion, the container we're talking about here isn't the same as the containers we're running in our microservices application. A container in Azure Storage is like a directory; it's a location to store files.

Click the + Container button in the toolbar to create your first container. Now enter a name for your container. You can call it anything you like at this point, but to make it work with the example code coming up, let's call it videos. Here you can also choose the access level, but we'll stick with the default, which is Private Access Only. Next, click OK to create the container.

You should see the videos container in the list now. Click it to drill down. When viewing the contents of your new container, you'll see a message like that in figure 4.10. If you're wondering what a *blob* is, it's simply a file, and we don't have any of those yet. Let's upload one now.

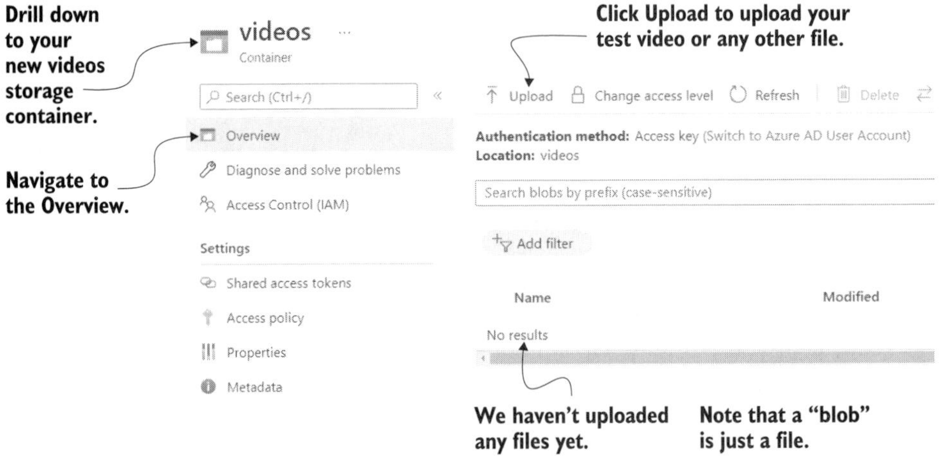

Figure 4.10   Drilling down into the videos container and clicking Upload to upload a video file

Click the Upload button in the toolbar to upload your video file, and select a file on your disk to upload. (If you don't have a video at hand, you can use the sample video under the example-1 subdirectory of the chapter-4 repository). After the video is uploaded, it appears in the list, as shown in figure 4.11.

Creating a microservice to read Azure Storage

We now have a test video uploaded to Azure Storage, so it's time to create our new video-storage microservice. This is our second official microservice, and it will be a REST API to retrieve videos from our storage provider.

> **NOTE**   We could directly integrate our video-streaming microservice with cloud storage, but instead, we'll abstract this connection behind another microservice. This makes it trivial to later replace the storage mechanism and can pave the way for our application to support multiple storage providers.

The first thing we need to do is create a new directory for our second microservice. You should either create a new subdirectory from scratch or just open example-2 from the chapter-4 code repository into VS Code. We'll name the subdirectory for the new

↑ Upload   🔒 Change access level   ↻ Refresh | 🗑 Delete   ⇄ Change tier   🖉 Acquire

Authentication method: Access key (Switch to Azure AD User Account)
Location: videos

Search blobs by prefix (case-sensitive)

⁺▽ Add filter

Name	Modified	Access tier
☐ 📄 SampleVideo_1280x720_1mb.mp4	7/19/2022, 10:41:16 …	Hot (Inferred)

**After uploading the test video, it appears in the
list of files under the videos storage container.**

Figure 4.11   Looking at the uploaded video in the videos container

microservice as azure-storage. We name this new project specifically to indicate that its purpose is related to Azure Storage. If we were to add different storage providers, we would give them different names (e.g., aws-storage or google-storage). You can see the layout of the example-2 project in figure 4.12.

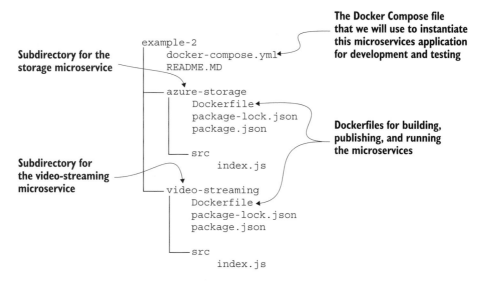

**The Docker Compose file
that we will use to instantiate
this microservices application
for development and testing**

**Subdirectory for the
storage microservice**

```
example-2
    docker-compose.yml
    README.MD

    azure-storage
        Dockerfile
        package-lock.json
        package.json

        src
            index.js

    video-streaming
        Dockerfile
        package-lock.json
        package.json

        src
            index.js
```

**Dockerfiles for building,
publishing, and running
the microservices**

**Subdirectory for
the video-streaming
microservice**

Figure 4.12   The layout of the example-2 project for chapter 4

NOTE   In case you were thinking of porting the code presented here over to Amazon Web Services (AWS) or Google Cloud Platform (GCP), converting from the Azure store microservice over to another provider isn't a simple task. The APIs to interface with AWS and GCP storage will be quite different from Azure, and you'll need to read their docs separately to figure out how to use them. Make sure you finish learning about the azure-storage microservice in this chapter before you attempt to convert to any other provider.

Now, open a terminal and change into the azure-storage directory. If you're creating the new microservice from scratch, you'll need to create a new package.json and install the express package like we did in chapter 2. You'll then need to install the @azure/storage-blob package like this:

```
npm install --save @azure/storage-blob
```

If you're following along with example-2 in the chapter-4 code repository, everything you need is already there:

- Package file
- Code
- Dockerfile

To run the new microservice directly under Node.js, you'll first need to change the directory to azure-storage and then install the dependencies:

```
npm install
```

Listing 4.2 (chapter-4/example-2/azure-storage/src/index.js) presents the code for our new microservice. Before we run this code, let's read it and understand what it's doing.

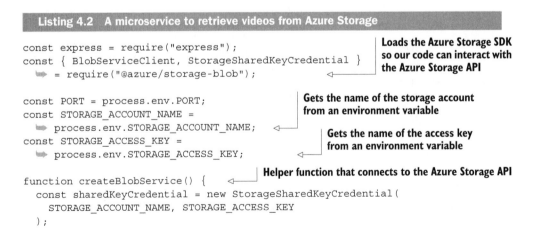

Listing 4.2   A microservice to retrieve videos from Azure Storage

```
const express = require("express");
const { BlobServiceClient, StorageSharedKeyCredential }
    = require("@azure/storage-blob");

const PORT = process.env.PORT;
const STORAGE_ACCOUNT_NAME =
    process.env.STORAGE_ACCOUNT_NAME;
const STORAGE_ACCESS_KEY =
    process.env.STORAGE_ACCESS_KEY;

function createBlobService() {
  const sharedKeyCredential = new StorageSharedKeyCredential(
    STORAGE_ACCOUNT_NAME, STORAGE_ACCESS_KEY
  );
```

Loads the Azure Storage SDK so our code can interact with the Azure Storage API

Gets the name of the storage account from an environment variable

Gets the name of the access key from an environment variable

Helper function that connects to the Azure Storage API

```
    const blobService = new BlobServiceClient(
      `https://${STORAGE_ACCOUNT_NAME}.blob.core.windows.net`,
      sharedKeyCredential
    );
    return blobService;
}

const app = express();

app.get("/video", async (req, res) => {

    const videoPath = req.query.path;

    const containerName = "videos";
    const blobService = createBlobService();
    const containerClient =
      ➥ blobService.getContainerClient(containerName);
    const blobClient =
      ➥ containerClient.getBlobClient(videoPath);

    const properties =
      ➥ await blobClient.getProperties();

    res.writeHead(200, {
      "Content-Length": properties.contentLength,
      "Content-Type": "video/mp4",
    });

    const response = await blobClient.download();
    response.readableStreamBody.pipe(res);
});

app.listen(PORT);
```

HTTP GET route for retrieving a video from Azure Storage. Note that the route handler uses the async keyword so that we can use JavaScript's async/await syntax within. This is why we installed Express v5 beta in chapter 2.

Specifies the path to the video in storage as an HTTP query parameter

Hardcoded container name. Later, we can vary this for some purpose (e.g., by user ID so we can keep videos for each user separately).

Connects to the Azure Storage API

Connects the client for the Azure Storage container

Connects the client for the "blob" (aka the file) that we'd like to retrieve

Retrieves the video's properties from Azure Storage

Writes content length and MIME type to the HTTP response headers

Starts the download of the specified file

Pipes the video stream from Azure Storage to the HTTP response

In listing 4.2, we use `@azure/storage-blob`, the Azure Storage SDK installed via npm. We also created an HTTP server using Express in the same way we did in chapter 2.

There are two new environment variables to configure this microservice; `STORAGE_ACCOUNT_NAME` and `STORAGE_ACCESS_KEY` set the authentication details for our Azure Storage account. Note that you'll have to set these environment variables to the authentication details from your own storage account. You'll do that in the next section. These authentication details are used in helper function `createBlobService` to create the API object that we need to access the storage SDK.

The most important thing in listing 4.2 is the HTTP GET route /video, by which we can retrieve a video from storage. The route handler streams a video from Azure Storage to the HTTP response.

TESTING OUR NEW MICROSERVICE INDEPENDENTLY

Before we try and integrate this microservice into our application, it's best if we test it independently. In this case, we could easily integrate it first and then test it later.

Working that way is feasible when our application is this small. However, as our application grows larger and more complicated, whole-application integration testing will become increasingly more difficult.

Testing microservices individually should be our first point of testing. It works better because we can start or reload a single microservice quickly (for rounds of development and testing) rather than doing the same for our application as a whole. Therefore, we should get into the habit of testing our microservices individually before testing the application as a whole.

Before running (and testing) our new microservice, we need to set the environment variables to configure it. We'll do this from the terminal. On macOS, Linux, or the WSL2 Linux terminal, it looks like this:

```
export PORT=3000
export STORAGE_ACCOUNT_NAME=<the name of your storage account>
export STORAGE_ACCESS_KEY=<the access key for your storage account>
```

On a regular Windows terminal, it looks like this:

```
set PORT=3000
set STORAGE_ACCOUNT_NAME=<the name of your storage account>
set STORAGE_ACCESS_KEY=<the access key for your storage account>
```

Note that we must insert the name and key for the storage account that we created earlier. When running the microservice, we can choose to run it in either production mode or in development mode, as we discussed in chapter 2. We can run it in production mode like this:

```
cd chapter-4/example-2/azure-storage
npm start
```

Alternatively, we can run it in development mode with nodemon for live reload like this:

```
npm run start:dev
```

Live reload is really important for rapid development because we can make changes to our code and have our microservice automatically restart. In the next chapter, you'll learn how to extend live reload to the entire microservices application. For now, we'll settle for using it during development and testing of an individual microservice.

With your microservice running, you can now open your browser and navigate to http://localhost:3000/video?path=SampleVideo_1280x720_1mb.mp4. If you used a different name for your video, you'll need to adjust the name of that video in this URL to fit. You should now see the familiar video playing, but this time, it's streamed from your Azure Storage account.

We'll talk more about testing microservices in chapter 9. For the moment though, let's move on and integrate our new microservice into the application.

4.4.2 Updating the video-streaming microservice

The first step of integrating the new microservice with our application is to update our video-streaming microservice. As a reminder, we ended chapter 3 with a video-streaming microservice that loaded the test video from the filesystem. Now, we're going to update that microservice so that it delegates the loading of the video to our new azure-storage microservice instead.

Here we update our video-streaming microservice to delegate storage to another microservice. We're *separating our concerns* so that the video-streaming microservice is solely responsible for streaming video to our user and so that it doesn't need to know the details of how storage is handled.

Listing 4.3 (chapter-4/example-2/video-streaming/src/index.js) shows the changes we'll make to the video-streaming microservice. Read through the code in the listing to see how we're forwarding the HTTP request for a video through to the new video-storage microservice.

> **Listing 4.3 Updated video-streaming microservice**

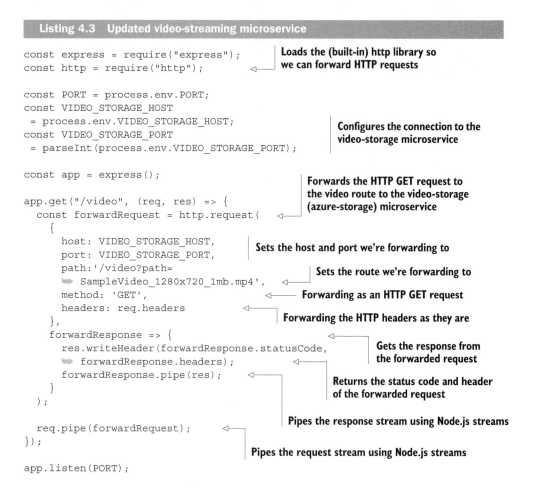

```
const express = require("express");
const http = require("http");
```
Loads the (built-in) http library so we can forward HTTP requests

```
const PORT = process.env.PORT;
const VIDEO_STORAGE_HOST
 = process.env.VIDEO_STORAGE_HOST;
const VIDEO_STORAGE_PORT
 = parseInt(process.env.VIDEO_STORAGE_PORT);
```
Configures the connection to the video-storage microservice

```
const app = express();

app.get("/video", (req, res) => {
  const forwardRequest = http.request(
```
Forwards the HTTP GET request to the video route to the video-storage (azure-storage) microservice

```
    {
      host: VIDEO_STORAGE_HOST,
      port: VIDEO_STORAGE_PORT,
```
Sets the host and port we're forwarding to

```
      path:'/video?path=
      SampleVideo_1280x720_1mb.mp4',
```
Sets the route we're forwarding to

```
      method: 'GET',
```
Forwarding as an HTTP GET request

```
      headers: req.headers
    },
```
Forwarding the HTTP headers as they are

```
    forwardResponse => {
```
Gets the response from the forwarded request

```
      res.writeHeader(forwardResponse.statusCode,
      forwardResponse.headers);
```
Returns the status code and header of the forwarded request

```
      forwardResponse.pipe(res);
    }
  );
```
Pipes the response stream using Node.js streams

```
  req.pipe(forwardRequest);
});
```
Pipes the request stream using Node.js streams

```
app.listen(PORT);
```

In listing 4.3, we use the Node.js built-in HTTP library to forward an HTTP request from one microservice to another. The response that is returned is then streamed to the client. The way this works might be difficult to understand, but don't worry too much about it right now. In the next chapter, we'll explore this more because communication between microservices is so important that it deserves its own chapter.

Note that we've hardcoded the path to the video in storage at this point. This is just a stepping stone, and we'll soon fix that. But for this code to work in the meantime, you must have uploaded the test video with this particular filename. If you've uploaded to a different filename, you should update the code to match that.

After updating our video-streaming microservice, we should test it independently. That's kind of difficult given that it depends on the video-storage microservice. We could do this if we had the tools and techniques in place to mock our dependencies.

Mocking is a technique used in testing where we replace the dependency with a fake or simulated alternative. We don't have those techniques yet, but this is something we'll explore in chapter 9, and you'll see an example of a mock microservice in chapter 10. Right now, let's just press on and finish the integration. Then, we can check that the application as a whole, simple as it currently is, works as expected.

4.4.3   *Adding our new microservice to the Docker Compose file*

We've done quite a lot of work to get to this point. We created an Azure Storage account, and we uploaded our test video. Then we created our second microservice, the azure-storage microservice, which is a REST API that abstracts our storage provider. After that, we updated our video-streaming microservice so that instead of loading the video from the filesystem, as it did in chapters 2 and 3, it now retrieves the video via the video-storage microservice.

> **NOTE**   The beauty of the Docker Compose file is that it simplifies defining and managing a whole suite of containers. It's a convenient way to manage a microservices application!

To integrate the new microservice into our application and test it, we now must add the microservice as a new section to our Docker Compose file. You can see what this looks like in figure 4.13, which shows what the Docker Compose file will look like later, after we add our second microservice and the database server. The Docker Compose file on the left has three sections that map to the three containers on the right.

You can think of the Docker Compose file as a kind of *aggregate* Dockerfile that we use to describe and manage multiple containers at once. It's an aggregate because we use it to tie together the multiple Dockerfiles for each of our microservices.

Listing 4.4 (chapter-4/example-2/docker-compose.yaml) shows our updated Docker Compose file with the addition of the azure-storage microservice. Note that we're reusing the environment variables STORAGE_ACCOUNT_NAME and STORAGE_ACCESS_KEY that we set in the terminal previously in section 4.4.1.

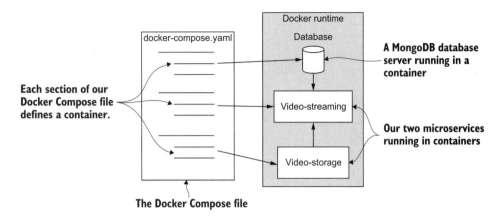

Each section of our
Docker Compose file
defines a container.

A MongoDB database
server running in a
container

Our two microservices
running in containers

The Docker Compose file

Figure 4.13   Each section in our Docker Compose file defines a separate container.

If you're working in a new terminal, you'll need to set those environment variables
again before running the updated application under Docker Compose.

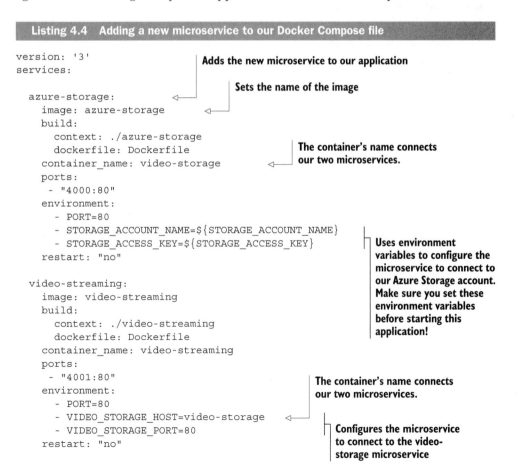

Listing 4.4   Adding a new microservice to our Docker Compose file

```
version: '3'
services:

  azure-storage:
    image: azure-storage
    build:
      context: ./azure-storage
      dockerfile: Dockerfile
    container_name: video-storage
    ports:
     - "4000:80"
    environment:
     - PORT=80
     - STORAGE_ACCOUNT_NAME=${STORAGE_ACCOUNT_NAME}
     - STORAGE_ACCESS_KEY=${STORAGE_ACCESS_KEY}
    restart: "no"

  video-streaming:
    image: video-streaming
    build:
      context: ./video-streaming
      dockerfile: Dockerfile
    container_name: video-streaming
    ports:
     - "4001:80"
    environment:
     - PORT=80
     - VIDEO_STORAGE_HOST=video-storage
     - VIDEO_STORAGE_PORT=80
    restart: "no"
```

Adds the new microservice to our application

Sets the name of the image

The container's name connects
our two microservices.

Uses environment
variables to configure the
microservice to connect to
our Azure Storage account.
Make sure you set these
environment variables
before starting this
application!

The container's name connects
our two microservices.

Configures the microservice
to connect to the video-
storage microservice

You might have a few questions on your mind at this point: Why is the container name set to `video-storage` instead of `azure-storage`? We called the microservice azure-storage, but we called the container `video-storage`; why is that? This is an intentional abstraction. It's a part of our design that the video-streaming microservice doesn't care where it retrieves its videos from! It's not interested in the fact that the videos are stored in Azure. From the microservice's point of view, these could just as easily be stored anywhere else, such as AWS S3 or Google Cloud Storage.

By naming our container as `video-storage`, we're now able to connect our microservices to it using a name that is independent of the underlying storage provider. This is good application structure put into practice. We've given ourselves the flexibility of later being able to swap out azure-storage and replace it with aws-storage or google-storage. We do this without interrupting the video-streaming microservice, so nothing has changed from its point of view. This kind of freedom to effect change in the future without knock-on effects is important, and it shows that we're making the most of our microservices architecture.

4.4.4   *Testing the updated application*

We've updated our Docker Compose file to include both of our microservices. Now, we're finally ready to boot our application and test it with our additional microservice. Before doing this, please make sure you've set the environment variables STORAGE_ACCOUNT_NAME and STORAGE_ACCESS_KEY as detailed in section 4.4.1, as that's what connects the application to your Azure Storage account.

Start the whole application on your local computer:

```
cd chapter-4/example-2
docker compose up --build
```

The difference now is that we've booted up two containers, rather than just one. You can see an example of the output in the following:

```
video-streaming   | > example-1@1.0.0 start /usr/src/app
video-streaming   | > node ./src/index.js
video-streaming   |
video-storage     |
video-storage     | > example-1@1.0.0 start /usr/src/app
video-storage     | > node ./src/index.js
video-storage     |
video-streaming   | Forwarding video requests to video-storage:80.
video-streaming   | Microservice online.
video-storage     | Serving videos from...
video-storage     | Microservice online.
```

Note in the output how the name of each container is printed on the left. This is an aggregate stream of logging from all containers. The name on the left allows us to differentiate the output from each microservice.

NOTE We're booting our application with multiple containers using a single command so we can test our application with multiple microservices.

Now that we've added our second microservice, this is where we start to see the real value of Docker Compose. We could have booted up the application without Docker Compose in either of the following ways:

- *Open two terminals and use Node.js directly to run the video-streaming microservice in one terminal and the azure-storage microservice in the other.* That's two terminals and two commands to run our application.
- *Use Docker to run two containers.* In this case, we have to run `docker build` and `docker run` once for each microservice. That's one terminal and four commands.

No one wants to spend all day repetitively typing commands. Instead, Docker Compose allows us to boot our application with a single command, and this is scalable to any number of containers.

Just imagine down the track a bit and say we've progressed development of our application to 10 microservices. Without Docker Compose, we'll have to type at least 20 commands to build and start our application. With Docker Compose, we can build and run our growing application with just one command! No matter how many containers we need, it's still just a single command.

At this point, we have two opportunities for testing. At a minimum, we must test the video-streaming microservice because, currently, that's the only customer-facing endpoint we have. To do that, open a browser and navigate to http://localhost :4001/video.

Yet again, you'll see the familiar test video. Testing the video-streaming microservice actually tests both microservices because the video-streaming microservice depends on the video-storage microservice, so they are both tested at the same time. We could stop here, but for completeness in testing, we can also independently test the video-storage microservice.

If you glance back to listing 4.4, you'll see that we've bound its port to 4000. We can navigate our browser to that port and see the video playing directly from the video-storage microservice. The video-storage microservice, however, expects us to tell it the path where the video is located. We do that via the URL. Let's navigate our browser to http://localhost:4000/video?path=SampleVideo_1280x720_1mb.mp4 and test the video-storage microservice.

Note that testing an internal microservice from the outside like this is normally only possible in development. Once we move this microservice to production, its REST API is only available within the Kubernetes cluster. In this case, we'll make it private because we don't want the outside world having direct access to our video storage. This is a security feature of microservices! We can control which microservices are exposed to the outside world, and we can use that to restrict access to parts of the application that should not be directly accessible by outsiders. We'll talk more about security in chapter 12.

Well, there we have it. We added external file storage to our application and, in the process, scaled it up to two microservices. Before we congratulate ourselves, however, let's consider some design theory.

4.4.5   Cloud storage vs. cluster storage

At this point, if you know anything about Kubernetes, you might be wondering why we haven't used Kubernetes volumes for file storage as opposed to cloud storage. That's an important design decision, and again, it's the kind of thing that depends on the needs of your project, your business, and your customers.

We used cloud storage instead of cluster storage because it's simple, it works when we run in development, it's cheap, and it's managed for us. These are the benefits of cloud storage and why it's in common use by many companies. Besides, we haven't learned anything about Kubernetes yet, so we definitely couldn't have used Kubernetes volumes at this point in the book. However, there's another important reason why I generally choose to use cloud storage over cluster storage.

We could store the files and data for our application in the Kubernetes cluster, but I prefer my production clusters to be *stateless* so I can destroy and rebuild any cluster at will without risk of losing any data. Later, this enables us to use *blue-green deployment* for our production rollouts, which we'll talk about in chapter 12. This makes it easy to build a new and updated instance of our application that runs in parallel with the previous version.

To upgrade our customers to the new version, we can then switch the Domain Name System (DNS) record so that the hostname now refers to the new instance. This gives us a low-risk way to do major upgrades to our application. It's low risk not because problems won't happen, but because if problems do happen, we can quickly switch the DNS back to the old instance so that our customers are (almost) immediately reverted to the previous (and presumably working) version.

4.4.6   What did we achieve?

Congratulations! We now have a small microservices application running! That's a big deal. Using Docker Compose, we created a scaffold into which we can easily add new microservices and grow our application. Take a moment to pat yourself on the back—this is a big milestone!

What did we achieve? We added file storage capability to our application. Our microservice now has the capability to store files in external cloud storage, and this gives our application a place to host its videos. You might be wondering at this point how we'll allow our customers to upload their own videos. We haven't implemented video upload yet, but that's coming in chapter 10, so hold tight.

We also added a second microservice. With Docker Compose in place, we can now continue to expand our application by adding new containers to it. We'll make use of this capability again in a moment when we add a database server to our application.

We added the second microservice as an abstraction over our storage provider. This is a design decision with benefits. We can now swap out and replace our video-storage microservice with a different storage provider and minimal effect on our application. We could even do this while the application is running in production! In the future, we might also want to have multiple storage microservices running in parallel. If it suited our product, we could upgrade to support Azure Storage, AWS S3, and Google Cloud Storage all at the same time!

The details of how storage works have been restricted to the internals of the video-storage microservice. That means we can change the details independently from the rest of the application without causing knock-on problems. This kind of protection might seem superfluous right now, but it becomes more important as our application grows.

> **NOTE** Eventually, our application will become a spider's web of communication among many microservices. Changes in one have the potential to cause an exponential ripple of problems across the application. Careful construction of the interfaces between microservices to minimize their coupling helps us make the most of our microservices architecture.

Separating our microservices based on what they do, called separation of concerns (mentioned in chapter 1), is important—each microservice should look after its own area of responsibility. We're also following the single responsibility principle (also mentioned in chapter 1) that says each microservice should look after one thing. Our microservices now look after their own areas of responsibility:

- The video-streaming microservice is responsible for streaming a video to a user.
- The video-storage microservice is responsible for locating and retrieving videos from storage.

The separation of the microservices in this way helps to ensure that each microservice is small, simple, and manageable.

4.5 Adding a database to our application

The other half of data management relates to the database. Most applications need some kind of database to store their dynamic data, and FlixTube is no exception.

> **NOTE** This chapter isn't intended to teach database design or data engineering; it just serves as an example of how to integrate one kind of database, MongoDB, with your microservices. To take your database and data engineering skills further than this, please see the references for more learning at the end of this chapter.

The first thing we need is metadata storage for each video. We'll start using our database by storing the path to each video. This fixes the problem from earlier of having a hardcoded path to the video file in our video-streaming microservice.

NOTE Practically all applications need some kind of database to store the data that will be updated by the application.

Figure 4.14 shows what our application will look like after we add the database. In addition to the two containers for our two microservices, we'll add a new container that hosts a MongoDB database. You can see in the diagram that only the video-streaming microservice connects to the database; the video-storage microservice doesn't require a database.

We add a database to our application.

For ease of development, we instantiate the database using Docker Compose.

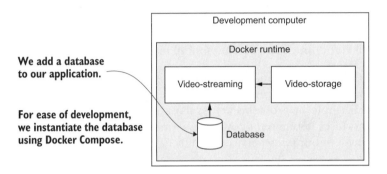

Figure 4.14 Adding a database to our application

4.5.1 Why MongoDB?

MongoDB is one of the most popular of the NoSQL variety of databases. Using Docker to bring up a MongoDB database allows us to have an almost instant database for use in development. We only need to specify the name of a database image, and Docker will pull it from Docker Hub and instantiate it on our development computer.

NOTE MongoDB is easy to use, provides a flexible database that stores schema-free structured data, and has a rich query API.

But there are many different databases that we could easily boot up with Docker, so why MongoDB? In my experience, even manually downloading and installing MongoDB is easy compared to older and more traditional databases; now that we have Docker, it's even easier. Like any database, we can use MongoDB to store rich structured data. MongoDB is also known to have high performance and is extremely scalable.

I work with a lot of unpredictable data, and it's hard to tell what's going to be thrown at me next. I like the fact that MongoDB doesn't force me to define a fixed schema. However, it's certainly possible to define a schema with MongoDB if you use an object-relational mapping (ORM) library such as Mongoose (www.npmjs.com/package/mongoose).

MongoDB is also easy to query and update in many different programming languages. It's well supported and has great documentation, and there are many examples in circulation. MongoDB is open source. You can find the code here: https://github.com/mongodb/mongo.

4.5.2 *Adding a database server in development*

We're going to add a database to our application in development using Docker Compose in the same way that we added our video-storage microservice earlier in this chapter. Now, in example-3, we'll add one new container to our Docker Compose file to host a single database server. We only need a single server, but we can host many databases on that server. This means we'll be set up for the future to easily create more databases as we add more microservices to our application. The layout of example-3, as you can see in figure 4.15, is mostly the same as example-2, except now we have the addition of a JSON file that contains some test data that we'll add to our database.

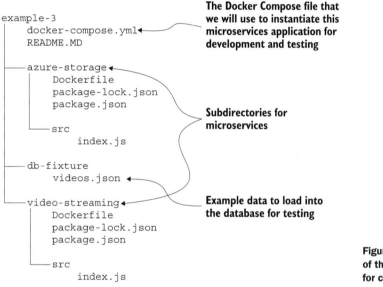

**Figure 4.15   The layout
of the example-3 project
for chapter 4**

ADDING THE DATABASE SERVER TO THE DOCKER COMPOSE FILE

To add the database server to our application, we must update our Docker Compose file. Docker Compose makes it easy to add a database to our application. We just add a few lines to the Docker Compose file to specify the public Docker image for the database and set some configurations. Abracadabra, instant database!

Listing 4.5 (chapter-4/example-3/docker-compose.yaml) shows the updated Docker Compose file. We're adding a new section to the top of the file with the name db (short for database). The configuration for this container is different from the configuration for the microservices we added earlier because now we don't need to build the image for the new container. Instead, we use the publicly published mongo image from Docker Hub.

Listing 4.5 Adding a MongoDB database

```
version: '3'
services:

  db:
    image: mongo:7.0.0
    container_name: db

    ports:
    - "4000:27017"
    restart: always

  azure-storage:
    image: azure-storage
    build:
      context: ./azure-storage
      dockerfile: Dockerfile
    container_name: video-storage
    ports:
    - "4001:80"
    environment:
      - PORT=80
      - STORAGE_ACCOUNT_NAME=${STORAGE_ACCOUNT_NAME}
      - STORAGE_ACCESS_KEY=${STORAGE_ACCESS_KEY}
    restart: "no"

  video-streaming:
    image: video-streaming
    build:
      context: ./video-streaming
      dockerfile: Dockerfile
    container_name: video-streaming
    ports:
    - "4002:3000"
    environment:
      - PORT=80
      - DBHOST=mongodb://db:27017
      - DBNAME=video-streaming
      - VIDEO_STORAGE_HOST=video-storage
      - VIDEO_STORAGE_PORT=80
    restart: "no"
```

Adds a MongoDB database server to our microservices application

Sets the image name and version. This is a public MongoDB image retrieved from Docker Hub.

Sets the name of the container that's instantiated in our application. Our microservices use this name to connect to the database.

Maps the MongoDB standard port 27017 to 4000 on our host OS. We can interact with and check the database on our development computer using port 4000.

Sets the restart policy to always. If MongoDB ever crashes, which hardly ever happens, this automatically restarts it.

Configures the microservice to connect to the database

Sets the name the microservice uses for its database

In our updated application, the video-streaming microservice will be connected to the database. Notice that we now have new environment variables, DBHOST and DBNAME, which configure the microservice's connection to its database.

It's also worth noting in the configuration for the db container how we've mapped the container's ports. Here, we've mapped the standard MongoDB port of 27017 to 4000. What does this mean? Within the Docker runtime, other containers can access the database using 27017. That's the conventional port for MongoDB, so we'll stick with that.

On our host operating system (OS), we've mapped the port to 4000. That's an arbitrary choice. We could have given it any number, including 27017. I prefer not to give it the standard MongoDB port because that would conflict with an instance of MongoDB that we might have running directly on our host OS.

This is a good setup. Our application can interact with MongoDB via the standard port, but we can also use tools (as you'll soon see) to directly query and edit our database from our development computer. This is great for development as it gives us the ability to directly interact with and query our database.

UPDATING THE VIDEO-STREAMING MICROSERVICE TO USE A DATABASE

We added environment variables to our Docker Compose file to connect our video-streaming microservice to its database. Now, we need to update the code for this microservice to make use of these environment variables to establish the database connection.

Listing 4.6 (chapter-4/example-3/video-streaming/src/index.js) shows the updated code for the video-streaming microservice that allows it to query and read data from its database. Browse this code to see how it differs from the previous incarnation.

Listing 4.6 Updating the microservice to use the database

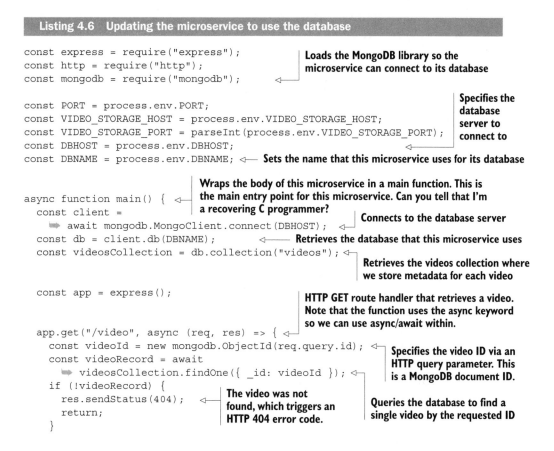

```
const forwardRequest = http.request(           ◁─┐  Forwards the request to the
  {                                                │  video-storage (azure-storage)
    host: VIDEO_STORAGE_HOST,                      │  microservice
    port: VIDEO_STORAGE_PORT,
    path:`/video?path=${videoRecord.videoPath}`, ◁─┐  When forwarding the HTTP
    method: 'GET',                                  │  request to the video-storage
    headers: req.headers                            │  microservice, this maps the
  },                                                │  video's ID to the video's
  forwardResponse => {                              │  location.
    res.writeHeader(forwardResponse.statusCode, forwardResponse.headers);
    forwardResponse.pipe(res);
  }
);

req.pipe(forwardRequest);
});

app.listen(PORT);
}

main()                    ◁─────  Starts the microservice
  .catch(err => {
    console.error("Microservice failed to start.");
    console.error(err && err.stack || err);
  });
```

Listing 4.6 queries its database by video ID to retrieve the location of a video in storage. It then passes that location to the video-storage microservice to retrieve the video that is stored there. The rest of the code here should be familiar. We're forwarding HTTP requests for videos to the video-storage microservice.

This update to the video-streaming microservice has removed the hardcoded video path. Instead, we now refer to videos by their database ID. We could have fixed this without using IDs by simply referring to videos by their path in storage. But as you might suspect, that's not a good idea. Let's consider why.

If we use paths to identify our videos, that makes it difficult to later move videos to a different location if we decide in the future that we'd like to restructure our storage filesystem. This is a problem because various other databases and records will need to refer to our videos. This includes a metadata database for recording information about a video, such as its genre. In addition, we'll later want a database for recording recommendations and views of each video.

Each of these databases must have a generic way to refer to a video. If we only record the ID for each video, we give ourselves much more freedom to make independent changes to our storage without causing any nasty problems to ripple through our microservices and databases.

This also makes it a bit simpler because the location of the video could potentially be a long path, and internal details like this aren't something we'd usually like to let leak out of our application. Why? Exposing details that hint at the internal structure can give a potential attacker an advantage. It's better to keep a lid on this kind of information.

LOADING SOME TEST DATA INTO OUR DATABASE

We've added a database to our Docker Compose file and updated the video-streaming microservice to use that database. We're almost ready to test our changes!

To test our updated code, we must now load some test data into our database. Later, we'll have a way for our users to upload their own videos and populate the database with relevant details, but we don't yet have any way to do this in our application.

We could test our code by replacing the database with some kind of simulated version of it. I'm talking about mocking the database, as mentioned earlier in this chapter. Another way we can do this is to use a *database fixture*, which is a piece of test data that we load into our database purely for testing.

There are various ways we can load data into our database. We can write custom code (you'll see examples of that later in the book), use the MongoDB Shell, or use Studio 3T (formerly known as Robo 3T and Robomongo). The latter is a fantastic UI tool for working with MongoDB. I use it all the time myself, which you already know if you read my first book, *Data Wrangling with JavaScript* (Manning, 2018). It's available for Windows, macOS, and Linux.

For download and install instructions for Studio 3T, see https://studio3t.com/. Studio 3T allows you to view the collections and documents in your database. You can easily create databases, collections, and data records.

But before we can load example data into our database, we first must have our database up and running. We can do that by booting our application. If you haven't yet done so, open a terminal and start your application:

```
cd chapter-4/example-3
docker compose up --build
```

> **NOTE** You should run this command from the same directory as the updated Docker Compose file shown earlier in listing 4.5. You can find this file in the example-3 subdirectory of the chapter-4 code repository.

After starting our application, we now have a MongoDB database server running in a container. Because we mapped the standard MongoDB port 27017 to port 4000 on our development computer, we can now access the database by starting our database viewer and then connecting it to localhost:4000.

Listing 4.7 (chapter-4/example-3/db-fixture/videos.json) shows the test data we'll add to our database. This is a single JSON document that is available under the example-3 directory and is suitable for a copy-and-paste insert using Studio 3T.

You can load this data using Studio 3T: create a new database called `video-streaming`, create a collection called `videos`, and then insert a new document into that collection using the content from listing 4.7.

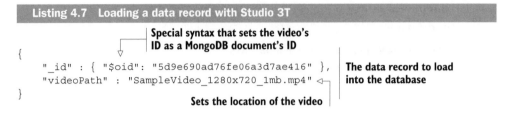

Listing 4.7   Loading a data record with Studio 3T

```
{
    "_id" : { "$oid": "5d9e690ad76fe06a3d7ae416" },
    "videoPath" : "SampleVideo_1280x720_1mb.mp4"
}
```

Special syntax that sets the video's ID as a MongoDB document's ID

The data record to load into the database

Sets the location of the video

We'll come back to mocking and database fixtures in chapter 9. For now, let's look at how to test our application.

> **NOTE**   If you want to invest a little more effort learning, you can also load your database fixtures from the terminal using the MongoDB Shell. This is a powerful way to read, write, and manipulate the data in your database. Learn more in the MongoDB Shell documentation: www.mongodb.com/docs/mongodb-shell/.

TESTING OUR UPDATED APPLICATION

At this stage, you can first test the microservice directly under Node.js if you like. It's always a good idea to test your microservices independently before you integrate them. If you're putting this code together by yourself and testing directly under Node.js, don't forget to install the mongodb driver package from npm:

```
npm install --save mongodb
```

There's no need for me to walk you through individual testing for each new microservice. In the interest of expediency, we'll skip that and go straight to running our integrated code in the application under Docker Compose.

You should already have the application running from the previous section. We needed it there for the database, so we could load our test data. If the application isn't running, start it now:

```
cd chapter-4/example-3
docker compose up --build
```

We can now test the application in the usual way with a web browser. This time, though, we must provide the ID of the video we'd like to watch. The ID that we specified in our test data was a big long string of numbers, and that's what we must now add to our URL to test the updated application. Open your browser, and navigate to this URL: http://localhost:4002/video?id=5d9e690ad76fe06a3d7ae416. If you change the ID in the test data, you also need to update the ID in this URL. You should now see the test video playing. You must know this video very well by now!

4.5.3   *Adding a database server in production*

So far, we've only covered the case of adding a database server to the development version of our application. This works well enough for the moment because we haven't yet talked about how to deploy our application to production; that's coming in chapters 6, 7, and 8. What we can do now, though, is briefly consider how we might deploy a database server for use by our production environment.

Docker Compose makes it easy to add a database server to our application for development, but what about production? For production, I recommend using a database external to the Kubernetes cluster. This keeps the cluster stateless, which, as we discussed in section 4.4.5, means that we can tear down and rebuild our cluster at any time without risk to our data.

Once we've built our production Kubernetes cluster, we can easily deploy a MongoDB database similar to what we've just done with Docker Compose. In fact, that's what we'll do in chapter 6 because that's the easiest way for us to get our database server into production.

Beyond that though, I recommend that you keep your database separate from your cluster. You can run it on a separate VM or, even better, in an external managed database. The reason to keep the database separate from the cluster is to keep the production cluster stateless. I mentioned this earlier: having a stateless cluster makes it easier to run multiple versions of our application in parallel. It also means we can destroy and rebuild our cluster without fear of losing our data.

Another advantage to using a managed database is security. The database provider takes care of maintenance for us, including protecting and backing up our data! If we work for a big company, our company will probably manage this in-house. But if we work for a small company or startup, we need all the help we can get.

4.5.4   *Database-per-microservice or database-per-application?*

At this point, we've only created a single database on our database server. But we're now set up to create many more additional databases.

You probably noticed that we named the database video-streaming to coincide with the microservice that uses it. This alludes to a rule we'll be following throughout the book: *each microservice should have its own database*. We do this because we'd like to encapsulate our data within the microservice in the same way we'd encapsulate data within an object in object-oriented programming (OOP).

Do we really need one database for each and every microservice? It's definitely worthwhile to stick to this rule. Your databases can be hosted on a single database server, but make sure that each individual microservice has its own individual database. If you share databases or make a database the integration point between microservices, you're inviting architectural and scalability problems.

We're restricting our data from all but the code that directly encapsulates it. This helps us to safely evolve the structure of our data over time because changes to the data can be hidden within the microservice. This is another technique that, if we structure our REST APIs carefully, allows us to avoid propagating breakages and problems from one microservice to other parts of the application. Care applied when designing our microservices equates to better design for our application.

You might think that sharing a database between microservices is a good way for them to share data. But using a database as an integration point or interface between microservices is a bad idea because it makes for a more fragile and less scalable application. It reduces our ability to evolve our microservices independently from each other.

At some point, you might find yourself wanting to share a database for performance or some other reason. After all, rules sometimes have to be broken if you're trying to achieve a difficult goal. Carefully consider why you want to do this and whether it's truly necessary. Bringing such anti-patterns into our application isn't something we should do blindly. We'll talk more about databases and scalability in chapter 12.

4.5.5 What did we achieve?

We added a database to our application. We now have two different methods at our disposal to manage our application's data: we can store files in external cloud storage and store data in a database. We made good use of Docker Compose to run an application composed of multiple containers, and we upgraded our application to two microservices and a database.

We hid our storage provider behind a video-storage microservice whose job is to retrieve videos from storage. The abstraction we put in place allows us to easily change our storage provider later without much disruption to our application.

We created a database server and added a database for use by our video-streaming microservice. We're following the rule that each microservice should have its own database, and, in the future, we can easily add more databases to our server and continue to satisfy this rule.

We've also briefly seen how one microservice can communicate with another. The HTTP GET request received by the video-streaming microservice was forwarded to the video-storage microservice. This is the first and simplest form of communication that one microservice can use to request or delegate tasks to another. In the next chapter, we'll more deeply explore this and other methods of communication between microservices. In addition, you'll further extend your skills with Docker Compose and learn how to apply automated live reload to the entire microservices application.

4.6 Docker Compose review

Throughout this chapter, we've seen increasing value from Docker Compose, using it to help manage the complexity of our growing application on our development computer. Even when running just a single container, Docker Compose was useful because it allowed us to capture and record configuration details. At that early stage, it magically turned two commands into one.

As we progressed through the chapter, we added two more containers to our application, and the value of Docker Compose became even clearer. We can add as many containers as we want to our application, we can record all their configuration details, and—no matter how many containers we have—we can manage them all as an aggregated entity using single commands.

Figure 4.16 shows the simple lifecycle of our application running under Docker Compose. We use the up command to boot our application and all of its microservices. We use the down command to destroy our application and return our development computer to a clean state.

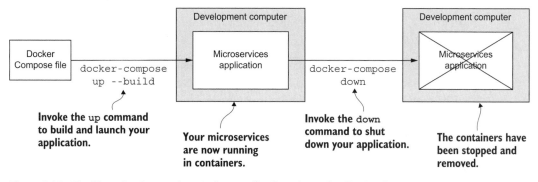

Figure 4.16   The lifecycle of your microservices application when using Docker Compose

Before you finish this chapter, scan table 4.2 for a quick review of the Docker Compose commands you've learned. Return here when you need help working with Docker Compose.

Table 4.2   Review of Docker Compose commands

Command	Description
docker compose up --build	Builds and instantiates an application composed of multiple containers as defined by the Docker Compose file (docker-compose.yaml) in the current working directory
docker compose ps	Lists running containers that are part of the application specified by the Docker Compose file
docker compose stop	Stops all containers in the application, but persists the stopped containers for inspection
docker compose down	Stops and destroys the application, which leaves the development computer in a clean state

4.7   *Continue your learning*

This chapter skimmed the surface of two big topics. We added a new microservice to our application and connected it to our Azure Storage account. We also added a MongoDB database to our application. Both Azure and MongoDB are technologies that have a world of their own. We'll explore Azure more in chapters 6, 7, and 10, but I'll leave you for now with some references to dig deeper in these areas:

- *Microsoft Azure in Action* by Lars Klint (Manning, est. Spring 2024)
- *Learn Azure in a Month of Lunches,* 2nd ed., by Iain Foulds (Manning, 2020)
- *MongoDB in Action,* 2nd ed. by Kyle Banker, Peter Bakkum, et. al (Manning, 2016)

To learn more about working with data in JavaScript, there's my earlier book:

- *Data Wrangling with JavaScript* by Ashley Davis (Manning, 2018)

To learn more about Docker Compose, read the documentation online:

- https://docs.docker.com/compose/
- https://docs.docker.com/compose/compose-file/
- https://docs.docker.com/compose/reference/

In this chapter, we scaled up to multiple microservices using Docker Compose. We also added data management capability to our application. In the next chapter, you'll learn in more detail how to make your microservices talk to each other. You'll also improve your skills with Docker Compose and learn how to extend live reload so that it works across the entire application.

Summary

- Docker Compose is a subcommand of Docker that allows us to script the building and running of multiple containers. It's a convenient way to simulate Kubernetes and run a many-microservices application for development and testing.
- A Docker Compose file is the script that configures a distributed application from multiple Docker containers. It aggregates together a collection of Dockerfiles.
- The command `docker compose up --build` builds and instantiates the distributed application.
- The command `docker compose down` shuts down the application.
- Cloud file storage is a method of storing files for an application in a service provided by a cloud platform such as Azure, AWS, or GCP.
- Azure Storage is the cloud file storage service provided by Microsoft Azure.
- MongoDB is an easy to use, flexible, and scalable database solution that is a perfect fit for microservices.
- In development, we can easily instantiate a MongoDB server under Docker Compose and share it between all the microservices we're running in development.
- It's okay to share a database server among microservices, but we should try to follow this rule: only one database per microservice. A good microservice encapsulates its database behind a REST API and doesn't share that data with any other service. So (for low cost and convenience of maintenance), just have a single database server, but make sure that each microservice has its own database on that server.
- Although it's possible to store files and run a database in a Kubernetes cluster, for production, we'd prefer to have a stateless cluster. Keeping our files and data outside the cluster can be safer and more flexible. It means that we can easily destroy and rebuild our cluster without fear of losing our files and data.

Communication
between microservices

This chapter covers

- Using live reload at the application level for faster iterations
- Sending direct messages between microservices with HTTP requests
- Sending indirect messages between microservices with RabbitMQ
- Choosing between using direct and indirect messages

A microservices application is composed of many microservices, each looking after its own area of responsibility. Because each microservice by itself is small, simple, and doesn't do much, our microservices must collaborate to create the complex behaviors needed to implement the feature set for our product. To work together, our microservices need ways to communicate. If they can't talk to each other, then they won't be able to coordinate their activities, and they won't achieve much.

In this chapter, we examine the different ways that microservices can communicate so that they can collaborate and fulfill the higher-level requirements of the application. In the process, we'll also revisit Docker and Docker Compose to set up live reload for our entire application. Moving forward, that's essential so that we aren't constantly rebuilding and restarting our application as we update our code.

We already saw in earlier chapters that HTTP requests are one way that microservices can communicate. In this chapter, we'll expand on using HTTP requests for direct messaging, and we'll also look at using RabbitMQ for indirect messaging. Throughout the chapter, you'll learn how to decide what type of messaging to use for a given situation.

5.1   New and familiar tools

This chapter introduces the RabbitMQ software for queuing messages, which will help us decouple our microservices. We'll use the npm package called *amqplib* to connect our microservices to RabbitMQ so they can send and receive messages. We'll also revise some familiar tools, and we'll explore in more detail how to use HTTP requests to send messages and upgrade our development environment to support application-wide live reload. The list of tools introduced in this chapter is shown in table 5.1.

Table 5.1   New and familiar tools in chapter 5

Tool	Version	Purpose
Docker Compose	Included with Docker 24.0.5	Docker Compose lets us configure, build, run, and manage multiple containers at the same time.
HTTP	1.1	HTTP is used to send direct (or synchronous) messages from one microservice to another.
RabbitMQ	3.12.4	RabbitMQ is the message-queuing software that we'll use to send indirect (or asynchronous) messages from one microservice to another.
amqplib	0.10.3	This npm package allows us to configure RabbitMQ and to send and receive messages from JavaScript.

5.2   Getting the code

To follow along with this chapter, you need to download the code or clone the repository. Download a zip file of the code from here: http://mng.bz/vPM1. You can clone the code using Git, like this:

```
git clone
⮡ https://github.com/bootstrapping-microservices-2nd-edition/chapter-5
```

For help on installing and using Git, see chapter 2. If you have problems with the code, log an issue against the repository in GitHub.

5.3   *Getting our microservices talking*

At this point in the book, we have an application with two microservices: video-streaming and video-storage. In the previous chapter, we added data storage capability, so now the video-streaming microservice has a database, and the video-storage microservice uses external cloud storage to store the video files. Figure 5.1 shows what our application looks like now.

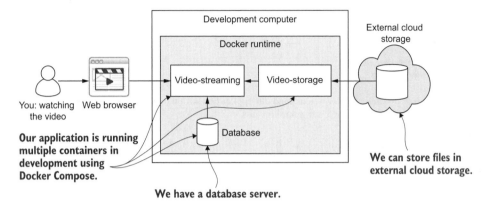

Figure 5.1   We finished the preceding chapter with two microservices and a database running under Docker Compose on our development computer. We also added external cloud storage via a connection to Azure Storage to store our videos.

A microservices application is built from services that collaborate to provide the application's features. Our application can't do much if our microservices can't communicate! Communication between microservices is therefore a crucial part of building with microservices, and it's essential that we have communication techniques at our disposal.

Actually, we wouldn't have gotten this far without having already used HTTP requests for communication between the video-streaming and video-storage microservices like we did in chapter 4. We glossed over it there, but it's very important. Without it, we would have stumbled at the first hurdle: separating out the streaming and storage capabilities for our application.

> **NOTE**   Our microservices must work together to implement the features of our application, so it's crucial that they be able to communicate for collaboration.

In this chapter, we add a third microservice to our application: the history microservice. The purpose of adding this new microservice is to demonstrate communication among microservices. You can see in figure 5.2 how the video-streaming microservice is sending a stream of messages to the history microservice.

Figure 5.2 shows conceptually what our application looks like at the end of this chapter, but it doesn't show the full technical details of what we'll add. To get the full picture, we need to know the various styles of communication we can use and the

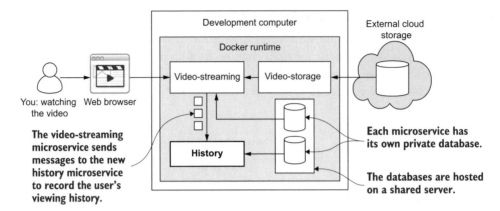

Figure 5.2   In this chapter, we expand our application with a new microservice and explore methods of communication between our microservices.

technologies that underpin these. Before that, let's better understand the history microservice.

5.4   *Introducing the history microservice*

We're using the history microservice in this chapter as an example of how microservices can send and receive messages to each other. Actually, this new microservice really does have a proper place in FlixTube, and as the name suggests, it records our user's viewing history.

There are multiple ways our application can use this history. For starters, our users might want to look at their own history to remember a video they watched in the past or to resume watching a video later. In addition, we might use the viewing history to provide recommendations for other users.

To keep the examples in this chapter simple, we'll drop out the video-storage microservice from the previous chapter, which simplifies the video-streaming microservice. In fact, for our starting point in this chapter, we'll revert to an earlier version of the video-streaming microservice that has the example video baked into its Docker image. We'll use the video-streaming microservice like it was after chapter 3. This simplification is just in effect while we get our heads around the communication techniques. After this chapter, we'll reinstate the video-storage microservice and restore the video-streaming microservice to its former glory.

The message we'll transmit between microservices is the "Viewed" message. This is how the video-streaming microservice informs the history microservice that the user has watched a video. Figure 5.3 shows you what the history microservice is doing: it receives a stream of messages from the video-streaming microservice and records them in its own database.

We haven't yet discussed the styles of messaging we could use—that's coming soon. For the moment, know that there are multiple techniques we can use to send the "Viewed" message. Through this chapter, we'll explore our options, and we can

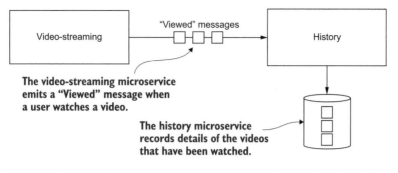

Figure 5.3   As a way to explore communication methods, we'll have the video-streaming microservice send a viewed message to the history microservice to record our user's viewing history.

decide later which one is best suited for any future situation. But first, let's upgrade our development environment for faster development cycles.

5.5   Live reload for fast iterations

In chapter 2, section 2.4, we talked about our philosophy of development and how small, fast increments are essential for a tight feedback loop and for maintaining a fast development pace. When directly running our first microservice under Node.js in chapter 2, we were able to use the npm package nodemon to make our microservice *live reload*. This means our microservice automatically reloads when we make changes to its code. Having an efficient live reload mechanism is even more important at the application level than it is at the microservice level. That's because building and booting up the whole application composed of multiple microservices is much slower than booting up each individual microservice.

In chapter 3, we used Docker and began to "bake" the code for our microservice into the Docker image. Docker is an incredibly useful way for us to package, publish, and deploy our microservices. That's why we use it, even though we've yet to see the deploy part of this puzzle; we'll see our microservices deployed to production in chapter 6.

In chapter 4, we used Docker Compose in our development environment as a convenient way to structure and manage a local version of our growing application. This is all well and good, but, unfortunately, in transitioning from direct use of Node.js to running our microservices in Docker containers, we lost our ability to automatically reload our code.

Because we're baking our code into our Docker images, we can't change it afterward! This is great for production because, for security reasons, many companies would like to be able to verify the software supply chain and know that no one has injected any (potentially malicious) code into the image that isn't supposed to be there. The problem now is that during development, we don't want to constantly rebuild our images and reboot our application to include updated code. Doing this is quite slow. For repeated rebuilds and restarts, the time really adds up, especially as our application grows in size.

NOTE Not being able to quickly update the code in a running application is a terrible thing for our development process and can be a huge drain on our productivity. We'll address this now and find a way to restore our live reload capability.

In this section, we'll upgrade our Docker Compose file to support sharing code between our development computer and our containers. Figure 5.4 shows you how the source code directory for the new history microservice is shared from our development computer into the microservice's container.

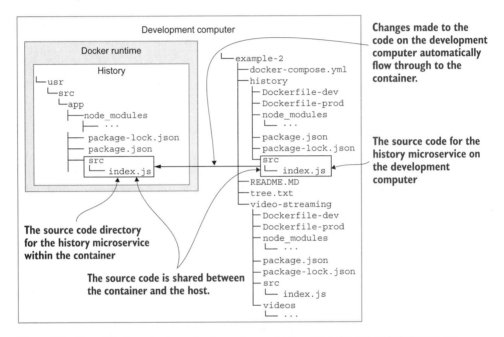

Figure 5.4   To enable live reload on a larger scale, we must synchronize the code between our development computer and the container so that changes to the code automatically propagate through to the container.

Again, we'll use nodemon for this across the board for all of our microservices. It will automatically restart each microservice when the code changes. This configuration might seem onerous to put in place, but it's going to make a huge improvement to our pace of development, so it's important to get this right!

5.5.1   Creating a stub for the history microservice

We'll create the live reload configuration only for the new history microservice, but after that, we apply this same configuration to each and every microservice. This way, live reload is supported for all the microservices in our application.

Before we get started, read through listing 5.1 (chapter-5/example-1/history/ src/index.js) and familiarize yourself with the newly born history microservice. This doesn't do anything yet. It's just a stub waiting to have features added. Once we have live reload working for this microservice, we'll be able to boot our application using Docker Compose. Then, we'll make live updates and incremental changes to evolve this new microservice without having to restart the application.

Listing 5.1   A stub for the history microservice

```
const express = require("express");

--snip--

const PORT = process.env.PORT;

async function main() {

  const app = express();

  // ... add route handlers here ...        ◁──┐  This is a stub microservice.
                                                 Later, we'll add HTTP routes
                                                 and message handlers here.
  app.listen(PORT, () => {
    console.log("Microservice online.");
  });
}

main()
  .catch(err => {
    console.error("Microservice failed to start.");
    console.error(err && err.stack || err);
  });
```

5.5.2 *Augmenting the microservice for live reload*

We don't need to do anything else to the basic code for our microservice, other than what we already learned in chapter 2, where we set up our first microservice and installed nodemon for live reload. Each microservice needs nodemon installed like this:

```
npm install --save-dev nodemon
```

We'll use the npm package, nodemon, to watch our code and to automatically restart our microservice when the code changes. The package.json file for the microservice includes an npm script called start:dev, according to the convention we started in chapter 2. You can see what this looks like in listing 5.2 (chapter-5/example-1/history/package.json).

Listing 5.2   Setting up package.json for live reload with nodemon

```
{
  "name": "history",
  "version": "1.0.0",
  "description": "",
```

```
  "main": "./src/index.js",
  "scripts": {
    "start": "node ./src/index.js",
    "start:dev":
➥     "nodemon --legacy-watch ./src/index.js"
  },
--snip--  "dependencies": {
    "express": "^5.0.0-beta.1"
  },
  "devDependencies": {
    "nodemon": "^2.0.21"
  }
}
```

> Uses nodemon to enable live reload for this microservice. When the code changes, nodemon automatically restarts the microservice.

With the `start:dev` npm script in place, we can run our microservice like this:

```
npm run start:dev
```

This invokes nodemon for our microservice like this:

```
nodemon --legacy-watch ./src/index.js.
```

Obviously, we could always type out the full nodemon command, but using `npm run start:dev` is shorter, and it's always the same for all of our microservices (assuming that we apply the convention to each and every microservice). If you just started the history microservice, now exit with Ctrl-C. Soon, we'll run our entire application again using Docker Compose.

You're probably wondering why I used the `--legacy-watch` argument with nodemon. I used this argument because I usually run Docker and Docker Compose under WSL2 on Windows. The `--legacy-watch` argument disables the filesystem watch and, instead, uses a frequent polling mechanism to monitor for code changes. If you do your development under WSL2 or on a virtual machine (VM), you need this because the automatic file watch required by live reload doesn't translate changes through from the host operating system. If you're not doing your development under WSL2 or a VM, you can safely remove the `--legacy-watch` argument, and your live reload will work with slightly better performance.

5.5.3   *Splitting our Dockerfile for development and production*

In chapter 2, we talked about being able to run our microservices in either development mode or production mode. We made this distinction so that we can optimize separately for the differing needs of development and production. In this section, you'll see this separation start to come to fruition.

> **NOTE** At this point, we'll create separate Dockerfiles for our development and production modes. In each case, our needs differ: we prioritize fast iteration for development, and we prioritize performance and security for production.

So, for all microservices, we'll create not just one but two Dockerfiles: one for development and another for production. We'll call the development one Dockerfile-dev and the production one Dockerfile-prod.

These names are chosen to avoid confusion. Naming is so important in software development and we should aim to select clear names to help avoid ambiguity. We're separating our Dockerfiles at this point so that we can enable live reload in development. That isn't something that we want enabled in production!

Listing 5.3 (chapter-5/example-1/history/Dockerfile-prod) shows a production Dockerfile for the new history microservice. There's nothing new here as this is a fairly standard Node.js Dockerfile and similar to the Dockerfile we created in chapter 3.

Listing 5.3   Creating the production Dockerfile

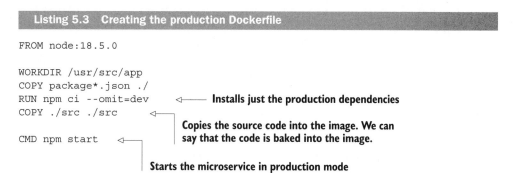

```
FROM node:18.5.0

WORKDIR /usr/src/app
COPY package*.json ./
RUN npm ci --omit=dev        ◁──── Installs just the production dependencies
COPY ./src ./src        ◁
                              Copies the source code into the image. We can
                              say that the code is baked into the image.
CMD npm start        ◁

                        Starts the microservice in production mode
```

We won't actually make use of the production Dockerfiles in this chapter, but we'll definitely need these starting in chapter 6, when we deploy to our production environment. It's a good idea to maintain our development and production Dockerfiles side by side so that the development version doesn't get too far ahead of the production one.

Listing 5.4 (chapter-5/example-1/history/Dockerfile-dev) shows the development Dockerfile for the history microservice. As you read through, compare it to the production Dockerfile in listing 5.3 to notice the differences between development and production for yourself.

Listing 5.4   Creating the dev Dockerfile

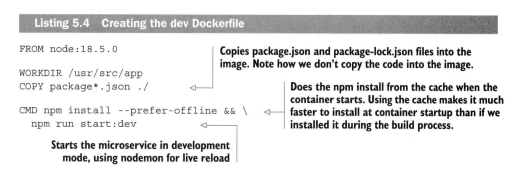

```
FROM node:18.5.0        Copies package.json and package-lock.json files into the
                        image. Note how we don't copy the code into the image.
WORKDIR /usr/src/app
COPY package*.json ./        ◁
                                    Does the npm install from the cache when the
                                    container starts. Using the cache makes it much
CMD npm install --prefer-offline && \   ◁── faster to install at container startup than if we
    npm run start:dev        ◁              installed it during the build process.

        Starts the microservice in development
        mode, using nodemon for live reload
```

Did you pick up the differences between the two different Dockerfiles? In listing 5.3, we installed production-only dependencies, whereas in listing 5.4, we installed all dependencies, including our development dependencies.

Did you spot the most important change? In listing 5.3, we baked our code into the production Docker image using the COPY instruction:

```
COPY ./src ./src
```

That command copies our code into the image. What's most interesting in the development version of the Dockerfile is what's missing. You'll note there is *no* COPY instruction for our code in listing 5.4 (although there is one for package.json), so we're excluding our code from the development Docker image! If we bake our code into the image, then we can't easily change it later. If we can't change our code, then we can't use live reload.

But if we aren't copying code into our development image, then how will it get into the container? We'll find an answer to this in the next section. For now, we still have one more big difference to look at between our development and production Dockerfiles.

Note the CMD instruction that specifies how to start our microservice within the container. In the production Dockerfile, we simply start the microservice using the npm start convention that was described in chapter 2:

```
CMD npm start
```

The CMD instruction in the development Dockerfile is different and does a lot more work:

```
CMD npm install --prefer-offline && \
  npm run start:dev
```

This command is separated over two lines using the backslash (\) line continuation character. The first line installs dependencies from the cache, and the second line starts the microservice.

In the production Dockerfile, we invoke npm install during the Docker build process, which means our dependencies are baked into the image, just as they should be in production. In the development version, though, we do the npm install at container startup. The reason for the difference in development is for better performance in subsequent rebuilds.

The npm install can take significant time. When we do it at container startup, we're able to cache the npm packages on the host operating system. That's why we configured the cache on the first line. Caching our npm packages in this way makes subsequent npm installs much faster, which in turn makes container startup faster. You'll learn more about how this works in the next section.

The second line of the CMD instruction in the development Dockerfile is what actually starts the microservice. It invokes npm script start:dev to start our microservice in development mode with live reload enabled.

5.5.4 *Updating the Docker Compose file for live reload*

The final part of getting our application-wide live reload working is to make some necessary changes to our Docker Compose file to share our code and the npm cache between the host operating system and the containers. In this section, we use Docker volumes to share the filesystem between our development computer and the container. This means we can edit code in Visual Studio Code (VS Code) and see the changes appear almost immediately in our microservice running in the application under Docker Compose.

Listing 5.5 is an extract from the example-1 Docker Compose file (chapter-5/example-1/docker-compose.yaml) that shows the configuration for our new history microservice. This is similar to the Docker Compose files we created in chapter 4, but there are some differences and new additions.

Listing 5.5 Updating the Docker Compose file for live reload

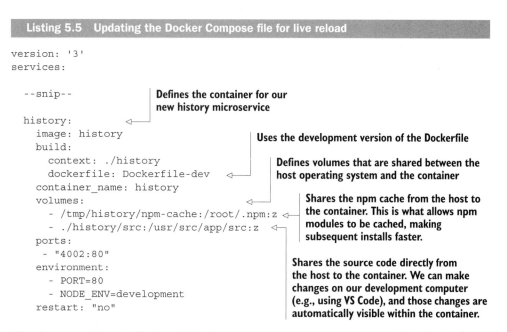

```
version: '3'
services:

  --snip--                    Defines the container for our
                              new history microservice
  history:
    image: history                  Uses the development version of the Dockerfile
    build:
      context: ./history            Defines volumes that are shared between the
      dockerfile: Dockerfile-dev    host operating system and the container
    container_name: history
    volumes:                        Shares the npm cache from the host to
      - /tmp/history/npm-cache:/root/.npm:z    the container. This is what allows npm
      - ./history/src:/usr/src/app/src:z       modules to be cached, making
    ports:                          subsequent installs faster.
      - "4002:80"
    environment:                    Shares the source code directly from
      - PORT=80                     the host to the container. We can make
      - NODE_ENV=development        changes on our development computer
    restart: "no"                   (e.g., using VS Code), and those changes are
                                    automatically visible within the container.
```

The first new thing in listing 5.5 is that we now use `Dockerfile-dev`, which is the development version of our Dockerfile. I mentioned back in chapter 4 that we could omit the `dockerfile` field and that it would default to `Dockerfile`. In chapter 4, we didn't leave it at the default value; instead, we explicitly set it to `Dockerfile`. I indicated that we'd need to explicitly set this in the near future. Well, this is where we're at now, and we're explicitly setting it to `Dockerfile-dev` to use the development version of our Dockerfile.

The next new thing is the addition of the `volumes` field, where we create some Docker volumes to connect the filesystem on our development computer with the filesystem of the container. This links our source code directly into the container and is why we didn't bake our code directly into the image.

To share the code, we use one Docker volume. The other volume creates a shared directory for the npm cache. This allows npm packages that are installed in the container to be cached on the host operating system so that if we destroy and recreate the container, subsequent npm installs are faster because we've retained the cache outside of the container.

In case you were wondering about the z flag used in the volume configuration in listing 5.5, that simply indicates to Docker that the volume is to be shared (potentially among multiple containers). If you like, you can read more about it here: https://docs .docker.com/storage/bind-mounts/.

This has been quite a lot to take in, and so far, it's only for the history microservice! We'll need to make these changes to all of our microservices. Fortunately, we can just use the same pattern and apply it to each microservice as follows:

1. Install nodemon for each microservice.
2. Update package.json, and implement the `start:dev` script to start the microservice with nodemon (as in listing 5.3).
3. Create development and production versions of our Dockerfiles. The development Dockerfile should not copy the code into the image (as in listing 5.4).
4. Do the `npm install` on container startup only for development, not production (this is for performance, as in listing 5.4).
5. Update the Docker Compose file so that it uses the development Dockerfile (as in listing 5.5).
6. Add Docker volumes to the Docker Compose file so that the source code and npm cache are shared into the container (as in listing 5.5).

I've gone ahead and done this already for all examples in the chapter 5 repository so you don't have to worry about it. But you should at least start example-1 and then make some code changes to the history microservice so that you can see live reload in action! Let's do that now.

5.5.5 *Trying out live reload*

Enough looking at code listings! It's time to see live reload in action so you can truly appreciate how useful it is. Open a terminal, and change directory to the example-1 subdirectory under the chapter-5 code repository. Then use Docker Compose to start the application:

```
cd chapter-5/example-1
docker compose up --build
```

This example contains the simplified video-streaming microservice and the new stub history microservice. Check the output from Docker Compose. You should see "Hello world!" printed out by the stub history microservice as it starts up. To test live reload, we'll change the message that is printed by the history microservice:

1   Open the example-1 directory in VS Code.
2   Find and open the index.js file for the history microservice.
3   Search for the line of code that prints the "Hello world!" message, and change this line of code to print "Hello computer!" instead.
4   Save the index.js file, and then switch back to the Docker Compose output.

If you switch over quickly enough, you'll see the history microservice being reloaded and printing your updated message. If you weren't quick enough, you should see that this has already happened. When you do this, note that the video-streaming microservice didn't reload because we didn't change its code. Only the history microservice was updated, so only that microservice reloaded.

This is the promise of live reload. We can update our code in quick iterations and receive fast and direct feedback. We don't have to wait to build and start the entire application. Instead, we can *hot reload* the code for each microservice that needs to be updated.

What happens if we introduce an error in our code? If a microservice reloads with an error, the error is displayed in the Docker Compose output. We can then correct the error and save the code file. The microservice automatically reloads, and assuming our change actually fixes the error, we should see clean output from the updated microservice.

At this point, I recommend that you try to break the history microservice on purpose to see what happens. Go on. Open its index.js file, and enter some random gibberish that's sure to break it. Save the file, and switch back to the Docker Compose output to see the result.

Consider what the error message means and what you did that caused it. Now I hear you say, "But Ash, we'd like to keep our code working, so why are we trying to break it?" It's actually good to practice breaking and fixing your code in a controlled and safe environment. That way, when it comes to encountering real problems in the wild, you'll be more experienced and have a better understanding of the error messages and how to deal with them. Spend some time now breaking the code; cause problems, and try to have some fun while you're at it.

Forcing a container to restart

Every so often, we might want to force a reload of a microservice that hasn't changed. Say the microservice has hung or crashed and is now stuck. With our live reload system, we can make a container restart simply by changing the code, for example, adding some whitespace and then saving the file.

Actually, we don't need to go that far. We can simply save the file in VS Code, and that's enough to make the container restart. We don't need to make the change!

If you have access to the `touch` command from your terminal, you can also trigger live reload from the command line for the history microservice as follows:

```
cd chapter-5/example-1
touch history/src/index.js
```

(continued)

If you don't have live reload set up for a particular container (you only need live reload for microservices whose code changes frequently), then you can use the Docker Compose `restart` command to make a container restart, for example, to force the history microservice to rebuild and restart:

```
docker compose build history
docker compose restart history
```

5.5.6   *Testing production mode in development*

So far, in this chapter, we've split our Dockerfiles into separate files so that we can have different versions for development mode and production mode, but we aren't making use of the production Dockerfiles yet. This will change in chapter 6, when we deploy to production. But just because we aren't ready to deploy to production yet doesn't mean we can't test in production mode. In fact, we should always and often be testing for both development and production on our local computer.

During development, we'll constantly make small incremental code changes and then test that our application still works. Even though we aren't making as frequent use of our production Dockerfiles as the development versions, we should update these at the same time we update the development versions. We should also regularly test in production mode, albeit less frequently than we test in development mode.

For example, we might be testing in development mode every few minutes as we make code changes. We still want to test production mode, but we may only do that every few hours after substantial code changes have accumulated. The main point is that we also need to test our production Dockerfiles on our local computer even before we deploy them to production. What we don't want is to unwittingly bank up hidden problems that will only be revealed after deployment to production.

We can easily and preemptively solve this problem by testing regularly in production mode on our development computer. To make this easier, I usually have two separate Docker Compose files: one for development and the other for production.

When we invoke Docker Compose, we can use the `-f` argument to specify the Docker Compose file. For instance, if we want to run our application in production mode on our development computer, we can create a separate production version of our Docker Compose file and run it like this:

```
docker compose -f docker-compose-prod.yml up --build
```

We can get away with having a single Docker Compose file that is parameterized by an environment variable, but I generally keep separate versions for testing development and production. That's because I like to have my production Docker Compose file mimic the real production environment as much as feasible. In addition, usually my development version will replace various microservices with mock versions for easier and faster testing, but when testing in production mode, it's better to test the real microservices and not the mock versions.

We'll talk about mocking microservices in chapter 10. In chapter 9, we'll cover automated testing, which can also enhance your productivity.

5.5.7 What have we achieved?

In section 5.5, we configured our microservices for live reload. We started with the history microservice and applied the same pattern to the video-streaming microservice. From now on, we'll use this for all of our microservices.

We did this because it takes significant time to build and start our application. We don't want to build and restart our application for each line of code that we change. Instead, we want to be able to rapidly change code to experiment and iterate quickly and have the application automatically update itself. Now, we can edit code, and our microservices will automatically restart. That's why this is called *live reload*—it reloads automatically while we're coding.

This makes for a very efficient and effective workflow. We can now continuously evolve our microservices application while receiving a constant stream of feedback. Browse the code in example-1, and make sure you understand how the live reload configuration is applied across the entire application.

5.6 Methods of communication for microservices

After that interlude of upgrading our development environment to support application-wide live reload, let's now return to the main topic of this chapter: exploring mechanisms for communication between microservices. But before we dive into the technology for communication, we'll start with a high-level overview of the two styles of communication used by microservices: direct messaging and indirect messaging, also commonly known as *synchronous* and *asynchronous* communication.

I prefer to use the terms direct and indirect messaging rather than synchronous and asynchronous messaging because the words "synchronous" and "asynchronous" have a different meaning in normal computer programming. In addition, the concept of asynchronous programming can be especially difficult to learn and has sent chills down the spines of many aspiring coders. Don't be concerned; let's avoid using the word asynchronous.

5.6.1 Direct messaging

Direct messaging simply means that one microservice directly sends a message to another microservice and then receives an immediate and direct response. We use messages for one of two purposes: to notify a microservice of some event in the system or to trigger an action in the microservice. You can think of any message as either a notification or a command (or something in between). Direct messaging is most useful when sending a command to another microservice, triggering some action in the microservice, and then immediately receiving a response as to whether that action succeeded or failed.

We can also use direct messaging to sequence a strict series of behaviors across multiple microservices. You can think of this as sending instructions to a set of microservices (e.g., *do this* or *do that* and then *tell me* if you were successful).

The recipient microservice can't ignore or avoid the incoming message. If it were to do so, the sender would know about it directly from the response. Figure 5.5 shows how the video-streaming microservice directs the "Viewed" message to the history microservice, which provides a direct and immediate response.

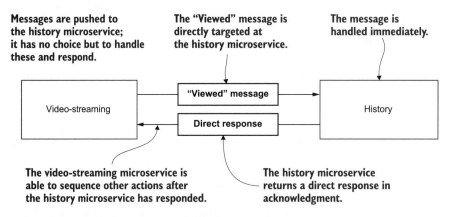

Figure 5.5   A direct message is sent to the history microservice explicitly by its name and is handled immediately.

Direct messaging is often required for certain use cases. It has the major drawback that it requires tight coupling of the two microservices that are at either end of the communication. Often, we'd prefer to avoid tight coupling between our microservices, so, for that reason, we'll make frequent use of indirect messaging instead of direct messaging.

5.6.2   *Indirect messaging*

Indirect messaging introduces an intermediary between the endpoints in the communication process. We add a middleman to sit between our microservices. For that reason, the two parties of the communication don't have to know about each other. This style of communication results in a much looser coupling between our microservices. It means two things:

- *Messages are sent via an intermediary so that both the sender and the receiver of the messages don't know which other microservice is involved.* In the case of the sender, it doesn't even know if any other microservice will receive the message at all!
- *Because the receiver doesn't know which microservice has sent the message, it can't send a direct reply.* This means that this style of communication can't be applied in situations where a direct response is required for confirming success or failure.

We should use indirect messages when the sending microservice doesn't care if any subsequent action is taken or not. We can also use it for broadcast-style notifications to the entire application (e.g., a notification of an important event that other microservices would like to know about).

> **NOTE** We use indirect messaging to announce important events that don't need a direct response. This kind of messaging allows a more flexible communication structure than direct messages and makes for less coupling between our microservices.

Figure 5.6 shows how the video-streaming microservice (on the left) sends an indirect message through a message queue (the intermediary) to the history microservice (on the right). Note that there is no direct connection between the video-streaming and history microservices. This is why we can say they are *loosely coupled*.

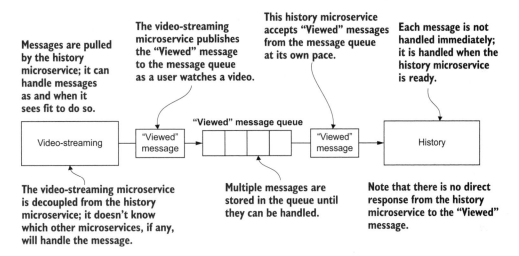

Figure 5.6 An indirect message isn't explicitly sent to a microservice; instead, the message is placed in a queue and can be handled later.

Indirect messaging can help us to build flexible messaging architectures to solve many complicated communication problems. Unfortunately, with this flexibility comes increased complexity. As your application grows, you'll find it more difficult to map the communication pathways precisely because they aren't direct and, therefore, aren't as obvious. With this overview of direct and indirect messaging out of the way, we can dive head first into actually trying out each of these communication methods.

5.7 *Direct messaging with HTTP*

In the previous chapter, we used HTTP for data retrieval, which retrieved our streaming video from storage. In this chapter, we use HTTP for a different purpose: sending messages directly from one microservice to another.

NOTE   Messages sent with HTTP requests have direct responses. We can know immediately if the handling of the message succeeded or failed.

Specifically, in this section, we'll use HTTP POST requests to send messages directly from the video-streaming microservice to the history microservice. Figure 5.7 shows this process.

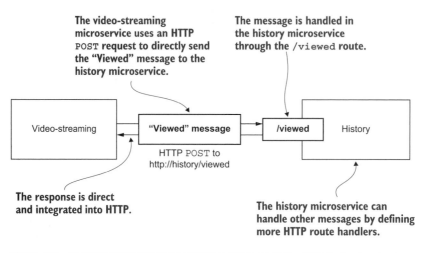

Figure 5.7   **An HTTP POST request explicitly targets another microservice by name.**

5.7.1   *Why HTTP?*

HTTP is the language and foundation of the World Wide Web and the de facto standard when creating a *web service*. HTTP is dependable and well understood by everyone.

HTTP is already ubiquitous for creating REST APIs, and we don't need to think too hard about why we should use HTTP. It was made for this kind of thing, and it's supported by every programming language we would care to work with. We also have easy access to huge amounts of learning resources related to HTTP, and, ironically, this information will most likely be delivered to us via HTTP that is underlying the World Wide Web.

5.7.2   *Directly targeting messages at particular microservices*

Before we can send a message to a microservice, we need a way to locate it. Accompanying HTTP is another internet protocol called *Domain Name System* (DNS). This gives us a simple and automatic means by which to direct messages to microservices using their names.

A key question with microservices communication is how do we direct a message to another microservice? The simplest answer to this question is to use the ubiquitous DNS, which translates hostnames to IP addresses. This works automatically with Docker Compose (the container name is the hostname) and also doesn't require much effort to have it work within our production Kubernetes cluster.

Figure 5.8 shows how we can send an HTTP POST message to a particular hostname. A lookup of the DNS is done automatically when sending an HTTP request, and it translates our hostname to the IP address of the microservice.

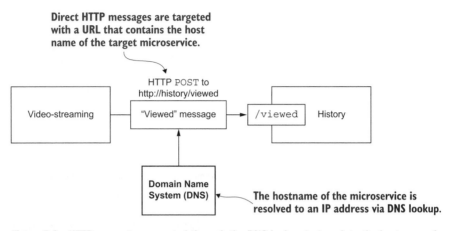

Figure 5.8   HTTP requests are routed through the DNS lookup to translate the hostname of the target microservice to an IP address.

The IP address is the string of numbers that represents the unique internet location for our microservice. Note that just because it's an IP address doesn't necessarily mean we're talking about the public internet. The IP address, in this case, actually represents a private server that is located in a private network, either operating under the Docker runtime on our development computer or operating within our production Kubernetes cluster. We need the IP address to direct a message at a recipient using an HTTP request, and DNS operates automatically and almost magically under the hood when we send the message.

Using Docker and Docker Compose for development as we've been doing means that DNS works automatically, and we can rely on it. When we deploy to our production Kubernetes cluster, we'll have some more work to do to make our microservices accessible via DNS, but we'll address that in chapter 6.

5.7.3   *Sending a message with HTTP POST*

There are two sides to the messaging equation: one microservice sends a message, and another receives it. In this section, we examine how to send a message using an HTTP POST request.

In chapter 4, section 4.4.2, we looked at an HTTP GET request that was forwarded from one microservice to another. We did that using the built-in Node.js HTTP library. We'll use that library again to make a request from one microservice to another.

Listing 5.6 is an extract from an updated index.js file from the example-2 video-streaming microservice (chapter-5/example-2/video-streaming/src/index.js) that shows how to send an HTTP POST message. It implements a new function, sendViewed-Message, that sends the "Viewed" message to the history microservice whenever a user starts watching a video.

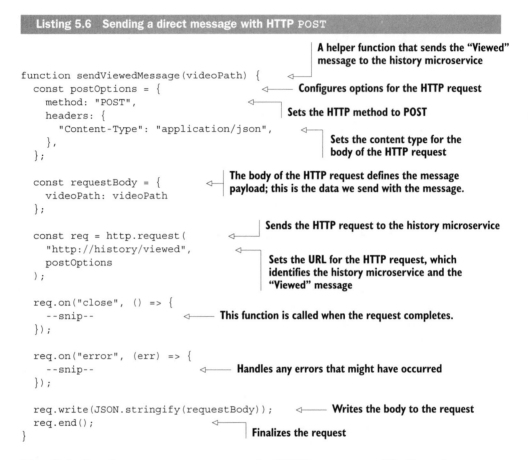

Listing 5.6   Sending a direct message with HTTP POST

```
function sendViewedMessage(videoPath) {
  const postOptions = {
    method: "POST",
    headers: {
      "Content-Type": "application/json",
    },
  };

  const requestBody = {
    videoPath: videoPath
  };

  const req = http.request(
    "http://history/viewed",
    postOptions
  );

  req.on("close", () => {
    --snip--
  });

  req.on("error", (err) => {
    --snip--
  });

  req.write(JSON.stringify(requestBody));
  req.end();
}
```

A helper function that sends the "Viewed" message to the history microservice

Configures options for the HTTP request

Sets the HTTP method to POST

Sets the content type for the body of the HTTP request

The body of the HTTP request defines the message payload; this is the data we send with the message.

Sends the HTTP request to the history microservice

Sets the URL for the HTTP request, which identifies the history microservice and the "Viewed" message

This function is called when the request completes.

Handles any errors that might have occurred

Writes the body to the request

Finalizes the request

We call the function http.request to create the HTTP POST request. We direct the request to the history microservice using the URL http://history/viewed. This URL incorporates both the hostname (history, in this case) and the route (viewed, in this case). It's this combination that identifies the target microservice and the message we send to it.

Separate callback functions handle the success and the failure of the request. It's here where we can detect an error and take subsequent remedial action. Otherwise, if it succeeds, we might want to invoke follow-up actions.

5.7.4   *Receiving a message with HTTP POST*

On the other side of the equation, we receive HTTP POST messages by creating an Express route handler in the receiving microservice. Listing 5.7 shows an extract of the index.js file for the history microservice (extract from chapter-5/example-2/history/src/index.js), which demonstrates this. The new HTTP POST handler for the viewed route receives incoming messages. In this listing, we simply store the received messages in the database to keep a record of the viewing history.

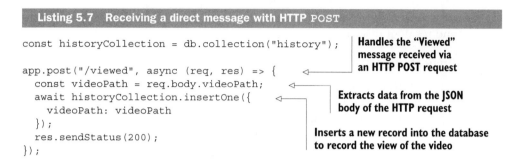

Listing 5.7   Receiving a direct message with HTTP POST

```
const historyCollection = db.collection("history");        Handles the "Viewed"
                                                           message received via
app.post("/viewed", async (req, res) => {                  an HTTP POST request
  const videoPath = req.body.videoPath;
  await historyCollection.insertOne({                      Extracts data from the JSON
    videoPath: videoPath                                   body of the HTTP request
  });
  res.sendStatus(200);                                     Inserts a new record into the database
});                                                        to record the view of the video
```

Did you notice in the HTTP POST handler how we access the body of the request through req.body? We treated the body of the request as the message *payload*. The body variable was automatically parsed from the JSON format because we used the JSON parsing middleware that is included with Express. If you're interested in seeing how the JSON parsing middleware is configured, look at the code file chapter-5/example-2/history/src/index.js.

5.7.5   *Testing the updated application*

Now it's time to test our latest code and see how this kind of messaging operates. Open a terminal, change to the example-2 directory, and start the application in the usual way:

```
cd chapter-5/example-2
docker compose up --build
```

If you get any errors about containers already created, it might be because you left the previous example running. When moving on from each example, be sure to shut it down using

```
docker compose down
```

Wait for the microservices to come online, and then point your browser to http://localhost:4001/video. The test video will play.

Switch back to the terminal to see the Docker Compose output. You should see output confirming that the video-streaming microservice sent a "Viewed" message, followed up by some text that shows the history microservice received the message.

At this point, we can directly check to make sure that the "Viewed" message was stored in the database. You'll need a database viewer installed. We can use either the MongoDB Shell or Studio 3T (refer to chapter 4, section 4.5.2) to see that data is being added to our database.

Connect your database viewer to the database (connect on localhost:4000 as the port that is configured in the Docker Compose file), then look at the videos collection of the history database, and confirm that a new record is created each time you refresh your browser. Checking the database is a simple and practical way to test the end result of this code.

5.7.6   *Orchestrating behavior with direct messages*

A potential benefit of direct messaging is the ability to have one controller microservice that can orchestrate complex sequences of behavior across multiple other microservices. A direct message has a direct response, allowing a single microservice to directly control the activities of other microservices.

The reason this type of messaging is called synchronous communication is that we're able to *synchronously* coordinate messages, as shown in figure 5.9. In the figure, Microservice A is coordinating the activities of the other microservices.

> **NOTE**   Direct messaging can be useful to coordinate behaviors in an explicit way or well-defined order.

With direct messages, it's easy to follow the code and understand the sequence of messages. You'll see in a moment that tracing the sequence of indirect messages isn't as easy.

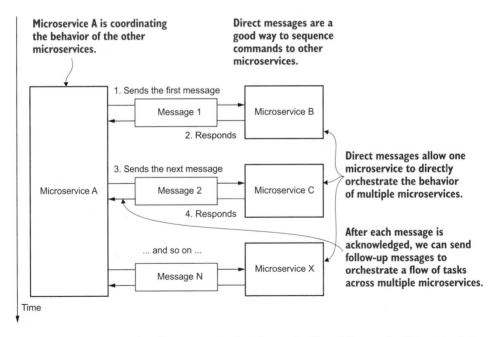

Figure 5.9   Direct messaging allows one controller microservice (here, Microservice A) to orchestrate complex behaviors across multiple other microservices.

5.7.7   *What have we achieved?*

In section 5.7, we explored using HTTP POST requests to directly send a "Viewed" message from microservice to microservice. This is called *direct messaging* because we can direct these messages to particular microservices by their name. We can also know immediately if the message was handled successfully or if it failed.

It's best to think of this type of message more as a command or a call to action and less as a notification. Due to the synchronous nature of direct messages, we can sequence multiple coordinated messages. This is useful when we want a controller microservice that orchestrates complex behaviors in other microservices.

Although direct messages can be useful and are sometimes necessary, these also have some major downsides. For a start, we can only target a single other microservice at a time. Direct messages, therefore, don't work easily when we'd like to have a single message received by multiple recipients.

In addition, direct messages are a point of high coupling between microservices. High coupling is necessary sometimes, but we'd prefer to avoid it where possible. The ability to centrally orchestrate multiple microservices from a controller microservice might seem like an advantage, and it certainly can make it easier to work out what's going on in your application. But the biggest problem is that this creates a single point of failure for what could be a large and complex operation. What happens if the controlling microservice crashes in the middle of the orchestration? Our application might now be in an inconsistent state, and data may have been lost. The problems that arise from direct messaging can be solved with indirect messaging, and that's why we now turn to RabbitMQ.

5.8   *Indirect messaging with RabbitMQ*

Now that we have a handle on using HTTP POST requests for direct messages, it's time to look at indirect messaging, which can help us decouple our microservices. On one hand, it can make the architecture of our application more difficult to understand. On the other hand, it has many positive side benefits for security, scalability, extensibility, reliability, and performance.

> **NOTE**   RabbitMQ allows us to decouple message senders from message receivers. A sender doesn't know which, if any, other microservices will handle a message.

Figure 5.10 shows the structure of our application after the addition of a RabbitMQ server. The video-streaming microservice is no longer directly coupled to the history microservice. Instead, it's publishing its "Viewed" messages to a message queue. The history microservice then pulls messages from the queue in its own time.

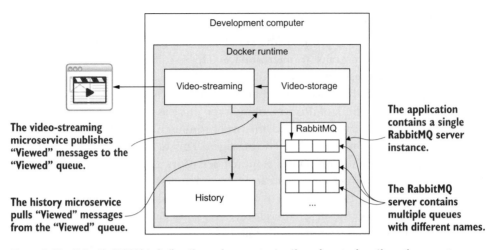

The video-streaming microservice publishes "Viewed" messages to the "Viewed" queue.

The history microservice pulls "Viewed" messages from the "Viewed" queue.

The application contains a single RabbitMQ server instance.

The RabbitMQ server contains multiple queues with different names.

Figure 5.10   Using RabbitMQ to indirectly send messages to other microservices through message queues

5.8.1   *Why RabbitMQ?*

RabbitMQ is well-known and established software for queuing messages. Many companies commonly use RabbitMQ, and it's my go-to solution for indirect messaging. Developed over a decade ago, RabbitMQ is stable and mature. Among other protocols, it implements the Advanced Message Queueing Protocol (AMQP), which is an open standard for message–broker communication.

> **NOTE**   RabbitMQ is well known for indirect communication between microservices, and it allows for complex and flexible messaging architectures.

RabbitMQ has libraries for all the popular programming languages, so you'll have no problems using it whatever your tech stack. We're using Node.js, so we'll use the amqplib library available on the npm registry. RabbitMQ is open source and fairly easy to get started with. You can find the code for the server here: https://github.com/rabbitmq/rabbitmq-server.

5.8.2   *Indirectly targeting messages to microservices*

With indirect messaging, we aren't directly targeting any particular microservice, but we do still need to direct our messages to something: a RabbitMQ server. In the RabbitMQ server, we direct our message to either a named queue or a message exchange. The combination of queues and exchanges gives us a lot of flexibility in how we structure our messaging architecture.

> **NOTE**   The message sender uses DNS to resolve the IP address of the RabbitMQ server. The message sender then communicates with RabbitMQ to publish a message on a particular named queue or exchange. The receiver also uses DNS to locate and communicate with the RabbitMQ server to retrieve the message from the queue. At no point do the sender and receiver communicate directly.

To publish a message to a queue or an exchange, we must first add a RabbitMQ server to our application. Then, we can use the AMQP code library (called amqplib) to send and receive messages.

Under the hood, DNS resolves the RabbitMQ hostname to an IP address. Now, rather than directing our message to a particular microservice as we did when sending messages via HTTP POST requests, we're instead directing these to a particular queue or exchange on our RabbitMQ server.

The transfer of an indirect message is conducted in two parts, so I'll use two diagrams to explain it. We'll first consider using queues, and later we'll look at using an exchange. Figure 5.11 shows the video-streaming microservice *pushing* its message to the *viewed* queue. Then, in figure 5.12, we can see the history microservice *pulling* the message from the queue.

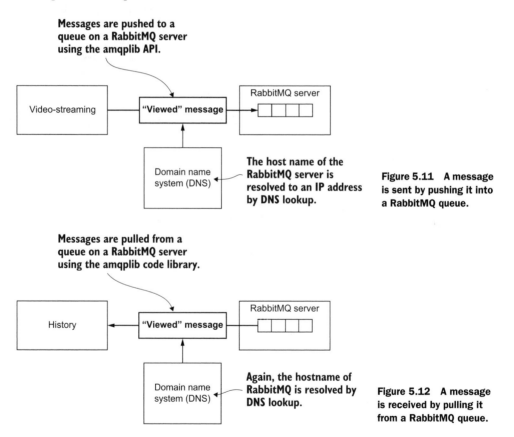

Messages are pushed to a queue on a RabbitMQ server using the amqplib API.

The host name of the RabbitMQ server is resolved to an IP address by DNS lookup.

Figure 5.11   A message is sent by pushing it into a RabbitMQ queue.

Messages are pulled from a queue on a RabbitMQ server using the amqplib code library.

Again, the hostname of RabbitMQ is resolved by DNS lookup.

Figure 5.12   A message is received by pulling it from a RabbitMQ queue.

I've used the verbs *pushing* and *pulling* here because that's a good way to visualize this transaction. As we did earlier with HTTP POST, we can imagine the video-streaming microservice is pushing its message onto the history microservice, which has no choice in the matter. The message is forced onto the history microservice with no regard for whether the microservice has the capacity to handle it.

With indirect messaging, more control is given to the history microservice. It now pulls messages from the queue when it's ready to do so. When the history microservice is overwhelmed and has no capacity to accept new messages, it's free to just ignore them, letting those pile up in the queue until the microservice is able to handle them.

5.8.3   Creating a RabbitMQ server

Let's add a RabbitMQ server to our application. Believe it or not, RabbitMQ is programmed in the Erlang language. There might have been a day when it was difficult to set up, but not anymore! These days, it's a no-brainer, thanks to the skills you've already learned with Docker and Docker Compose.

Listing 5.8 is an extract from the example-3 Docker Compose file (chapter-5/example-3/docker-compose.yaml) that shows adding a RabbitMQ server to our application. This is another example of instantiating a container from an image on Docker Hub, as we did in chapter 4 for our MongoDB database.

Listing 5.8   Adding a RabbitMQ server to the Docker Compose file

```
version: '3'          Defines the container that hosts our RabbitMQ server
services:
                                              We use the management version of the RabbitMQ
  --snip--                                    image. This gives us the RabbitMQ dashboard.

  rabbit:    <                                Sets the name of the container. This is the name
    image: rabbitmq:3.12.4-management  <      we'll use to connect to the RabbitMQ server.
    container_name: rabbit    <
    ports:                          Configures port mappings from the host
      - "5672:5672"                 operating system to the container
      - "15672:15672"
    restart: always    <
                              If something goes wrong with the RabbitMQ
  --snip--                    server, this makes it restart automatically.
```

5.8.4   Investigating the RabbitMQ dashboard

You might have already noticed in listing 5.8 how the RabbitMQ ports were configured. Port 5672 is the port number we'll soon use with amqplib to send and receive messages through RabbitMQ. The other port is 15672, which we'll use to access the RabbitMQ management dashboard.

> **NOTE** RabbitMQ's dashboard is a great way to learn about how RabbitMQ works and to better understand the messages that are being passed around your application.

We booted our RabbitMQ server from the image named rabbitmq:3.12.4-management because this one comes with a built-in management dashboard. The dashboard is pictured in figure 5.13 and serves as a graphical way to explore message flow in our application. Let's have a look at that now. Start the application for yourself so you can try it out!

Open a terminal, and change to the example-3 directory. Start the application in the normal way (if nothing else, I'm going to make sure you remember this command!):

```
cd chapter-5/example-3
docker compose up --build
```

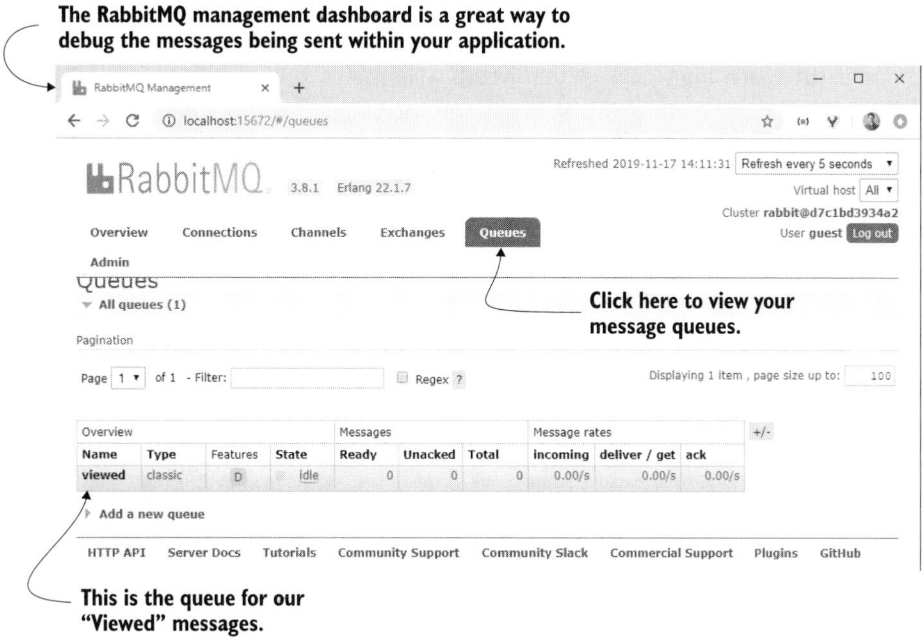

The RabbitMQ management dashboard is a great way to debug the messages being sent within your application.

Figure 5.13   The RabbitMQ management dashboard

In addition to the output from the database and your microservices, you should also see a stream of output from your RabbitMQ server. Give it some time to start, and then point your web browser at http://localhost:15672/. You can log in with the default username, *guest*, and default password, *guest*.

You should now see the RabbitMQ dashboard. But unlike figure 5.13, you won't yet see any queues or exchanges. I took that screenshot after the viewed queue was created. We'll trigger the queue to be created in a moment, and then you can come back to the dashboard to see what it looks like.

The RabbitMQ dashboard is a useful tool for debugging. It's always better to be able to visualize what's happening rather than just assuming we know what's happening. The dashboard is one of those great visual tools that make it obvious what our application is actually doing.

You might note that we don't have to include the RabbitMQ dashboard. We could, instead, use the image `rabbitmq:3.12.4`. This is a version of the image that doesn't include the dashboard. This might be your preference if you're building a lean, mean production application or if you have particular security concerns. But generally, I prefer to leave the dashboard in place for production (behind a private network, of course) because it's so valuable to have these tools to help us understand what's happening in our production environment.

5.8.5   *Connecting our microservice to the message queue*

With our RabbitMQ server in place, we can now update our microservices to connect to it. If you're coding this from scratch, you must first install the amqplib npm package into each microservice that needs to connect to RabbitMQ:

```
npm install --save amqplib
```

If you're running the code from example-3 directly under Node.js, you must first install all dependencies:

```
npm install
```

Listing 5.9 is an extract from the index.js file for the history microservice (chapter-5/example-3/history/src/index.js). It shows how we make the connection to the RabbitMQ server.

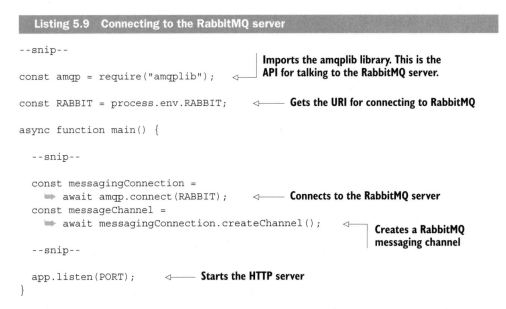

Listing 5.9   Connecting to the RabbitMQ server

```
--snip--

const amqp = require("amqplib");          ◁──┐  Imports the amqplib library. This is the
                                              │  API for talking to the RabbitMQ server.

const RABBIT = process.env.RABBIT;        ◁────── Gets the URI for connecting to RabbitMQ

async function main() {

  --snip--

  const messagingConnection =
    ➡ await amqp.connect(RABBIT);        ◁────── Connects to the RabbitMQ server
  const messageChannel =
    ➡ await messagingConnection.createChannel();   ◁──┐ Creates a RabbitMQ
                                                       │ messaging channel
  --snip--

  app.listen(PORT);      ◁────── Starts the HTTP server
}
```

One of the most important parts of listing 5.9 and listing 5.10, which follows, is how the RABBIT environment variable configures the connection to the RabbitMQ server. Listing 5.10 is an extract from the example-3 Docker Compose file (chapter-5/example-3/docker-compose.yaml). It sets the RABBIT environment variable to include the username (guest), the password (also guest), the hostname for the server (rabbit), and the port number (5672) for the connection.

NOTE   In production, you might want to choose a username and password rather than accept the defaults, but for this book, it won't matter so much because we'll be running RabbitMQ on a private and trusted network.

Listing 5.10   Configuring the history microservice

```
version: '3'
services:

  --snip--

  history:
    image: history
    build:
      context: ./history
      dockerfile: Dockerfile-dev
    container_name: history
    volumes:
      - /tmp/history/npm-cache:/root/.npm:z
      - ./history/src:/usr/src/app/src:z
    ports:
    - "4002:80"
    environment:
      - PORT=80
      - RABBIT=amqp://guest:guest@rabbit:5672
      - DBHOST=mongodb://db:27017
      - DBNAME=history
      - NODE_ENV=development
    depends_on:
      - db
      - rabbit
    restart: "no"
```

Sets the URI for connection to RabbitMQ. The password is hardcoded in the URI, but please note that this isn't a security problem. This is the default RabbitMQ password (that everyone already knows), and this configuration is only ever intended for development. For production, in chapter 10, we'll take a different approach.

The history microservice now depends on the rabbit container that we defined in listing 5.8.

There's yet another piece to this puzzle that may not have occurred to you until you start this version of our application. The RabbitMQ server is fairly heavyweight, and it takes time to start up and get ready to accept connections. Our tiny microservices, on the other hand, are lightweight and ready in just moments. So, what happens when our microservice attempts the connection to RabbitMQ and it's not ready yet? It will error and abort! We now have a problem because we have startup dependencies in our application that need to be resolved in a particular order.

To be a fault-tolerant and well-behaved microservice, it should really wait until the RabbitMQ server is ready before it tries to connect. Better yet, if RabbitMQ ever goes down (say, because we're upgrading it), we'd like our microservices to handle the disconnection and automatically reconnect as soon as possible—but that's more complicated. For the moment, we'll solve this with a simple workaround. In chapter 11, you'll learn a more sophisticated way to handle this.

The simplest way to solve this problem is to add an extra command to our Dockerfile that delays starting our microservice until the RabbitMQ server is ready. We'll use the handy `wait-port` command installed using npm:

```
npm install --save wait-port
```

Listing 5.11 (chapter-5/example-3/history/Dockerfile-dev) shows the history micro-service's updated Dockerfile with the addition of the `wait-port` command. We use this to delay the start of the microservice until after RabbitMQ has started.

Listing 5.11 Delaying the history microservice for RabbitMQ

```
FROM node:18.17.1

WORKDIR /usr/src/app
COPY package*.json ./

CMD npm install --prefer-offline && \
  npx wait-port rabbit:5672 && \
  npm run start:dev
```

> Uses npx to invoke the locally installed wait-port command to wait until the server at hostname rabbit is accepting connections on port 5672

> Starts the history microservice after the wait-port command has completed

At the same time, we should update the production version of the Dockerfile. It's good to keep both versions in sync as we work.

Using `wait-port` is a simple and effective way to get up and running when we first start building our microservices application. It's not very robust, though. The startup ordering problem isn't the only problem. We generally want our microservice to be fault tolerant and able to survive the inevitable outages of other servers and micro-services. We'll come back to this in chapter 11.

At this point, you might be wondering why we didn't have this startup order prob-lem in chapter 4 when we started using the MongoDB database. Surely the database also takes time to start up, but we didn't have to wait for it to be ready before we con-nected to it. Well, this is simply down to good software engineering in the MongoDB library. It's already programmed for automatic reconnections, so thank the MongoDB engineers for going to this level of effort for you. This should give you some pause for thought. When writing code libraries, a little time considering the perspective of our users translates into a much better experience for them.

5.8.6 *Single-recipient indirect messaging*

There are many ways to configure message routing in RabbitMQ to achieve various messaging architectures. We'll focus on just two simple configurations that will handle many of the communication problems you'll face when building your application.

The first is a setup for single-recipient messages that we'll use to create a one-to-one, but still indirect, messaging conduit between microservices. Although, in this configuration, you're allowed to have multiple senders and receivers participating, you're guaranteed that only a single microservice will receive each individual message. This is great for when you're distributing a job to a pool of microservices, but the job should be handled only by the first one that is capable of dealing with it.

NOTE Single-recipient messages are *one-to-one*: a message is sent from one
microservice and received by only one other microservice. This is a great way
of making sure that a particular job is done only once within your application.

RECEIVING SINGLE-RECIPIENT MESSAGES

Let's add code to the history microservice so that it can receive single-recipient messages. We already added code in section 5.8.5 to connect to our RabbitMQ server.
Once connected, we can now *assert* a message queue and start pulling messages from
that queue. Note the new terminology used here: "assert" a message queue instead of
"create" a message queue. The difference is that multiple microservices can assert a
queue, so it's like checking for the existence of the queue and then only creating the
queue when it doesn't already exist. That means the queue is created once and shared
between all participating microservices. Don't get this confused with the other kind of
assert that is commonly used in programming—these are two separate concepts.

Listing 5.12 is an extract of index.js from the history microservice (chapter-5/
example-3/history/src/index.js) that asserts the viewed queue and calls `consume` to
start receiving messages. Our function receives messages and is called for each new
message that arrives. It then records the message in the database. This is it! There
really isn't very much code needed to receive messages from RabbitMQ.

Listing 5.12 Consuming "Viewed" messages from a RabbitMQ queue

```
--snip--

async function main() {

  --snip--

  const historyCollection = db.collection("history");     // Asserts the existence of the
                                                          // "Viewed" message queue for
  await messageChannel.assertQueue("viewed", {})          // incoming messages

  await messageChannel.consume("viewed", async (msg) {    // Receives messages from
                                                          // the viewed queue
    const parsedMsg =
      JSON.parse(msg.content.toString());                 // Parses the JSON message
                                                          // to a JavaScript object
    await historyCollection.insertOne({                   // Records the view in
      videoPath: parsedMsg.videoPath                      // the history database
    });

    messageChannel.ack(msg);                              // If there was no error,
  });                                                     // acknowledges the message

  --snip--
}
```

The code in listing 5.12 is only slightly complicated by the fact that we'd like to send messages in the JSON format; unfortunately, RabbitMQ doesn't natively support JSON. We must therefore manually parse the incoming message payload.

RabbitMQ is actually agnostic about the format for the message payload, so from its point of view, a message is just a blob of binary data. This can be useful in performance-critical cases where we'd probably like to replace JSON with a more efficient binary format.

SENDING SINGLE-RECIPIENT MESSAGES

Sending a simple message with RabbitMQ is even easier than receiving a message. Listing 5.13 is an extract of the index.js file from the video-streaming microservice (chapter-5/example-3/video-streaming/src/index.js). Assume that we've already added code like that shown in listing 5.9 and connected this microservice to the RabbitMQ server. We now call `publish` by specifying the name of the queue (viewed) and providing the message payload.

> #### Listing 5.13   Publishing viewed messages to a RabbitMQ queue

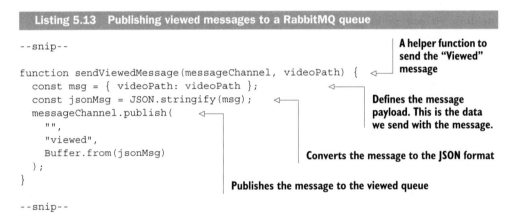

```
--snip--

function sendViewedMessage(messageChannel, videoPath) {
  const msg = { videoPath: videoPath };
  const jsonMsg = JSON.stringify(msg);
  messageChannel.publish(
    "",
    "viewed",
    Buffer.from(jsonMsg)
  );
}

--snip--
```

A helper function to send the "Viewed" message

Defines the message payload. This is the data we send with the message.

Converts the message to the JSON format

Publishes the message to the viewed queue

Again, listing 5.13 is only slightly complicated by the fact that we have to manually *stringify* (or serialize) our message payload to JSON before sending the message. Other than that, it's pretty straightforward. Now we have the video-streaming microservice publishing a "Viewed" message whenever a user watches a video.

TESTING SINGLE-RECIPIENT MESSAGES

We have everything we need in place to do another test run: a RabbitMQ server, the video-streaming microservice sending the "Viewed" message, and the history microservice receiving it. If you haven't already, start the example-3 application:

```
cd chapter-5/example-3
docker compose up --build
```

Wait for the database and RabbitMQ to start and the microservices to establish their connections. Now, point your web browser at http://localhost:4001/video. Check the output to see that the message has been sent and received. Again, we can use the

MongoDB Shell or Studio 3T (see chapter 4, section 4.5.2) to check that the history microservice has created a new record for the view in its database.

5.8.7   *Multiple-recipient messages*

Sending single-recipient messages is the first common use case for RabbitMQ. It's also the simplest to understand—that's why we started with it. Potentially, even more useful are multiple-recipient (or broadcast-style) messages. Put simply, one microservice sends the message, but many others can receive it.

We use this type of message for *notifications* (e.g., messages that indicate an important event has occurred in the application, such as a video having been viewed). This is the kind of message that multiple other microservices would like to know about.

> **NOTE**   Multiple-recipient messages are *one-to-many*: a message is sent from only a single microservice but potentially received by many others. This is a great way of publishing notifications within your application.

To make this work with RabbitMQ, we must now use a message exchange. Figure 5.14 shows the video-streaming microservice publishing its message to the "Viewed" exchange. From the exchange, the message is routed to multiple anonymous queues to be handled by multiple microservices simultaneously.

When you look at figure 5.14, you might wonder where the recommendations microservice came from. No, you didn't miss anything! I've literally just snuck a new microservice in while you weren't looking. I had to do this; otherwise, I don't have a way to show you how these broadcast-style messages work.

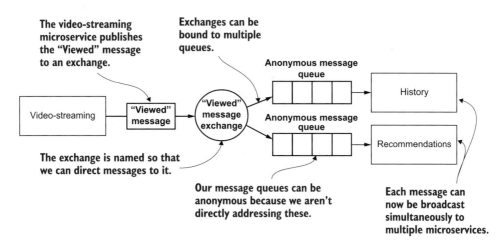

Figure 5.14   Broadcasting a message to be handled by multiple recipients

The recommendations microservice will later suggest videos to watch to our users. It's appearance here and now is only so that we can see multiple-recipient messages in action.

RECEIVING MULTIPLE-RECIPIENT MESSAGES

Receiving multiple-recipient messages isn't much different from receiving single-recipient messages. Listing 5.14 is an extract of the index.js file from the history microservice (chapter-5/example-4/history/src/index.js) and shows the configuration for receiving messages from a RabbitMQ exchange.

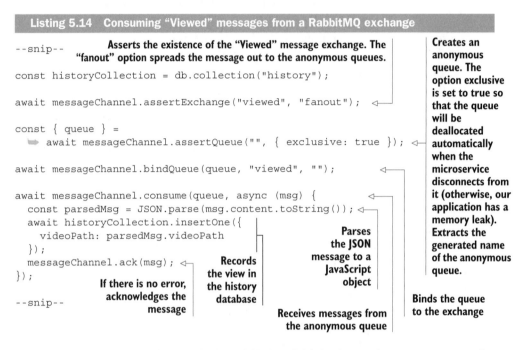

Listing 5.14 Consuming "Viewed" messages from a RabbitMQ exchange

```
--snip--              Asserts the existence of the "Viewed" message exchange. The      Creates an
                  "fanout" option spreads the message out to the anonymous queues.      anonymous
const historyCollection = db.collection("history");                                     queue. The
                                                                                        option exclusive
await messageChannel.assertExchange("viewed", "fanout");                                is set to true so
                                                                                        that the queue
const { queue } =                                                                       will be
    await messageChannel.assertQueue("", { exclusive: true });                          deallocated
                                                                                        automatically
await messageChannel.bindQueue(queue, "viewed", "");                                    when the
                                                                                        microservice
await messageChannel.consume(queue, async (msg) {                                       disconnects from
    const parsedMsg = JSON.parse(msg.content.toString());                               it (otherwise, our
    await historyCollection.insertOne({                                                 application has a
        videoPath: parsedMsg.videoPath                      Parses                      memory leak).
    });                                                      the JSON                    Extracts the
    messageChannel.ack(msg);                                 message to a               generated name
});                           Records                        JavaScript                 of the anonymous
            If there is no error,     the view in            object                     queue.
            acknowledges the   the history
--snip--         message          database                                             Binds the queue
                                              Receives messages from                    to the exchange
                                              the anonymous queue
```

The difference between listing 5.14 and listing 5.12 is that we're now *asserting* the "Viewed" exchange (there's that assert terminology again) rather than the viewed queue. After that, we assert an anonymous queue. By creating an unnamed queue, we get one that was created uniquely for this microservice. The "Viewed" exchange is shared among all microservices, but the anonymous queue is owned solely by this microservice. That detail is an important part of how this works.

In creating the unnamed queue, we're returned a random name generated by RabbitMQ. The name that RabbitMQ assigned to our queue is only important because we must now bind the queue to the "Viewed" exchange. This binding connects the exchange and the queue, such that messages published on the exchange are then routed to the queue.

Every other microservice that wants to receive the "Viewed" message (e.g., the recommendations microservice that I snuck in here) creates its own unnamed queue to bind to the "Viewed" exchange. We can have any number of other microservices bound to the "Viewed" exchange, and these will all receive copies of messages on their own anonymous queues as messages are published to the exchange.

SENDING MULTIPLE-RECIPIENT MESSAGES

Sending multiple-recipient messages is, again, similar to sending single-recipient messages. Listing 5.15 is an extract of the index.js file for the video-streaming microservice (chapter-4/example-4/video-streaming/src/index.js). I've included more code in this extract because it's important to see how the connection to the RabbitMQ service is different in this situation because we're asserting the existence of the "Viewed" message exchange when the microservice starts.

Doing this once at startup means we can rely on the existence of the exchange for the lifetime of the microservice. In the listing, we're still sending the message with the `publish` function, except we're now specifying that the message is published to the "Viewed" exchange rather than the "Viewed" queue.

Listing 5.15 Publishing "Viewed" messages to a RabbitMQ exchange

```
--snip--

async function main() {

  const messagingConnection = await amqp.connect(RABBIT);

  const messageChannel = await messagingConnection.createChannel();

  await messageChannel.assertExchange(          Asserts the
    "viewed",                                   existence of the
    "fanout"                                    "Viewed" message
  );                                            exchange
                                                                A helper function to
                                                                send the "Viewed"
  function broadcastViewedMessage(messageChannel,              message
      videoPath) {
    const msg = { videoPath: videoPath };          Defines the payload of the message
    const jsonMsg = JSON.stringify(msg);
    messageChannel.publish(                         Converts the message to the JSON format
      "viewed",
      "",                                           Publishes the message to the "Viewed" exchange
      Buffer.from(jsonMsg)
    );
  }

  app.get("/video", async (req, res) => {
                                                    Sends the view message
    --snip--                                        in response to the video
                                                    being streamed to the
    sendViewedMessage(messageChannel, videoPath);   web browser
  });

  --snip--
}
```

TESTING MULTIPLE-RECIPIENT MESSAGES

Let's test our updated code. For this test, I added the recommendations microservice to our application. The new microservice is really just a stub; it does nothing except print out the messages it receives. That's just enough to show that multiple microservices can handle these messages. Open a terminal, change to the example-4 directory, and do the usual thing:

```
cd chapter-5/example-4
docker compose up --build
```

Give it a bit of time to start up. Then, when you get to http://localhost:4001/video in your web browser, you should see messages being printed to the console to show that both the history microservice and the recommendations microservice are receiving the "Viewed" message.

This works because we have one exchange that is bound to two queues: we have one queue for each receiving microservice. We can't achieve this behavior with only a single queue. When we publish a message to a single shared queue, the receiving microservices compete to be the first one that pulls the message and handles it, which you can view as a kind of load balancing. That's a useful technique sometimes, but broadcast-style messages are generally more useful.

5.8.8   *Emergent behavior with indirect messages*

Indirect messages have plenty of positive benefits, but they can make it harder to understand and control the behavior of our application. There's no way to get a direct response for an indirect message, and from the sender's point of view, the receiver may as well not even exist! The sender has no way of knowing if there is a receiver out there waiting to pick up its message.

> **NOTE** Because there is no "central control" over indirect messages, these allow for much more flexible, extensible, and evolvable messaging architectures. Each separate microservice is in charge of how it responds to incoming messages and can generate many other messages in response.

With indirect messaging, unlike direct messaging, there is no single microservice in charge of orchestrating the others. So instead of directly creating a controlled set of behaviors, the behavior of the application emerges automatically from the interplay of indirect messages between microservices. This isn't necessarily a bad thing. Consider that having a single controlling microservice means we have a single point of failure, and that's undoubtedly a bad thing. If that controlling microservice crashes in the middle of a complex orchestration, whatever was in progress will be lost! That can be the terrible side effect of direct messages.

Direct messaging is sometimes useful, but indirect messaging generally allows for much more complex and resilient networks of behaviors. We might struggle to understand how it all fits together in its complexity, but at least we know that it's reliable! That's because, when using indirect messages, there is no single point that can fail, and the connections between microservices are implemented by reliable and fault-tolerant message queues (well, RabbitMQ can fail, but it's much less likely to do so than one of our own microservices).

Any particular microservice can fail, but even if it does so while handling a message, we know that the message won't be lost. Because messages aren't acknowledged when a microservice crashes, these will eventually be handled by another microservice (usually a replica of the one that crashed). It's the sum of small techniques like this that contribute to building a rock-solid and reliable microservices application. Cast your eyes over figure 5.15 for a more visual understanding of how indirect messages can be sequenced into a dynamic flow of messages within your application.

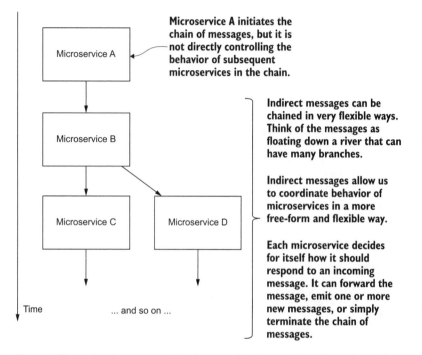

Figure 5.15   Indirect messages allow for more free-form and flexible orchestration of microservices, resulting in emergent behavior.

5.8.9   What have we achieved?

In this section, you've learned how to use RabbitMQ to send indirect messages between microservices. First, we tried sending single-recipient messages. Then, we changed to multiple-recipient messages so that we can broadcast application-wide messages.

> **NOTE** Using indirect multiple-recipient messages seems like the right way to go for the "Viewed" message, and our microservices are less coupled as a result. That's a good win.

We could have easily planned ahead and headed straight for the indirect broadcast-style messages, but that's the benefit of experience. Now that we've worked through all the options, you have that experience and are better placed to decide for yourself what style of messaging you'll need case by case as you add more messages to your application.

5.9   *Microservices communication review*

You now have at your disposal two different styles of messaging that you can use to make your microservices talk to each other. You've learned how to send direct messages with HTTP requests and indirect messages with RabbitMQ. With RabbitMQ, you can send single-recipient and multiple-recipient (or broadcast) messages.

We have a flexible structure for messaging that can be extended in the future. Later, we'll add more microservices to this application, and each one may or may not care about the "Viewed" message. But those that do can simply handle it without us having to modify the original sender of the message.

We've talked through various reasons why you might want to choose one style of messaging over the other. For your convenience, this information is summarized in table 5.2. You can refer back to this table later when you're deciding what style of messaging you need in particular situations.

Table 5.2   **When to use each type of communication**

Situation	What to use
I need to direct a message to a particular microservice by name.	Direct messaging: HTTP
I need confirmation that the message handling was successful or that it failed.	Direct messaging: HTTP
I need to sequence subsequent messages after completion of the first.	Direct messaging: HTTP
I want one microservice to orchestrate the activity of other microservices.	Direct messaging: HTTP
I need to broadcast a message across the application to notify zero or more microservices of an event in the system (and I don't care if the messages are handled or not).	Indirect messaging: RabbitMQ
I want to decouple the sender and the receiver (so they can more easily change and evolve independently).	Indirect messaging: RabbitMQ
I want the performance of sender and receiver to be independent (the sender can emit as many messages as it likes, and the receiver will process these in its own time).	Indirect messaging: RabbitMQ
I want to be sure that if message handling fails, it will automatically be retried again later until it succeeds (so no messages are lost due to intermittent failures).	Indirect messaging: RabbitMQ
I need to load balance handling of a message so it's handled by one out of a pool of workers.	Either HTTP or RabbitMQ
I need to distribute the handling of a message to multiple workers who can act in parallel.	Indirect messaging: RabbitMQ

5.10   *Continue your learning*

This chapter has been a tour through the various ways we can make our microservices communicate. We've used HTTP for direct messages and RabbitMQ for indirect messages. As usual, we only briefly touched on each of these subjects, and there is a whole lot more you can learn. Here are some great resources for you to learn more:

- *API Design Patterns* by JJ Geewax (Manning, 2021)
- *The Design of Web APIs* by Arnaud Lauret (Manning, 2019)
- *RabbitMQ in Depth* by Gavin M. Roy (Manning, 2017)
- *RabbitMQ in Action: Distributed Messaging for Everyone* by Alvaro Videla and Jason J. W. Williams (Manning, 2012)

To learn more about the amqplib package, read the documentation here: https://amqp-node.github.io/amqplib/. To learn more about the `wait-port` command, see https://github.com/dwmkerr/wait-port.

We've come a long way to this point. After building our first microservice, we quickly scaled up to developing multiple communicating microservices. Each microservice can have its own database and/or file storage. We're now using live reload to efficiently reload our whole application while we're coding.

What's next? We have a fledgling app. It can't do much yet, but that's no reason to avoid moving to production. Getting our application to run in a production environment can be a difficult affair, and it's best done while the application is small and simple. So, without further ado, starting in chapter 6, we'll take our application to production!

Summary

- We can use Docker volumes to share code between our development computer and the containers in our application.
- Using nodemon for live reload means we can update our code and have the relevant microservices in our application automatically reload without having to rebuild and restart the entire application.
- There are two styles of communication between microservices: direct and indirect.
- Direct (aka synchronous) messaging is most useful when we want to explicitly sequence the flow of messages or carefully orchestrate the behavior of other microservices.
- With direct messages, we know immediately if the message handling succeeded or failed.
- Indirect (aka asynchronous) messaging helps us decouple our microservices from each other, which promotes the development of flexible and evolvable applications.
- With indirect messages, we can broadcast a message throughout the application to notify other microservices of important events in the system.
- HTTP POST requests are useful for sending direct messages between microservices.

- RabbitMQ is software for queuing messages. We can use it to send indirect messages between microservices.
- Although we used the `wait-port` npm package to wait until the RabbitMQ server was ready before our microservice connected to it, we'll learn a better way of waiting for other services that aren't currently available in chapter 11.
- Deciding to use either HTTP or RabbitMQ depends on the needs of the situation. Refer to table 5.2 in section 5.9 for help deciding which to use based on your needs.

The road to production

This chapter covers

- Deploying a microservice to a Kubernetes cluster
- Using a local Kubernetes instance for development, experimentation, and learning
- Creating a managed Kubernetes cluster through the Azure portal UI

Finally, we arrive at the most exciting chapters of the book! The next three chapters cover the three tools we need to deploy our application to production. These three chapters will also be the most difficult so far, but just follow along with the examples to learn the most and gain real experience by bringing your own application to production.

Starting in this chapter, we'll deploy our first microservice to Kubernetes. You'll discover how easy it is to use a local Kubernetes instance to experiment and learn.

Then, we'll take the easiest route to a production Kubernetes cluster by creating a managed cluster in the Azure portal UI. In subsequent chapters, you'll learn how to create your Kubernetes cluster through code using Terraform and then how to put your deployment process on automatic using GitHub Actions.

6.1   *New tools*

This chapter introduces Kubernetes, the Kubernetes command-line tool (kubectl), and the Azure command-line tool (the Azure CLI), as described in table 6.1. Kubernetes is pretty important: that's why it's on the cover of this book. Kubectl is the command-line tool that we'll use from our local computer to interact with our Kubernetes cluster. The Azure CLI is very useful because it can easily create the configuration we need to connect kubectl to our Kubernetes cluster running on Azure. We can then use kubectl to deploy our microservice and interact with our cluster.

Table 6.1   New tools in chapter 6

Tool	Version	Purpose
Kubernetes	1.25.12	Kubernetes is the computing platform that we use to host our microservices in production.
Kubectl	1.27.2	Kubectl is the command-line tool for interacting with a Kubernetes cluster.
Azure CLI	2.51.0	We'll use the Azure CLI to configure kubectl for access to our Kubernetes cluster.

6.2   *Getting the code*

To follow along with this chapter, you need to download the code or clone the repository.

- Download a zip file of the code from here: http://mng.bz/467D
- You can clone the code using Git like this:

```
git clone
⮩ https://github.com/bootstrapping-microservices-2nd-edition/chapter-6.git
```

For help on installing and using Git, see chapter 2. If you have problems with the code, log an issue in the repository in GitHub.

6.3   *Going to production*

The day has arrived. We're taking our application to production, that is, the customer-facing environment. So "going to production" means deploying our application somewhere so that our customers can see it and use it. For us, that place will be a Kubernetes cluster in the cloud.

It might seem like it's too early to take this small application to production, but actually, in normal development situations, I advocate going to production as early as possible. Maybe not as early as this, but it's a good idea to go to production while your application is still small. Why is that? Putting our product in front of users is essential to getting feedback, adapting to their needs, and building valuable features. If we don't go to production, we won't get that feedback.

In addition, the easiest time to go to production is precisely when our application is small. As our application grows larger, it will become more unwieldy and more difficult to get working in production. It's best to start deploying to production while the application is small and then evolve to a bigger and more complicated application through development and continued deployments.

6.4 Hosting microservices on Kubernetes

By the end of this chapter, we'll have practiced deploying a single microservice to Kubernetes. You'll learn how to deploy a microservice to Kubernetes with just one example microservice. We're not bringing our full application online yet, we're just warming up with Kubernetes by starting with one microservice. Later, in chapter 10, we'll see how to deploy the full FlixTube application to Kubernetes.

We're taking small steps here to bring our application to life. Ultimately, we'll have many microservices running in our cluster, but the work has to start somewhere. So, for this chapter, we'll return to our simple video-streaming microservice as it was at the end of chapter 3 (where we first published it to our container registry).

> **NOTE** Kubernetes is a computing platform for managing container-based applications. It was originally created by Google but is now managed by the Cloud Native Computing Foundation (CNCF), a committee that has huge industry support and is also responsible for many other interesting projects.

Kubernetes is commonly known as a *container orchestration platform*, which tells us all we need to know. The platform can manage and automate the deployment and scaling of our containers. Kubernetes is the production backbone of our microservices application. I like to think of Kubernetes as *a platform for microservices*.

Figures 6.1 and 6.2 show what we'll do in this chapter. First, we'll take advantage of the local Kubernetes instance that comes with Docker Desktop (figure 6.1) and

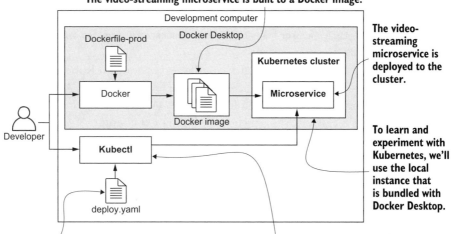

Figure 6.1   Deploying a microservice to the local Kubernetes instance that is bundled with Docker Desktop

deploy our video-streaming microservice to it. Using the local instance is a good starting point when learning Kubernetes because it's an easy way to learn and gain experience. There's nothing to install, so you most likely already have it on your computer and just need to enable it.

After you're a bit more comfortable with Kubernetes, we'll create a managed Kubernetes cluster on Microsoft Azure (figure 6.2) and then deploy our video-streaming microservice to that.

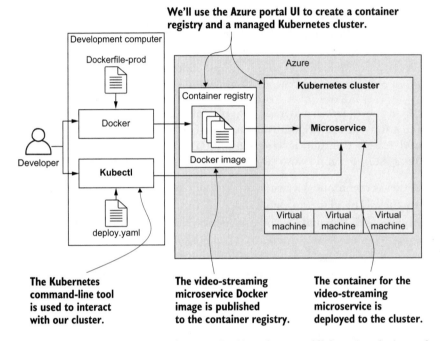

Figure 6.2   Deploying a microservice to a cloud-based managed Kubernetes cluster on Azure

Yes, in the second half of this chapter, you'll create your own Kubernetes cluster! Does that sound difficult? Don't worry, it's not; with a few clicks in the Azure UI, you'll have a cluster up and running in only a few minutes. (We're saving the more complicated task of creating a cluster through code until the next chapter.)

6.4.1   *Why Kubernetes?*

There are many reasons to use Kubernetes. The simplest reason is to avoid vendor lock-in. All the main cloud vendors offer their own container orchestration services, which are good in their own right. But each of these also offers a managed Kubernetes service, so why use a proprietary service when you can instead use Kubernetes? Using Kubernetes means our application is portable to virtually any cloud vendor.

It's worthwhile to learn Kubernetes (at least the basics) because the knowledge is transferable. Although, in this book, we host our Kubernetes cluster on Azure, you can take your Kubernetes skills with you and use them on whichever cloud you prefer.

In addition, Kubernetes is rapidly becoming the standard platform for hosting distributed applications. We can use it for any kind of distributed application, not just the microservices kind.

Kubernetes has a reputation for being complicated, which it is if you manage it directly in your own data center or take a deep dive and become an expert. Fortunately, for the rest of us, building a managed Kubernetes cluster in our favorite cloud platform is much easier; in fact, at least on Azure, we can create the cluster in the GUI with just a handful of clicks. Just learning Kubernetes is even simpler than that because, since the first edition of this book, Kubernetes now comes bundled with Docker Desktop. So, if you have Docker Desktop (which we've been using since chapter 3), you should already have Kubernetes installed and ready to go (although you need to switch it on in the Docker Desktop settings).

Kubernetes emerged from the vast experience of Google, and then it was turned over to the community. This means you can fork the code and contribute to Kubernetes yourself—assuming you have a desire to be lost down that particular rabbit hole!

Kubernetes allows us to build applications that are scalable in multiple ways, which we'll talk about in chapters 11 and 12. In this chapter, you'll learn the absolute basics—just enough to deploy a single microservice to a production Kubernetes cluster.

Most importantly, Kubernetes has an automatable API, which allows us to build our automated, continuous deployment pipeline in chapter 8. Kubernetes is becoming an industry standard for microservices, and I expect it to continue in that direction. It's well supported and has a great community and a large ecosystem of tools.

Kubernetes is the *universal computing platform* as it's supported by all the major cloud players. No matter where we end up, we can take Kubernetes with us. Kubernetes is open source and you can find the code at https://github.com/kubernetes/kubernetes.

6.4.2 Pods, nodes, and containers

A Kubernetes cluster is normally composed of multiple computers called *nodes*. For our purposes, each node will be a virtual machine (VM), although you can also run Kubernetes on physical hardware as well if you do all the setup work yourself. We can add as many nodes as we need to our cluster to expand the amount of computing power available to our application. Each node can host multiple pods. (A *pod* is the basic unit of computation in Kubernetes.)

Figure 6.3 shows an example arrangement of nodes and pods. The depicted cluster has three nodes (it's powered by three VMs). However, the cluster we'll create in this chapter will only have a single node because our simple application doesn't need more computing power than that. It also means we won't pay for more VMs than we need. Scaling up to more nodes is easy though, and you'll see an example of that in chapter 12.

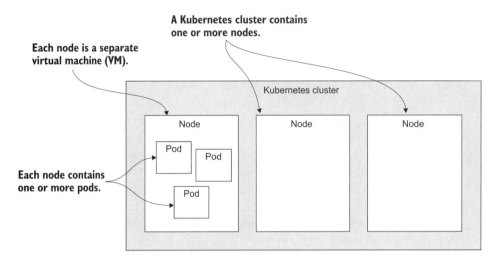

Figure 6.3   The structure of a Kubernetes cluster

Each pod can host multiple containers, as figure 6.4 shows. This can be the basis for many interesting architectural patterns, such as the well-known sidecar pattern for proxies and authentication. In this book, though, we're keeping things simple. Each pod will host only a single container or microservice. To help simplify things, you can think of a pod and a container as one and the same thing. That's not really true, but it works in this book because we're keeping things that simple.

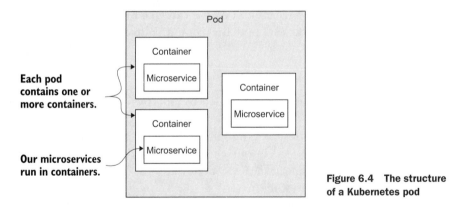

Figure 6.4   The structure of a Kubernetes pod

6.4.3   *Pods, deployments, and services*

We could just deploy our microservice to our cluster as a pod. That would keep things simple, and that's how most books on Kubernetes start. The problem, though, is that deploying a pod on its own isn't really good enough for a production application. When we use a pod by itself, and the microservice in the pod crashes or stops responding (hangs), there's no convenient way to know that our microservice has failed.

So, in this book, we'll jump directly to the idea of using a Kubernetes "deployment" to manage our microservice in production (see figure 6.5). It's the Kubernetes

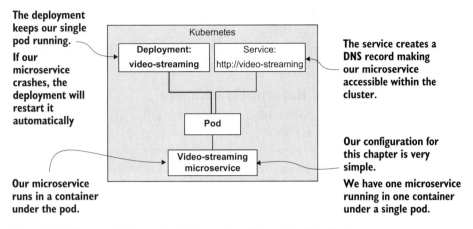

Figure 6.5 The simple Kubernetes deployment we'll create in this chapter

deployment that will continuously monitor the pod, and if the microservice crashes or hangs, then the deployment will detect that and automatically start a new instance of the microservice.

You can see the structure of our first microservice running on Kubernetes in figure 6.5. Notice how the microservice runs in the pod, which is managed by the deployment, and a domain name system (DNS) record is created for the pod by the service. Pods, deployments, and services are the main concepts from Kubernetes that we need to know to instantiate our microservice in production.

In this book, we're keeping things simple. We're only running one microservice under a single pod that is managed by a Kubernetes deployment and exposed by a Kubernetes service. However, figure 6.6 shows where we might take this in the future.

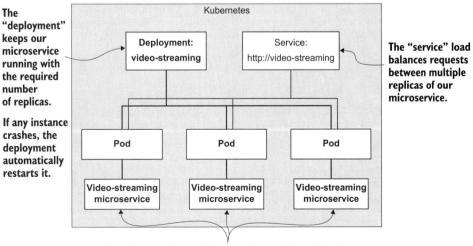

Figure 6.6 Kubernetes can run multiple copies of our microservice for scalability and redundancy.

We can scale up the number of pods for redundancy and load balancing. The Kubernetes deployment will keep multiple copies of our microservice running. If any should crash or hang, the deployment instantiates new microservices to take the place of those that failed. We'll talk more about scaling and redundancy in chapters 11 and 12.

6.5   *Enabling your local Kubernetes instance*

One of the best things that's happened since the first edition of this book is that Kubernetes now comes bundled with Docker Desktop, so you just have to turn it on. That's right, you can now experiment and learn with a local Kubernetes instance without having to install it (assuming you installed Docker Desktop already, which we've been using since chapter 3) or having to invest any time in configuration or management. This is the best starting point for learning Kubernetes because you can start using it on your own computer at no cost, and you don't even have to worry about authenticating with it.

Figure 6.7 shows how to enable your local Kubernetes instance. Open the Docker Desktop window, click the Settings button at the top, select the Kubernetes tab, click Enable Kubernetes, and, finally, click Apply & Restart. When enabling Kubernetes, the system might need to install an update to Kubernetes at this point, so it could take a few minutes before the instance is ready to go.

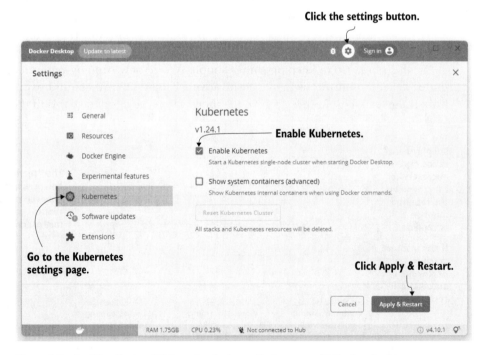

Figure 6.7   Enabling the local Kubernetes instance that comes with Docker Desktop

As you can see in figure 6.8, after enabling your local Kubernetes instance, the Reset Kubernetes Cluster button appears. Using this button is the fastest way to clean out your local cluster after you've finished a session of experimenting or learning.

Whatever you've deployed to the cluster can be quickly wiped away using this button, leaving you with a fresh cluster for your next session. The Reset Kubernetes Cluster button is also the best way to solve any problem that might be happening. For example, if your Kubernetes instance stops responding or seems to have crashed, or you need to update your Kubernetes version—which might be necessary if you installed Docker Desktop a long time ago—come back to this Settings page, and click the Reset Kubernetes Cluster button.

When you've finished a session of working with the local Kubernetes instance, and assuming you won't need it again soon, go back into Docker Desktop settings and disable Kubernetes. You don't want to leave this running, especially on an underpowered computer, because it consumes valuable system resources (not to mention your laptop's battery).

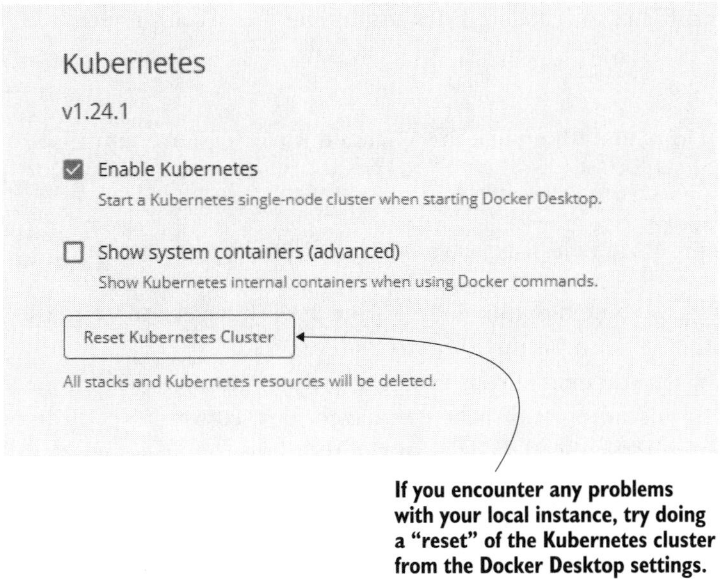

If you encounter any problems with your local instance, try doing a "reset" of the Kubernetes cluster from the Docker Desktop settings.

Figure 6.8   Resetting your local Kubernetes instance can sometimes solve any problems you're experiencing.

NOTE   To learn more about Kubernetes running under Docker Desktop, see their documentation at https://docs.docker.com/desktop/kubernetes/.

6.6   *Installing the Kubernetes CLI*

To interact with our Kubernetes cluster and deploy our microservice to it, we'll use the Kubernetes CLI tool called kubectl. If you're wondering how to say "kubectl," I've heard it pronounced "coob-cuttle" or "coob-CTL," but I tend to say "coob-control," which is fairly common. Sometimes, I say the full "Kubernetes CLI tool" to avoid ambiguity.

The good news is that kubectl, along with Kubernetes itself, comes with Docker Desktop, so you should already have it installed. To make it available, you might have to enable Kubernetes in the Docker Desktop settings, which we did in the previous section.

For some reason, kubectl isn't bundled with Docker Desktop when installed on Linux. So, if you're working on Linux, you'll have to install kubectl according to the instructions in the Kubernetes documentation: http://mng.bz/QR5R.

To check if you have access to kubectl, invoke the version subcommand:

```
kubectl version
```

If the output is difficult to read, consider adding the --short argument:

```
kubectl version --short
```

The output will look something like this (cleaned up for easier reading):

```
Client Version: v1.27.2
Kustomize Version: v5.0.1
Server Version: v1.25.12-eks-2d98532
```

From the output, we can extract the information about the version we're using for the kubectl client (1.27.2) and for the Kubernetes server (1.25.12).

By default, when you enable your local Kubernetes instance (see the previous section), kubectl should automatically be connected to it. However, if you've previously installed or configured kubectl or have previously connected to some other Kubernetes cluster, you might now be connected to something other than the local Kubernetes instance. If that's the case, you might see a connection error like this:

```
Unable to connect to the server: dial tcp: lookup <some cluster name>: no
such host
```

Don't worry if you're seeing an error like that; you'll soon see how to be sure you're connected to the correct Kubernetes cluster.

6.7   *Project structure*

Before we attempt to deploy our microservice to Kubernetes, let's briefly look at the structure of our example microservice project and see how it relates to Kubernetes deployment. Figure 6.9 is an overview of example-1 for chapter 6. It should have a familiar structure by now. You can see the JavaScript source code (index.js), the

Node.js project file (package.json, covered in chapter 2), and the production Docker-file (Dockerfile-prod) that we use to build the production Docker image for the microservice (covered in chapter 3).

You can see that, just like in chapter 3, we're baking a video directly into the Docker image. This isn't a good production practice, but we're doing it to keep things simple while we learn how to deploy a single microservice to Kubernetes. You'll see when we come to chapter 10 that the real FlixTube application uses cloud storage to store its files and a MongoDB database to store metadata (like we set it up in chapter 4).

The thing that's new here is the deploy.yaml file, which you can see in figure 6.9. This file contains the configuration to deploy our microservice to Kubernetes. In a moment, we'll take a look inside this file.

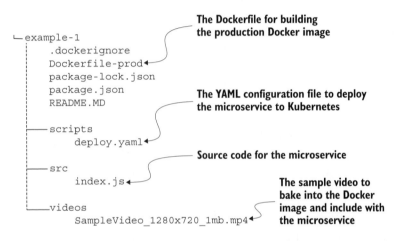

Figure 6.9   The structure of a microservice project that is deployable to Kubernetes

6.8   Deploying to the local Kubernetes instance

Our main aim in this chapter is to deploy to a Kubernetes cluster in the cloud, but we haven't yet discussed how to create a cluster in the cloud. We'll do that soon.

An easier starting point is to first practice deploying our video-streaming microservice to our local Kubernetes instance. We already have that, so there's nothing we need to install; we can simply practice deploying our microservice.

6.8.1   Building the image for the microservice

Before we can deploy a microservice, we need to build the image for it. We already did this in chapter 3, but let's run through the steps again here. For this image, we'll be using example-1 from the chapter-6 code repository.

Open a terminal, clone the chapter-6 code (see section 6.2), change directory into example-1, and then build the image:

```
cd chapter-6/example-1
docker build -t video-streaming:1 --file Dockerfile-prod .
```

Note how we've tagged the image as `video-streaming:1`. The version number appears after the colon, and we're starting with version 1 for the first deployment of the video-streaming microservice. For future builds, after the code has changed, you should increment this version number for each new deployment of your microservice.

> **NOTE**   For a more detailed explanation of the Docker `build` command, refer to chapter 3, section 3.8.

6.8.2   No container registry needed (yet)

When we published our first microservice in chapter 3, you might recall that we tagged our image (using the Docker `tag` command) and then we published the image to our private container registry (using the Docker `push` command). Right now, though, we don't need to tag or publish our image to deploy it to our local Kubernetes instance. Because Kubernetes is running locally on our computer, it already has access to our locally built Docker images, so we don't need a separate container registry to share our images with our Kubernetes cluster. Any images that we build on our development computer are already where they need to be for deployment to our local Kubernetes instance.

Later in this chapter, we'll be working with a Kubernetes cluster in the cloud. At that point, we'll need to publish to a container registry before deployment but, right now, working with a local cluster, we just don't need it. This is one of the things that makes it much easier and more convenient to learn and experiment with a local Kubernetes instance, rather than jumping straight to a cloud-hosted cluster.

6.8.3   Creating configuration for deployment to a local Kubernetes instance

Let's take our first look at a Kubernetes deployment configuration file. Listing 6.1 shows the deploy.yaml file from the scripts directory in example-1 (chapter-6/example-1/scripts/deploy.yaml) that we saw in figure 6.9. We'll use this configuration file to create the deployment, service, and pod structure for our microservice that was shown earlier in figure 6.5.

By the way, there's nothing special about the scripts directory, that's just the name that I use for keeping the deployment scripts for a project. You can call this directory whatever you like.

Listing 6.1   Deploying our microservice to Kubernetes

```
apiVersion: apps/v1          Creates a Kubernetes deployment that keeps our
kind: Deployment             microservice alive (restarting it automatically if it crashes)
metadata:
  name: video-streaming      ◁──── Sets the name of the deployment
spec:
  replicas: 1        ◁─────  Requests that this deployment keep only a single replica of our
  selector:                  microservice running. You can increase this number for performance
    matchLabels:             (handling more requests) or redundancy (increased fault tolerance).
```

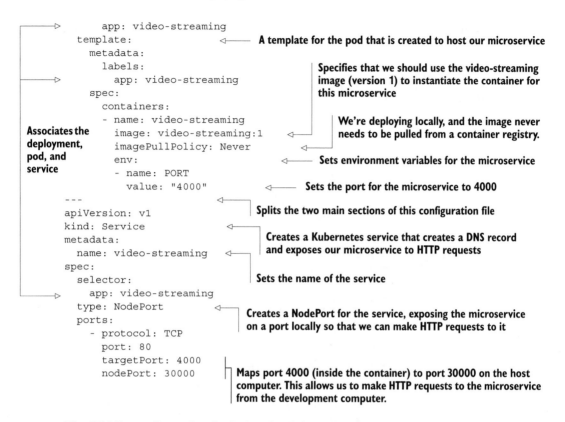

The YAML configuration in listing 6.1 is broken up into two main sections that are separated by three hyphens (---). The first section creates the Kubernetes deployment that keeps our microservice alive (automatically restarting it when it crashes).

The second section creates the Kubernetes service that exposes our microservice to HTTP requests via DNS. Having these two sections in the same file is optional. If we wanted, we could create a different structure, for instance, with each section in its own file. But it's convenient to group these together like this because they are the complete configuration for one single microservice.

Within the first section, notice the subsection for the pod template. The deployment uses this configuration template to instance the pod, its containers, and therefore our microservice. Whenever the microservice crashes or stops responding, the deployment will replace it with a new instance, freshly created from this template. Note how we're referencing the image via the tag video-streaming:1 that we applied earlier, including the version number, starting at version 1. As you build new versions of the image for your microservice, you'll need to increment this version number and update the configuration in listing 6.1 to match (if that sounds tedious, rest assured that in chapter 8 we'll talk about templating our configuration so that updated version numbers are plugged in automatically).

Deployments, services, and pods are associated with each other using labels, illustrated in figure 6.10. In listing 6.1, you can see `labels`, `matchLabels`, and `selector` that tie together the pieces of our configuration by setting the `app` label to `video-streaming`. There's nothing special about the `app` label or the name `video-streaming`. We could have called these anything.

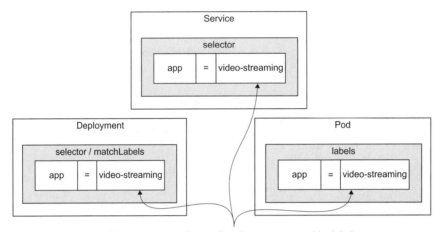

Deployment, service, and pods are connected by labels.

Figure 6.10   Deployments, services, and pods are associated with each other by labels.

Toward the end of listing 6.1, notice that the type of the service is set to `NodePort`. If we didn't specify a type here, the type of the service would default to `ClusterIP`, which would expose the service (and hence our microservice) only within the cluster—it would not be accessible outside the cluster.

Using `NodePort` here is the simplest way to make this service accessible from outside the cluster. In this case, it's a local Kubernetes instance, so we're only talking about making the service (and our microservice) accessible from our local computer.

Kubernetes allows us to choose a port in the range from 30000 to 32767, and it will pick a port at random if we don't specify a particular one. Notice in listing 6.1 that we've chosen to use port 30000 to access our microservice—that's just the first port in the allowed range. If you find any problem with port 30000 (e.g., it's not available on your computer), choose a higher port number within the allowed range, or simply delete the line `nodePort:30000` to have it choose a port number for you.

> **NOTE**   You can read more about `NodePort` configuration in the Kubernetes documentation at http://mng.bz/XqX1.

Later, when we start using a cloud-hosted Kubernetes cluster, we'll have to be more careful when exposing our microservices outside the cluster because it opens us up to attacks and abuse from the outside world. That doesn't matter right now because we're working with a Kubernetes cluster on our local computer, and the cluster itself isn't exposed to the world.

6.8.4 Connecting kubectl to local Kubernetes

At this point, we've built an image for our microservice and we've created a Kubernetes configuration to deploy it. Before we can deploy, we need to connect kubectl to our local Kubernetes instance.

If this is your first time using Kubernetes and you've just installed Docker Desktop (and enabled Kubernetes in section 6.5), then you should already be connected. The installation process sets this up for you by default.

To be sure though, let's check which cluster you're connected to. Open a terminal and invoke this command:

```
kubectl config current-context
```

If you're already connected to your local cluster, the output should be something like this:

```
docker-desktop
```

If you've used kubectl before and connected to other clusters (say, if you're already using it for work), you might find that you're connected to some other cluster, or you might not be connected to any cluster and see the error mentioned earlier in section 6.6. If that's the case, you can connect to your local cluster using the following command:

```
kubectl config use-context docker-desktop
```

To see the list of connection contexts you've configured, invoke this command:

```
kubectl config get-contexts
```

With Docker Desktop installed and Kubernetes enabled (see section 6.5), you should see `docker-desktop` (or something similar) in the list.

Once connected to your local Kubernetes, let's run a test to make sure the connection is working. The following command lists all pods that are running in your cluster:

```
kubectl get pods
```

If you're running a new Kubernetes instance, you should see a list that contains nothing because you don't have any pods running yet. If you had been experimenting with Kubernetes already, you might see some pods running that you deployed previously. If so, you might want to click the Reset button to get a fresh empty cluster (see section 6.5).

Another good test is to view the system pods:

```
kubectl get pods --namespace kube-system
```

You should see a short list of the Kubernetes system pods that are running in your cluster. By default, these are hidden when you view pods, but we've exposed them here by explicitly requesting to show pods in the namespace `kube-system`.

NOTE For more information on working with Kubernetes under Docker Desktop, see the Docker documentation at https://docs.docker.com/desktop/kubernetes/.

To explore the commands available under kubectl, invoke `kubectl --help` or check out the kubectl reference in the Kubernetes documentation at https://kubernetes.io/docs/reference/kubectl/.

6.8.5 *Deploying a microservice to local Kubernetes*

It's time to deploy our video-streaming microservice to our local Kubernetes cluster. Make sure you're connected to your local Kubernetes cluster, as described in the previous section. Then, in your terminal, change directory to example-1, and invoke kubectl to deploy the microservice:

```
cd chapter-6/example-1
kubectl apply -f scripts/deploy.yaml
```

The `-f` argument specifies which configuration file to use, and the `apply` subcommand creates the specified objects in your Kubernetes cluster. If the deployment succeeded, you should see output like this:

```
deployment.apps/video-streaming created
service/video-streaming created
```

Now let's check that the requested objects are running in your local Kubernetes instance (like the structure that was shown earlier in figure 6.5). To check the pods now running, invoke the following:

```
kubectl get pods
```

You should see output showing that our video-streaming microservice is now running as a pod:

```
NAME                             READY   STATUS    RESTARTS   AGE
video-streaming-56d66b75c7-fp44x  1/1     Running   0          92s
```

See how the name of the pod starts with `video-streaming-` but ends with a unique number? Kubernetes has generated a unique number for this pod because it could be one of a number of replicas that have been created for this deployment. In this case, we're keeping things simple, and our configuration file (refer to listing 6.1) only creates a single replica, so we should only see a single pod in this list of pods.

To check the deployments that are now running, invoke the following:

```
kubectl get deployments
```

You should see the video-streaming deployment listed in the output:

```
NAME             READY   UP-TO-DATE   AVAILABLE   AGE
video-streaming  1/1     1            1           5m25s
```

To check the services that are now running, invoke the following:

```
kubectl get services
```

In the output, you'll see at least two things: our video-streaming service and the service for the Kubernetes API:

```
NAME            TYPE       CLUSTER-IP    EXTERNAL-IP   PORT(S)        AGE
kubernetes      ClusterIP  10.96.0.1     <none>        443/TCP        11m
video-streaming NodePort   10.98.29.135  <none>        80:30000/TCP   6m16s
```

When we see the pod, deployment, and a service running in our local cluster, it means we've successfully deployed our microservice. Note in the preceding output how it tells us that the video-streaming service is available on port 30000 (that's how we configured it). This is a useful way to check the port number (and later the IP address) where our service is exposed.

Did you have any problems deploying the microservice? If so, please see chapter 11 for help debugging deployment problems.

6.8.6   *Testing the locally deployed microservice*

Now we must test that our microservice is actually working. Because we set the type of the service to `NodePort` and configured the port number to be `30000` (refer to listing 6.1) we should now be able to test our microservice and see the streaming video by pointing our browser at http://localhost:30000/video. If everything worked, and you can see the video playing, then congratulations: your video-streaming microservice is now running on Kubernetes.

If the microservice isn't working, the most common problem is not being able to access the port from the host computer. Check your configuration to make sure the ports match up, and use `kubectl get services` to double-check the port number of the service. If port 30000 isn't working for you, try another port in the range of 30000–32767 that is allowed by Kubernetes, or delete the `nodePort` line from the configuration to use an available port. We'll talk more about debugging microservices in chapter 11.

At this point, feel free to experiment by doing code updates and more deployments. Change the code in the video-streaming microservice, and then run `docker build` again to rebuild the image (make sure you update the version number of the image for each new build). Then, run `kubectl apply` again to deploy the updated microservice to your local cluster.

6.8.7   *Deleting the deployment*

When we're done testing our microservice, we can delete the deployment now to clean up our cluster:

```
kubectl delete -f scripts/deploy.yaml
```

This removes the deployment, the pod, and the service—everything that was created from that configuration file should now be deleted. If you like, you can confirm that everything is deleted by invoking `kubectl get pods`, `kubectl get deployments`, and `kubectl get services` to confirm that it really is all gone. Practice deploying and deleting your microservice multiple times to get more experience with it.

In addition, don't forget that you can reset your whole cluster by clicking Reset Kubernetes Cluster in the Kubernetes settings in Docker Desktop (refer to section 6.5). If you've been experimenting for a while and have done a few different deployments, it can be faster to just reset the cluster than trying to delete everything that you created.

6.8.8   *Why not use local Kubernetes for development?*

We have a local Kubernetes cluster that is super convenient and ready to use, so why don't we use that during development instead of Docker Compose? Why should we use Docker Compose for development and then Kubernetes for production?

We've spoken about Kubernetes versus Docker Compose already in chapter 4, section 4.3.6. But here, just let me say that you can absolutely use your local Kubernetes for development if that's how you want to work. It's a legitimate choice, so long as you can make it work well in your situation. You'll have to write a set of scripts for deployment to your local Kubernetes. Of course, this is the first problem and probably the main reason I prefer Docker Compose for development and testing. There's simply less that needs to be done to get our application running during development.

In my experience, I've loved having access to my local Kubernetes instance; it's been amazing for experimentation and continuing to learn about Kubernetes. But I don't use my local Kubernetes instance for development because I think it creates unnecessary friction in the development process.

Here are my reasons:

- Starting a multimicroservice application in Kubernetes is tedious. You need to run the deployment scripts for each and every microservice that you want to deploy. (If someone were to invent the Kubernetes version of Docker Compose, e.g., *Kubernetes Compose*, I might change my mind on this.)
- Changing between projects is tedious. You need to reset your local instance and then rerun the deployment scripts for all of your microservices.
- Configuration for the local Kubernetes will be different from your production configuration (you'll see the difference soon). That means you still need separate deployment scripts for development and production.
- The biggest problem is that the local Kubernetes instance is kind of heavyweight and doesn't have the best performance, especially when running on a laptop. Think about it: Kubernetes was designed to run over multiple computers, so how's it going to perform on your development laptop? On my development laptop, I have Kubernetes disabled most of the time so that it isn't draining my battery! However, I do leave it running permanently on my desktop computer.

For those reasons, I prefer to use Docker Compose in development instead of using a local Kubernetes instance. But it's still great to have that local Kubernetes instance, and you can decide for yourself which way you prefer to work during development. My advice is that when you've finished experimenting with your local Kubernetes instance, disable it in Docker Desktop settings so it doesn't consume resources on your computer.

6.8.9 What have we achieved?

To this point, we've built a Docker image for our microservice and deployed it to the local Kubernetes instance that came bundled with Docker Desktop. We created a Kubernetes deployment, pod, and service within the Kubernetes cluster by invoking `kubectl apply` and thus instantiated our video-streaming microservice in a *production-like* environment.

I say production-like because we've really only done a simulation of what it's like to run our microservice in production. There's a few more hoops we must jump through to really get our microservice into production—and that's exactly what we're doing next.

6.9   Creating a managed Kubernetes cluster in Azure

It's time to create a real production Kubernetes cluster in the cloud and deploy our video-streaming microservice to it. Deployment to our cloud-based Kubernetes cluster will be very similar to how we deployed to our local Kubernetes instance, but there are some differences. For example, to deploy our microservice, we'll first need to build it and publish it to our container registry, which you first learned about in chapter 3. Before we can get to deployment, though, we must create our container registry and Kubernetes cluster and then connect to our cluster with kubectl.

If you didn't sign up for Azure in chapter 3, now is the time to do that. See chapter 3, section 3.9.1, to sign up for Azure, and then create your container registry. If you still have that container registry from chapter 3, then feel free to continue using it in this chapter.

Next, we'll go through the steps to create our Kubernetes cluster. Open the Azure portal (https://portal.azure.com), and search for "kubernetes," as shown in figure 6.11. Click the Create dropdown, and then click Kubernetes Service.

Now we configure the details for our Kubernetes cluster, shown in figure 6.12. Be sure to choose your Free Trial subscription (if you have multiple subscriptions) so that's it paid for by your trial credits. You might have to add your credit card details to Azure in order to create a cluster; even if you have to do this, the cluster should be paid for by your trial credits, but be careful because if you exhaust those credits, Microsoft will proceed to charge you real money. Once we've finished with this Kubernetes cluster, we'll delete it anyway, just to be on the safe side.

Choose or create a resource group to contain your new Kubernetes cluster. Resource groups in Azure allow us to group and organize our cloud resources. You

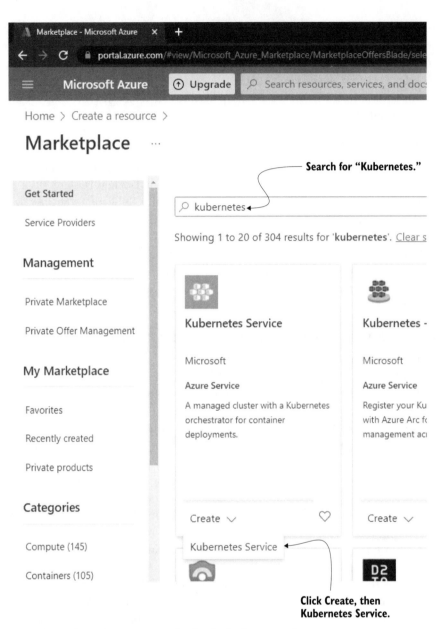

Figure 6.11   Selecting Kubernetes Service in the Azure portal

must also choose a name for your Kubernetes cluster. Take note of the name you use for the resource group and the cluster; you'll need to remember these details again soon.

Choose the location where you'll host your cluster. For the purposes of experimentation and learning, it doesn't matter where you place your cluster, so feel free to use the default. However, if the default location isn't available, you might have to create the cluster in a different location.

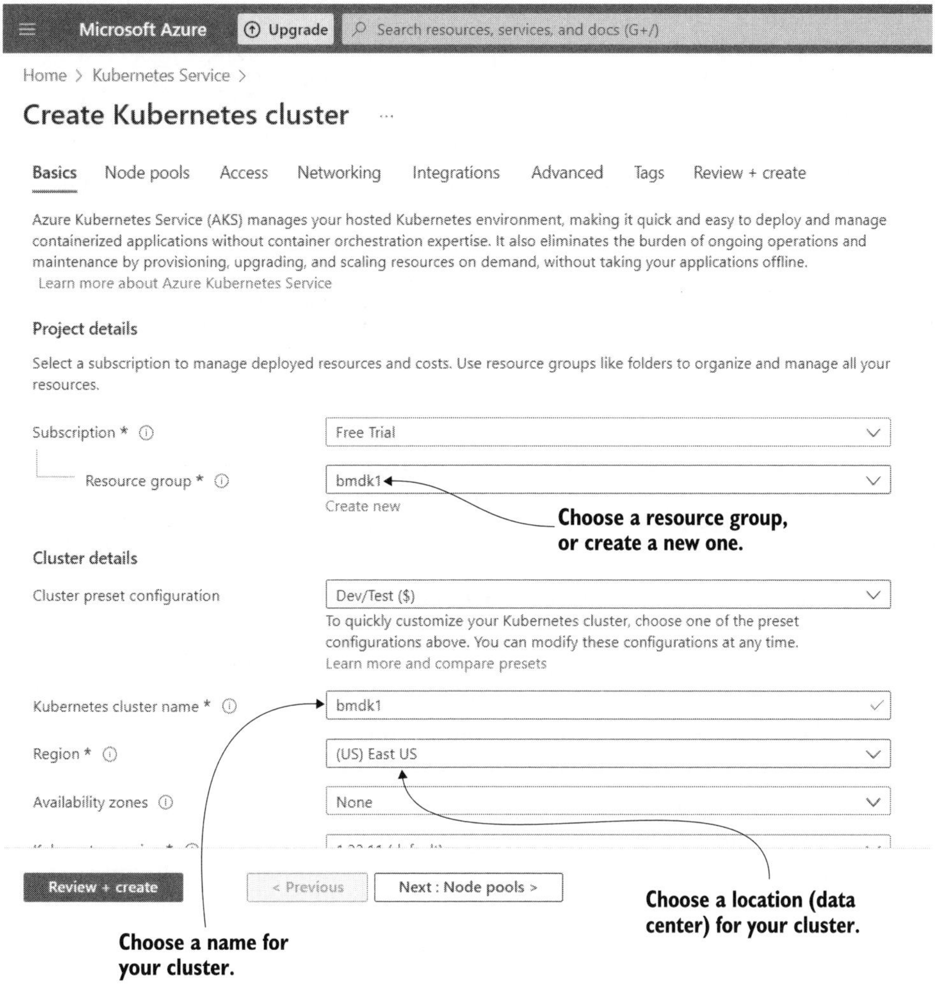

Figure 6.12   Creating a Kubernetes cluster, part 1

Next, we scroll down and continue to configure our Kubernetes cluster, shown in figure 6.13. Here, we can choose a VM size—I recommend clicking through to see the list of options, waiting until it computes the estimated cost for each VM, and then selecting the cheapest one (we don't want to burn through our credits too quickly).

To make it more affordable, you can also select Manual for the Scale Method and a single node for the Node Count (unless you're experimenting with scalability; if that's the case, feel free to experiment with autoscaling and a larger number of nodes—just know that it's going to burn through your credits much faster).

When you're happy with the configuration for your cluster, click Review + Create. It will take some time to create your cluster. When it's finished, you'll see a notification in the Azure portal, and you can click through that to see the details of your new Kubernetes cluster. You can also find your cluster at any time through the All

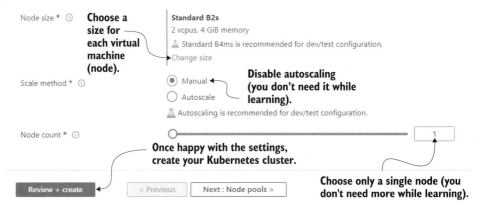

Figure 6.13   Creating a Kubernetes cluster, part 2

Resources list in the Azure portal (just like we found our container registry back in section 3.9.1—check there for a reminder).

Now we need to look at the connection details for the cluster. In the Overview page for your cluster, click the Connect button, shown in figure 6.14. This pops out a section on the right that shows you the Azure CLI commands you need to invoke locally on your computer to download your Azure credentials and connect kubectl to your shiny new cluster running on Azure. So, the next thing you must do is install the Azure CLI tool.

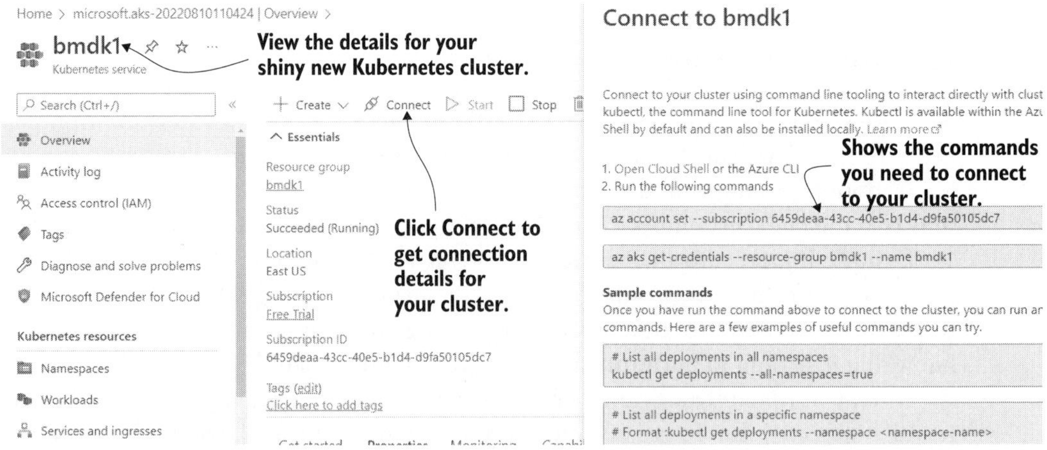

Figure 6.14   Finding the connection details for your new Kubernetes cluster

6.10   *Working with the Azure CLI*

Using the Azure portal UI is a convenient and easy way to get started creating infrastructure on Azure. At this point, though, we need to move to the command line and start using the Azure CLI tool because that's the easiest way to connect kubectl to our cloud-based cluster. We also need the Azure CLI for other tasks later in this chapter and in the next chapter. Let's get it installed.

6.10.1   *Installing the Azure CLI*

You can find the instructions for installing the Azure CLI here: http://mng.bz/yZeo. Choose your platform, and follow the instructions to install it. After installing the Azure CLI, you can test it from your terminal with the following command:

```
az --version
```

At the time of writing, I'm using version 2.51.0. Future versions should be backward compatible.

6.10.2   *Authenticating the Azure CLI*

Before using the Azure CLI, we must authenticate it with our Azure account from the terminal with this command:

```
az login
```

Running this command opens a browser where you can sign into your Azure account. If it doesn't automatically open your browser, follow the instructions in the output:

```
A web browser has been opened at ...
Please continue the login in the web browser.
If no web browser is available or if the web browser fails to open,
use device code flow with `az login --use-device-code`.
```

When the `az login` command completes, it displays a JSON-formatted list of your Azure subscriptions. If you only just signed up for Azure for this book, you should see only one subscription. If you already use Azure for work, you might see multiple subscriptions listed.

The authentication is saved locally, and from now on, you can issue other commands against your Azure account without having to sign in each time. We can see which Azure subscription we're working with using this command:

```
az account show
```

The output from this command shows us the current default subscription. We can also view a list of all subscriptions:

```
az account list
```

The output is a JSON-formatted list of subscriptions. Each subscription has an `id` field that is a unique ID for the subscription. You'll also notice that the current default subscription is marked by having its `isDefault` field set to `true`. This field is set to `false` for any other subscriptions in the list.

At this point, you should verify that you're using the right subscription to follow along with the examples in this book. For example, if you have access to subscriptions from your employer, you probably shouldn't use those for your own learning and experimentation (or at least, check with your boss first). If you need to change the current working subscription, you can set a new default like this:

```
az account set --subscription=<subscription-id>
```

Replace `<subscription-id>` with the ID of the subscription that you want to set as the default. After changing the default subscription, double-check it just to be sure you're using the right subscription:

```
az account show
```

6.10.3 *Connecting kubectl to Kubernetes*

Now that we have the Azure CLI installed and authenticated against our Azure account, we can invoke the `aks get-credentials` subcommand that downloads the credentials and connects our kubectl command to our Kubernetes cluster on Azure. You can find the details of the command by clicking the Connect button in the page for your Kubernetes cluster in the Azure portal, which was shown earlier in figure 6.14.

The command that I invoked looks like this:

```
az aks get-credentials --resource-group bmdk1 --name bmdk1
```

You'll need to use the name of your own resource group and your own cluster. You selected those names earlier when you created your cluster (refer to section 6.9).

Here's the general format of the command to which you add your own details:

```
az aks get-credentials --resource-group <resource-group> --name <cluster>
```

You can read the documentation for the `aks get-credentials` subcommand here: http://mng.bz/yZeo.

> **NOTE** There's a lot more that we can do with the `aks` command to interact
> with our Kubernetes cluster. Scan the docs to see the other subcommands
> that are available: https://learn.microsoft.com/en-us/cli/azure/aks.

With kubectl configured, we can now use it to send commands to our cloud-based Kubernetes cluster. To be sure, just like we did earlier with our local Kubernetes instance, let's check which cluster we're connected to. Open a terminal and invoke this command:

```
kubectl config current-context
```

This tells you the name of the cluster you're connected to. For me, it was `bmdk1`. The output will be different for you depending on the name you gave to your cluster in section 6.9.

To see the list of connection contexts, invoke the following:

```
kubectl config get-contexts
```

You can easily change between any of your connection contexts with this command:

```
kubectl config use-context <context-name>
```

Once connected to your Kubernetes cluster, you can do a test to make sure the connection is working. The following command lists all pods that are running in your cluster:

```
kubectl get pods
```

It's a new cluster, so you shouldn't see anything running! Just to be sure, let's test that you can view the system pods with this command:

```
kubectl get pods --namespace kube-system
```

You should see a list of the Kubernetes system pods running in your cluster. Note that there will be some differences from the list of system pods from your local Kubernetes instance that we looked at earlier.

6.11   Deploying to the production cluster

At this point, we've created our Kubernetes cluster, and we're almost ready to deploy our microservice to it. Before we can deploy, however, we must first publish our image.

6.11.1   Now we need a container registry

To deploy to a cloud-based cluster, the image for our microservice must be published to our cloud-based container registry. Feel free to reuse the container registry you created in chapter 3 if you still have that. Otherwise, return to chapter 3, and follow the steps in section 3.9.1 to create your container registry through the Azure portal.

6.11.2   Publishing the image to the container registry

Before we publish our image to our container registry, we must build it. To do so, open a terminal, change directory into example-2, and build the image for our video-streaming microservice:

```
cd chapter-6/example-2
docker build -t video-streaming:1 --file Dockerfile-prod .
```

Don't forget that period at the end of the `docker build` command, it's so easy to miss or forget that!

Now we must tag our image according to the name of our container registry where we intend to publish it. You'll need to insert the URL for your container registry when you invoke this command:

```
docker tag video-streaming:1 <registry-url>/video-streaming:1
```

As we build and publish successive versions of our microservice, don't forget that we need to increment that version number. The next version of the image will be tagged `video-streaming:2`, then `video-streaming:3`, and so on.

Prior to publishing the image, we must log in to our container registry. You just need to insert the URL for your container registry, invoke this command, and then enter your username and password:

```
docker login <registry-url>
```

Now we can actually publish our image by pushing it to the container registry. Again, just insert the URL for your own container registry:

```
docker push <registry-url>/video-streaming:1
```

When `docker push` succeeds, we've published our microservice, and it's ready for deployment to Kubernetes.

Did you have any problem pushing the image? If so, check that you tagged the image correctly according to the URL for your container registry. It's a common problem to get the tag wrong and then not be able to push the image.

Need more details on the process of building, tagging, and publishing an image? Refer back to sections 3.8 and 3.9 in chapter 3 for a longer and more detailed description of how to do this.

6.11.3 Connecting the container registry to the Kubernetes cluster

There's one more thing we need to do before we deploy the microservice. We need to connect our container registry and our Kubernetes cluster so that the cluster can pull images from the registry without having to authenticate. Not having to configure authentication between the registry and cluster is a significant simplification of the setup process.

Here's the command I used to "attach" my container registry to my cluster:

```
az aks update --resource-group bmdk1 --name bmdk1 --attach-acr bmdk1
```

The `aks update` subcommand allows us to update the configuration of our Kubernetes cluster running on Azure.

You'll need to insert the name of your own cluster, resource group, and container registry. Here's the general format of the command:

```
az aks update --resource-group <resource-group>
 --name <cluster> --attach-acr <registry>
```

If we connect our cluster and container registry, it makes things so much easier because we don't have to encode registry authentication credentials in our Kubernetes deployment configuration. It's a perfectly safe way to make our deployment setup much simpler; given that we control and trust both our container registry and our Kubernetes cluster, we can safely "pre-authenticate" the cluster to talk to the container registry. This is a simplification that works great for a simple setup like we have in this book, but it might not work for you in production, depending on where and how you're hosting your cloud resources and what security model you're using. We'll talk more about security in chapter 12.

Note that if you don't attach your container registry to your cluster, then your cluster will fail to pull your microservice's image from the container registry. You can also make this work by encoding the container registry authentication in your deployment configuration file, but that's more complicated and unnecessary when you can just attach your registry to your cluster. If you later see an error such as `ErrImagePull` or `ImagePullBackOff`, that indicates you didn't get this step right.

NOTE You can read more about the `aks update` command here: http://mng .bz/amG9.

6.11.4 Creating a configuration for deployment to Kubernetes

The Kubernetes configuration for production deployment from example-2 that is shown in listing 6.2 (chapter-6/example-2/scripts/deploy.yaml) creates a deployment, pod, and service for our microservice. It's almost the same as the configuration we used earlier in listing 6.1 for deployment to our local Kubernetes instance. The differences are indicated by the annotations in the code listing.

Listing 6.2 Deploying our microservice to Kubernetes on Azure

```
apiVersion: apps/v1
kind: Deployment
metadata:
  name: video-streaming
spec:
  replicas: 1
  selector:
    matchLabels:
      app: video-streaming
  template:
    metadata:
      labels:
        app: video-streaming
    spec:
      containers:
      - name: video-streaming
        image: bmdk1.azurecr.io/video-streaming:1
        imagePullPolicy: IfNotPresent
        env:
        - name: PORT
```

The image is referenced in the container registry. Make sure you update this to the URL for your own container registry!

Pulls the image from the container registry when it's not already present in the Kubernetes cluster

```
              value: "4000"
---
apiVersion: v1
kind: Service
metadata:
  name: video-streaming
spec:
  selector:
    app: video-streaming
  type: LoadBalancer
  ports:
    - protocol: TCP
      port: 80
      targetPort: 4000
```

Sets the type of the service to LoadBalancer, which creates an Azure load balancer that makes this microservice accessible by the outside world. We must be careful with this because it means anyone can access our microservice without authentication. This example is just a simple way to expose our microservice, meaning we can easily send it HTTP requests to test it from our development computer.

At this point, let's take a moment to reflect on the differences between our local and production configurations. The following differences can be seen in listing 6.2:

- The image being deployed is the one we just published to our container registry. Before you can deploy this code, you'll have to change this URL to the URL for your own container registry.

- The image pull policy is set to IfNotPresent, meaning that if the image doesn't exist within the cluster, it will be pulled from our container registry. This is how the image gets to the cluster in the first place. New versions will also be pulled as necessary, but if we attempt to deploy an existing version again, the locally cached image will be used, and it doesn't need to be pulled again from the container registry.

- The type of the service is now set to LoadBalancer, which causes Azure to create a load balancer and allocate an IP so we can access our microservice from the outside world. This allows us to send HTTP requests to our microservice from our development computer to test that the microservice is functional. We have to be very careful when using type LoadBalancer: it's useful for our own testing, but it also exposes our microservice to the outside world (and thus attacks and abuse). It doesn't matter in this case because we're only experimenting, and very soon after we'll simply delete this deployment.

These differences between local and production deployment are one of the reasons I generally don't use the local Kubernetes instance for development. If we have to maintain two sets of configuration anyway, it doesn't help much to replace Docker Compose with our local Kubernetes instance, especially when Docker Compose is convenient for development in other ways (see chapter 4, section 4.3.6, and section 6.8.8 in this chapter for a reminder).

6.11.5 *Deploying the microservice to Kubernetes*

With our image published, our container registry connected to our cluster, and our configuration ready to go, let's deploy our video-streaming microservices to Kubernetes.

The nice thing is that deploying to a cloud-based cluster is no different from deploying to our local Kubernetes instance:

```
cd chapter-6/example-2
kubectl apply -f scripts/deploy.yaml
```

Again, the -f argument chooses the configuration file that specifies the objects we'd like to create in our cluster.

With the deployment completed, invoke the following commands to check what we just created:

```
kubectl get pods

kubectl get deployments

kubectl get services
```

We should see that we've created one deployment, one pod, and one service for our video-streaming microservice.

Did you have any problems deploying the microservice? If so, please see chapter 11 for help debugging deployment problems.

6.11.6 Testing the deployed microservice

Our microservice is deployed, but we still have to test that it's functioning correctly. This is why we set the type to LoadBalancer in listing 6.2, so that an externally accessible IP was allocated. We can use this to send HTTP requests to our microservice to test it. The question is, how do we find out the IP address?

Well, you might have noticed earlier how the external IP address was listed when you invoked the following:

```
kubectl get services
```

Here's what the output looked like for me. When you see this, you see that a different IP address has been allocated for your own microservice:

```
NAME             TYPE          CLUSTER-IP     EXTERNAL-IP     PORT(S)
kubernetes       ClusterIP     10.0.0.1       <none>          443/TCP
video-streaming  LoadBalancer  10.0.221.252   20.127.176.147  80:32545/TCP
```

We can pluck the IP address from the output and use it to test our microservice. In this case, the IP address is 20.127.176.147, so I point my browser at http://20.127.176.147/video. If the streaming video plays, it means the microservice is working. You can do the same, but you'll have to use the IP address that was allocated to your microservice. You can't use my IP address because my version of this microservice won't even be running by the time you read this. Figure 6.15 shows the

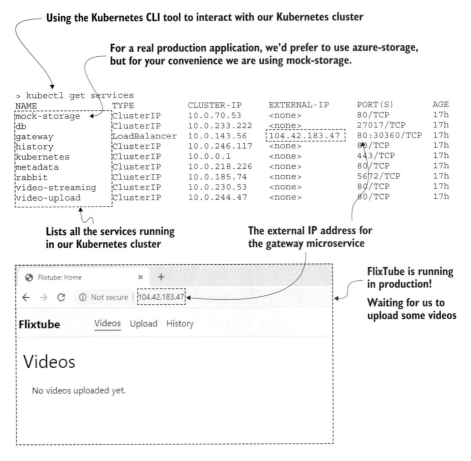

Figure 6.15   Shows how we find our external IP address from the output of `kubectl get services`

complete suite of microservices we'll deploy in chapter 10 and how the output from `kubectl get services` relates to what we see in the browser.

For a production microservice, normally we wouldn't make it accessible to the outside world unless it really does have to be available to the public. Exposing the video-streaming microservice like this is just a temporary measure while you're experimenting and learning Kubernetes. In chapter 11, we'll talk about other ways to test your production microservices without exposing them to the whole world.

6.11.7 Deleting the deployment

When we're done testing our microservice, we can delete the deployment now to clean up our cluster. Invoke this command to delete the deployment:

```
kubectl delete -f scripts/deploy.yaml
```

This removes the deployment, the pod, and the service: everything that was created from that configuration file should now be gone. If you like, you can invoke `kubectl get pods`, `kubectl get deployments`, and `kubectl get services` to confirm that everything we created is now gone. Practice deploying and deleting your microservice as many times as you like. Remember to increment the version number each time you change the code and rebuild the image for your microservice.

6.11.8   Destroying your infrastructure

After we've finished experimenting with our cloud-based Kubernetes cluster, we can delete it to save the cluster from consuming all of our free trial credits, assuming there's nothing else we want to do with it. In the next chapter, we'll be rebuilding our container registry and our Kubernetes cluster through code using Terraform, so you don't need to keep this particular container registry or cluster around for anything else in this book. Of course, feel free to leave your Kubernetes cluster running if you'd like to continue experimenting, learning, or running your application.

To delete your Kubernetes cluster, open the Azure portal, find the page for your cluster (click through All Resources to find it), and then click the Delete button near the top of the page. This will delete your cluster and associated resources (e.g., nodes). Check in All Resources to make sure it's gone. In a similar way, you can delete your container registry.

6.11.9   What have we achieved?

Up to now, we've built the Docker image for our microservice and published it to our container registry. We then created a Kubernetes cluster through the Azure portal and deployed our microservice to it. This is very close to how our production environment will work; the key difference is that later the creation of our infrastructure and the deployment of our microservices will be automated. At this point, we've deployed just one single microservice, but each step forward brings us closer to the full deployment of the FlixTube microservices application.

6.12   Azure CLI tool review

The Azure CLI tool is what we use to create and configure Azure cloud resources from our terminal. In this chapter, we used it to connect to Azure and download the credentials so we could connect to our Kubernetes cluster. Table 6.2 provides a review of the CLI commands.

NOTE   You can learn more about it from Azure CLI documentation page: https://learn.microsoft.com/en-us/cli/azure/.

Table 6.2   Review of Azure CLI commands

Command	Description
`az --version`	Shows the version number of the Azure CLI tool
`az login`	Logs in to your Azure account and connects the Azure CLI tool
`az account show`	Shows which Azure account you're currently using
`az account list`	Shows all Azure accounts you've configured
`az account set --subscription=<id>`	Sets the Azure account you're currently using
`az aks get-credentials --resource-group <resource-group> --name <cluster>`	Downloads credentials and connects kubectl to your Kubernetes cluster
`az aks update --name <cluster> --resource-group <resource-group> --attach-acr <registry>`	Attaches your container registry to your Kubernetes cluster. This means the cluster can pull images from the registry without being authenticated; not having to set up authentication between cluster and registry makes setup significantly simpler.

6.13   *Kubectl review*

Kubectl is the command-line tool we used to interact with our Kubernetes cluster to deploy and manage our microservices. We used it to deploy our video-streaming microservice first to our local Kubernetes instance and then to our cloud-based managed Kubernetes cluster that we created on Azure. Table 6.3 provides a review of the kubectl commands.

> **NOTE** To learn more about kubectl, see its documentation page: https://kubernetes.io/docs/reference/kubectl/.

Table 6.3   Review of kubectl commands

Command	Description
`kubectl version`	Shows the version number of the Kubernetes client and server
`kubectl config current-context`	Shows which Kubernetes cluster you're currently connected to
`kubectl config use-context <cluster-name>`	Connects to a named Kubernetes cluster, assuming you have the context already configured for it
`kubectl config use-context docker-desktop`	Connects to the local Kubernetes cluster running under Docker Desktop
`kubectl config get-contexts`	Shows all connections you've configured
`kubectl apply -f <file>`	Applies a Kubernetes configuration (YAML) file to the cluster, creating the requested objects there. We used this command to deploy our microservice to Kubernetes.
`kubectl delete -f <file>`	Deletes all objects specified in the configuration file from the cluster

Table 6.3 Review of kubectl commands

Command	Description
kubectl get pods	Shows the pods that have been created in the cluster
kubectl get deployments	Shows the deployments that have been created in the cluster
kubectl get services	Shows the services that have been created in the cluster. This is particularly useful to find the IP address and port for externally accessible services.

6.14 *Continue your learning*

In this chapter, you started learning how to create a production environment on Kubernetes. We started simply using the local Kubernetes instance that comes with Docker Desktop and then graduated to creating a managed Kubernetes cluster through the Azure portal UI.

Kubernetes is a deep and complex technology—definitely the most complex technology we'll talk about in this book. You can spend many months working with it before you dig all the way to the bottom! In this book, we'll barely scratch the surface of what Kubernetes has to offer. To dive deeper, I recommend the following books:

- *Core Kubernetes* by Jay Vyas and Chris Love (Manning, 2022)
- *Kubernetes in Action, 2nd ed,* by Marko Lukša (Manning, est. March 2024)
- *Kubernetes for Developers* by William Denniss (Manning, est. February 2024)
- *Learn Kubernetes in a Month of Lunches* by Elton Stoneman (Manning, 2021)

Of course, there's always so much more we can learn by reading the relevant documentation. Following are some links that will keep you busy for a while:

- You can learn more about Kubernetes under Docker Desktop by reading the Docker documentation: https://docs.docker.com/desktop/kubernetes/.
- You can learn more about Kubernetes by reading the Kubernetes documentation here: https://kubernetes.io/docs/home/.
- To learn more about Kubernetes objects and how to express them in YAML configuration files, start here: http://mng.bz/g7W8.
- To find out what else you can do with the Azure CLI tool, read the documentation here: https://docs.microsoft.com/en-us/cli/azure/.
- You can read more about the managed Kubernetes service on Azure here: https://docs.microsoft.com/en-au/azure/aks.

Summary

- Going to production early—putting our application in front of our customers as soon as we can—is a good idea because that's where we need to put our product so customers can see it and give feedback. In addition, it's easier to go to production while our application is still small.

- Kubernetes is a container orchestration platform that is becoming an industry standard for running microservices.
- A Kubernetes cluster is composed of nodes (VMs), pods, and containers.
- The pod is the unit of computation for Kubernetes, and it can host multiple containers.
- A Kubernetes deployment is responsible for keeping the pod (or pods) for our microservice running. If a pod crashes or becomes unresponsive, the deployment will automatically replace it with a fresh instance.
- A Kubernetes service is responsible for creating a DNS record that exposes our microservice within the cluster and, if we choose to, makes it available to the outside world.
- Using the local Kubernetes instance that is bundled with Docker Desktop is a great way to learn, experiment, and practice creating deployments using Kubernetes.
- We use kubectl, the Kubernetes CLI tool, to interact with Kubernetes and create deployments.
- A Kubernetes deployment is created by applying a YAML configuration file to our cluster.
- Although setting up Kubernetes on your own hardware is complicated and difficult, creating a managed Kubernetes cluster through the Azure portal UI is simple in comparison.
- We can use the Azure CLI tool to connect our container registry and Kubernetes cluster. This effectively pre-authenticates the cluster to pull images from the container registry, which is the simplest setup of our deployment.

Infrastructure as code

In this chapter, we scale up the difficulty significantly and start using code to script the creation of our infrastructure. That is, we'll now be using the technique known as *infrastructure as code* to automate the creation of our infrastructure.

So far, we've manually created our cloud-based infrastructure through the Azure portal. We manually created a container registry in chapter 3 and manually created a Kubernetes cluster in chapter 6. In this chapter, we'll be creating these same things again; however, instead of creating them manually using the Azure portal, we'll write code and run it on our local computer to create our infrastructure in the cloud.

This chapter is significantly more difficult than anything before it. As such, I've designed this chapter to be skipped, so if this is too much or not interesting, move directly to chapter 8 if you like. You can come back to this chapter again in the future. But if you're keen to learn Terraform and infrastructure as code, or you just want to fully automate the creation of your infrastructure alongside the deployment of your microservices application, please continue reading.

7.1   New tool

This chapter introduces Terraform, another tool important enough to be in the title of the book, as shown in table 7.1. We'll use Terraform to create the infrastructure for our microservices application, including our Kubernetes cluster.

Table 7.1   New tool in chapter 7

Tool	Version	Purpose
Terraform	1.5.6	Terraform allows us to script the creation of cloud resources and application infrastructure.

7.2   Getting the code

To follow along with this chapter, you need to download the code or clone the repository:

- Download a zip file of the code from here: http://mng.bz/ZR5A
- You can clone the code using Git like this:

```
git clone https://github.com/bootstrapping-microservices-2nd-edition/
➥ chapter-7.git
```

For help on installing and using Git, see chapter 2. If you have problems with the code, log an issue against the repository in GitHub.

7.3   Prototyping our infrastructure

How do we go about writing code that creates infrastructure? It's not that different from writing any code that we eventually want running in production. We start by writing and testing the code on our local development computer. This works a bit differently from normal coding, though. With normal coding, we'll test locally and see the results locally. When coding with Terraform, we'll run the code locally to test it, but we'll see the results, that is, infrastructure being created, in the cloud. Figure 7.1 shows how we'll use Terraform from our local computer to build a cloud-based infrastructure.

That's how we're working in this chapter: running Terraform locally, but seeing the results appear in the cloud. Running code to create infrastructure is a valuable technique that helps make the creation of our infrastructure repeatable.

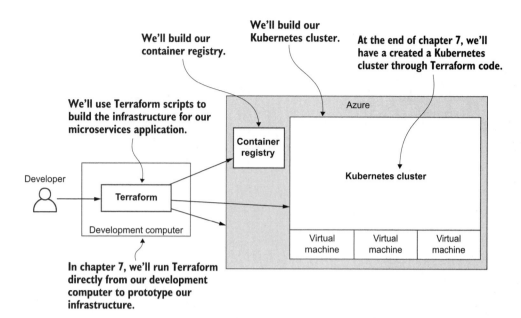

Figure 7.1   Creating infrastructure with Terraform

7.4   *Infrastructure as code*

The technique we're using to create our infrastructure is called *infrastructure as code* because rather than manually creating infrastructure (say, through a GUI—the Azure portal—like we did in chapters 3 and 6), we're now writing code so that we can automate the creation of our infrastructure. Not only will this code describe our infrastructure, but we'll also execute it to actually create our infrastructure. Using code to create infrastructure means that we can reliably and repeatedly create and recreate our infrastructure on demand and as often as we like.

The fact that this code both describes and builds our infrastructure makes it a form of *executable documentation*. It's a statement about how we want our infrastructure to look, and unlike normal (i.e., nonexecutable) documentation, it's a form of documentation that's never going to go out of date.

Through infrastructure as code, creating and updating our infrastructure becomes a kind of coding task. The best form of infrastructure as code uses a declarative language instead of a procedural one. This means it describes the configuration and layout of the infrastructure instead of the step-by-step instructions for building it. We prefer the declarative format because we can let our tools do the heavy lifting—that is, let our tools figure out the best way to make changes to our infrastructure.

Figure 7.2 illustrates the concept of infrastructure as code. The code for our infrastructure lives in a code repository such as Git. From there, we execute it to create, configure, and maintain our cloud-based infrastructure.

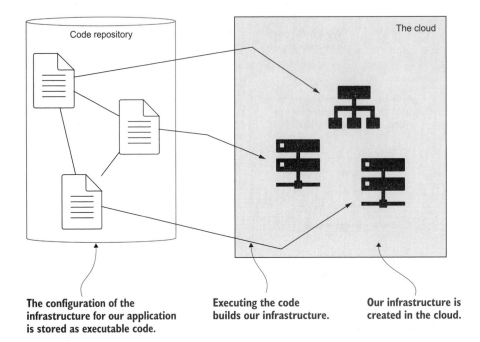

The configuration of the infrastructure for our application is stored as executable code.

Executing the code builds our infrastructure.

Our infrastructure is created in the cloud.

Figure 7.2   Infrastructure as code uses executable code to create the infrastructure.

7.5   *Authenticate with your Azure account*

Before Terraform can create infrastructure in Azure on our behalf, we must first authenticate with Azure using the Azure CLI tool just like we did in chapter 6, section 6.10. If you aren't already logged in, do that now with the Azure CLI:

```
az login
```

> **NOTE**   For the full details on installing the Azure CLI and authenticating with Azure, refer to chapter 6, section 6.10.

7.6   *Which version of Kubernetes?*

We use the Azure CLI now to determine which versions of Kubernetes are available in the particular region where we'd like to create our cluster. Here's an example that lists versions of Kubernetes in the Eastern US region:

```
az aks get-versions --location eastus
```

The output is in JSON and shows the available versions of Kubernetes in that location, but it isn't very readable. We can make it readable using table output formatting like this:

```
az aks get-versions --location eastus --output table
```

The output will look something like this:

```
KubernetesVersion      Upgrades
-------------------    -----------------------
1.27.3                 None available
1.27.1                 1.27.3
1.26.6                 1.27.1, 1.27.3
1.26.3                 1.26.6, 1.27.1, 1.27.3
1.25.11                1.26.3, 1.26.6
1.25.6                 1.25.11, 1.26.3, 1.26.6
```

From this list, you should select the most recent version of Kubernetes. That's 1.27.3 at the time of writing. But by the time you read this, there will be a more recent version. It's quite possible that version 1.27.3 will have expired (no longer available through Azure). Be sure to choose a version number that's currently available! Make a note of your chosen version number because you'll need it soon to create your cluster.

You might note that the version of Kubernetes we're using here is different from the version we used in the previous chapter. It appears that the local version of Kubernetes that comes with Docker Desktop is a couple of steps behind the latest version available on Azure. However, it shouldn't matter because Kubernetes is usually backward compatible so that what we learn for an older version will still work on later versions.

7.7 Creating the infrastructure with Terraform

Now we're coming to the point where we'll actually start to create our infrastructure! We could build our infrastructure manually, either using the GUI (e.g., the Azure portal) like we did in the previous chapter or by using the Azure CLI tool. To see how to use the Azure CLI, see my blog post at www.codecapers.com.au/kub-cluster-quick-2/.

In this chapter, though, we're building our infrastructure in an automated fashion using code. From here on in, we're using infrastructure as code to automate the process of infrastructure creation and, hence, making it reliable, repeatable, and automatic. We'll do this with Terraform, an amazingly flexible tool for executing HashiCorp Configuration Language (HCL) code. HCL is the declarative configuration language in which we'll define our infrastructure. Executing this code with Terraform actually creates our infrastructure in the cloud.

> **NOTE** In the future, I'll refer to HCL simply as *Terraform code.*

Terraform supports multiple cloud vendors through plugin providers as figure 7.3 illustrates. For the examples in this chapter, we're using Terraform to script the creation of infrastructure on Microsoft Azure.

If learning HCL seems in any way daunting, remember that HCL is actually just like YAML or JSON, but it's a different format. HashiCorp created HCL to be a human-readable configuration format that is also machine translatable to YAML and JSON. Think of it as YAML or JSON but structured to be more friendly for humans.

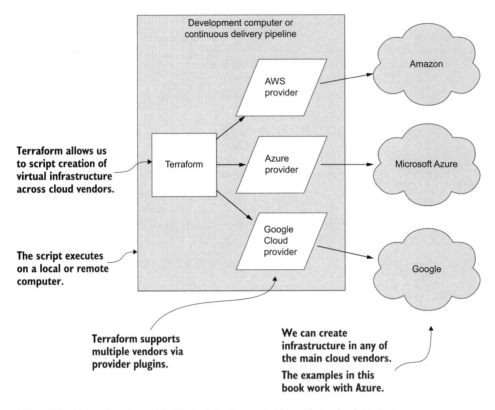

Figure 7.3   Using Terraform to build the infrastructure with various cloud vendors

7.7.1   Why Terraform?

Terraform is a tool and a language for configuring infrastructures for cloud-based applications. Terraform makes it easy to reliably and repeatedly create and configure cloud infrastructure. It's incredibly flexible, as its functionality is extended through plugin providers, which is how it supports multiple cloud vendors. Terraform already has robust providers implemented for Azure, Amazon Web Services (AWS), and Google Cloud.

Just like with Kubernetes, you're learning transferable skills that can be used with all the major cloud vendors. No matter which cloud we use, we can make use of Terraform to build our infrastructure. We can even create our own providers and extend Terraform to work with platforms that it doesn't yet support.

Terraform seems like the *universal configuration language*—it's one language we can use to create all of our infrastructure. Terraform is open source, and you can find the code here: https://github.com/hashicorp/terraform.

7.7.2   Installing Terraform

Installing Terraform is simply a matter of downloading the binary executable for your operating system and moving it to a directory that's included in your system's PATH environment variable. Download the latest version of Terraform from www.terraform .io/downloads.html.

After installing Terraform, test it from your terminal with the following command:

```
terraform --version
```

At the time of writing, I'm using version 1.5.6. Future versions should be backward compatible.

7.7.3 Terraform project setup

Before we get started with Terraform, let's become familiar with what a Terraform project looks like. In figure 7.4, we take a peek at a more complete Terraform project that is example-3 from later in this chapter. We're jumping ahead just to get an idea of the structure of a Terraform project.

As you can see in figure 7.4, a Terraform project is composed of a number of Terraform code files; those are the files ending in the .tf extension. These files contain the Terraform code that, when executed by Terraform, creates the infrastructure for our application.

You should be able to read the filenames in figure 7.4 and get the gist of their purpose. I've used a naming convention where each script file is named according to the piece of infrastructure that it creates. When you read through the filenames in figure 7.4, you can read it like this: container-registry.tf creates the container registry, kubernetes-cluster.tf creates the Kubernetes cluster, and resource-group.tf creates the Azure resource group.

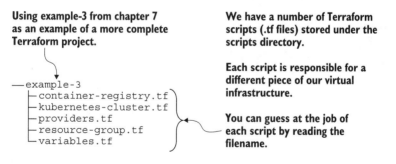

Figure 7.4   The structure of a more complete Terraform project (example-3 from later in this chapter)

The structure and filenames in this example project aren't dictated by Terraform. This just happens to be a convention that I like to use. For your own projects, a different structure might be better, so feel free to experiment and find the best structure for your own project.

7.8   *Creating an Azure resource group for your application*

After looking at the project structure of example-3, let's now dial back the complexity and reset back to the much simpler example-1. We need to start our Terraform journey somewhere, and our starting point should always be simple. This is the case with example-1, which contains the simplest Terraform code from which to start creating our infrastructure.

The first thing we must do is create an Azure resource group that groups together all the other Azure resources we'll create in this chapter. Back in chapter 3, we manually created a resource group through the GUI in the Azure portal. Now, we create a resource group again, but this time, we aren't doing it manually—we'll build it through code using Terraform.

Example-1 contains two Terraform code files: providers.tf and resource-group.tf. The script file, resource-group.tf, is the one that actually creates the resource group. The other file, providers.tf, contains configurations for the Terraform provider plugins; we'll talk more about that soon.

We'll use the command `terraform apply` to execute our Terraform code. Figure 7.5 shows how our code files are input to Terraform, which executes our code and creates the `flixtube` resource group in Azure.

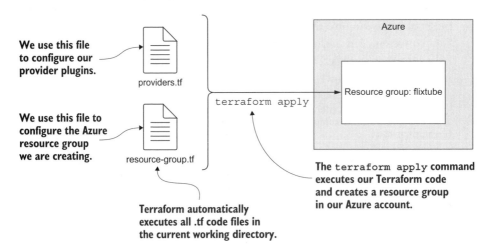

Figure 7.5   Using Terraform to create an Azure resource group

7.8.1   *Evolutionary architecture with Terraform*

Terraform is a tool for building out our infrastructure little by little in an iterative fashion—something we call *evolutionary architecture* (see figure 7.6). Each of the examples in this chapter can be run standalone, so you can easily create the infrastructure at each point by jumping to any of the examples and invoking Terraform for that code. However, the usual way to develop infrastructure is through iterative prototyping. Write a bit of code in Terraform, apply it, and then test that the right infrastructure

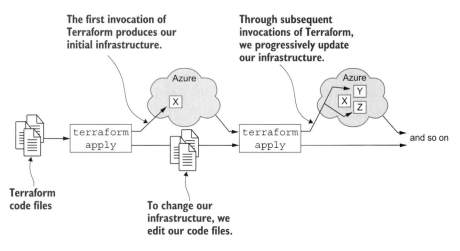

The first invocation of Terraform produces our initial infrastructure.

Through subsequent invocations of Terraform, we progressively update our infrastructure.

Terraform code files

To change our infrastructure, we edit our code files.

Figure 7.6 Iterative evolution of infrastructure with Terraform

was created. Then, write some more code, apply it, and test it again. This is just like normal coding, except that the results we're getting, that is, the infrastructure we're creating, appears in the cloud. This is the process we're emulating in this chapter: repeatedly writing code, applying it, and testing it until we've built out the infrastructure the way we want it.

7.8.2 Scripting infrastructure creation

Listing 7.1 shows our first Terraform code file (chapter-7/example-1/resource-group.tf). It doesn't get much simpler than this. Using the Azure provider, we'll create an Azure resource group simply by declaring it in three lines of Terraform code.

Listing 7.1 Creating an Azure resource group

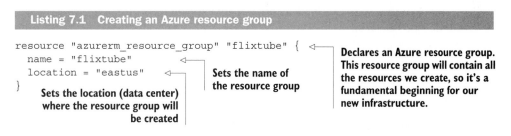

```
resource "azurerm_resource_group" "flixtube" {
  name = "flixtube"
  location = "eastus"
}
```

Declares an Azure resource group. This resource group will contain all the resources we create, so it's a fundamental beginning for our new infrastructure.

Sets the name of the resource group

Sets the location (data center) where the resource group will be created

Through Terraform code, we're defining the components of our infrastructure. In listing 7.1, we've defined the first piece of our infrastructure. We've declared an Azure resource group called `flixtube` with the type `azurerm_resource_group`. This is a Terraform resource type that comes from the Azure provider and gives us the ability to create a resource group on Azure. Soon we'll run Terraform, and it will create this resource group in our Azure account just how we've configured it in listing 7.1.

7.8.3   *Fixing provider version numbers*

Before we initialize our Terraform project, let's talk about that other file in our project. Listing 7.2 shows the code for providers.tf (chapter-7/example-1/providers.tf). This is the file where we define and configure all of our Terraform provider plugins. Here we're only requiring the Azure provider and aren't passing any parameters to the provider, so this file is quite small.

Listing 7.2   Configuring Terraform provider plugins

```
terraform {
  required_providers {            Requires the Azure provider
    azurerm = {
      source = "hashicorp/azurerm"
      version = "~> 3.71.0"         Fixes the version number that is required. We
    }                               can remove this line to make Terraform install
  }                                 the latest version.

  required_version = ">= 1.5.6"     Sets the minimum version of Terraform
}

provider "azurerm" {     Configuration for the Azure
  features {}            provider can be placed here.
}
```

Note that the line of code in listing 7.2 that fixes the Azure provider to version 3.71.0 can be omitted, which causes Terraform to download the latest version. This is a useful way to upgrade to a new version of a provider. Delete the specified version, and Terraform downloads the latest version. Its version number is printed to the output, so we can copy it and then plug it back into providers.tf, thus fixing our project to the new version.

You should always fix the version numbers for our dependencies when that's possible. Not doing so can lead to unexpected problems down the road. If you don't fix your project to a particular version, your project will automatically be upgraded to new versions as they are released. As a result, your Terraform code can break in ways that are often difficult to predict or understand. Therefore, take care to preemptively fix version numbers for dependencies in your projects so that you aren't exposed to the risk of having your dependencies automatically changed beneath you.

7.8.4   *Initializing Terraform*

We've taken the first steps in creating our infrastructure. We wrote a simple script that creates an Azure resource group. But before we invoke Terraform and execute this script, we must first initialize Terraform.

When we initialize Terraform, it downloads the provider plugins required for our script. At this point, we only need the Azure provider. To initialize Terraform, first change directory to the location of the Terraform code:

```
cd chapter-7/example-1
```

Now, run the `terraform init` command:

```
terraform init
```

You should see some output indicating that the Azure provider plugin is downloaded, for example:

```
Initializing the backend...

Initializing provider plugins...
- Finding hashicorp/azurerm versions matching "~> 3.71.0"...
- Installing hashicorp/azurerm v3.71.0...
- Installed hashicorp/azurerm v3.71.0 (signed by HashiCorp)

--snip--

Terraform has been successfully initialized!
```

Once this completes, we're now ready to execute our Terraform code. We must always run the `terraform init` command at least once for each Terraform project before we execute any Terraform code in that directory. We must also run it at least once for each new provider that we use. Each time we invoke `terraform init`, it only downloads those providers that it hasn't yet cached.

Don't worry if you forget to run `terraform init`, it won't cause you any problem. When you forget, Terraform reminds you that you need to do that first.

7.8.5 *By-products of Terraform initialization*

With Terraform initialized, we can now inspect the files that the `init` command has created or downloaded. Have a look through the example-1 directory to see what you can find. You won't normally need to do this, but it can be interesting to understand a little more about how Terraform works. Figure 7.7 shows the example-1 project after running `terraform init`.

Notice that the hidden subdirectory `.terraform` was created and contains a bunch of files. This is where Terraform stores the provider plugins that it has downloaded. These are cached here to be reused each time we invoke Terraform.

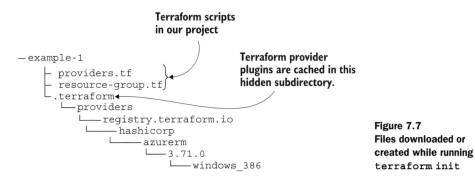

Figure 7.7
Files downloaded or created while running
`terraform init`

7.8.6   *Building your infrastructure*

After initializing our Terraform project, we're ready to invoke `terraform apply`, executing our Terraform code and building the first iteration of our infrastructure. If you need to, refer to figures 7.5 and 7.6 for a graphical depiction of the `apply` command.

From the same directory where you invoked the `init` command, now invoke this command:

```
terraform apply
```

The `apply` command gathers together and executes all the Terraform code files in our project. (So far, we only have two code files, but soon we'll have more.)

You should see output like this:

```
Terraform used the selected providers to generate the following
execution plan. Resource actions are indicated with the
following symbols:
  + create

Terraform will perform the following actions:

  # azurerm_resource_group.flixtube will be created
  + resource "azurerm_resource_group" "flixtube" {
      + id       = (known after apply)
      + location = "eastus"
      + name     = "flixtube"
    }

Plan: 1 to add, 0 to change, 0 to destroy.

Do you want to perform these actions?
  Terraform will perform the actions described above.
  Only 'yes' will be accepted to approve.

  Enter a value:
```

This output describes the planned update to our infrastructure. Terraform is telling us the changes that it's about to make. (If you like, you can do this in two phases: create the plan first with `terraform plan` and then invoke the plan with `apply`.)

Terraform is now waiting for us to approve the plan before it continues and updates our infrastructure. It's a good idea at this point to scan the output and check that the upcoming changes are okay and what we expect. Once happy with the plan, type `yes` and press Enter to allow Terraform to proceed.

Terraform now creates the infrastructure we requested. In this case, on our first invocation of Terraform, the `flixtube` resource group is created in our Azure account. This should happen pretty quickly (because at the moment it's still a small script and doesn't do much). You'll see a success message like this:

```
azurerm_resource_group.flixtube: Creating...
azurerm_resource_group.flixtube: Creation complete after 3s [--snip--]

Apply complete! Resources: 1 added, 0 changed, 0 destroyed.
```

The output gives a quick summary of what was added, changed, and deleted. In this case, it confirms that we've created one cloud resource, our Azure resource group.

Now let's manually check what the change looks like. Open your web browser, and navigate to the Azure portal at https://portal.azure.com/. Check for yourself that an Azure resource group has indeed been created in your Azure account. In the portal, click Resource Groups, and verify that the flixtube resource group is now in the list. This is what running your first Terraform code has just created!

Of course, you don't always need to check that every resource has been created by manually inspecting the Azure portal. Normally, if Terraform succeeds, you can assume that the requested resources were created. We're just doing this in the first instance so that you can connect the dots about what has just happened.

7.8.7 Understanding Terraform state

At this point, after invoking `terraform apply` in our project for the first time, Terraform will have generated its state file terraform.tfstate. You should see this file in the same directory as your Terraform code files.

It's important that we understand Terraform's persistent state management. Most of the time, we won't care what's in the state file, but it's good to know why it's there and how to deal with it.

Let's take a look at our Terraform state file and see what it looks like after we've created our first piece of infrastructure. This is a good time to look at the state file because it's still small and easily understandable. Invoke the `cat` command to display the state file:

```
cat terraform.tfstate
```

In Windows, you can use the `type` command instead:

```
type terraform.tfstate
```

Your output will look something like this:

```
{
  "version": 4,
  "terraform_version": "1.5.6",
  "serial": 1,
  "lineage": "b10f693f-e27f-f223-a8ef-011948c56f9c",
  "outputs": {},
  "resources": [
    {
      "mode": "managed",
      "type": "azurerm_resource_group",
```

```
    "name": "flixtube",
    "provider": "provider[\"registry.terraform.io/hashicorp/azurerm\"]",
    "instances": [
      {
        "schema_version": 0,
        "attributes": {
          "id": "/subscriptions/snip/resourceGroups/flixtube",
          "location": "eastus",
          "managed_by": "",
          "name": "flixtube",
          "tags": null,
          "timeouts": null
        },
        "sensitive_attributes": [],
        "private": "snip"
      }
    ]
  }
],
"check_results": null
}
```

You can see that our Terraform state file has one item in the resources field. The details of the resource group we just created were recorded in this state file.

The first time we invoke terraform apply, the state file is generated. Subsequent invocations of terraform apply will use this state file as input. Terraform loads the state file and then refreshes it from the live infrastructure. Figure 7.8 shows how successive invocations of Terraform are connected by both the live infrastructure and the state file.

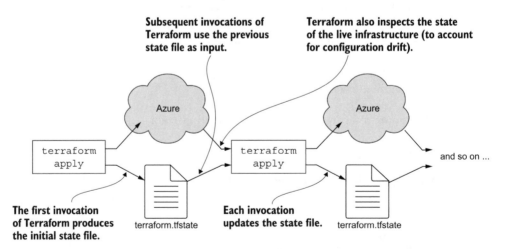

Figure 7.8   Understanding Terraform state is crucial to working with Terraform.

So, what exactly is the point of the state file? If our infrastructure is defined in our Terraform code, and Terraform can know the current state directly from the live infrastructure, why must it persist the state in a separate file? There are two points to consider to understand why the state file is necessary:

- This Terraform project doesn't *own* all the infrastructure in your Azure account.
- As we make changes to our Terraform code (to change our infrastructure), it becomes out of sync with the live infrastructure. (We're relying on Terraform to change the live infrastructure to make it look like our declared infrastructure.)

Let's consider the first point. An Azure subscription may well be shared among multiple projects. Infrastructure in that account might have been created by other Terraform projects or even by entirely different means (e.g., created manually in the Azure portal or with the Azure CLI tool).

As you follow the examples in this book, you might have an entire Azure subscription dedicated to it. But this won't be the case if you're working for a company that is managing multiple projects or if you're managing multiple projects yourself. In that case, an Azure subscription is shared between projects, with the subscription containing multiple sets of infrastructure.

The point I'm making is that Terraform can't and, indeed, doesn't assume that it owns everything in the Azure account that we're allowing it to access and modify. What this means is that Terraform doesn't just read the live infrastructure and assume that it owns everything. It only assumes ownership of infrastructure that is either declared in our infrastructure code or that is recorded in the state file. The first thing that Terraform does is load our code and our state file. That's how it knows the set of infrastructure that it owns.

Terraform always wants to be up to date though, so after loading the state file, it refreshes the state directly from the live infrastructure. This allows Terraform to handle configuration drift when the actual state has changed (e.g., because someone tweaked it manually) from the previously recorded state.

You can hopefully see how this affects performance. Terraform only queries those parts of the live infrastructure for which it's responsible; those parts which it knows about because of the recorded state. If, instead, it queried *all* live infrastructure, that could be an expensive and time-consuming operation, depending on the total amount of infrastructure that exists in our Azure account.

Now, let's consider the second point mentioned. As we change our Terraform code (to change our infrastructure), it becomes out of sync with our live infrastructure. That's because we're leading changes to the infrastructure with changes in the code. That's why we call it *infrastructure as code.*

We can add, update, and delete infrastructure by modifying our code. How does Terraform know what's changed? Terraform compares its recorded state with what's in our code. Terraform then automatically figures out the precise set of changes it needs to update our infrastructure. It's amazing when you think it through, just how smart Terraform is and how much work it can do on our behalf.

Now you know more than you probably wanted to about Terraform state, but it's important that you have a good understanding of Terraform state. As you proceed through the examples in this chapter and the next, feel free to look at the state file again to see how it grows and changes.

7.8.8   *Destroying and recreating our infrastructure*

We've bootstrapped our infrastructure! It's not much yet, but it's a good start. Before we continue evolving our infrastructure, let's take some time out to experiment with destroying and rebuilding it.

The reason we're choosing this moment to experiment is that it's more efficient to do this experimentation while our infrastructure is small. At the end of this chapter, we'll have added a Kubernetes cluster, which will take much more time to destroy and rebuild.

Not to mention that, eventually, you'll need to clean up these Azure resources anyway. You don't want to end up paying for them (unless, of course, you're developing a real product). It costs money to run this infrastructure, but I hope you're starting with the free credit from Azure. Either way, don't leave it running longer than you need it!

Now, go ahead and destroy your current infrastructure with the Terraform `destroy` command like this:

```
terraform destroy
```

Your output will look something like this (abbreviated):

```
Terraform used the selected providers to generate the following
execution plan. Resource actions are indicated with the
following symbols:
  - destroy

Terraform will perform the following actions:

  # azurerm_resource_group.flixtube will be destroyed
  - resource "azurerm_resource_group" "flixtube" {
      - id       = "/subscriptions/snip/resourceGroups/flixtube" -> null
      - location = "eastus" -> null
      - name     = "flixtube" -> null
      - tags     = {} -> null
    }

Plan: 0 to add, 0 to change, 1 to destroy.

Do you really want to destroy all resources?
  Terraform will destroy all your managed infrastructure, as shown above.
  There is no undo. Only 'yes' will be accepted to confirm.

  Enter a value:
```

Just like the `apply` command, `destroy` shows us its plan. These are the changes it will make. To continue, we type `yes` and press Enter. Terraform then does the work and displays a summary:

```
azurerm_resource_group.flixtube: Destroying... --snip--
azurerm_resource_group.flixtube: Still destroying... —snip--
--snip--
azurerm_resource_group.flixtube: Destruction complete after 1m23s

Destroy complete! Resources: 1 destroyed.
```

As you finish with each example in this chapter, you should invoke `destroy` to clean up the infrastructure that you created. However, if you're doing your own iterative prototyping, you don't need a `destroy` before doing each new `apply`. Instead, just make the changes to your Terraform code, and then invoke `terraform apply` again. You can do this repeatedly as you feel your way through the creation of your infrastructure.

You could also clean up by manually deleting Azure resources through the Azure portal or the Azure CLI tool. But it's easier to do this with the `destroy` command because you don't have to think about it. It also means you won't accidentally delete other infrastructure, say, if you're sharing the Azure subscription with other projects.

After a practice run with `terraform destroy`, it's simple to recreate the infrastructure by invoking `terraform apply` again:

```
terraform apply
```

Practice this as many times as you want. This process of destroying and rebuilding your infrastructure helps you comprehend the fact that you're actually managing infrastructure with executable code! You can destroy and create your infrastructure at will with no manual effort. At this early stage, it might not seem like much, but the significance of this increases as your infrastructure and application grow larger and more complex.

In fact, you may have already realized that we can use our Terraform code to create multiple copies of our infrastructure! In chapter 12, you'll learn how to parameterize your Terraform code to create separate instances for development, testing, and production. If that doesn't excite you, I don't know what will.

7.8.9   *What have we achieved?*

We now have Terraform installed and we've coded a fledgling infrastructure. Terraform is the tool we use for infrastructure as code. This is the technique where we store our infrastructure configuration as executable code (e.g., in Terraform code files) that we can use to create, manage, and destroy our infrastructure.

We created our first Terraform code files and initialized our project using `terraform init`. Then we invoked `terraform apply` running the code to create an Azure resource group. Finally, you learned how to destroy and recreate the infrastructure using `terraform destroy` followed by `terraform apply`.

7.9   *Creating our container registry*

The next step for our infrastructure is to create a private container registry, which we need to publish our Docker images before we deploy our microservices. If you remember, back in chapter 3, you learned how to build and publish Docker images. In that chapter, we manually created a container registry through the GUI in the Azure portal. Now that you have a basic understanding of Terraform, we'll revisit that territory and create our container registry with code.

7.9.1   *Continuing the evolution of our infrastructure*

We're now moving to example-2 in the chapter-7 code repository, which continues on from example-1. You can move directly to the example-2 project and run `terraform init` to get started:

```
cd chapter-7/example-2
terraform init
```

When moving to the second example, don't forget to first destroy any infrastructure you created for the first example.

7.9.2   *Creating the container registry*

Listing 7.3 shows the newest Terraform code file that creates our container registry (extract from chapter-7/example-2/container-registry.tf). To run this code for yourself, you must first change the name of the registry. That's because Azure container registry names must be unique. It won't let you use a name that has already been used (e.g., flixtube).

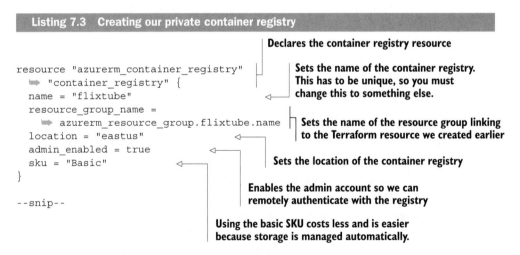

Listing 7.3   Creating our private container registry

```
resource "azurerm_container_registry"
    ➥ "container_registry" {
    name = "flixtube"
    resource_group_name =
        ➥ azurerm_resource_group.flixtube.name
    location = "eastus"
    admin_enabled = true
    sku = "Basic"
}

--snip--
```

Declares the container registry resource

Sets the name of the container registry. This has to be unique, so you must change this to something else.

Sets the name of the resource group linking to the Terraform resource we created earlier

Sets the location of the container registry

Enables the admin account so we can remotely authenticate with the registry

Using the basic SKU costs less and is easier because storage is managed automatically.

NOTE   In case you were wondering, a SKU (stock keeping unit) is a different version of a product. It's a weird name, I know. What this means here is that we're using the Basic version of the container registry.

Take note of how the value of `resource_group_name` is set from the properties of a resource that is defined in another file (the file resource-group.tf that we looked at in figure 6.1). These two resources are now linked via the Terraform *resource graph*. This is how Terraform manages the dependencies between resources and knows the order in which it should execute our script files. This link is how Terraform knows it must create the resource group before it creates the container registry.

Let's invoke the `apply` command to create our updated infrastructure:

```
terraform apply -auto-approve
```

Note that we use the `-auto-approve` argument this time. That means we don't have to type `yes` each time to approve the changes. This is convenient while we're prototyping our infrastructure, but it becomes essential later if we want to run this code in an automated deployment pipeline.

At that point, we'll need to invoke Terraform in an automated and unattended manner. There will be no person there to do the approval! Because of this, we'll now start using `-auto-approve` to run Terraform in *noninteractive* mode.

As we start to create more complex infrastructure now, we might have to wait a bit longer than last time. Once it's finished, we'll see output similar to before; Terraform is showing us what's changed in our infrastructure.

7.9.3   *Terraform outputs*

Tacked on the end of the output, you can see values displayed from Terraform outputs. These give us the details of our new container registry:

```
Outputs:

registry_hostname = "flixtube.azurecr.io"
registry_pw = <sensitive>
registry_un = "flixtube"
```

Terraform (or the underlying plugin providers) often produces configuration information that we'd like to know. We can use Terraform outputs to extract generated configuration details from our Terraform code. In listing 7.4 (extract from chapter-7/example-2/container-registry.tf), you can see outputs declared to output the URL, username, and password for our new container registry. This causes Terraform to display these values in the terminal. Output like this can be useful to debug Terraform code and understand the details of the infrastructure it has created on our behalf.

Listing 7.4   Terraform outputs

```
--snip--

output "registry_hostname" {          ⟵——— Creates an output
  value = azurerm_container_registry          | Sets the values
    ⇛ .container_registry.login_server        | to be output
```

```
}
output "registry_un" {                    ◄──────┐  Creates an output
  value = azurerm_container_registry               │  Sets the values
    ➥ .container_registry.admin_username           │  to be output
}
                                          ◄──────┐  Creates an output
output "registry_pw" {
  value = azurerm_container_registry
    ➥ .container_registry.admin_password   ◄───── Sets the values to be output
  sensitive = true                     ◄─────┐
}                                            │  Terraform will refuse to run this code unless we acknowledge
                                             │  that the container registry password is a sensitive value.
```

7.9.4   *Outputting sensitive values from Terraform*

You may have noted in the output from the previous section that the container registry's password was redacted. Instead of the actual value for the password, Terraform has replaced it with <sensitive>.

This password isn't displayed because it's a sensitive value. In fact, in listing 7.4, we added the line sensitive = true. Without it, Terraform refuses to run this code (feel free to remove it and try running the code). Terraform forces us to acknowledge that this value is sensitive so that we understand that we might not actually want to output it from our code.

So, what's the point of outputting this password if it's redacted and we can't even see it? Well, we can retrieve the redacted value, we just have to ask for it by name through Terraform:

```
terraform output -raw registry_pw
```

If you do this, you'll see the actual value of the password displayed in the terminal. You do need to know this password soon (along with the URL and username) to log in to the container registry with Docker to publish your images to it.

But why are sensitive values redacted in the first place? Terraform is designed to run in an automated deployment pipeline, which means the pipeline records all the output to the terminal so that we can browse it after the fact. We need this recorded information because it's the only way to know what has happened in past deployments that were fully automated. It wouldn't be good for the security of our deployment process to store that password in plain text output where potentially anyone in the company might be able to see it. Terraform understands that values like this are sensitive, so it makes us (the Terraform coders) acknowledge that they are sensitive, and it then redacts these sensitive values from its output in the terminal so they can't be recorded by our deployment pipeline.

But wait—doesn't the fact that we've requested this sensitive output and been able to retrieve it mean that the sensitive value is actually stored somewhere locally? Yes, it does! In fact, if you simply invoke cat terraform.tfstate to show the contents of the Terraform state file (try it yourself), you'll see the password right there in plain text!

Okay, so any good continuous deployment pipeline should nuke this local state when it has finished running, but still, this doesn't feel great leaving a plain-text password in the filesystem where who knows who might later be able to see it.

7.9.5 *Just don't output sensitive values*

Of course, the answer to the problem of outputting sensitive values is, just don't output them. It's as simple as that. I've included the container registry password in example-2 just so that we could talk about it and the problems it presents. Feel free to use sensitive values in outputs when you're learning Terraform and experimenting with it. However, it's best if we don't use these in real production code where security is important, and you'll see if you look in container-registry.tf in example-3 that I've removed the output for `password`. In fact, I've removed all the outputs. Terraform outputs are useful for debugging, but we don't need them to get the details of the cloud resources we're creating. In the next section, we'll see a better way to retrieve the details of our container registry.

7.9.6 *Getting the details of your container registry*

We've established that we prefer not to output sensitive values, which is good because we don't actually have to output anything. Instead, we can easily retrieve the details of our container registry using the Azure CLI tool without having to store sensitive details locally.

Invoke these two commands:

```
az acr show --name flixtube --output table
az acr credential show --name flixtube --output table
```

The first command shows general details for the container registry. The second shows the password for the registry. Note that we've added the option `--output table` for more readable output; without that, these commands display JSON-formatted output.

Don't forget to use the name for your own container registry. Here is the general format:

```
az acr show --name <your-container-registry-name> --output table
az acr credential show --name <your-container-registry-name> --output table
```

Invoking these commands shows you the details (URL, name, and password) that you need to interact with your container registry using the Docker command. You can also find this information by looking up the page for your container registry in the Azure portal.

7.9.7 *What have we achieved?*

We've continued to evolve our infrastructure by adding a container registry. This is what we need to publish Docker images for our microservices.

In this section, we added a new Terraform code file and executed it, creating the new container registry in our Azure account. You learned about Terraform outputs for debugging our Terraform code and that we probably shouldn't output sensitive values.

7.10 *Refactoring to share configuration data*

You might have noticed in recent code listings that we're starting to repeat certain configuration values from file to file. This can be a problem when it comes to changing these values. Ideally, we'd like to be able to change important values in one place and have these shared between all of our Terraform code files. We can achieve this with *Terraform variables*, so now we'll refactor our code to use variables and share configuration data.

7.10.1 *Continuing the evolution of our infrastructure*

We now move to example-3 in the chapter-7 code repository. If you like, jump directly to example-3, and invoke `terraform init`. If you do this, don't forget to first destroy any infrastructure you created for earlier examples.

7.10.2 *Introducing Terraform variables*

Example-3 in the chapter-7 code repository is a refactoring of example-2, modified to share configuration values between code files and adding a new file called variables.tf. Listing 7.5 (chapter-7/example-3/variables.tf) shows the new code file.

In the listing, you can see how Terraform variables are defined for some of our most important configuration values. We have variables defined for the name of our application (`flixtube`), the location of our data center (`eastus`), and similar.

Listing 7.5   Setting Terraform variables

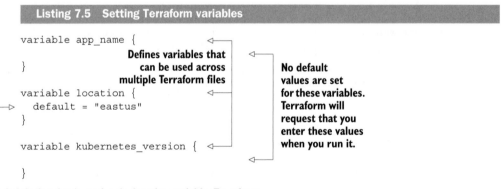

```
variable app_name {         ◄──┐
                    Defines variables that   ◄──┐
        }           can be used across          │    No default
                    multiple Terraform files    │    values are set
variable location {         ◄──┘                │    for these variables.
┌─▷   default = "eastus"                        │    Terraform will
│                                               │    request that you
│       }                                       │    enter these values
│                                               │    when you run it.
│  variable kubernetes_version {  ◄──┘          │
│                                               ◄──┘
│       }
```

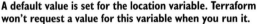
A default value is set for the location variable. Terraform won't request a value for this variable when you run it.

Note that the variables `app_name` and `kubernetes_version` in listing 7.5 don't have default values set. When you run this code in Terraform, it will request that you enter values for these variables that don't have defaults.

Listings 7.6 (chapter-7/example-3/resource-group.tf) and 7.7 (chapter-7/example-3/container-registry.tf) show how we use our new variables. You can see that the name of our resource group and the name of our container registry are both set from the value of the `app_name` variable. We can also set the locations of these resources from the `location` variable.

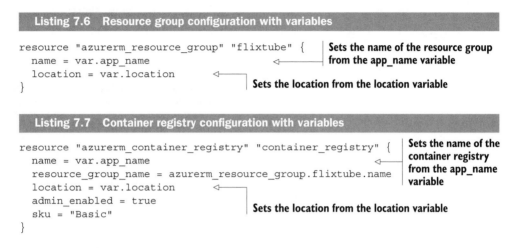

Listing 7.6   Resource group configuration with variables

```
resource "azurerm_resource_group" "flixtube" {          Sets the name of the resource group
  name = var.app_name                                    from the app_name variable
  location = var.location
}                                            Sets the location from the location variable
```

Listing 7.7   Container registry configuration with variables

```
resource "azurerm_container_registry" "container_registry" {   Sets the name of the
  name = var.app_name                                          container registry
  resource_group_name = azurerm_resource_group.flixtube.name   from the app_name
  location = var.location                                      variable
  admin_enabled = true
  sku = "Basic"                               Sets the location from the location variable
}
```

We've refactored our Terraform code and shared some pertinent configuration values between our code files using Terraform variables. We now have one convenient place to go to change these values. For example, let's say that we want to change the location of our application. We can do this simply by changing the `location` variable in variables.tf.

7.11 *Creating our Kubernetes cluster*

Now we arrive at our most vital piece of infrastructure: a platform on which to host our microservices in production. For this, we'll use Terraform to create a Kubernetes cluster in our Azure account.

7.11.1 *Scripting creation of your cluster*

Continuing with example-3, now let's look at the code to create our Kubernetes cluster. Listing 7.8 (extract from chapter-7/example-3/kubernetes-cluster.tf) is an extract from a new Terraform code file, kubernetes-cluster.tf, that defines the configuration of our cluster.

We're making continued use of our Terraform variables here, and some of these fields will already be familiar to you. Fields such as `name`, `location`, and `resource_group_name` require no new explanation. However, there are other fields here that will be completely new.

Listing 7.8   Creating our Kubernetes cluster

```
resource "azurerm_kubernetes_cluster" "cluster" {     Declares the resource for
  name = var.app_name                                 our Kubernetes cluster
  location = var.location
  resource_group_name = azurerm_resource_group.flixtube.name
```

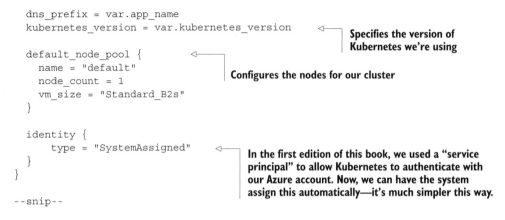

```
    dns_prefix = var.app_name
    kubernetes_version = var.kubernetes_version          ◁──┐  Specifies the version of
                                                            │  Kubernetes we're using
    default_node_pool {              ◁──┐
      name = "default"                   │  Configures the nodes for our cluster
      node_count = 1
      vm_size = "Standard_B2s"
    }

    identity {
        type = "SystemAssigned"      ◁──┐
    }                                    │  In the first edition of this book, we used a "service
}                                        │  principal" to allow Kubernetes to authenticate with
--snip--                                 │  our Azure account. Now, we can have the system
                                         │  assign this automatically—it's much simpler this way.
```

Listing 7.8 is where we define the nodes and VM size that powers our cluster. Note that we're building our cluster on only a single node. Although we could easily add more, we'll save that for chapter 12.

7.11.2 *Attaching the registry to the cluster*

We're almost ready to create our Kubernetes cluster. There's just one more thing to understand. Just like in chapter 6, we must "attach" our container registry to our cluster so that our cluster is pre-authenticated to pull images from it. In chapter 6, we did that by invoking an Azure CLI command; in this chapter, we'll do the same but through Terraform.

Listing 7.9 (extract from chapter-7/example-3/kubernetes-cluster.tf) shows how we create a *role assignment* that gives our cluster permission to pull images from the container registry.

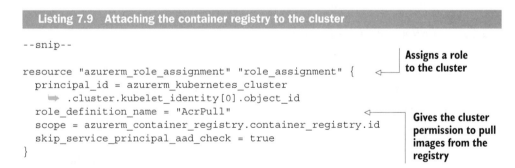

Listing 7.9   Attaching the container registry to the cluster

```
--snip--
                                                             ┌  Assigns a role
                                                             │  to the cluster
resource "azurerm_role_assignment" "role_assignment" {   ◁──┘
  principal_id = azurerm_kubernetes_cluster
    ⟹ .cluster.kubelet_identity[0].object_id
  role_definition_name = "AcrPull"                         ◁──┐  Gives the cluster
  scope = azurerm_container_registry.container_registry.id     │  permission to pull
  skip_service_principal_aad_check = true                      │  images from the
}                                                              │  registry
```

7.11.3 *Building our cluster*

We're now ready to run our latest Terraform code to create our Kubernetes cluster. Invoke the apply command:

```
terraform apply -auto-approve
```

At this point, Terraform prompts us to enter the variables that don't have default values. We must now enter values for `app_name` and `kubernetes_version` because we didn't specify default values for these in variables.tf:

```
var.app_name
  Enter a value: flixtube

var.kubernetes_version
  Enter a value: 1.24.6
```

The value I choose for `app_name` is `flixtube`, but you can't use that. Because the name of the container registry is derived from `app_name` and must be unique, you'll have to choose a new unique name for your app. Use whatever name you like, as long as it isn't taken already. (I was going to suggest a humorous name for you to use, but then I realized whatever name I suggest will already be taken by the time you read this.)

It's interesting to note that by parameterizing our code by `app_name`, we now have the ability to deploy multiple parallel versions of infrastructure just using different names. For example, you could deploy separate instances with names `flixtube-prod` and `flixtube-test` to separate your production and testing environments. We'll talk more about this in chapter 12.

The value for `kubernetes_version` is the value you noted earlier in section 7.6. If you don't have that, you'll need to return to that section for instructions on how to choose an available version of Kubernetes.

Terraform now creates your Kubernetes cluster. This can take some time, so you might like to grab a cup of coffee. When it completes, your Kubernetes cluster will be ready to use.

NOTE If you're trying to use the Kubernetes version number I've used (1.27.3) and that isn't working, it's probably because that version is no longer available on Azure. See section 7.6 for instructions on how to choose an available version.

7.11.4 *What have we achieved?*

Well done! We created a Kubernetes cluster through Terraform code. If you had previously been convinced that creating a Kubernetes cluster is very complicated, you might be surprised at just how much simpler it is than you thought! (Or is it just that I think it's simple because I have done it so many times?)

This is a significant achievement on the road to production. We evolved our infrastructure code, step by step, and finally added a Kubernetes cluster. Along the way, we did some refactoring and used Terraform variables to share important values between our various Terraform code files.

7.12   *Deploying to our cluster*

Now that we have a Kubernetes cluster, we should try deploying a microservice to it and make sure that everything is in working order. To test our new cluster, we'll deploy the microservice from the example-4 subdirectory in the chapter-7 code repository. There's nothing new in this example; it's the same as example-2 from chapter-6. We'll deploy it again now to test the cluster we created using Terraform.

Just like in chapter 6, we'll start by ensuring that Kubectl is connected to our new cluster:

```
az aks get-credentials --resource-group <resource-group> --name <cluster>
```

Be sure to plug in the details of your resource group and your cluster name. These are simply derived from the app_name variable whose value you entered in the previous section. So, if your app_name was flixtube, the command looks like this:

```
az aks get-credentials --resource-group flixtube --name flixtube
```

Now, in the example-4 project from chapter-7, build the Docker image:

```
cd chapter-7/example-4
docker build -t video-streaming:1 --file Dockerfile-prod
```

At this point, we must know the details of our container registry. Refer to section 7.9.6 to look up those details. Now tag the image with the URL of your container registry:

```
docker tag video-streaming:1 <registry-url>/video-streaming:1
```

Now we can log in to our container registry:

```
docker login <registry-url>
```

After logging in, we can publish the image for our microservice to the registry:

```
docker push <registry-url>/video-streaming:1
```

(This part can take some time, so this is another good time to make your favorite hot beverage.)

Before doing the test deployment, you must update deploy.yaml so that it points to the correct container registry. Enter the URL for your container register at the correct location in the file:

```
spec:
  containers:
  - name: video-streaming                              Use the name of your
    image: <registry-url>/video-streaming:1            container registry here
    imagePullPolicy: IfNotPresent        ◁────────────  in deploy.yaml.
    env:
    - name: PORT
      value: "4000"
```

With the image published and after updating deploy.yaml to point to the correct registry, we can now deploy the microservice to our Kubernetes cluster:

```
kubectl apply -f scripts/deploy.yaml
```

Afterward, we can check that our deployment was successful:

```
kubectl get pods
kubectl get deployments
kubectl get services
```

From the output of `kubectl get services`, we can pull the `EXTERNAL-IP` value and use that to test the web page served by our video-streaming microservice. Be sure to view the `video` route of the web page, or you won't see anything. When finished testing, we can delete the deployment and clean up our cluster:

```
kubectl delete -f scripts/deploy.yaml
```

We've moved very quickly through testing our cluster. For more details on using Docker to build and publish images, refer to chapter 3. For more on deploying to Kubernetes, refer to chapter 6.

7.13 Destroying our infrastructure

Unless you're really building a production application, there's no need to leave your infrastructure running. Ultimately, it will exhaust your free credits on Azure and will start costing real money. So, when you're finished experimenting with Terraform and Kubernetes, destroy your infrastructure with this command:

```
terraform destroy
```

Don't be afraid to destroy your infrastructure. Because our infrastructure is created through code, we can easily destroy it and create it again as many times as we like. Of course, if we have people (customers or team members) depending on our infrastructure, we can't just destroy it while they are using it! But in chapter 12, we'll talk about ways to minimize the risk of upgrading or replacing our infrastructure while people are using it.

7.14 Terraform review

It seems like we're getting through big chapter after big chapter! Remember that you can come back to any of these chapters at any time to practice what you've learned.

To review, Terraform is a universal tool for the creation and configuration of cloud-based infrastructures. We've used it to create the entire infrastructure for our microservices application. Before continuing, let's review the Terraform commands we've added to our toolkit in table 7.2.

Table 7.2 Review of Terraform commands

Command	Description
`terraform init`	Initializes a Terraform project and downloads the provider plugins
`terraform apply -auto-approve`	Executes Terraform code files in the working directory to incrementally apply changes to our infrastructure
`terraform destroy`	Destroys all infrastructure that was created by the Terraform project

7.15 *Continue your learning*

In this chapter, we used Terraform and the technique called *infrastructure as code* to create a production environment based on Kubernetes. But there's much to learn on infrastructure as code and Terraform, so here are some books that will be useful if you'd like to dive deeper:

- *Terraform in Action* by Scott Winkler (Manning, 2021)
- *Terraform in Depth* by Robert Hafner (Manning, est. Spring 2024)
- *Infrastructure as Code, Patterns and Practices* by Rosemary Wang (Manning, 2022)

In addition, the best resources are the Terraform docs. I recommend you start at their website and click through to the tutorials and documentation. As an exercise, try to find and learn more about the Terraform resources we've used in this chapter at www.terraform.io/.

Summary

- Infrastructure as code is a technique where we store our infrastructure configuration as code. Editing and executing that code is how we update our infrastructure.
- Terraform is a tool and language for scripting the creation of cloud resources and application infrastructure through code.
- Writing code that creates infrastructure isn't that much different from writing any code that we eventually want running in production, except that, even though we can run Terraform code on our local development computer, the results always appear in the cloud. The resources that are created by running Terraform code are always created in the cloud.
- Terraform allows building out our infrastructure little by little in an iterative fashion, something we call *evolutionary architecture.*
- Terraform is powered by provider plugins, which means it can be used to create infrastructure on all the major cloud platforms: AWS, GCP, Azure, and more.
- Terraform must be initialized before it can be used, and we should fix our provider version numbers to avoid nasty surprises.
- A Terraform project is initialized with `terraform init`.

- A Terraform project is executed with `terraform apply`, which runs the code and creates the resources in the cloud.
- Cloud resources created by a Terraform project can be destroyed with `terraform destroy`.
- Terraform state maintains a record of the system we created and makes future modifications to the system more efficient.
- Terraform outputs can be useful to get output from Terraform for debugging and understanding what our code is doing, but for production code, we shouldn't output sensitive values from Terraform.
- Terraform variables are useful for sharing configuration and data through a Terraform project.

Continuous deployment

This chapter covers

- Using GitHub Actions to create automated workflows
- Creating a CI pipeline to run automated tests for a microservice
- Creating an automated deployment pipeline to deploy a microservice to Kubernetes

In this chapter, we'll reap the benefits of the work we've done in the previous two chapters. In chapters 6 and 7, you learned how to create infrastructure using code and how to manually deploy our microservices to that infrastructure.

In this chapter, you'll learn how to put your deployments on automatic. Importantly, you'll learn how to build an automated, continuous deployment pipeline for a microservice using GitHub Actions. This kind of automation will prove to be a vital part of your success with microservices. To keep things simple, we'll focus on deploying a single microservice, but that will give us a recipe that we can apply to all of our microservices moving forward.

We're in very advanced waters now and you might find this quite difficult. It's not that it's that difficult to build an automated workflow; I'm sure you'll find the basics quite easy in the first and second examples of this chapter. But the third example relies on everything that you learned in chapters 3 and 6. If you aren't yet confident using Docker and kubectl, that will make completing this chapter more difficult.

If you're happy tinkering with your microservices using manual deployments, feel free to skip this chapter and come back to it later. After all, you really need to feel the pain and tedium of manual deployments before you can truly appreciate how amazing it is to have a fully automated deployment system.

Again, practice and experimentation are the key to making the most of your learning here. By the end of this chapter, with some work on your part, you'll be able to trigger the deployment of your microservices simply by pushing your code to GitHub.

8.1   New tool

This chapter introduces GitHub Actions (see table 8.1), a service on top of GitHub that runs automated workflows in response to actions on our code repository. In this chapter, we'll use GitHub Actions to automatically test and deploy our code whenever we push updated code to the main branch of our code repository.

Table 8.1   New tool in chapter 8

Tool	Version	Purpose
GitHub Actions	N/A	GitHub Actions is a cloud-based service for running automated workflows triggered by certain events, such as pushing code to a GitHub code repository.

8.2   Getting the code

The example code for this chapter is structured differently from the code for the rest of the book. The examples from previous chapters were located side by side in a single code repository for each chapter. In this chapter, however, each example is contained in its own separate code repository. The reason for this is to make it easy for you to fork the code repository and try out GitHub Actions for yourself for each example. If forking a code repository is new for you, don't worry; instructions are coming up soon.

There are three example projects presented in this chapter with the first one starting here: http://mng.bz/RmWv. You can easily find each example by replacing *example-1* with the next number sequentially, such as *example-2* and then *example-3*.

For help with installing and using Git to clone a code repository, see chapter 2. If you have problems with the code, log an issue against the relevant code repository in GitHub.

8.3   Running the examples in this chapter

Running the code for the example projects in this chapter is pretty different from every other chapter. For each chapter so far, we've run the code on our personal development computers. However, when we run automated deployment pipelines, like the examples in this chapter, our code will run in the cloud.

To try out GitHub Actions for yourself, you must fork each of the example code repositories that accompany this chapter. *Forking* essentially means to take your own copy of the code. There's no need to do that all at once, though; you can just fork each code repository as you work through this chapter. At this stage, though, you should try to practice forking the code repository for the first example, just to be sure you know how to do that.

First thing, you must sign up for a GitHub account, if you don't have one already, at https://github.com/. Once logged in to your own GitHub account, you can click the Fork button for the example-1 code repository, as indicated in figure 8.1.

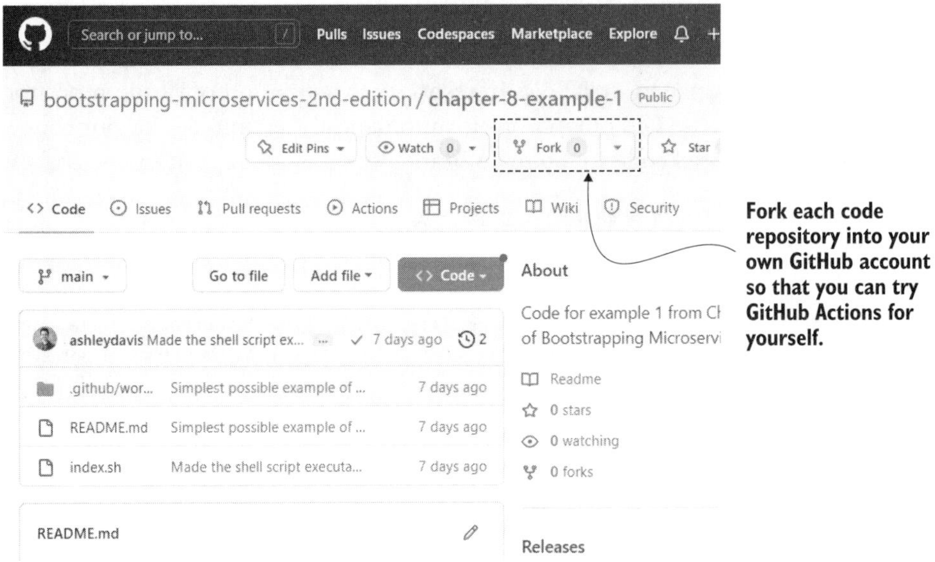

Figure 8.1   Forking the example code repository. You need to do this so you can try out GitHub Actions for yourself.

Follow the instructions presented there, and it makes a copy of the code repository in your own GitHub account. You own the forked copy of the repository and therefore can make whatever changes you like to it. Most importantly, you can now push code changes to your version of the repository to trigger the GitHub Actions workflow that is included in the code repository. What that means and how you can make use of it will be explained soon. Before you can trigger a workflow, you must enable workflows for your forked repository. Go to the Actions tab for your repository, and then click the button to enable workflows, as shown in figure 8.2.

When you clone a local copy of the code examples for this chapter, be sure to clone your own fork of the code repository like this, adding your GitHub account name to the following command:

```
git clone git@github.com:<your-name>/chapter-8-example-1.git
```

Workflows aren't being run on this forked repository

Because this repository contained workflow files when it was forked, we have disabled them from running on this fork. Make sure you understand the configured workflows and their expected usage before enabling Actions on this repository.

View the workflows directory

Figure 8.2 After forking the repository, go to the Actions tab, and click to enable workflows for the repository.

8.4 *What is continuous integration?*

Before learning about continuous deployment (CD), let's first learn about continuous integration (CI). In many respects, CI is a stepping stone to CD, and usually setting up a CI pipeline is simpler than setting up a CD pipeline because CD pipelines have basically grown out of CI pipelines. Indeed, a CD pipeline is often the same as a CI pipeline, but with the additional feature that it also does deployment. So, in the spirit of learning through simple and incremental steps, we'll first cover how to create a GitHub Actions workflow for continuous integration.

But what exactly is a CI pipeline? A CI pipeline is an automated process that detects changes in our codebase and runs various checks and balances against the code to make sure that it still functions. Often, a CI pipeline includes building the code and running a linter against it, but usually the most important purpose of most CI pipelines is to run automated tests against our code. You'll learn how to create some automated tests in chapter 9, but in this chapter, you'll see how to have the automated tests be automatically invoked whenever you push code changes to GitHub.

CI pipelines have traditionally been most useful when we have a team of developers contributing to a codebase. In fact, they are called continuous *integration* pipelines because they are designed to test the *integrated* code being merged in from multiple developers. It can be very difficult to keep code working in the midst of constant changes from a busy development team. But a CI pipeline can automatically detect problems the moment they are created. In this sense, we can think of a CI pipeline as an early warning system for problems in our codebase.

Figure 8.3 shows the process. We have multiple developers each committing code to their local code repositories. At some point, they merge changes with their fellow developers and then push the merged code to the code repository hosted on GitHub. The code push (or, in other cases, a *pull request*) triggers the CI pipeline that we've implemented as a workflow in GitHub Actions. Usually, our CI pipeline runs various checks and automated tests against our code. If all tests pass, this particular run of the

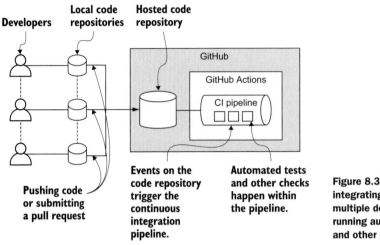

Developers **Local code repositories** **Hosted code repository**

GitHub

GitHub Actions

CI pipeline

Pushing code or submitting a pull request

Events on the code repository trigger the continuous integration pipeline.

Automated tests and other checks happen within the pipeline.

Figure 8.3   A CI pipeline integrating code from multiple developers and running automated tests and other validations

workflow is marked successful. If anything fails, it's instead marked as failed, and typically an email is sent to the team to let them know that something was broken.

8.5   What is continuous deployment?

Now that we've learned what CI is, we can move on to continuous deployment (CD). CD is a technique where we do frequent automated deployments of our code to a production (or testing) environment. Essentially, making updates to our code automatically triggers new deployments of our software. A CD pipeline builds on a CI pipeline: it's very similar but adds extra steps to deploy our code to production.

To automate our deployments, we must write deployment code that can be invoked automatically and run in an unattended fashion in the cloud. The deployment code that we write must be as bulletproof as possible, and we must do thorough testing to confirm that it's reliable. We'd prefer that our deployment code doesn't fail. When it fails in production, it's going to be more difficult to debug because it's running in the cloud rather than on our local machine. So, the code we write for deployment should be simple, have minimal moving parts, and be very well tested.

Like any other code, we'll test our deployment code on our local development computer before we try to run it in production. So, a part of this chapter consists of creating and testing our deployment pipeline locally, even though the ultimate goal is to have all this code running automatically on *some other computer in the cloud* under GitHub Actions.

Figure 8.4 shows a CD pipeline. Similar to figure 8.3 earlier, it shows multiple developers integrating their code into a code repository on GitHub. Their changes to the codebase trigger the CD pipeline implemented in GitHub Actions. The CD pipeline does much of the same work as the CI pipeline in figure 8.3. It runs checks and tests against the code. The addition in figure 8.4 is that our CD pipeline also deploys our microservice to our Kubernetes cluster. What this means is that any changes to the

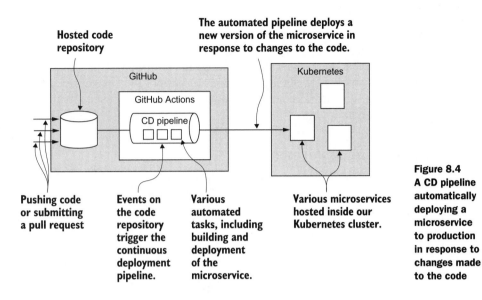

Figure 8.4
A CD pipeline automatically deploying a microservice to production in response to changes made to the code

code for our microservice triggers its deployment to production. This assumes, of course, that building and testing the microservice succeeds. If a developer introduces a change that breaks the build or fails the automated tests, the CD pipeline will be aborted and marked as failed, the deployment won't happen, and the team will be emailed the details of the failure.

Although building a real CD pipeline can be very challenging, just understanding the concept and implementing the basics aren't so difficult. Building a CD pipeline isn't much more difficult than writing a shell script, a point that I'm sure to belabor throughout this chapter.

I like to explain CD as automatically running a shell script in the cloud. I know that's an absurd reduction, but hopefully it helps to get the point across. And often, writing a reliable shell script is the hardest part of creating a CD pipeline. Implementing your CD pipeline as a shell script also has the very positive side effect that it makes testing much easier on your local computer. Testing locally is something we must do, and using a shell script is a very practical way to achieve that.

For the examples in this chapter, we'll create various shell scripts that invoke Docker to build and publish our microservices, as well as kubectl to deploy our microservices to Kubernetes.

Continuous delivery vs. continuous deployment

The terms *continuous delivery* and *continuous deployment* have both been used in our industry. These terms sound similar and are very similar in their meaning. It can be quite confusing because they both abbreviate to CD and are very close in meaning, making it difficult to remember which is which (even for me). Hopefully this makes it simple:

- Continuous delivery means we're always ready to deploy our software to production, but deployment can be automated or manual.
- Continuous deployment means that every change we make to our software is automatically *deployed* to production (assuming it passes tests and other checkpoints).

8.6 *Why automate deployment?*

Maybe we should address the elephant in the room. Why should we even bother automating our deployments in the first place? Automated deployment provides numerous benefits:

- Manual deployments are tedious and take time. We risk mistakes every time we do them. Seriously, don't you want to automate them to minimize time spent and risk taken?
- Automated deployment creates a pipeline for delivering product features to our customers, allowing us to make changes quickly and get fast feedback. I believe that automated deployment should be feature number 1 for any new product because that's how we get the product in front of our customers (of course, this all depends on what you're building).
- When deployment is automatic, reliable, and responsive, it starts to feel like a kind of magic that just fades into the background. This means we can focus on the important work of delivering useful features to customers and not get distracted by a complicated, tedious, or error-prone deployment process.
- The recorded history of our deployments forms a kind of audit trail for our product, showing what was changed, why it was changed, and who triggered the deployment.

Okay, that's enough with the benefits. Let's talk about the necessity of automated deployment. Quite simply, if you can't afford to automate your deployments, you probably can't afford to use microservices. As you build out a microservices application and scale it up, as the number of microservices increases, you'll find yourself overwhelmed with the increased workflow of manual deployment. Success with microservices ultimately hinges on having robust, automated deployment pipelines for them.

I sometimes wonder if this is the reason for much of the fear around microservices. Is it because of the bad experience people have when they don't successfully automate deployment of their microservices? Or maybe their automated deployment pipelines are badly implemented and constantly breaking down (for whatever reason). I believe success in automated deployment can either make or break our experience with microservices. That's how important this is.

Fortunately, automated deployment isn't that difficult (relatively speaking). If you're already confident with Docker and Kubernetes, then you should have few problems implementing a reliable deployment pipeline. This is one of the major advantages of using Docker and Kubernetes in the first place: these technologies were designed for automated deployments.

8.7   An introduction to automation with GitHub Actions

Let's start with a simple introduction to creating an automated workflow with GitHub Actions. If you already know GitHub Actions, you might want to skip this section and move directly to section 8.8.

8.7.1   Why GitHub Actions?

Using GitHub Actions is one good way to create automated workflows that are triggered in response to events around our code, such as pushing our code or submitting a pull request. But there are actually many good services that can do this. Bitbucket and GitLab have similar services for their hosted code repositories. Then, there are dedicated services for automation, such as Travis CI and CircleCI.

Most of these services are configured using YAML (similar to what you'll see soon for GitHub Actions), and mostly they just amount to running commands for us automatically in response to some event. All of these services are pretty similar, so if you learn one, you won't find it difficult to learn any of the others.

GitHub Actions is kind of special, but only because it accompanies GitHub, which as you know is the most popular and most mainstream version control provider and has practically taken over the software industry. (There are alternatives to Git and GitHub, but you practically wouldn't know that if you had just entered the industry recently.)

GitHub Actions integrates with GitHub almost seamlessly, allowing our code and our automated pipelines to live side by side. This makes it trivial to trigger our automated workflows from events on the code repository. It also gives the workflow easy access to the content of the code repository.

GitHub Actions is very good, very mature, and quite extensible (by adding custom actions). I personally use it extensively in production for various projects. To a large extent, GitHub and GitHub Actions are free, meaning you can experiment for free and then actually go a long way on the limitations of the free account.

8.7.2   What is a workflow?

By now, I've mentioned the word *workflow* many times, but what exactly does this mean? The concept of the workflow is exactly as it sounds: a flow of work or a sequence of tasks that are performed one after the other. This is also basically what I mean when I say *pipeline*, except there's a slightly different connotation with pipeline: the pipeline is some kind of conduit. In the case of a CD pipeline, it's a conduit that delivers working code to our production environment.

I singled out the word *workflow* because that is what an automation pipeline is actually called in GitHub Actions. If you read the GitHub Actions documentation (and I recommend that you do), you'll read that word many times.

A workflow in GitHub Actions is written as a YAML file that runs through a series of *jobs*, and in those jobs run *steps*. Each step can be a command or series of commands, but as I'm sure to mention many times, we can also call out to a shell script containing the commands we'd like to run. The concept of a workflow is illustrated in figure 8.5.

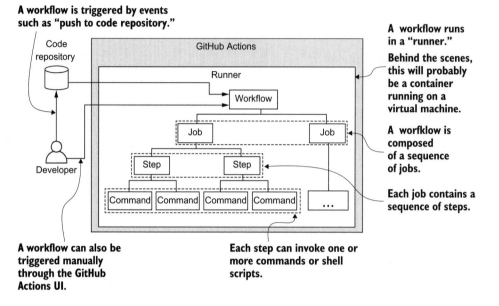

Figure 8.5   An illustration of the parts of a GitHub Actions workflow

A workflow is triggered by events on our code repository, such as code has been pushed or a pull request has been submitted. A workflow that has been invoked is instanced on a *runner*, that is, a container or virtual machine, that executes the jobs and steps as laid out in the workflow.

In this book, we won't be going too far into the depths of a GitHub Actions workflow. Even though a workflow can do many things, such as running jobs sequentially or in parallel, creating dependencies between jobs, or running the workflow on a particular OS, we won't need anything so advanced—just enough so we can trigger some shell scripts to deploy our microservices. At the end of this chapter, I'll give you a link to the GitHub Actions documentation in case you'd like to dive deeper.

8.7.3   Creating a new workflow

The simplest way to create a new workflow for your code repository starts by changing to the Actions tab for our code repository on GitHub. If you forked the chapter-8-example-1 code repository earlier in section 8.3, you can navigate to that and follow along.

When looking at a code repository that doesn't yet have a workflow, we're presented with the Get Started With GitHub Actions page, shown in figure 8.6. Otherwise, if we're looking at a code repository that already has one or more workflows (e.g., your fork of chapter-8-example-1), instead click through the New Workflow button to arrive at the Choose a Workflow page, which should also look similar to figure 8.6.

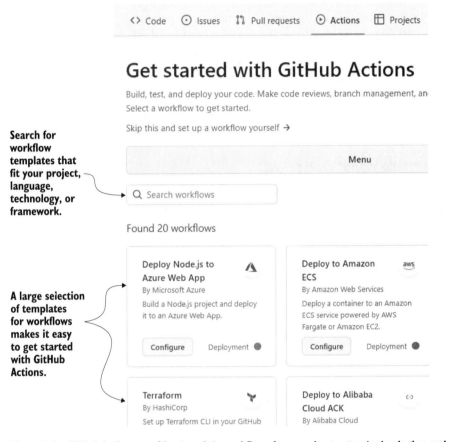

Figure 8.6   GitHub Actions provides template workflows for many languages, technologies, and frameworks, making it very easy to get started creating a CI or CD pipeline for your project.

From here, we can find many useful templates to use as starting points for new workflows. Some popular languages, frameworks, and deployment targets are automatically listed. We can also search based on a keyword. Try searching for "Node.js" to see some templates for building, testing, and deploying Node.js projects. Feel free to choose any of these options and create a workflow just to see what the result looks like. Of course, you might not be using Node.js—you might be creating your microservices with C#, Python, Go, Rust, or some other language. Whatever language or framework you're using, search for that, and you'll find a template for your new workflow.

8.7.4   *Example 1 overview*

Let's learn the basics of GitHub Actions by starting with example-1 for this chapter. The code is available here: http://mng.bz/RmWv.

This is the "hello world" of GitHub Actions workflows. Seriously, all it does is print "hello world" into the output of the workflow, but it's enough to see how we can trigger a workflow by pushing changes to our code repository.

Figure 8.7 shows the layout of this very basic project. There are only two important files: the configuration file for the workflow and the shell script that prints "hello world."

Figure 8.7   An overview of the project for example-1

8.7.5   *The "Hello World" shell script*

The core of the workflow—the commands that it invokes—are contained within the shell script index.sh. To be sure, this is the world's simplest shell script, and you can see it in listing 8.1 (chapter-8-example-1/index.sh). It runs one command that prints "hello world" into the terminal. Open a terminal and try it for yourself:

```
cd chapter-8-example-1
./index.sh
```

If you're working on a Windows computer, you'll have to open a Linux terminal under WSL2 to run this shell script.

Listing 8.1   The "Hello World" shell script

```
echo "Hello world!"              ⟵─── Prints "Hello world!"
```

Usually before running a shell script, we must mark it as executable:

```
chmod +x ./index.sh
```

In this case, you shouldn't have to do that because I marked the script as executable within the Git repository. When you create your own code repository and add your own shell scripts, you'll probably have to do this as well, using the following command:

```
git update-index --chmod=+x <path-to-the-script-file>
```

When marking your shell script as executable in the Git repository, you then must add, commit, and push the changes to your hosted code repository.

I didn't have to implement the workflow using a shell script. It would have been simpler to just invoke the commands directly from within the workflow (I'll show you that as well in a moment). But I wanted to drive home my point that if you can write a shell script, it's not a big leap to creating a CD pipeline.

8.7.6   The "Hello World" workflow

Listing 8.2 (chapter-8-example-1/.github/workflows/hello-world.yaml) shows the workflow that runs our "hello world" shell script under GitHub Actions. This YAML file implements (almost) the world's simplest workflow. Workflows can, of course, get a lot more complicated than this.

We can see that the workflow can be triggered both by code push and manually through the GitHub Actions UI. Notice how the steps section in the workflow first checks out the code repository and then invokes the shell script index.sh, which simply prints "hello world." When the workflow is invoked, the runner is empty, so it must explicitly check out the code repository to take a copy of it and make its contents available within the workflow runner.

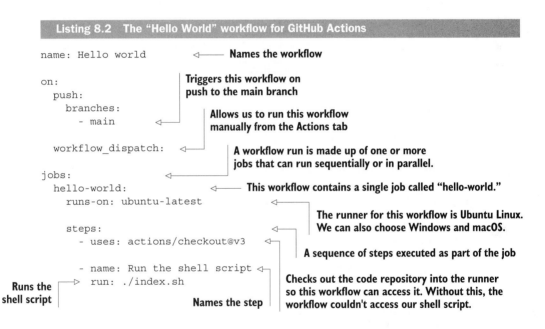

Listing 8.2   The "Hello World" workflow for GitHub Actions

8.7.7   Invoking commands inline

I did say this was *almost* the world's simplest workflow. As I indicated, we could make it even simpler by eliminating the shell script and just invoking commands directly from the workflow. For the "hello world" example, it would look like this:

```
steps:
  - uses: actions/checkout@v3

  - name: Prints hello world
    run: echo "Hello world!"
```

Runs the command directly within the workflow

We can also use a slightly different syntax to invoke multiple commands in sequence:

```
steps:
  - uses: actions/checkout@v3

  - name: Prints hello world          ┐  Using a vertical bar to start
    run: |                         ◁──┘  a multiline command block
        <command1>                   ┌ Multiple commands
        <command2>                   └ over several lines
        <etc>
```

You might already have imagined that we can also have multiple steps, each with its own set of commands:

```
steps:
  - uses: actions/checkout@v3

  - name: First step
    run: |                        ◁─┐
        <command1>                   │
        <command2>                   │  Workflow
        <etc>                        │  steps that run
  - name: Second step                │  sequentially
    run: |                        ◁─┘
        <command1>
        <command2>
        <etc>
```

Many times, I've seen and created workflows that invoke commands directly without using shell scripts. There's really no problem doing it that way. The reason I've used a shell script in example-1 is just to make my point about shell scripts; we really don't need it in this case. But soon, we'll look at a real example that does very much benefit from using a shell script to separate its commands from the workflow file.

8.7.8   *Triggering a workflow by code change*

We've created a simple workflow and have a job for it to do (albeit only printing "hello world"). Let's see this workflow in action.

As mentioned in section 8.3, to try the examples in this chapter, you need to fork each of the code repositories. If you haven't already, do that now for example-1: http://mng.bz/RmWv.

Then, clone your own copy of the repository. Go to the Actions tab for your fork, and enable workflows if you haven't done that yet. There should be no workflows listed in the history because we haven't triggered any yet.

Now try making a change; for example, in the file index.sh, try changing "hello world" to "hello computer." After that, commit your changes to the code repositories, and then invoke `git push` to push your code change to GitHub. This triggers the workflow that we defined in listing 8.2 earlier.

After invoking `git push`, while still at our terminal, it won't be obvious that anything has happened. To see the result, we must return to GitHub and view the workflow history.

8.7.9 *Workflow history*

You can see the workflow history by visiting your code repository on GitHub and then switching to the Actions tab. Figure 8.8 shows the history of my version of example-1. You can see that, when I was creating this example, I had two runs of the workflow. You can see at a glance that the first run failed, and the second run (at the top) was successful. A little later, I'll show you why the first run failed.

Your fork of example-1 is going to look different, of course, but you should still see a list of workflow runs. If you just pushed your first code change for this repository, you should see one run. If you haven't triggered your workflow yet, your list will be empty.

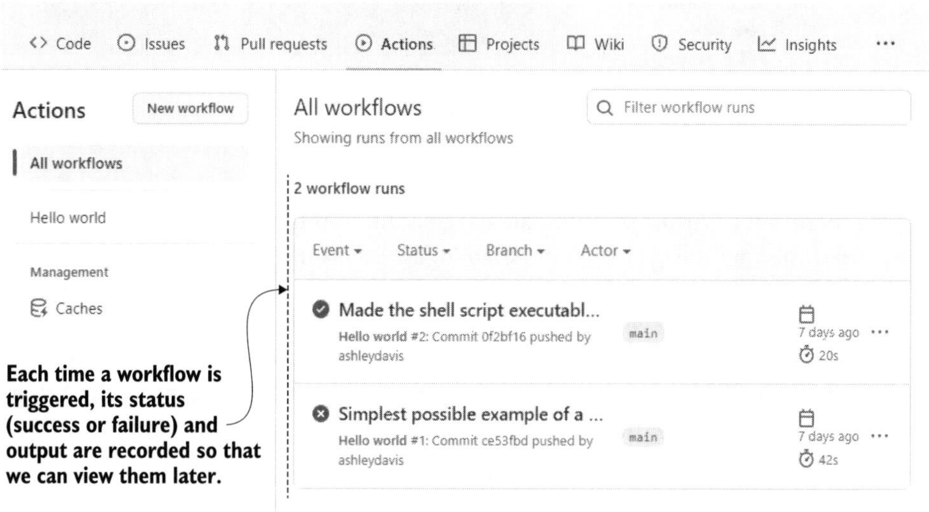

Figure 8.8   The history of workflow runs for example-1 in GitHub Actions

If you don't have time to fork the repository (we're all busy) and just want to see what it looks like, feel free to check out the workflow history for my version of example-1 at http://mng.bz/27xa.

Now click through into one of the runs. In figure 8.9, I've clicked through the successful run (the top one). You can see in the output how the workflow has invoked our shell script index.sh and that it has printed `Hello world!` into the output for the workflow. It's a simple and unexciting example, but in the next section, we'll start taking this to a more advanced level.

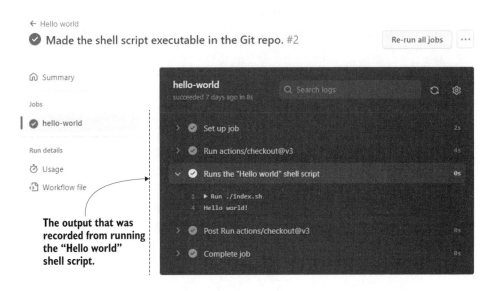

The output that was recorded from running the "Hello world" shell script.

Figure 8.9   Viewing the successful output of the "Hello world" workflow in GitHub Actions

8.7.10   *Triggering a workflow through the UI*

I mentioned earlier that we can trigger our workflow in one of two ways. We've just tried the first way: pushing code changes. But you'll notice in listing 8.2 that we also added a second event that triggers our workflow: we enabled *manual invocation* for our workflow (read the code again if you missed it the first time). That means we can click a button in the GitHub Actions UI to trigger our workflow without having to make any code changes. We do this by selecting the workflow (in this case, the "Hello World" workflow), clicking the Run Workflow dropdown, and then clicking the Run Workflow button. You can see what this looks like in figure 8.10.

This invokes the workflow and does the same thing as if we had pushed code changes. It's really useful that we can manually trigger our workflow and makes it easier to test. It's also useful if we want to change configuration and then rerun the workflow to read in the new configuration. I'll refer back to this section later when we start configuring our microservice deployment workflow with environment variables.

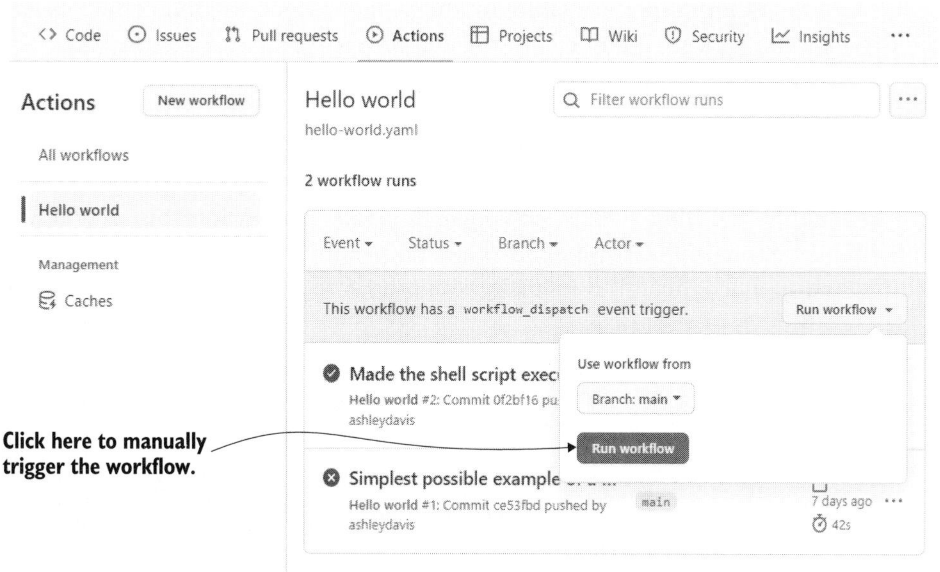

Figure 8.10   Triggering a workflow manually in GitHub Actions

8.7.11   *What have we achieved?*

So far, we've created a simple and not very useful workflow for GitHub Actions, but hopefully you can see that this isn't rocket science. If you can write a small YAML file and a small shell script, you basically now have everything you need to build CI and CD pipelines. My job is done.

I'm only joking, of course. We can't just leave it at that. Our next steps are to learn how to integrate various commands into our workflows, for example, commands to build and deploy our microservices. These are nothing new, though. We built and published our first microservice way back in chapter 3. We deployed our first microservice to Kubernetes in chapter 6. You'll soon learn how to integrate these commands into our GitHub Actions workflow, and thus we'll have automated the deployment of our first microservice.

8.8   *Implementing continuous integration*

Before creating a CD pipeline, let's first create a CI pipeline. CI is not only a good stepping stone toward CD but also useful in its own right.

In this section, we'll see our first glimpse of automated testing. We haven't covered automated testing yet—that's still to come in chapter 9—but here we'll see how to trigger automated tests from within our CI pipeline.

8.8.1   *Example 2 overview*

Moving on to example-2 for this chapter, you can find the code here: http:// mng.bz/1Jxq.

This example project contains the Node.js video-streaming microservice we've been working with, but now with the addition of some automated tests.

The layout of the project is shown in figure 8.11. There's no shell script in this example. Typically, a CI pipeline is implemented in one or two commands (which we'll see in a moment), so there's really no need to have a shell script because the commands we'll run in our CI pipeline just aren't that complicated, and it's easy enough to test them locally. Of course, this will change after this section, when we're implementing our CD pipeline. The complexity introduced by the addition of the deployment commands does make wrapping it up in a shell script very desirable.

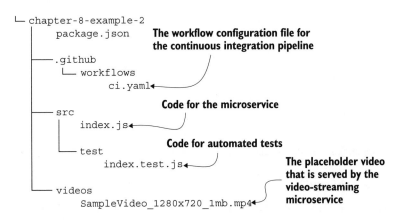

Figure 8.11   An overview of the project for example-2

8.8.2   *A workflow for automated tests*

Listing 8.3 (chapter-8-example-2/.github/workflows/ci.yaml) shows the workflow that runs the automated tests. There are two commands to look out for. The first is `npm ci`, which is like `npm install` (that you learned about in chapter 2) in that it installs dependencies, but it's designed to run in an unattended CI pipeline (in case you were wondering, the *ci* in `npm ci` actually means *clean install*). It installs only the specific dependencies listed in package-lock.json (ignoring package.json) for a deterministic and stable set of dependencies, resulting in more reliable and repeatable deployment pipelines.

The second command is the one that invokes the automated tests. The command `npm test` is the conventional Node.js command used to run automated tests. You'll learn more about how to implement this command in the next chapter.

This example is for Node.js, but you can easily adapt it to any other language or framework just by changing a few commands. In fact, you don't even have to think very hard about it—just search for a workflow template to use as a starting point as described in section 8.7.3. GitHub Actions has templates ready to use for every language and framework.

Listing 8.3 A workflow running automated tests for a Node.js microservice

```
name: CI          ◁——— Names the workflow

on:
  push:
    branches:            The workflow is invoked on
      - main         ◁—┘ push to the main branch.

jobs:
  build:
    runs-on: ubuntu-latest
                              Gets a copy of the code repository,
    steps:                    including the Node.js microservice
                              project that we'd like to run
    - uses: actions/checkout@v3   ◁—┘ automated tests against

    - uses: actions/setup-node@v3    ◁——— Installs Node.js version 18
      with:
        node-version: 18.x      Installs dependencies. This is like npm
        cache: 'npm'            install but designed to be noninteractive
                                and run in an automated pipeline.
    - run: npm ci       ◁—┘
    - run: npm test     ◁——— Runs automated tests against our Node.js project.
```

To try out this example for yourself, you'll need to fork and clone the code repository. Make sure you go into the GitHub Actions tab and enable running workflows. Then, try making a change to the code, and push your code. This triggers the workflow and runs the automated tests. You might like to try breaking the automated tests. Causing a problem on purpose (in a controlled environment) is a great way to see what a failed workflow looks like. Soon you'll learn how to tackle a failed workflow.

8.8.3 *What have we achieved?*

We've now created a useful workflow for GitHub Actions, a workflow that can automatically test a microservice each and every time we push our code to GitHub. I probably don't need to spell out how useful this can be. We can easily see how an automated testing pipeline will test all our code changes every time without ever skipping a beat. If we push broken code, our CI pipeline detects the problem quickly and lets us know so that we rectify the situation. You'll learn about how to create automated tests in the next chapter.

8.9 *Continuous deployment for a microservice*

Now we arrive at the main event and one of the most important reasons to use GitHub Actions. In this section, we'll create a workflow that automatically deploys our video-streaming microservice to Kubernetes whenever we push code changes to GitHub.

8.9.1 *Example 3 overview*

Now we move to example-3 for this chapter; you can find the code here: http://mng .bz/PR9R

The project layout is illustrated in figure 8.12. This is very similar to example-2 that we saw earlier in figure 8.11. Take note of the new files here, which include various shell scripts that are useful for building, publishing, and deploying our microservice. There is a YAML file to deploy the microservice to Kubernetes and a Dockerfile to create the production image for our microservice.

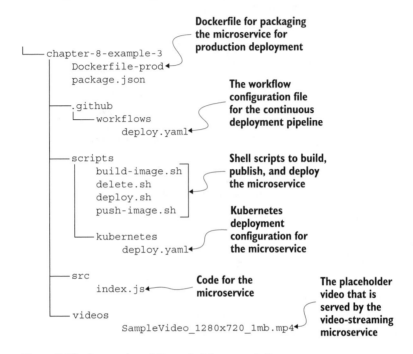

Figure 8.12   An overview of the project for example-3

8.9.2   *Templating our deployment configuration*

Before we can set up our microservices project for automated deployment, we first need a way to configure our deployment pipeline. We need this because there are various details relating to our deployment that we'd prefer not to hardcode into our project. We need a way to parameterize our deployment configuration file so that we can fill in the blanks for certain values during the execution of the CD pipeline.

In previous chapters, we've used environment variables to configure our microservices, and environment variables also turn out to be a good way (not to mention a simple way) to configure our CD pipelines. It doesn't make sense to hardcode details such as container registry and version number into our code. We might like to change the location of our container registry later, and this would be very difficult if its URL were hardcoded across the many code repositories for the numerous different microservices we'll have in the future.

The version number for our microservice can't be hardcoded because it's going to be changing frequently. If we hardcoded that, it would mean we had to make regular updates to our code just to keep the version number up to date, which is tedious and impedes fast deployments. These are just two examples of things that we don't want to hardcode in a microservice project, but any real-world project is likely to have many more examples of configurable values that we'd prefer to have separated out from the code.

So, instead of hardcoding these values, we'll use environment variables for details such as the container registry and the version number. We need to plug these values into our Kubernetes deployment configuration file, but how do we do this? There are several sophisticated (read: unnecessarily complicated) ways to achieve this. Fortunately for us, we can use a simple command-line tool called envsubst that's included with Linux. Because we're running our CD pipeline on Ubuntu Linux (defined in the workflow file), we can rely on it to inject values into our configuration file from environment variables.

This is illustrated in figure 8.13, which shows an extract of deploy.yaml, our Kubernetes deployment configuration file (see GitHub for the full file). Notice how we've set environment variables for VERSION and CONTAINER_REGISTRY and that invoking the command envsubst injects these values into the configuration file deploy.yaml.

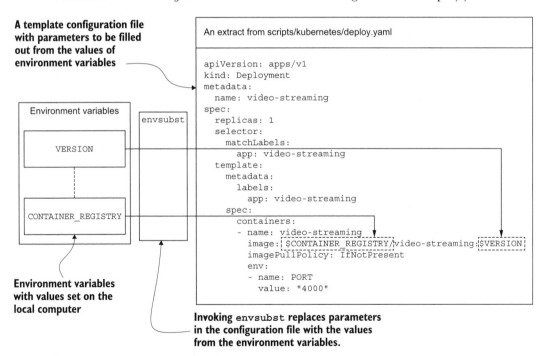

Figure 8.13 Using the envsubst command to inject parameters into our deployment configuration file deploy.yaml

For any tool that we include in our automated deployment pipeline, we should already be familiar with how to use it and have practiced using it on our local computer. We can't automate something unless we already know how to use it manually! So, if you haven't used `envsubst` before, now is your chance to try it out directly before we add it to our workflow. Just open a terminal, and try it out. If you're on Windows, you'll need to open a Linux terminal under WSL2.

Set the following environment variables:

```
export CONTAINER_REGISTRY=<url-for-your-registry>
export VERSION=1
```

You'll need to use the URL for your own container registry. You can use the container registry you created earlier or create a new one the easy way (through the UI) like we did in chapter 3, section 3.9.1, or the more difficult way (through Terraform code) as we did in chapter 7, section 7.9.2.

Now, invoke `envsubst` in the chapter-8-example-3 project, inputting the file deploy.yaml:

```
cd chapter-8-example-3
envsubst < ./scripts/kubernetes/deploy.yaml
```

In the output, you should see that the parameters in deploy.yaml have been replaced by the values from the environment variables `CONTAINER_REGISTRY` and `VERSION`.

> **NOTE** To learn more about `envsubst`, you can easily find many tutorials, guides, and videos on the internet.

8.9.3 *Manual deployment precedes automated deployment*

Before we automate our deployment process, we need to have something that we can automate. If we can't work through a process manually, we have no business trying to automate it. Like any coding task, we must first be able to run it locally from our development computer before we try to get it running in production.

This is nothing more than the manual deployment process we've been through already in chapter 6, except, this time, we'll create shell scripts to contain the commands for building, publishing, and deploying our microservice. Using shell scripts creates a framework or scaffolding for our deployment, making it easier to test locally and be sure it works before we move it into the cloud. Shell scripts also give us a way to test our deployment code again in the future after we make changes.

If you jump straight to trying to run these commands directly under GitHub Actions, you'll likely hit problems that would have been easier to debug and solve if only you had first tried running them locally. It's always easier to solve problems locally where possible, rather than trying to figure them out when running in production because debugging a remote machine is usually a fair bit harder than debugging locally. So, running our code locally first makes us much more effective than if we committed it with no testing and pushed it, just hoping everything works out in production. We'll talk more about debugging in chapter 11.

WE NEED A TARGET FOR DEPLOYMENT

To be able to deploy our code to production, we must have a place to which we can deploy it. We can't use our local Kubernetes instance (in Docker Desktop) because, ultimately, we want to run our deployment code in the cloud under GitHub Actions, and code that runs there won't be able to access our local machine. So, at this point, we must have a Kubernetes cluster that is also running in the cloud. We'll also need a container registry.

If we were doing this for real, for example, working for a tech company, we'd probably already have multiple production or production-like environments at our disposal. But in any case, as you've seen in chapter 6, it's easy enough for us to create our own Kubernetes cluster for learning, testing, and experimentation.

So now make sure you have a Kubernetes cluster (chapter 6 or 7) and a container registry (chapter 3 or 7) ready to use. You'll need to know the details of each, including the URL of the container registry and its username and password. You'll also need to know how to authenticate kubectl with your Kubernetes cluster, but we'll cover that again soon.

SHELL SCRIPTS FOR BUILDING AND PUBLISHING IMAGES

Let's now create shell scripts to codify the commands to build and publish images for our microservices that we learned in chapter 3. Listing 8.4 (extract from chapter-8-example-3/scripts/build-image.sh) is the first of three shell scripts that we need to build the CD pipeline for our microservice.

It makes sense to break up this deployment process into three independent parts. The first part is for building an image, the second part is for publishing the image, and the third part is for deploying the microservice to Kubernetes. We could, of course, combine all of this into a single large shell script, but separating it into three makes each of the shell scripts smaller and easier to test in isolation. It's also a good way to break up the work into pieces. Then later, when something goes wrong with our CD pipeline, debugging will be easier because it will be clearer in which stage of the deployment (which shell script) the problem has occurred.

The shell script in listing 8.4 encapsulates the command to build the image for our microservice. As input, it takes the environment variables we've already seen: CONTAINER_REGISTRY and VERSION. These are used to tag the image with the registry we'll publish it to and to set the version number of the image.

Listing 8.4 A shell script for building an image

```
docker build -t
    ⇒ $CONTAINER_REGISTRY/video-streaming:$VERSION
    ⇒ --file ./Dockerfile-prod .
```
Builds the images and tags it based on environment variables

Now let's test our first shell script locally. If you haven't done this already, open a terminal, and set the following environment variables (in Windows, open a Linux terminal under WSL2):

```
export CONTAINER_REGISTRY=<url-to-your-container-registry>
export VERSION=1
```

You'll need to enter the URL for your own container registry.

Now run the shell script yourself:

```
cd chapter-8-example-3
./scripts/build-image.sh
```

This builds the image so that it's ready to be published. Afterward, you can invoke `docker image list` to check that you now have the image locally. We can tell which image it is by scanning the list and looking for the one that is tagged with the URL for our registry and the version number that we set.

If you're running the shell script from the example-3 code repository, its permissions should already be set correctly. If not, you'll need to mark the shell script as executable before you run it:

```
chmod +x ./scripts/build-image.sh
```

If you need to do this, remember to do it for the upcoming shell scripts as well.

Moving on to the second shell script in listing 8.5 (extract from chapter-8-example-3/scripts/push-image.sh), we can see the commands for publishing the image to our container registry. This shell script takes input from the environment variables we set already, plus REGISTRY_UN and REGISTRY_PW, which are the username and password, respectively, to authenticate with our container registry.

> **Listing 8.5   A shell script for publishing an image**

```
                                                                Logs in to the container
                                                                registry. Username and
                                                                password are supplied by
echo $REGISTRY_PW | docker login $CONTAINER_REGISTRY            environment variables.
  ➥ --username $REGISTRY_UN --password-stdin
docker push $CONTAINER_REGISTRY/video-streaming:$VERSION        ◁─┐
                                                                  │
            Publishes the image to the container registry. The registry
            and image version are specified by environment variables.
```

Back in your terminal, set these additional environment variables:

```
export REGISTRY_UN=<registry-username>
export REGISTRY_PW=<registry-password>
```

You'll need to enter the username and password for your own container registry as the values for these environment variables.

Now run the shell script for yourself:

```
./scripts/push-image.sh
```

This publishes the image to our container registry. If you'd like to test this, follow the instructions in chapter 3, section 3.9.3, to boot the microservice from the image that we've published to the registry.

A SHELL SCRIPT FOR DEPLOYMENT

Now we arrive at the third and final shell script for deployment of our microservice. Listing 8.6 (extract from chapter-8-example-3/scripts/deploy.sh) contains the commands to fill parameters in our Kubernetes configuration file (using `envsubst` that we talked about in section 8.9.2), and it pipes the resulting configuration to kubectl, which then deploys our microservice to Kubernetes. This is just like what we did in chapter 6, except then we were sending a static (unchanging) configuration file into kubectl, and now we're using a dynamic configuration file whose content depends on parameters injected from environment variables.

> **Listing 8.6   A shell script for deployment to Kubernetes**

```
envsubst < ./scripts/kubernetes/deploy.yaml
    ⇨ | kubectl apply -f -
```

Invokes envsubst to fill parameters in the configuration file from environment variables, and then pipes the expanded configuration to kubectl to deploy the microservice to the Kubernetes cluster

Our new shell script and the configuration file it fills out depend on the environment variables we set earlier, so we can simply run the shell script:

```
./scripts/deploy.sh
```

This takes the image we published earlier and instantiates a container into the Kubernetes cluster, thus deploying our microservice to production.

Congratulations! By running these three shell scripts, we've tested our deployment pipeline locally. If we hit any problems, we should solve them here and now before moving on. Don't save problems until you hit production; they'll be so much more difficult to solve if you do that.

Now, it's time for the end goal: we'll get our microservice deployment running automatically under GitHub Actions. But first, we should clean up our cluster and remove the test deployment we just made. The example-3 code repository includes a shell script for this:

```
./script/delete.sh
```

This is a shell script that looks a lot like listing 8.6, except that instead of `kubectl apply`, it invokes `kubectl delete` to delete the microservice deployment.

8.9.4 *A workflow to deploy our microservice*

Now that we've created and tested our shell scripts for deployment, we can invoke them from our GitHub Actions workflow. Looking at listing 8.7 (chapter-8-example-3/.github/workflows/deploy.yaml), you can see how we run each of the shell scripts in sequence.

This procedure (running three shell scripts) looks the same as what we've done locally, except that by including them in this workflow, our deployment will now happen automatically each and every time we push code changes to GitHub. Whenever we make changes to our code, GitHub will allocate a runner to do the deployment for us. No more manual deployments for us, thank you very much. What a wonderful day this is turning out to be!

Listing 8.7   A workflow to deploy a microservice

```
name: Deploy microservice

on:
  push:
    branches:
      - main          ⟵──┐ Deploys the microservice on push to the
                           main branch of this code repository

  workflow_dispatch:   ⟵──┐ Allows deployment to be invoked
jobs:                       manually through the GitHub Actions UI

  deploy:
    runs-on: ubuntu-latest

    env:
      VERSION: ${{ github.sha }}
      CONTAINER_REGISTRY:                      Loads secret values into
        ➥ ${{ secrets.CONTAINER_REGISTRY }}   environment variables (more
      REGISTRY_UN: ${{ secrets.REGISTRY_UN }}  about this in a moment)
      REGISTRY_PW: ${{ secrets.REGISTRY_PW  }}

    steps:

      - uses: actions/checkout@v3

      - name: Build
        run: ./scripts/build-image.sh   ⟵── Builds the Docker image

      - name: Publish                       Publishes the Docker image
        run: ./scripts/push-image.sh   ⟵── to the container registry

      - uses: tale/kubectl-action@v1   ⟵── Installs kubectl and
        with:                               connects it to the cluster
          base64-kube-config:
            ➥ ${{ secrets.KUBE_CONFIG }}  ⟵── Sets authentication credentials for
          kubectl-version: v1.24.2            connection to Kubernetes from a
                                              GitHub secret
      - name: Deploy
        run: ./scripts/deploy.sh   ⟵──  Expands templated configuration based on
                                        environment variables and then invokes
                                        kubectl to deploy the microservice to the
                                        Kubernetes cluster
```

There are two key elements to understand in listing 8.7:

- How kubectl is installed and authenticated within the workflow
- How the environment variables are set (the inputs to our shell scripts)

Let's cover each of these items in turn.

8.9.5 *Authenticating kubectl*

How exactly do we authenticate kubectl to connect to our Kubernetes cluster from within the runner that is executing our workflow? There are a few ways to do this. Let's look at the simplest.

First of all, you need to have authenticated with your Kubernetes cluster so that you can run kubectl locally and connect to your cluster. If you successfully worked through section 8.9.3, you've done this already.

If you haven't already, authenticate the Azure CLI tool with Azure:

```
az login
```

Then, download the configuration for kubectl that authenticates it to your cluster:

```
az aks get-credentials --resource-group <resource-group-name>
    --name <cluster-name>
```

Remember to insert the name of your cluster and the Azure resource group that contains it.

Now look at the kubectl configuration file under your home directory at ~/.kube/config. Try printing it out like this:

```
cat ~/.kube/config
```

You should see a (possibly rather complex) YAML file that configures your connection(s) to your Kubernetes cluster. This file contains the authentication details to connect to your cluster. Keep it safe.

If you're running on Windows (even under the WSL2 Linux terminal), you may find the file is located at c:\Users\<username>\.kube\config. To access it under WSL2, use the path /mnt/c/Users/<username>/.kube/config (taking care to insert your username into the path).

We're about to take a copy of our kubectl configuration and put it in a GitHub secret (this will be explained soon). You should be careful at this point that your local kubectl configuration only has the connection details for the one cluster that we're currently working with. For security reasons, we'd like to constrain our CD pipeline to only access the single cluster that it needs to deploy to. So, if you've previously connected to other clusters (meaning you're now connected to multiple clusters), you might want to delete your kubectl configuration file and invoke az aks get-credentials again to ensure that you only have the one set of credentials stored locally. To check how many clusters you're connected to, invoke kubectl config get-contexts. If there is only one item in the output, it means you've only configured the connection to one cluster, so we're good to proceed.

To make our kubectl configuration available to our workflow through an environment variable, we first have to Base64 encode it:

```
cat ~/.kube/config | base64
```

You might want to copy the Base64-encoded version to a new file to make it easier to copy:

```
cat ~/.kube/config | base64 > ~/kubeconfig.txt
```

Now we have a kubectl configuration that we can use in our workflow to allow it to connect to Kubernetes on our behalf, yet it has to remain secret. This is where GitHub secrets comes into play.

8.9.6 *Installing and configuring kubectl*

The next question is, how do we install and configure kubectl so that we can use it in the runner that executes our workflow? Recall the following lines of code from listing 8.7 earlier:

This is an example of using a *custom action* in our workflow. Anyone can make a custom action to package a reusable code module and share it with other users of GitHub Actions. There are many useful actions available on the GitHub Marketplace (https://github.com/marketplace?type=actions).

This action installs kubectl into our workflow, targeting the particular version we've specified (1.24.2), and extracts the kubectl configuration from a GitHub secret using the following syntax:

```
${{ secrets.KUBE_CONFIG }}
```

> **NOTE** You can learn more about `kubectl-action` at http://mng.bz/JdOZ.

8.9.7 *Environment variables from GitHub secrets*

If you didn't know already, you might have guessed by now that GitHub secrets is a service for storing secret and sensitive values (like our Kubernetes configuration details, mentioned previously) and for making those secrets available for use within our workflow.

The main use of secrets is to set environment variables. Recall these lines of code from listing 8.7 earlier:

Sets the version for our deployed image based on the Git commit hash. This is a convenient way to set the version number without ever having to increment a value manually.

```
env:
  VERSION: ${{ github.sha }}
  CONTAINER_REGISTRY: ${{ secrets.CONTAINER_REGISTRY }}
  REGISTRY_UN: ${{ secrets.REGISTRY_UN }}
  REGISTRY_PW: ${{ secrets.REGISTRY_PW }}
```

Sets container registry authentication details from GitHub secrets

Sets the URL for the container registry where the image should be published

Here, we're extracting various values from GitHub secrets and setting them as environment variables within the workflow. These are the environment variables we use to provide inputs to our shell scripts. GitHub secrets give us a secure and secret place to store values when we'd prefer that no one is able to view them later. Then, we use the syntax in listing 8.7 to set environment variables that we can use in our shell scripts for building, publishing, and deploying our microservices.

Note that we could hardcode each of these values in our YAML file (or even in our shell scripts!) and not have to worry at all about configuring GitHub secrets. There are two problems with that. First, *not* hardcoding these values into our code makes our deployment code (e.g., our YAML files and shell scripts) more reusable, thus making it easier to use this setup for future microservices. Second, we really don't want to put secret and sensitive values in our code at all. When we commit values like this to our code, we run the risk of other people being able to easily read them (like all developers who can access the code at our company, or worse, all developers in the world for an open source project). So, using GitHub secrets can help us reuse our deployment pipeline and, more importantly, keep our secrets safe.

> **NOTE** You can learn more about setting environment variables in your workflow at http://mng.bz/wjd5.

8.9.8 *Environment variables from GitHub context variables*

In the code presented in listing 8.7, there was an exception. Note that setting the VERSION environment variable didn't extract its value from a secret; instead, it extracted it from a so-called context variable:

```
VERSION: ${{ github.sha }}
```

In this case, `github.sha` represents the hash of the commit that triggered the workflow. This is a unique ID, and I found it to be a simple and effective way to create a version number for the image. It means we never have to manually increment a version number for our microservice (some people do this by tagging a commit with a version number, e.g., v1.2.3, and then using the addition of the tag to trigger the workflow).

Using context variables allows us to extract contextual information about the workflow, the run, the environment, the code repository, and many other things. When it proves to be useful, we can extract these values to environment variables as inputs to our shell scripts.

> **NOTE** You can learn more here, but be prepared for a long reading session: http://mng.bz/qj8x.

8.9.9 *Adding GitHub secrets*

Only one question remains: how do we set a GitHub secret? Setting the secrets required by the workflow is the final step, and if you trigger your workflow before you do this, it will cause the workflow to fail.

Don't worry, though, that's not a problem. In fact, I'd encourage you to push your code or trigger the workflow manually just to see it fail. Causing failures on purpose is a great way to see error messages in a controlled environment, allowing you to explore and understand them without the fear and panic that can sometimes set in at other times when you've unintentionally broken your workflow.

We can add secrets to the organization (if we're running a GitHub organization for our company), or we can keep them isolated and add them to just the single repository. Adding secrets to the organization is a great way to share values between many microservices, but for this example, we'll add secrets to just this one repository. Of course, you'll need to add them to your fork of the example-3 repository; you can't add them to my version because you won't have permission to modify the settings of my code repository.

Navigate to the Settings tab for your fork of the example-3 repository, as shown in figure 8.14. Before you've added any secrets, you'll see the following message: "There are no secrets for this repository." After you've added secrets, you'll see the list of the ones you've added here. Click New Repository Secret to create your first secret.

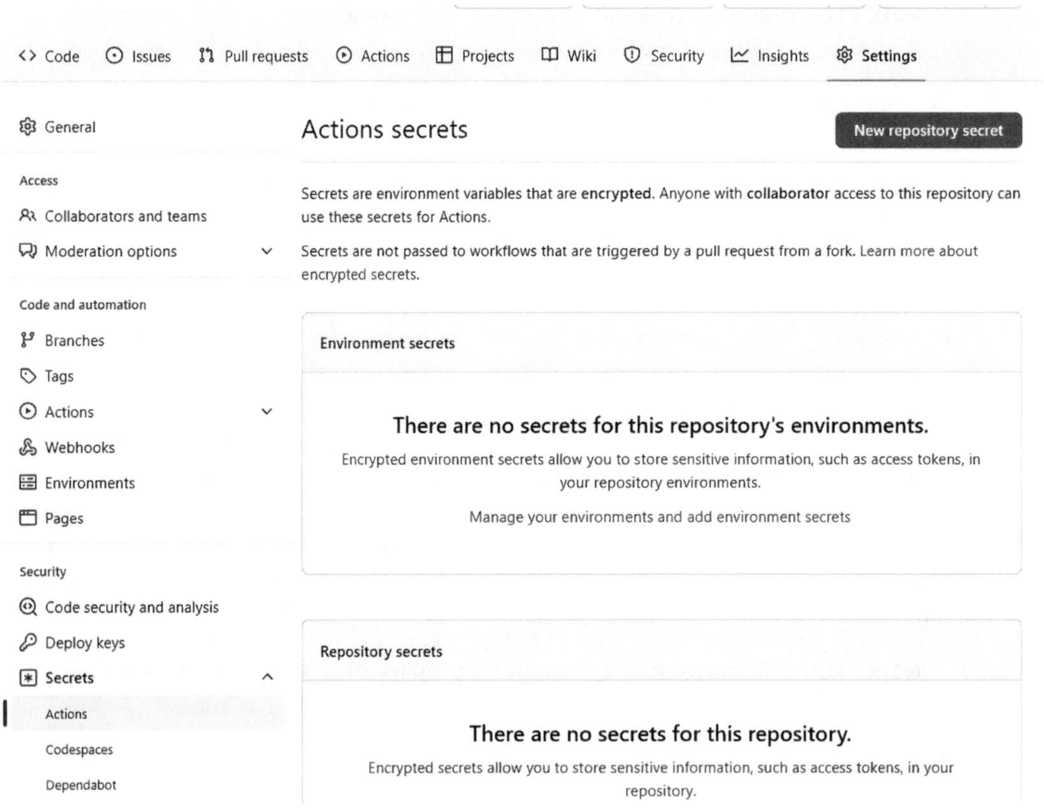

| <> Code   ⊙ Issues   ⇊ Pull requests   ⊙ Actions   ⊞ Projects   ▥ Wiki   ⊙ Security   ⟋ Insights   ⚙ **Settings** |

⚙ General

Actions secrets   [New repository secret]

Access

ᴀ Collaborators and teams

Secrets are environment variables that are **encrypted**. Anyone with **collaborator** access to this repository can use these secrets for Actions.

ᔓ Moderation options   ⌄

Secrets are not passed to workflows that are triggered by a pull request from a fork. Learn more about encrypted secrets.

Code and automation

ᛃ Branches

Environment secrets

◯ Tags

⊙ Actions   ⌄

There are no secrets for this repository's environments.

⅋ Webhooks

Encrypted environment secrets allow you to store sensitive information, such as access tokens, in your repository environments.

⊞ Environments

Manage your environments and add environment secrets

▭ Pages

Security

ᯊ Code security and analysis

⌿ Deploy keys

Repository secrets

⊞ Secrets   ⌃

Actions

There are no secrets for this repository.

Codespaces

Encrypted secrets allow you to store sensitive information, such as access tokens, in your repository.

Dependabot

Figure 8.14   The Secrets page in GitHub Actions

Now, add the name and value for the secret, as shown in figure 8.15. When you're done, click Add Secret to save it. Once saved, we can never view the value here again; after all, it's supposed to be a secret. So, if we need to remember these values (hint: you probably do), then we must save them somewhere else, such as in password management software.

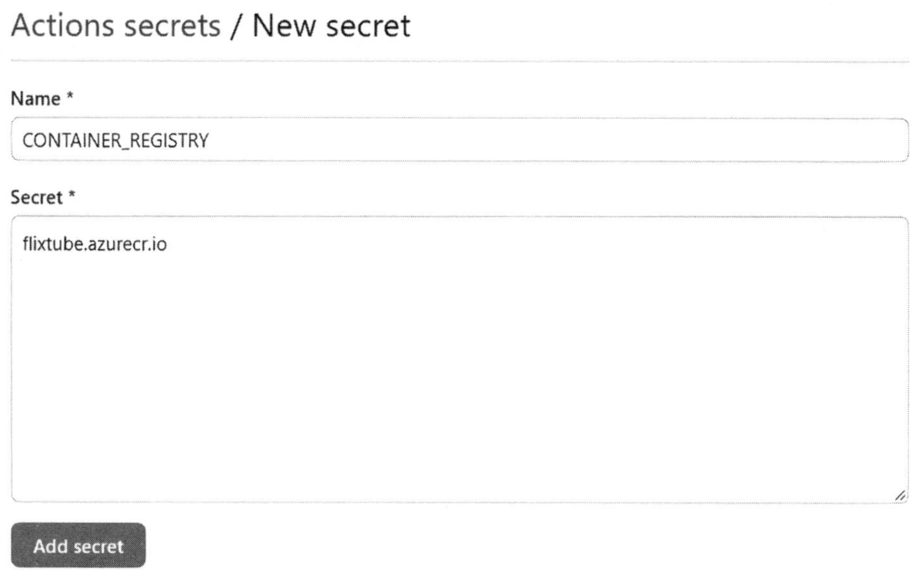

Actions secrets / New secret

Name *

```
CONTAINER_REGISTRY
```

Secret *

```
flixtube.azurecr.io
```

Add secret

Figure 8.15   Adding a new GitHub Actions secret to the code repository for use in our workflow

We must now add each of the secrets that is required by our workflow. You should have these details noted down from when you created your Kubernetes cluster and container registry:

- `CONTAINER_REGISTRY`—The URL to your container registry
- `REGISTRY_UN`—The username for your registry
- `REGISTRY_PW`—The password for your registry
- `KUBE_CONFIG`—Base64-encoded configuration that authenticates kubectl with your cluster (copy this value from the file you created earlier in section 8.9.5)

With all the secrets added, you can now trigger the workflow in your own fork of example-3 and hope to achieve a successful deployment. Trigger your workflow by pushing code or triggering it manually in the GitHub Actions UI. Will it work? If you follow all the steps correctly, then yes it should, but there's also a very good chance that it's going to fail. We'll talk about that in the next section.

> **NOTE**   As always, there is limited space to cover everything in this book. To learn more about GitHub secrets, here's a good place to start: http://mng.bz/7v7Q.

8.9.10 *Debugging your deployment pipeline*

It's quite difficult to get a deployment working properly on the first go, so don't be disheartened at the first failure of your deployment pipeline. You'll probably miss some environment variable or some authentication detail that will cause the deployment to fail immediately. Sometimes, you'll have to work through multiple failures like this before you get it working. The process of debugging in production is very slow, which is why it's so important that we thoroughly test our process (as far as we can) on our local computer and fully understand all the environment variables that must be set for it to work.

The first step in debugging your failed workflow is to drill down into the GitHub Actions workflow history and read the error messages. In figure 8.16, you can see the failure from my first deployment of the "Hello world" workflow from earlier in section 8.7. Yes, I am not immune to failure, and you might take some solace in knowing (or at least find it amusing; don't worry—I'm also laughing as I write this) that my first attempt at the most basic deployment pipeline was a failure!

The error is "Permission denied" and relates to the shell script index.sh. This might have been a very perplexing error for me if I hadn't seen it a dozen times before. Fixing it required marking the shell script as executable in the Git repository (like I mentioned earlier in section 8.7.5). A fact of life for software developers is that we'll continually see new error messages as we cause new kinds of problems. If we don't know what the error message means, we must then research it (hint: start with Google or ChatGPT) to help figure out what caused the problem and learn how we can fix it.

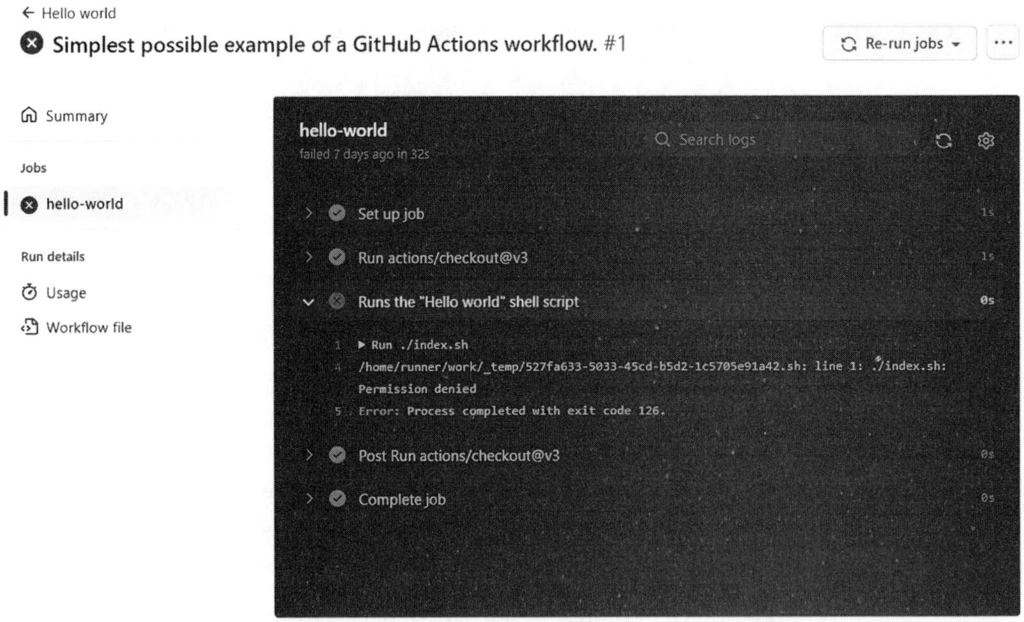

Figure 8.16 Output from a failed workflow in GitHub Actions

Solving a problem in our deployment code is similar to solving problems in any production code. We must ask the question: what caused the error? It can take some detective work and experimentation to figure that out. For problems we can't immediately figure out, can we reproduce the error locally? If the code works locally without error, then we must try to understand the differences between local and production. We need to study the differences between local environment variables and the ones in the workflow. Are they all correct? Have all required values been added to GitHub secrets?

For difficult problems, being able to reproduce the error locally gives us the best and quickest chance of finding the cause and fixing the problem. Figuring out how to replicate our production configuration on our local computer can be tricky, but it can also help us solve the most difficult problems.

In addition, if you didn't realize it, you can use any Linux command in your workflow (obviously, this depends on the OS you're using for your runner, but we've used Ubuntu Linux in these examples). This gives us an extensive toolkit for debugging our workflow in production, even though we can't create an interactive shell into the runner.

For example, try adding the commands `ls` and `pwd` to your workflow to show the current directory in the runner and the list of files it contains. Then, feel free to change directory using `cd` and print the contents of files using `cat`. It's worthwhile playing with these commands experimentally in your workflow even if it's working okay. That can help you understand what's happening and help you recognize these commands as a valuable technique for debugging your workflow. Debugging is an art form unto itself, and it's hard to do it justice in the space we have, but we'll return to debugging in chapter 11.

Running a workflow locally

Having trouble getting a complex workflow to run under GitHub Actions?

`act` is a tool that allows you to run a workflow locally. By default, it works best when your workflow needs to run under Linux (which is the case for this book).

You can trigger a particular workflow by filename like this:

```
cd my-repo
act -W .github\workflows\my-workflow.yml
```

Learn more here: https://github.com/nektos/act.

8.9.11 Deploying directly to production is dangerous

Note that deploying to production directly from the main branch of our code is very dangerous. Our main branch is typically where *integration* happens, the merging of code changes from the development team, after which it must be tested thoroughly before launching it on your customers.

So, we shouldn't deploy directly from our main branch, but to keep things simple in this chapter, that's exactly what we've done. However, in chapter 12, we'll change this. We'll talk about using a branching strategy where we have a main branch that triggers our CI pipeline (automatically testing code as the development team merges it) and a separate production branch (maybe with *branch protection* enabled—we'll talk about that later) that triggers our CD pipeline. Keeping these branches separate gives us a gateway where we can manually test and verify our code in development before we merge it into production and release it to our customers. A strategy like this helps stop embarrassing mistakes (and even malicious changes) from going to production.

8.9.12 What have we achieved?

We've come a long way from our "Hello world" workflow. We've automated the deployment of a single microservice. When we change the code for this microservice, it's automatically tested and then deployed to production. It might seem like some kind of magic, except that it's not, now that you understand how it works.

We covered the basics on templating our code configuration, and you can take this further to make it easier to reuse your deployment pipeline (everything in the scripts directory of example-3) across every other microservice that you create in the future. This is a recipe that we can scale across many microservices, and we'll talk more about it in chapter 12.

8.10 Continue your learning

As always, there is so much more to be learned than we can cover here. Here is an entire book on automated deployment, should you want to go deeper:

- *Grokking Continuous Delivery* by Christie Wilson (Manning, 2022)

I can also thoroughly recommend reading the documentation for GitHub Actions, especially the pages Quickstart and Understanding GitHub Actions: https://docs .github.com/en/actions.

Summary

- GitHub Actions is a service from GitHub that we can use to run automated workflows in response to various actions on our code repository.
- A continuous integration (CI) pipeline runs automated tests against our code (and other checks) automatically as we push changes to our code repository. It's like an early warning system for problems that appear in our codebase as changes are merged in from the development team.
- A continuous deployment (CD) pipeline automatically deploys our microservices to production in response to pushing code or submitting a pull request.
- Automated deployment is the conduit that conveys our code to our customer, making it easy to release code changes and get fast feedback.

- Creating a CI or CD pipeline isn't much more complicated than creating a YAML file (to configure our pipeline) and a shell script (to run commands, even though the commands within can be quite complicated).
- Success with microservices very much depends on having reliable automated deployments. It's increasingly difficult to scale up microservices if your deployments are manual or unreliable.
- Wrapping our deployment process in a shell script makes it convenient to test locally to ensure that it works correctly, before running in the cloud, where it's more difficult to debug.
- Environment variables are used to configure the shell scripts we run in our automated workflows.
- Values for environment variables can be set from GitHub secrets, a service for storing secret and sensitive values and keeping them safe.
- There are many useful GitHub context variables, such as `github.sha`, which we used to create a version number for the image created by our workflow.
- We can template our deployment configuration by using `envsubst` to fill parameters from environment variables.

Automated testing for microservices

To this point in the book, while building microservices, we've tested our code manually. In this chapter, though, we'll shift up a gear and learn how to apply automated testing to our microservices.

So far, we've primarily done our testing by running our code and visually inspecting the output. Methods of manual testing are many and varied. I want you to know that manual testing is okay, to a point. You should start with manual testing and continue with it until you're comfortable enough to use automated testing.

Your product should also be well enough understood that it's worth investing in automated testing. Doing automated testing for minimum viable products (MVPs) or prototypes is often a waste of time and slows down development—in those cases, manual testing is adequate.

When repetitive manual testing becomes tedious and time consuming, we'll want to turn to automated testing. Of course, automated testing is generally useful in the realm of software development, but with microservices, it becomes essential as we grow our application. It's also important for small teams because, at some point, the burden of manual testing becomes overwhelming to the point that all we're doing is that testing. There's no reason we should carry a heavy testing burden when such great automated testing tools are within easy reach!

Think of this chapter as a guided tour through the testing landscape as it applies to microservices. We'll start with an introduction to testing, and then we'll look at more advanced examples of unit testing, integration testing, and end-to-end testing.

Automated testing is an advanced topic. I've included it in this book because I believe it's essential for scaling microservices. If you haven't done automated testing before, you might find this chapter a little overwhelming. Hopefully not, but otherwise, feel free to skip this chapter and come back to it again later. Just know that automated testing is important and that even though you don't need it in the early days, eventually you'll need it to scale up to beyond a handful of microservices.

9.1   New tools

In the previous chapter, we added automated tests to our continuous integration/ continuous deployment (CI/CD) pipeline. In this chapter, you'll learn the basics of how to create automated tests to help ensure our microservices are reliable and robust. As modern developers, we're spoiled with great testing tools that are free, easily available, and straightforward to learn. Here, we'll use two great testing tools, Jest and Playwright (see table 9.1), to run our automated tests.

Table 9.1   New tools in chapter 9

Tool	Version	Purpose
Jest	29.6.4	Jest is a tool for automated testing of JavaScript code.
Playwright	1.37.1	Playwright is a tool for automated testing of web pages.

9.2   Getting the code

To follow along with this chapter, you need to download the code or clone the repository:

- Download a zip file of the code from here: http://mng.bz/eEgq
- You can clone the code using Git like this:

```
git clone https://github.com/bootstrapping-microservices-2nd-edition/
➥ chapter-9.git
```

For help on installing and using Git, see chapter 2. If you have problems with the code, log an issue in the repository in GitHub.

9.3   *Testing for microservices*

Like any code that we write, microservices need to be well tested so we can know the code is robust, is difficult to break, and can gracefully handle problems. Testing gives us peace of mind that our code functions in both normal and unexpected circumstances.

Effective testing emulates production as closely as possible. This includes the environment, the configuration of the code, and the test data that we use. Using Docker and Docker Compose allows us to configure our testing environment to be like the production environment.

This makes the "it worked on my computer" excuse for broken code much less common in modern development. Usually, when it works on our computer (in a correctly configured Docker environment), we can be fairly sure it's going to work in the production environment. Having a stable environment for our code is a crucial factor for reliable testing.

Manual testing is a good starting point and is a skill worth cultivating. But beyond a certain point, as mentioned earlier, automated testing is necessary to scale up our application. As the number of microservices grows, we'll rely more and more on automation to keep the application running and to help us maintain a rapid pace of development. In the previous chapter, we created our CI/CD pipeline to automatically run tests and deploy our microservices. Now, you'll learn how to write the automated tests.

9.4   *Automated testing*

Automated testing, put simply, is *code-driven* testing. We write code to exercise our code and verify that it works correctly. Often, the test code directly invokes the code under test, but it can also be invoked indirectly, for example, through HTTP requests or RabbitMQ messages. The test code then verifies that the result is correct, either by checking the output or checking the behavior.

Throughout this chapter, you'll learn a handful of automated testing techniques. You'll be able to apply these techniques over and over again to create a comprehensive suite of tests for your application.

Automated testing for microservices can be applied at multiple levels. We can test individual functions, whole microservices, groups of microservices together, or the whole application (until the application grows too large; more about that later). These levels of testing are related to the following three types of automated testing:

- *Unit testing*—Tests isolated code and individual functions
- *Integration testing*—Tests whole microservices
- *End-to-end testing*—Tests groups of microservices and/or the entire application, including the frontend

You may have heard of these types of testing before because they aren't specific to microservices. If not, don't worry because we'll look at each in turn.

Figure 9.1 shows a diagram that is called the *testing pyramid*. It relates the types of automated testing to each other and gives us an idea of how many of each type of test we should have in our test suite.

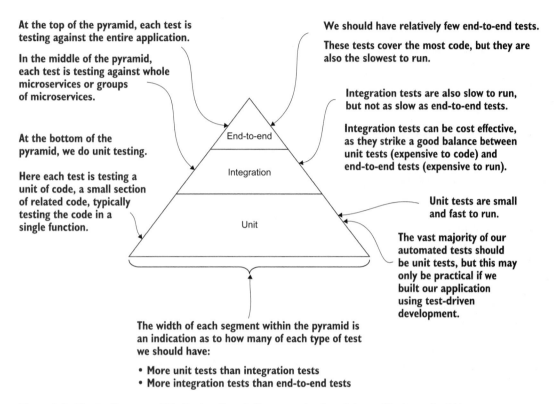

At the top of the pyramid, each test is testing against the entire application.

In the middle of the pyramid, each test is testing against whole microservices or groups of microservices.

At the bottom of the pyramid, we do unit testing.

Here each test is testing a unit of code, a small section of related code, typically testing the code in a single function.

We should have relatively few end-to-end tests.

These tests cover the most code, but they are also the slowest to run.

Integration tests are also slow to run, but not as slow as end-to-end tests.

Integration tests can be cost effective, as they strike a good balance between unit tests (expensive to code) and end-to-end tests (expensive to run).

Unit tests are small and fast to run.

The vast majority of our automated tests should be unit tests, but this may only be practical if we built our application using test-driven development.

End-to-end

Integration

Unit

The width of each segment within the pyramid is an indication as to how many of each type of test we should have:

• More unit tests than integration tests
• More integration tests than end-to-end tests

Figure 9.1   The testing pyramid indicates the relative amounts of each type of test we should have.

Unit tests run quickly, so we can afford to have many of them. They are, therefore, at the foundation (the base) of the testing pyramid. Integration testing and end-to-end testing are higher in the pyramid. These types of tests are slower to run, so we can't afford to have as many of those. (The diminishing area as we go up the pyramid indicates that we'll have fewer and fewer of these types of tests.) This means we should have fewer integration tests than unit tests and fewer end-to-end tests than integration tests.

Figure 9.2 illustrates what end-to-end testing looks like for a cut-down version of FlixTube. End-to-end testing is the easiest type of testing to understand because it's like we're simulating how the customer uses our product; therefore, it's the closest type of automated testing to manual testing. We load the entire application to test it, just like we do when testing manually. Figure 9.2 shows running Playwright tests against a cut-down version of our application that is running on Docker Compose.

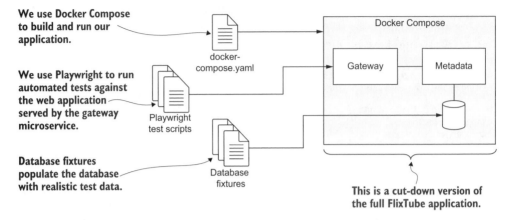

We use Docker Compose to build and run our application.

docker-compose.yaml

We use Playwright to run automated tests against the web application served by the gateway microservice.

Playwright test scripts

Database fixtures populate the database with realistic test data.

Database fixtures

Docker Compose

Gateway

Metadata

This is a cut-down version of the full FlixTube application.

Figure 9.2   **End-to-end testing of a simplified version of FlixTube using Playwright**

Automated testing coupled with a CI/CD pipeline is like an early warning system. When the alarm goes off, we can be thankful, as it gives us the opportunity to stop problems before going into production and potentially affecting our customers.

> **NOTE**   The true payoff with automated testing is that it will save us from countless hours of routine testing, not to mention that it can stop deployment of broken code that might have otherwise gone into production and caused havoc.

As amazing as automated testing is, it's not a panacea! It's not a replacement for good exploratory testing (e.g., manual testing) by actual humans. That still needs to happen because it's the only way to find the bugs that the development team couldn't even imagine.

Automated testing isn't just about proving that our code works. It also serves as an invaluable communication tool, a kind of *executable documentation* that demonstrates how the code is intended to be used. It also gives us a safe framework in which to refactor and restructure our application, allowing continuous movement toward a simpler and more elegant architecture. Let's work through each type of testing and look at examples of tests applied to the metadata microservice and then to the Flix-Tube application.

9.5   *Automated testing with Jest*

Testing is a huge topic, so let's start with simple examples that aren't directly related to microservices. The code we'll look at in this section is generally applicable for testing JavaScript code, regardless of whether that code is in a frontend, a backend, or even a mobile or desktop application.

If you can already write an automated test with Jest and you understand mocking, feel free to skip this section and move directly to section 9.6. In that section, we'll start to relate automated testing to microservices.

For this section, imagine we're creating a JavaScript math library for use in our microservices. We'll use Jest to do our testing, as shown in figure 9.3.

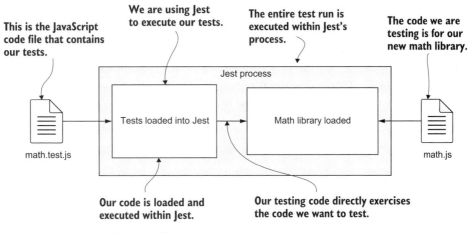

Figure 9.3   Automated testing with Jest

On the left side of the figure, we have the math.test.js file, which contains the tests that we'll run against our math library. On the right, we have the math.js file that contains the code for our math library. When we run Jest, it loads our test code, which, in turn, runs the code we're testing. From our tests, we directly invoke our code to test it and then verify it operated as expected.

9.5.1   *Why Jest?*

Jest is arguably the most popular testing tool and framework for JavaScript. It's easy to set up with minimal configuration, so it's great for beginners. Jest is fast, and it can run tests in parallel. Jest also has great support for live reloading; you can run it in *watch* mode, where it reloads by itself while you're coding.

Jest was created by Facebook, so it not only has great support behind it but also a huge following and many contributors outside of Facebook. The API is extensive, supports multiple styles of testing, and has various ways of validating tests and creating mocks.

There are other great features that we won't even touch on in this chapter. (At the end of the chapter, you'll find a link to learn more about Jest.) Jest is open source and free to use. You can find the code here: https://github.com/facebook/jest.

9.5.2   *Setting up Jest*

We'll start by looking at example-1 in the chapter-9 code repository. You can run these tests for yourself and make changes to those to see what happens. Example-1 already has Jest in its package.json file, so we can simply install dependencies for the project:

```
cd chapter-9/example-1
npm install
```

If you're starting a new project, you can install Jest like this:

```
npm install --save-dev jest
```

We used the `--save-dev` argument to save Jest as a development dependency in package.json. We'll only use Jest in our development or testing environment, so we save it as a development dependency to exclude it from our production environment.

Listing 9.1 shows the Jest configuration from example-1 (chapter-9/example-1/jest.config.js). This is actually the default configuration that was generated by Jest. I didn't change it, except to remove the numerous helpful comments that had been generated into it.

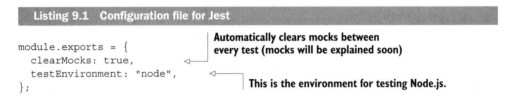

Listing 9.1   Configuration file for Jest

```
module.exports = {
  clearMocks: true,
  testEnvironment: "node",
};
```

Automatically clears mocks between every test (mocks will be explained soon)

This is the environment for testing Node.js.

When starting a fresh project, create your own Jest configuration file like this:

```
npx jest --init
```

Just to remind you, `npx` is a command that comes with Node.js and allows us to run npm modules as command-line applications. There are many npm installable modules that work this way, including Jest. You might recall the `wait-port` command we used with `npx` back in chapter 5.

Figure 9.4 shows the structure of the example-1 project with Jest installed. You can see the familiar package.json and package-lock.json files that are in every Node.js project (from chapter 2). As for Jest, note that this project contains the Jest configuration file (content shown in listing 9.1) and the files for our code and tests. The code for our math library is in math.js, and the code for our tests is in math.test.js. As with any other npm module, Jest itself is installed under the node_modules directory.

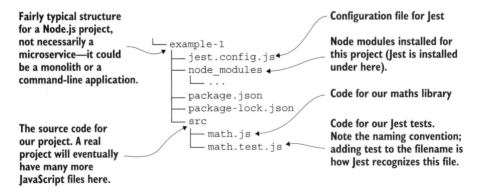

Fairly typical structure for a Node.js project, not necessarily a microservice—it could be a monolith or a command-line application.

Configuration file for Jest

Node modules installed for this project (Jest is installed under here).

```
└─ example-1
   ├─ jest.config.js
   ├─ node_modules
   │  └─ ...
   ├─ package.json
   ├─ package-lock.json
   └─ src
      ├─ math.js
      └─ math.test.js
```

Code for our maths library

The source code for our project. A real project will eventually have many more JavaScript files here.

Code for our Jest tests. Note the naming convention; adding test to the filename is how Jest recognizes this file.

Figure 9.4   The structure of a fairly typical Node.js project with Jest installed

Note that the test file is named after the code that it tests. When creating math.test.js, we simply appended .test.js to the name of our library. This naming convention is how Jest locates our test code. This is the default convention with Jest, but we can configure it differently if we want a different naming convention.

Notice how the test file (math.test.js) is right next to the code file (math.js) in the same directory. This is a fairly common convention. We could also have placed these two files anywhere within the directory structure of our project, and it wouldn't make much difference. Another common convention is to have all tests separated from the application code and located under a test or tests subdirectory that is next to or just under the src subdirectory.

You might have noticed that the Jest configuration file is actually a JavaScript file itself. This means you can use JavaScript code in your configuration. It's quite common for JavaScript and Node.js tools to have an executable configuration file, and I think it's pretty cool that JavaScript can be used as its own configuration language.

9.5.3 *The math library to test*

Now imagine we've added the first function to our new math library. The following listing (chapter-9/example-1/src/math.js) shows the `square` function. This is a simple function that takes one number and returns the square of that number.

> **Listing 9.2   A starting point for our new math library**

```
function square(n) {          A simple JavaScript function computes the
  return n * n;               square of a number. This is the code we'll test.
}

--snip--        ⟵   We can add more functions for our
                    math library here as we develop it.

module.exports = {
  square,       ⟵   Exports the "square" function so we can use
                    it in our code modules. This is also how we
                    access it from our test code.

  --snip--    ⟵
};              Other functions are exported here as we add them to our math library.
```

In the future, we would add many more functions to math.js. But for now, we'll keep it short so it can be a simple demonstration of automated testing.

9.5.4 *Our first Jest test*

The `square` function is a simple function with a simple result, and more complex functions always depend on simpler functions like this. To be sure that the complex functions work, we must first test the simple functions. Yes, even though this function is simple, we still want to test it.

Listing 9.3 (chapter-9/example-1/src/math.test.js) shows the code that tests our nascent math library. The `describe` function defines a test suite called `square` function. The `test` function defines our first test called `can square two`.

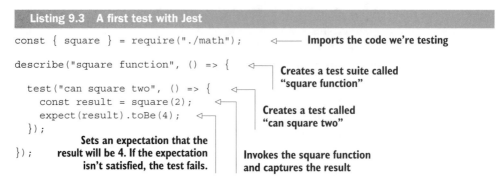

Listing 9.3   A first test with Jest

```
const { square } = require("./math");        ◁——— Imports the code we're testing

describe("square function", () => {          ◁—┐ Creates a test suite called
                                                 "square function"
  test("can square two", () => {       ◁—┐
    const result = square(2);      ◁—   │ Creates a test called
    expect(result).toBe(4);    ◁—┐      │ "can square two"
  });                                    │
        Sets an expectation that the     │ Invokes the square function
});     result will be 4. If the expectation   and captures the result
        isn't satisfied, the test fails.
```

We've named this test suite *square function* after the function that it's testing. You can imagine in the future that we might have other test suites in this file for other functions in our math library.

In listing 9.3, we imported our `square` function from the math.js file. In our `can square two` test, we then called it with the number 2 as input. You can see that we've carefully named the test to indicate its purpose.

> **NOTE**   A good name for a test allows us to instantly understand what is being tested.

We then use the `expect` and `toBe` functions to verify that the result of the `square` function is the number 4. Various combinations of functions can be chained onto the `expect` function (see the Jest docs for more examples at https://jestjs.io/docs/en/expect), which gives a rich syntax for describing the expected output of the code being tested.

9.5.5   *Running our first test*

Now we're ready to run Jest and see what a successful test run looks like (spoiler alert, I already know ahead of time that this code works). From the terminal in the example-1 directory, run the tests as follows:

```
npx jest
```

You can see the output of the successful test run in figure 9.5. We have one test and one test suite; both have completed successfully.

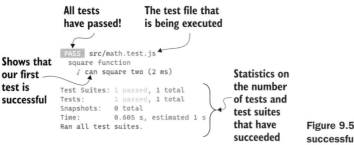

Figure 9.5   The output of our successful test run with Jest

9.5.6　*Live reload with Jest*

Live reloading is important for developer productivity, especially while testing. While coding and writing tests, we can run Jest in live reload mode as follows:

```
npx jest --watchAll
```

That command works for all projects and runs all tests when any code changes. If you're using Git, you can also use this command:

```
npx jest --watch
```

The second version has better performance because it uses Git to know which files have changed (rather than just blindly running all the tests).

Using live reload is a great way to work. We can change some code and the tests automatically run to show us if the change we made has broken anything.

9.5.7　*Interpreting test failures*

All is good and well when our tests are passing, but what about when we have a problem in our code and our tests are failing? Don't wait until you accidentally break your code to find out!

Let's try it now. It's as simple as changing the behavior of our code. For instance, try changing the square function to return the wrong result:

```
function square(n) {
  return n & n;
}
```

Notice how I replaced the multiplication operator with the binary AND operator (&). Let's see what our tests have to say about this.

You can see the output of the failing test in figure 9.6. When a test fails, Jest finishes with a nonzero exit code. This indicates that a failure happened. This is how our CI/CD pipeline can detect that our tests have failed.

This test failed because we changed the expected behavior of our code. In this case, we broke our own code on purpose to see the result, but you can also imagine how a simple typo in our regular development process can cause problems like this in production code. If you didn't have the automated test in place, this problem could easily fall through the cracks of manual testing and later be discovered by a customer. That's embarrassing, to say the least, but it can cause real problems for the business, depending on the nature of the actual bug.

Of course, the intention here isn't just to test the square function. Just that test by itself won't be very effective. We need to have a large proportion of our code covered by many such tests.

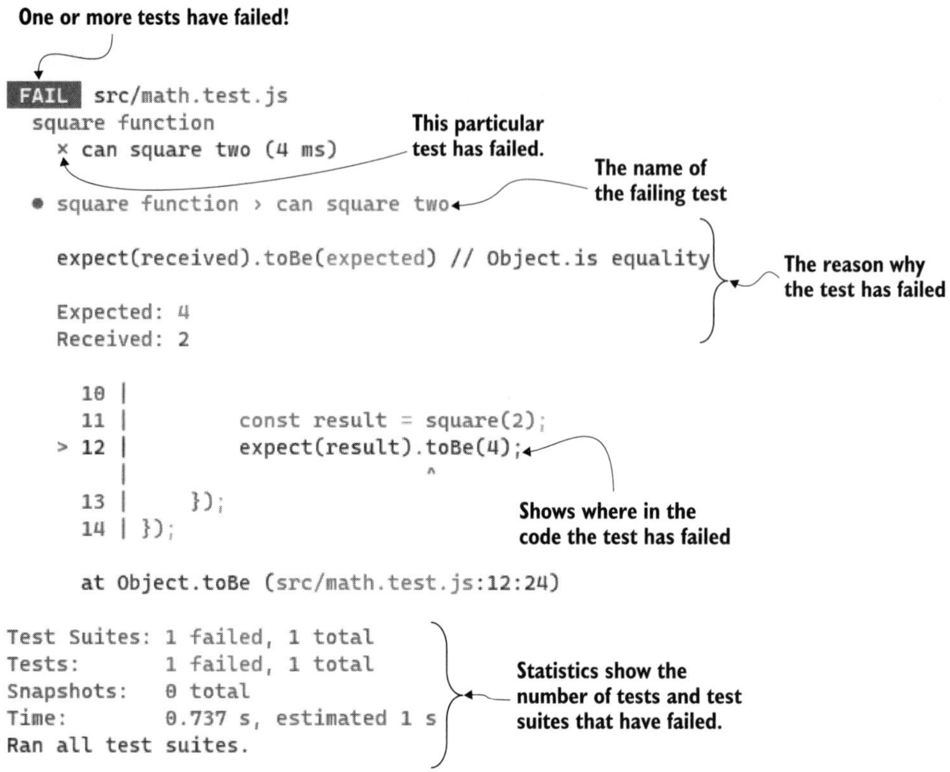

One or more tests have failed!

```
FAIL   src/math.test.js
  square function
    × can square two (4 ms)          This particular
                                     test has failed.
                                                          The name of
  ● square function › can square two ◄               the failing test

    expect(received).toBe(expected) // Object.is equality
                                                              The reason why
                                                              the test has failed
    Expected: 4
    Received: 2

      10 |
      11 |          const result = square(2);
    > 12 |          expect(result).toBe(4); ◄
         |                          ^
      13 |      });                       Shows where in the
      14 |    });                         code the test has failed

      at Object.toBe (src/math.test.js:12:24)

Test Suites: 1 failed, 1 total
Tests:       1 failed, 1 total          Statistics show the
Snapshots:   0 total                    number of tests and test
Time:        0.737 s, estimated 1 s     suites that have failed.
Ran all test suites.
```

Figure 9.6   The output of a failed test in Jest

A large body of tests gives us an automatic verification system that we run to prove, without a doubt, that our code (still) works as intended. More importantly, it proves in the future that our code continues to work as we evolve it.

It's handy to note that we can simulate failing code anywhere we like by throwing an exception like this:

```
throw new Error("This shouldn't happen.");
```

The best way to be fearless in the face of errors is to ruthlessly try to cause them in our own code. When we have seen all the errors, it takes away the fear, and we can focus on understanding and fixing the problem. Simulating or causing problems in code to make sure that our application handles it gracefully is known as *chaos engineering* (check the end of chapter 11 for a reference to learn more about this).

9.5.8   *Invoking Jest with npm*

In chapter 2, we introduced the idea of adding npm scripts to our package.json file so that we can use the conventional npm commands such as `npm start`. Here we'll config-ure the `test` script so that we can run our test suite like this:

```
npm test
```

This convention means that we can easily run tests for any Node.js project without hav-ing to know any details about the project. For example, we don't have to know if it's Jest or some other testing tool. Indeed, you'll see later in this chapter how we'll also run Playwright tests with the same command. Listing 9.4 (chapter-9/example-1/package.json) shows package.json with the test script configured to run Jest.

Listing 9.4   Package.json with npm scripts for running Jest

```
{
  "name": "example-1",
  "version": "1.0.0",
  "scripts": {                          Setup for running Jest by invoking npm test
    "test": "jest",
    "test:watch": "jest --watchAll"
  },                                    Setup for running Jest in live reload mode
  "devDependencies": {
    "jest": "^29.6.4"          ⟵———— Installs Jest as a development dependency
  },
  "dependencies": {
                     ⟵———— This project doesn't have any production dependencies yet.
  }
}
```

Note also in listing 9.4, there's an npm script called `test:watch`. This is configured so that we can run our tests in live reload mode like this:

```
npm run test:watch
```

The `test:watch` script is my own personal convention—it isn't an npm standard. I use it so that no matter which testing tool I use, I can easily remember how to run my tests with live reload enabled.

9.5.9   *Populating our test suite*

So far, we've only seen a single test, but I'd also like to give you a taste of what it looks like as we grow to a suite of tests (containing many tests). Listing 9.5 (additions to chapter-9/example-1/src/math.test.js) shows what math.test.js looks like after adding a second test. (Example-1 doesn't actually contain this new test, but feel free to add it yourself and experiment with it.)

Listing 9.5   Adding the next test

```
const { square } = require("./math");

describe("square function", () => {

  test("can square two", () => {
    --snip--                        ⟵——— Omits the previous test for brevity
  });

  test("can square zero", () => {   ⟵—┐
                                        │ Creates the test
    const result = square(0);           "can square zero"
    expect(result).toBe(0);
  });                               ⟵—┘

  --snip--        ⟵——— Add more tests to our square function test suite here.

});

--snip--        ⟵——— Add more tests suites for the math library here.
```

As listing 9.5 shows, we can add more tests to our `square` function test suite by adding more instances of the `test` function nested inside the test suite's `describe` function.

The new test, `can square zero`, is an example of an edge case. We don't need to add any more tests for squaring positive numbers; `can square two` is enough to cover all positive cases, so we could rename it `can square positive number`. If you'd like to complete this small test suite, you should probably also add a test called `can square negative number`.

As we develop our math library, we'll add more math functions and more test suites. For example, we'll add functions such as `squareRoot` and `average` and their test suites `square root function` and `average function`. Remember, we named our test file math.test.js, and that name is general enough that we can add new test suites to it using the `describe` function.

We could also have separate JavaScript code files for each test suite, for example, square.test.js, square-root.test.js, and average.test.js. Note that these are all appended with .test.js so that Jest can automatically find them. As we add new libraries in the future, we'll add new test files, as many as we need, to contain all the tests that we create.

You can structure your tests in any way you want. You can name the tests how you like and structure them across various files to suit your own needs. When working for a company, however, you'll be expected to follow their existing style and conventions. Whatever convention you follow, I only ask (on behalf of developers everywhere) that you use meaningful names for your tests—names that make it easy to understand the purpose of the test.

9.5.10 *Mocking with Jest*

JavaScript is a great language for creating mocks! The dynamic nature of JavaScript makes it particularly easy to create automated tests as well. But what is mocking?

DEFINITION *Mocking* is where we replace real dependencies in our code with fake or simulated versions of them.

The dependencies that we replace with mocks can be functions, objects, or even entire code modules. In JavaScript, it's easy to create functions and piece together new objects and data structures that we can use as mocks.

Why do we do this? The purpose of mocking is to isolate the code we're testing. Isolating particular sections of code allows us to focus on just testing only that code and nothing else. Isolation is important for unit testing and test-driven development (TDD).

Not only does mocking help isolate the code we're testing, but it can also entirely eliminate the code and processes that would make testing slow. For example, we can eliminate database queries, network transactions, and filesystem operations. These are the kinds of things that can take a huge amount of time compared to the code we're testing.

In section 9.6, you'll learn about unit testing and see a real example of mocking, but let's first understand mocking by examining a simple example. Let's say that instead of using the multiply operator (*) in our `square` function, we'll use the `multiply` function as follows:

```
function square(n) {
  return multiply(n, n);
}
```

If you're wondering why we're using a function to do multiplication when there's already a perfectly good operator, that's a good point. Well, I introduced the `multiply` function here primarily because I need a simple example by which to explain mocking. But if you'd like, I can also concoct a great reason why we need this!

Let's just say that we want our math library to work with abstract data types. Instead of working with ordinary numbers, we want it to be able to work with vectors (arrays of numbers). In this case, the `multiply` function could very well be an extremely complex function that does the computation in parallel on a graphics processing unit (GPU). That seems like a good reason to use a separate function for multiplication.

Now to isolate our code in the `square` function (which arguably isn't much), we need to mock the `multiply` function. That means we must replace it with another function—one that we can control. We can do this using a primitive form of *dependency injection* (DI). DI is a technique where we inject dependencies into our code rather than hardcoding them. We control what the dependencies are, which is useful for isolating code for unit testing. In this case, we inject the `multiply` function into the `square` function like this:

```
function square(n, multiply) {
  return multiply(n, n);
}
```

This works because functions are first-class citizens in JavaScript, and these can be passed around like any other value or object.

Now let's make use of this from our test. When we call the `square` function, we'll pass in our mock version of `multiply`:

```
test("can square two", () => {
    const mockMultiply = (n1, n2) => {
        expect(n1).toBe(2);
        expect(n2).toBe(2);
        return 4;
    };

    const result = square(2, mockMultiply);

    expect(result).toBe(4);
});
```

Expects the square function to pass the right inputs to the multiply function

Hardcodes the mock function to return 4

Passes the mock function into the square function instead of the real multiply function

Creates a mock version of the multiply function

Expects to get back the hardcoded value of 4

You're now probably wondering, what's the point of all this? Given that our mock function returns a hardcoded value of 4, what are we actually testing here? You can read it like this: "We're testing that the `square` function invokes the `multiply` function with inputs 2 and 2, and the result received from `multiply` is the value returned from the `square` function."

You might note at this point that we've just implemented the `square` function, tested it, and proved that it works—and the real version of the `multiply` function doesn't even exist yet! (We can write the GPU-powered version of `multiply` later.) This is one of the superpowers of test-driven development (TDD). TDD allows us to reliably test incomplete versions of our code.

To make this code work for real, we still need to implement the `multiply` function. This can, in turn, have automated tests applied to it.

Okay, so this is a crazy made-up example, but we needed a way to introduce the concept of mocking. It's pretty rare to see DI implemented at such a granular level as just demonstrated. Coming up soon, though, you'll see a more realistic example that replaces an entire code module with a mock.

9.5.11 What have we achieved?

We've seen a simple example of unit testing JavaScript code with Jest. We used mocking to isolate the code we were testing, ensuring that we were running only that code and nothing else.

9.6   *Unit testing for microservices*

Unit testing for microservices works the same as any other kind of unit testing. We aim to test a single *unit* of code by itself and in isolation from other code. What is a unit? Typically, each test exercises a single function or one aspect of a single function.

What's important with unit testing is the isolation. When we test isolated code, we focus our testing efforts on just that small piece of code. For example, we'd like to test the code for our metadata microservice, but we don't care to test the code for, say, the Express library or the MongoDB library. Those are dependencies that we assume have already been tested. Instead, we want to test only the code that we've created. To focus on our own code, we must eliminate all other code.

Isolation of a piece of code is achieved by mocking its dependencies. What this means in terms of our metadata microservice is that we'll substitute the real Express and MongoDB libraries with fake instances that we can control and can bend to our will.

Isolation is what makes unit tests run fast. Integration and end-to-end tests don't isolate code. In those types of testing, we exercise the integration of code modules rather than isolated pieces of code.

When running unit tests, we won't start a real HTTP server or connect to a real database. Excluding slow dependencies is the kind of thing that makes unit tests run quickly, and it's why they are at the foundation of the testing pyramid (refer to figure 9.1). We can afford to have hundreds or even thousands of unit tests for our code, and we won't have to wait a long time for our suite of unit tests to complete.

We'll be using Jest to execute our unit tests. Figure 9.7 shows what we'll do with it. Our test code from index.test.js (on the left) is loaded by Jest. Our code to be tested, the code for our metadata microservice from index.js (on the right), is loaded by our test code.

We'll mock Express and MongoDB instead of using the real thing. The test code "starts" our microservice, but not in the usual way. Unlike in normal execution, Express is mocked so we aren't starting a real HTTP server. Likewise, MongoDB is mocked so we aren't connecting to a real database.

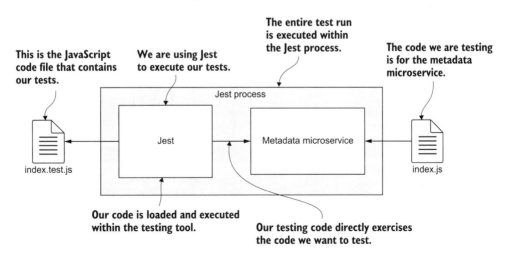

Figure 9.7 Unit testing the metadata microservice with Jest

9.6.1   *The metadata microservice*

We now move on to example-2 in the chapter-9 code repository. To follow along, you'll need to install dependencies:

```
cd chapter-9/example-2
npm install
```

Listing 9.6 (chapter-9/example-2/src/index.js) shows the code we'll test. This is a fledgling microservice that will become FlixTube's metadata microservice. This is a REST API whose purpose is to collect, store, search, and manage the metadata associated with each video. The basic setup in the listing isn't too different from our first microservice back in chapter 2.

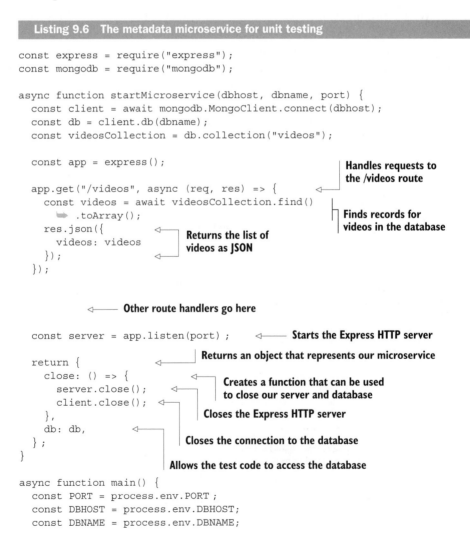

Listing 9.6   The metadata microservice for unit testing

```
const express = require("express");
const mongodb = require("mongodb");

async function startMicroservice(dbhost, dbname, port) {
  const client = await mongodb.MongoClient.connect(dbhost);
  const db = client.db(dbname);
  const videosCollection = db.collection("videos");

  const app = express();

  app.get("/videos", async (req, res) => {            ◁──  Handles requests to
    const videos = await videosCollection.find()           the /videos route
      ➥ .toArray();                                    ┐ Finds records for
    res.json({               ◁──┐ Returns the list of  ┘ videos in the database
      videos: videos              videos as JSON
    });                      ◁──┘
  });

            ◁────── Other route handlers go here

  const server = app.listen(port);    ◁──── Starts the Express HTTP server
  return {            ◁──┐ Returns an object that represents our microservice
    close: () => {    ◁──┐ Creates a function that can be used
      server.close();  ◁─┘ to close our server and database
      client.close();  ◁── Closes the Express HTTP server
    },
    db: db,       ◁──┐ Closes the connection to the database
  };              ◁──┘
}                      Allows the test code to access the database
async function main() {
  const PORT = process.env.PORT;
  const DBHOST = process.env.DBHOST;
  const DBNAME = process.env.DBNAME;
```

```
  await startMicroservice(DBHOST, DBNAME, PORT);
}

if (require.main === module) {            Starts the microservice normally
  main()                              ◄──┐ if this script is the main module
    .then(() => console.log("Microservice online."))
    .catch(err => {
      console.error("Microservice failed to start.");
      console.error(err && err.stack || err);
    });
}                                         Otherwise, running under test, so
else {                                    exports the function to allow the test
  module.exports = {               ◄──── to control how the microservice starts
    startMicroservice,
  };
}
```

Listing 9.6 starts an HTTP server using the Express library and connects to a MongoDB database using the MongoDB library. We added a single handler function for the HTTP GET /videos route. This route retrieves an array of video metadata from the database.

The code we test here will be exercised by calling the function startMicroservice. This is a new function we added to our microservice to help make it more testable. Calling startMicroservice returns a JavaScript object that represents the microservice. We aren't storing the returned object yet. We don't need that for unit testing, but we'll need it later when we come to integration testing. We've made this change to the structure of our microservice in an effort to *design for testing*, and we'll often find ourselves doing this, adapting our code to make it more amenable to testing.

Note that we aren't limited to calling startMicroservice. We could, in fact, call any exported function from any of our code modules; for example, we could add our math library from earlier and test that in the same way we did before. Keep this in mind because it's what unit testing is really all about: testing each and every function individually.

9.6.2 Creating unit tests with Jest

Before we can unit test our code, we need to be able to create mocks for the dependencies. For this example, the dependencies we have are Express and MongoDB. In other situations, we'll have different dependencies; for example, with another microservice, we might need to mock the amqp library for interacting with RabbitMQ.

Listing 9.7 (an extract from chapter-9/example-2/src/index.test.js) shows the code for our tests. This file defines a single test suite called metadata microservice that contains three tests. We've called the file index.test.js to indicate that it tests code contained in the main source file index.js. As we continue to develop our microservice, we'll end up having many more files like this, with tests to cover all the code in our microservice.

The first part of the test suite is devoted to setting up mocks for the Express and MongoDB libraries. Note the use of jest.fn to create mock functions that we can use to detect if the function was called, and, if so, then what arguments were passed to it. Next, note the use of `jest.doMock`, which allows us to mock entire Node.js modules. These tools are powerful and allow us to replace Express and MongoDB without having to adjust the code we're testing.

A bunch of tests have been omitted from listing 9.7 that you can see in the full example code if you like. The test that I have included in listing 9.7 directly invokes the `/videos` route handler function and checks that it retrieves the required data from the database.

This example is advanced, but I wanted to get straight to the point and show you some unit testing that is relevant to microservices. If you struggle to understand this code, don't be too concerned. Just read it, get the gist of it, and understand which parts of it are for mocking and which parts are for testing.

Listing 9.7   Testing the metadata microservice with Jest

```
                                          Defines the test suite for
                                          the metadata microservice
describe("metadata microservice", () => {         Creates a mock listen function

                                          Creates a mock get function
  const mockListenFn = jest.fn();
  const mockGetFn = jest.fn();             Creates a mock for the
                                           Express library
  jest.doMock("express", () => {
    return () => {               The Express library is a factory
      return {                   function that creates the Express
        listen: mockListenFn,    app object.
        get: mockGetFn,
      };                         Returns a mock for the Express app object
    };
  });

  const mockVideosCollection = {};      A mock for the MongoDB videos collection

  const mockDb = {                 A mock for the MongoDB database
    collection: () => {
      return mockVideosCollection;
    }
  };

  const mockMongoClient = {        A mock for the MongoDB client object
    db: () => {
      return mockDb;
    }
  };

  jest.doMock("mongodb", () => {       Creates a mock for the MongoDB module
    return {
      MongoClient: {              A mock for MongoClient
        connect: async () => {
          return mockMongoClient;      A mock for the connect function
```

```
        }
      }
    };
  });
                                        Imports the code we're testing       Tests that the
                                                                              /videos route
  const { startMicroservice } = require("./index");                          retrieves data
                                                                              from the videos
  --snip--                                                                    collection in
                                                                              the database
  test("/videos route retrieves data", async () => {

    await startMicroservice("dbhost", "dbname", 3000);                       Invokes the code
                                                                              to initialize the
                                                                              microservice
    const mockRequest = {};
    const mockJsonFn = jest.fn();            Mock Express request
    const mockResponse = {                   and response objects
      json: mockJsonFn                       passed to our Express
    };                                       route handler

    const mockRecord1 = {};
    const mockRecord2 = {};
                                                     Mocks the find function to return
    mockVideosCollection.find = () => {              some mock database records
      return {
        toArray: async () => {
          return [ mockRecord1, mockRecord2 ];
        }
      };
    };
                                                                            Invokes the route
                                                                            handler function,
    const videosRouteHandler =          Extracts the /videos               which executes the
      mockGetFn.mock.calls[0][1];       route handler function             code under test
    await videosRouteHandler(mockRequest, mockResponse);

    expect(mockJsonFn.mock.calls.length).toEqual(1);       Expects that the json
    expect(mockJsonFn.mock.calls[0][0]).toEqual({          function is called
      videos: [ mockRecord1, mockRecord2 ],
    });                                     Expects that the mock records
  });                                       were retrieved from the database

  --snip--          More tests go here!

});
```

You might be wondering where the jest variable actually comes from because there is no require statement in listing 9.7 that imports it! This is standard JavaScript, and normally, it would be a problem, but this code is running under Jest, which automatically imports the jest variable for us. How nice of it to save us a whole line of code like that.

A large section at the start of listing 9.7 is dedicated to creating the mocks that replace Express and MongoDB. We used jest.fn and jest.doMock to create mocks. Jest has many other useful functions for mocking and specifying the expectations of the test. See the reference at the end of this chapter to read more about mocking with Jest.

We replaced Express and MongoDB with new JavaScript objects, thus providing our own implementations for the dependencies of the code we're testing. When the code calls these functions, it calls our replacement versions and not the usual ones from the real Express and MongoDB libraries.

If we didn't replace Express and MongoDB, then calling `startMicroservice` would start the real HTTP server and connect to the real database. That normal operation is exactly what we want to avoid when unit testing! It's the kind of thing that makes automated tests run slowly. It won't seem like much of a difference right now because, for the moment, we're only talking about a tiny number of tests. But when you get to running hundreds or even thousands of tests, you'll definitely see a big difference.

9.6.3   *Running the tests*

After writing the code and the tests, we're ready to run Jest. From the terminal in the example-2 directory, run the tests as

```
npx jest
```

or

```
npm test
```

The output should show one passing test suite with three passing tests.

9.6.4   *What have we achieved?*

You've learned the basics of unit testing against our microservice using Jest. We mocked the Express and MongoDB libraries, and we tested that our microservice can start and that its `/videos` route can retrieve records from the database.

This might not seem like much, but you can continue to create tests like this to cover code across all of your microservices. You might even want to try TDD, where you write code for tests before writing the actual code being tested. That's a powerful technique that puts testing first and helps us write more testable code and, therefore, more reliable code.

9.7   *Integration testing*

The next step up the testing pyramid (refer to figure 9.1) is integration testing. It's called *integration testing* because, instead of testing code modules in isolation (as we did with unit testing), the emphasis is now on testing code modules functioning together in an integrated fashion. When it comes to microservices, integration testing usually means that we're testing an entire microservice, including all the code modules and code libraries that it depends on.

It would be nice if unit testing was enough to solve all of our problems. Unit testing is very effective because unit tests are extremely fast to run. The speed of unit tests means that we'll be more likely to run them frequently and thus catch problems quickly. Unfortunately, many problems can still be hidden in the spaces between code modules where they can't be detected by unit tests.

> **NOTE** Using the right combination of tests is a balancing act, and we need integration tests because that's the only way to find problems in the integrated code.

Typically, when we run integration tests against a microservice, we'll interact with the microservice through its official HTTP interface instead of directly calling its functions as we did for unit testing. There are other ways we could interact with it, depending on how the microservice is implemented. For example, if the microservice uses RabbitMQ, then we can also interact with it by sending it messages.

Figure 9.8 shows what we'll do with integration testing in this section. Again, we're using Jest to test our metadata microservice, but, this time, we won't be making use of Jest's mocking facilities. Instead of directly calling code in our microservice to test it, we'll send it HTTP requests and check the responses that come back.

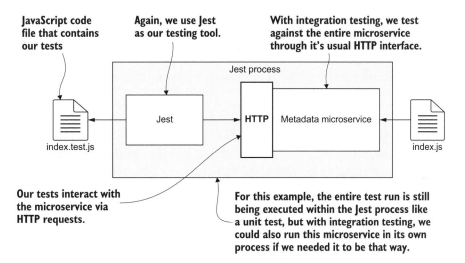

Figure 9.8   Integration testing a microservice with Jest

9.7.1   The code to test

Now we can move to example-3 in the chapter-9 code repository. You can continue to follow along and run these tests. The code we'll test is the same code as in example-2; nothing has changed, so look back to listing 9.6 if you'd like to revise that code.

9.7.2   Running a MongoDB database

When doing integration testing, we won't replace our database with a mock version. Instead, we need a real database, and we need to be able to load realistic test data.

To run the integration tests for example-3, you'll need a real MongoDB database up and running. It's not too difficult to download and install MongoDB. You can install it on your development computer if you haven't already done so. Follow the instructions for your platform here: https://docs.mongodb.com/manual/installation/.

As an alternative, I've included a Docker Compose file in example-3 that starts MongoDB in a Docker container. You can start it like this:

```
cd chapter-9/example-3
docker compose up
```

9.7.3 *Loading database fixtures*

With a database up and running, now we need a way to load database fixtures on demand. A *database fixture* is a set of test data that we can load into our database for testing. It's called a fixture because we use it to seed our database with a fixed (a well-known or specific) set of data.

Doing this is particularly easy with Jest as we can simply create a JavaScript helper function to load data directly into our database through the regular MongoDB Node.js library. MongoDB is already included in the example-3 package.json, and you can install all dependencies for example-3 like this:

```
npm install
```

If you are starting a new project, MongoDB can be installed as follows:

```
npm install --save mongodb
```

Note that we'll use the `--save` argument instead of `--save-dev` because MongoDB is actually used in our production microservice, not just in the test code. Even though we use it for testing, we also need it installed as a production dependency rather than a development dependency.

Listing 9.8 (extract from chapter-9/example-3/src/index.test.js) shows a simple function that we can use for loading test data. We can call this function from our test code, and you'll see an example of that soon. We simply need to specify the name of the collection and the data records to load. Note how we're accessing the microservice's database through the `db` field of the `microservice` object, which is saved in a variable, as shown earlier in listing 9.6. This saves us having to make multiple connections to the database. We don't need to do that because the microservice has already made the connection, and we can just reuse it.

Listing 9.8   A helper function to load a database fixture

```
--snip--

async function loadDatabaseFixture(collectionName,        ⟵  A helper function to
    records) {                                                load a database fixture

    await microservice.db.dropDatabase();        ⟵  Resets the database (don't
                                                     try this in production!)
```

```
    const collection = microservice.db.collection(collectionName);
    await collection.insertMany(records);         ◁──┐
}                                                      Inserts the test data (our database
                                                       fixture) into the database
--snip--
```

9.7.4 Creating an integration test with Jest

Creating an integration test with Jest is much the same as creating a unit test. Because we aren't doing any mocking, it simplifies our test code quite a bit.

Instead of invoking code directly in our microservice, we'll use HTTP requests to trigger the code we'd like to test. To make HTTP requests, we can use either the Node.js low-level HTTP library that we used in chapter 5 or a library installed through npm. In this case, we'll use the Axios library, which is a more modern library that directly supports async/await, so it fits nicely with Jest's support for asynchronous coding.

Example-3 already has Axios added to the package.json file. If you installed all dependencies for example-3, then you already have it. Otherwise, you can install Axios in a new project like this:

```
npm install --save-dev axios
```

We're using the --save-dev argument here because, in this case, we'll only use Axios in our tests. For that reason, it can be a development dependency. If you plan to use Axios in your production code though, be sure to install it as a regular dependency using --save instead of --save-dev.

Listing 9.9 (chapter-9/example-3/src/index.test.js) shows the code for our integration tests. This is similar to the code for our unit tests, but instead of mocking dependencies and directly calling into the code to be tested, we're starting our metadata microservice as a real HTTP server. We then use Axios to send HTTP requests to it.

Be careful that you don't run listing 9.9 against a production database! The function that loads the database fixture first deletes the entire database. Make sure you only ever run this against a test database!

Listing 9.9 Integration testing the metadata microservice with Jest

```
const axios = require("axios");
const mongodb = require("mongodb");

describe("metadata microservice", () => {         ┌─ Sets the base URL for the
                                                   │  microservice we're testing
    const BASE_URL = "http://localhost:3000";    ◁─┘
    const DBHOST = "mongodb://localhost:27017";  ◁──┐
    const DBNAME = "testdb";                          Sets the URL for our database,
                                                      which we're running locally
    const { startMicroservice } = require("./index");

    let microservice;
```

```
beforeAll(async () => {
  microservice =
    ⇒ await startMicroservice(DBHOST, DBNAME);
});
```
Starts the microservice, including the HTTP server and the database connection

```
afterAll(async () => {
  await microservice.close();
});
```
Shuts down the microservice

```
function httpGet(route) {
  const url = `${BASE_URL}${route}`;
  return axios.get(url);
}
```
The helper function that loads test data (a database fixture) into our database. We defined this function in listing 9.8.

```
async function loadDatabaseFixture(collectionName,
  ⇒ records) {
  await microservice.db.dropDatabase();

  const collection = microservice.db.collection(collectionName);
  await collection.insertMany(records);
}
```

```
test("/videos route retrieves data", async () => {
  const id1 = new mongodb.ObjectId();
  const id2 = new mongodb.ObjectId();
  const videoPath1 = "my-video-1.mp4";
  const videoPath2 = "my-video-2.mp4";

  const testVideos = [
    {
      _id: id1,
      videoPath: videoPath1
    },
    {
      _id: id2,
      videoPath: videoPath2
    },
  ];

  await loadDatabaseFixture("videos", testVideos);

  const response = await httpGet("/videos");
  expect(response.status).toEqual(200);

  const videos = response.data.videos;
  expect(videos.length).toEqual(2);
  expect(videos[0]._id).toEqual(id1.toString());
  expect(videos[0].videoPath).toEqual(videoPath1);
  expect(videos[1]._id).toEqual(id2.toString());
  expect(videos[1].videoPath).toEqual(videoPath2);
});
```
Tests that a list of videos can be retrieved via an HTTP request to the /videos route

Creates test data to load into the database

Loads the database fixture into the videos collection of the database

Makes an HTTP request to the route we're testing

Expects that the received data matches our test data

```
--snip--
```
More tests go here!

```
});
```

In listing 9.9, there is only one test, but we can easily add more as we develop the microservice. Here again, we test the /videos route. This time, though, we do it through its normal HTTP interface, and the microservice is using a real database instead of a mock.

Note in listing 9.9 how we use Jest's beforeAll function to start our microservice before testing, and then the afterAll function to shut down the microservice. See how we're saving a reference to the microservice object. This means we can access its database connection and shut down the microservice when the test is done. Shutting down our microservice is something we never considered before, but it's important here because this might not be the only test suite, and we don't want to leave this microservice running longer than necessary.

You might have realized that as we add more tests to this test suite, we'll run multiple tests against the same microservice. It's not ideal to share the microservice across multiple tests in this way because it makes it difficult to know if each test is independent of the others. But it's significantly faster to do it this way than to separately start and stop the microservice for each test in turn. We could do that to make the test suite more reliable, but it makes running the test suite much slower.

Other tools for integration testing microservices

Here are some other useful ways to do integration testing for your microservices for you to explore later:

- *Supertest*—A nice API that integrates with Express and makes it easy to send requests to your microservices and test their responses
- *Pact*—A more advanced tool for testing your microservices in pairs to ensure that the contract (i.e., communication) they have with each other continues to work into the future

---

9.7.5 *Running the test*

Running integration tests with Jest is the same as running unit tests. Invoke the following:

```
npx jest
```

Because we configured it in package.json, you can also invoke this:

```
npm test
```

Try running this integration test for yourself. In addition, try changing code to break the test and see what error messages come up, like we did earlier when unit testing.

9.7.6 *What have we achieved?*

In this section, you learned the basics of running integration tests with Jest. It's pretty much like unit testing, but we left out the mocking. As a result, we ran our code integrated with all of its dependencies.

When doing integration testing, we're not trying to isolate the code under test (that was the point of unit testing), and we aren't trying to mock any dependencies, which is what helps achieve that isolation. We are, instead, aiming to test the code in its integrated state! That is, we're testing it in combination with all the other code it depends on: code in other modules and code in external libraries.

In a sense, integration testing is easier than unit testing because we don't have the concerns of isolation and mocking. Creating integration tests can also be a more effective use of our time than writing unit tests because integration tests tend to cover more code, so you need to spend less time writing tests.

The big problem with integration tests is that they are slow compared to unit tests. That is why they have a higher position in the testing pyramid. Consider the unit and integration tests that we've already seen in this chapter. They have basically tested the same thing. But in the case of integration testing, we started a real live HTTP server that connects to a real database. Using real dependencies makes integration tests much slower to execute than unit tests.

9.8   *End-to-end testing*

Now we take the final step up the testing pyramid (refer to figure 9.1) and arrive at end-to-end testing. This is similar to integration testing except we aim to test against our whole application or, at least, some cut-down version of it. We hope to test our application in its entirety and as close as we can get to its production configuration.

With end-to-end testing, we'll be running tests against the UI—in this case, against FlixTube's frontend. We don't have to do any mocking as we did with unit tests, so that makes things a bit easier, but we do need database fixtures like we used with integration testing, so that we can load realistic test data.

Traditionally, it would have been difficult to do end-to-end testing against a distributed application because it takes a lot of effort to configure and start all the services. Fortunately, we're now empowered by Docker Compose, which you learned in chapters 4 and 5 and have used since to develop our application. We'll now use Docker Compose as a convenient way to boot our microservices application for automated end-to-end testing.

At this point, we're leaving Jest behind and moving on to Playwright, a testing tool for loading and testing web pages. Playwright is powerful and has many features, but we'll just learn some basics, enough to get started and get a taste of what it can do. We'll use Playwright to run tests against FlixTube, through its frontend that is served by the gateway microservice, as illustrated in figure 9.9.

Running end-to-end tests requires that we start our whole application (including the database) and do the testing against the frontend running in a web browser. This makes end-to-end tests the slowest of all the types of testing, earning them their place at the top of the testing pyramid.

That said, having a handful of end-to-end tests should be an important part of our testing strategy. End-to-end testing covers a lot of ground, so even though these can

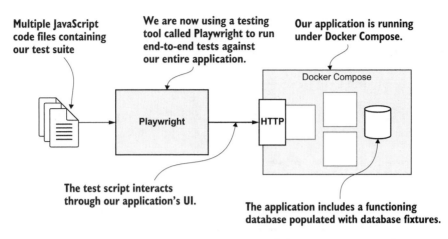

Figure 9.9   End-to-end testing our entire application with Playwright and Docker Compose

take significant time to run, they deliver a lot of bang for buck. In addition, this type of testing exercises our application through the frontend, which happens to be the point of view of our customer. Needless to say, this is the most important perspective from which we can test our application, and it's the primary reason we place such a high value on end-to-end tests.

9.8.1   Why Playwright?

Playwright is a fantastic all-in-one-tool for testing web pages. It's simple to install and start using and has a great automated configuration generator, which includes running tests on multiple browsers (it even transparently downloads the browsers for you). By default, Playwright runs in *headless* (not visible) mode, which makes it easy to get working in your CI/CD pipeline. On top of that, it also has great visual reporting and debugging tools.

Playwright was created by Microsoft as an open source project. You can find the code for it on GitHub here: https://github.com/microsoft/playwright.

9.8.2   Installing Playwright

For this book and for FlixTube, we integrate Playwright, our end-to-end tests, and some microservices into a single code repository. But there are other ways you could structure this. You might like to have your Playwright tests in their own code repository or have your frontend and the tests together in their own repository that is separate from the other microservices. I've included everything you need under the example-4 repository just to make it easy for you to try out.

You can install dependencies like this:

```
cd chapter-9/example-4
npm install
```

You don't need to do it for the example-4 project, but if you wanted to install Playwright in a new project (as per the Playwright getting started guide), you can install Playwright like this:

```
npm init playwright@latest
```

This isn't the same as installing other npm modules. We could, I imagine, also install it like this:

```
npm install --save-dev @playwright/test
```

Except, if we install it in the usual way, we'll have to set up our own configuration. When we install the first way, using `npm init`, it does the setup for us, which includes creating a configuration file, plus example tests to help us get started, and it will even ask us if we'd like to generate a GitHub Actions workflow file (it creates a CI pipeline for us!). It's an impressive starting point for writing end-to-end tests.

You can see the structure of the example-4 project with Playwright installed in figure 9.10. This is similar to other project structures we've worked with in earlier chapters. We have a docker-compose.yaml file to build and run our application, and we have code for our microservices in subdirectories. In addition, now we have a Playwright configuration file, our end-to-end tests, and a new REST API for loading database fixtures.

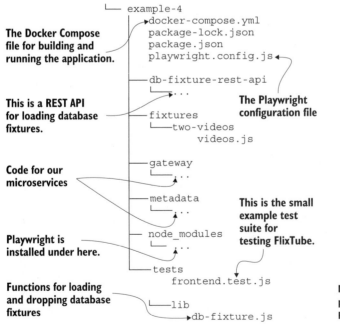

Figure 9.10 Example-4 project structure with Playwright installed

Listing 9.10 (extract from chapter-9/example-4/playwright.config.js) shows a cut-down (the actual one is quite long) version of the Playwright configuration file that was generated during the Playwright installation.

Listing 9.10   Configuration file for Playwright

```
const config = {
  testDir: './tests',     ⟵――| Sets the subdirectory in the
                                 project that contains our tests

  use: {
    baseURL: 'http://localhost:4000',     ⟵―┐ Sets the base URL for the web page
                                              we'll run tests against. This is where
    --snip--                                  the FlixTube frontend will be running.
  },

  --snip--
};

module.exports = config;
```

Note in listing 9.10 how we set the base URL in the configuration file. This lets Playwright know where we're running our frontend (the FlixTube frontend). It's a shortcut so that we don't have to specify the full URL when visiting each page in every test.

9.8.3 Setting up database fixtures

Before we start our application, we must be able to load database fixtures. When using Jest earlier, we were able to load data into our database directly from the test code. We could probably also do this directly from code running under Playwright, but then our tests would need the code and configuration to connect to our database (with Jest, we didn't need this because we piggybacked directly on the microservice's database connection). Instead, I prefer to delegate this to another REST API, one that I can reuse from project to project without having to clutter up my tests with database connection details.

So, to load test data into our database, we'll use a separate REST API. That means we can make HTTP requests to load and unload database fixtures. We're already using Docker Compose, so it's not difficult to add an extra container into our application. Figure 9.11 shows the structure of our application, including the new database fixtures REST API.

Creating a REST API like this is quite a bit of work. However, I already have one that I've used for testing projects in the past. I've included a copy of the code for it under the example-4 various projects (find it under example-4/db-fixtures-rest-api). You can also find a standalone copy of the code on GitHub: https://github.com/ashleydavis/db-fixture-rest-api.

We won't cover the internals of the database fixtures REST API in this book. We have to draw the line somewhere, but feel free to look over this code on your own. Be assured that you won't find anything particularly new here; after all, it's just a Node.js

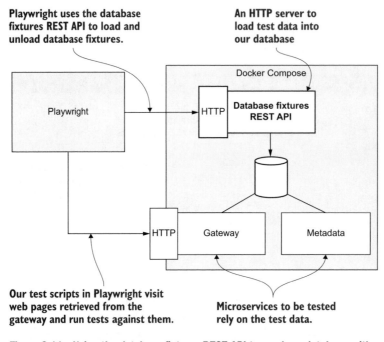

Playwright uses the database fixtures REST API to load and unload database fixtures.

An HTTP server to load test data into our database

Our test scripts in Playwright visit web pages retrieved from the gateway and run tests against them.

Microservices to be tested rely on the test data.

Figure 9.11   Using the database fixtures REST API to seed our database with test data prior to running tests with Playwright

REST API built on Express and is similar to the microservices you've already seen in this book.

Listing 9.11 is an extract from the example-4 docker-compose.yaml file (chapter-9/example-3/docker-compose.yaml). It shows how we integrate the database fixtures REST API into our application the same way as any other microservice.

Listing 9.11   Loading the database fixtures REST API with Docker Compose

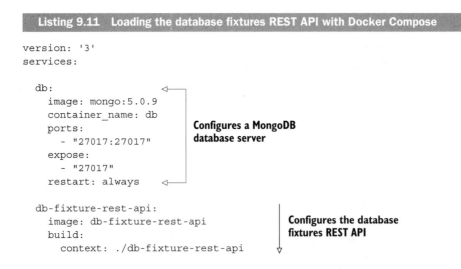

```
version: '3'
services:

  db:
    image: mongo:5.0.9
    container_name: db
    ports:
      - "27017:27017"
    expose:
      - "27017"
    restart: always

  db-fixture-rest-api:
    image: db-fixture-rest-api
    build:
      context: ./db-fixture-rest-api
```

Configures a MongoDB database server

Configures the database fixtures REST API

```
    dockerfile: Dockerfile
  container_name: db-fixture-rest-api
  ports:
   - "9000:80"
  environment:
   - PORT=80
   - DBHOST=mongodb://db:27017        Configures the database
   - FIXTURES_DIR=fixtures            fixtures REST API
  volumes:
   - ./fixtures:/usr/src/app/fixtures:z
  depends_on:
   - db
  restart: always

  --snip--        The gateway and metadata microservices are
                  defined here, but omitted from this code listing.
```

Listing 9.11 adds the database fixtures REST API to our application, but we still need a way to talk to it from our Playwright tests. For that, we'll create some JavaScript functions that we can use from Playwright tests to load database fixtures. Listing 9.12 (chapter-9/example-4/tests/lib/db-fixture.js) is an extract that shows the function we can use to load a database fixture.

Listing 9.12   Loading a database fixture under Playwright

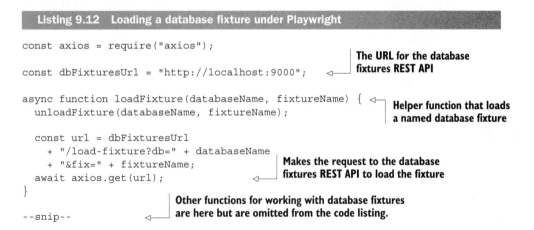

```
const axios = require("axios");

const dbFixturesUrl = "http://localhost:9000";      The URL for the database
                                                    fixtures REST API

async function loadFixture(databaseName, fixtureName) {    Helper function that loads
  unloadFixture(databaseName, fixtureName);               a named database fixture

  const url = dbFixturesUrl
    + "/load-fixture?db=" + databaseName      Makes the request to the database
    + "&fix=" + fixtureName;                  fixtures REST API to load the fixture
  await axios.get(url);
}
                         Other functions for working with database fixtures
--snip--                 are here but are omitted from the code listing.
```

The loadFixture function uses Axios to make an HTTP GET request to the database fixtures REST API and causes it to load a database fixture from a file (in this case, example-4/fixtures/two-videos/videos.js). In a moment, you'll see how we invoke this command from our test code.

9.8.4   Booting your application

We have Playwright installed and ready to go, and we have the ability to load database fixtures. Before we can test our application, we must boot it!

Listing 9.11 was an extract of the Docker Compose file for example-4. The complete file contains the configuration for a cut-down version of FlixTube with only the gateway and metadata microservices (other microservices are omitted; we only include what we need to test). This is nowhere near the full application, but it's enough that we can write a test to confirm that the list of videos is retrieved from the database and displayed in the frontend.

In this chapter, I've simplified FlixTube just so that I can present it as a simple example. But it's interesting to note that this technique of crafting cut-down versions of our application is quite useful. In the future, when our microservices application has grown too big to run on any single computer, we might be required to chop it up into smaller configurations to make each part of it testable. This could be the only way to do end-to-end testing in the future when our application has grown large and unwieldy!

Now, let's start the application using our old friend Docker Compose:

```
cd chapter-9/example-4
docker compose up --build
```

9.8.5 *Creating an end-to-end test with Playwright*

Writing end-to-end tests with Playwright is similar to writing tests with Jest, but there are some differences. Listing 9.13 (extract from chapter-9/example-4/tests/frontend .test.js) shows an example Playwright test; notice the familiar overall structure composed of `describe` and `test` functions. See the `page` argument that is passed to each test? This is the interface provided to us by Playwright that allows us to control the web page we're testing against.

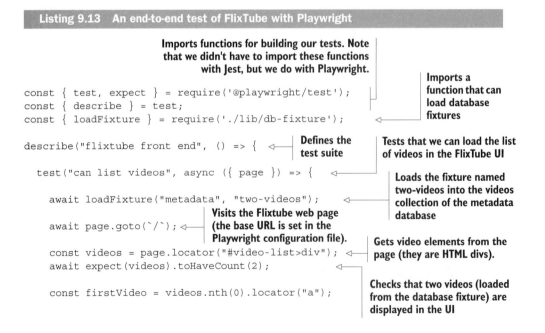

Listing 9.13   An end-to-end test of FlixTube with Playwright

```
    await expect(firstVideo)
       .toHaveText("SampleVideo_1280x720_1mb.mp4");
    await expect(firstVideo).toHaveAttribute("href",
       "/video?id=5ea234a1c34230004592eb32"
    );

    const secondVideo = videos.nth(1).locator("a");
    await expect(secondVideo)
       .toHaveText("Another video.mp4");
    await expect(secondVideo).toHaveAttribute("href",
       "/video?id=5ea234a5c34230004592eb33"
    );
  });
```

> **Verifies the details displayed for the first video**

> **Verifies the details displayed for the second video**

⟵——— **Other tests go here.**

```
});
```

The first line of code in our test is a call to our `loadFixture` function. On the next line, we call `page.goto` to make Playwright visit a web page. All other Playwright functions operate relative to the page that is visited. Here we're visiting the / (root) route for the FlixTube web page. Note that this is relative to the base URL that we specified earlier in the Playwright configuration file.

Next, we use `page.locator` to retrieve elements from the browser's document object model (DOM) hierarchy and run tests against them. Our code then checks that we have two videos in the video list and then verifies the names and links for each. We know these videos should be displayed in the frontend because we've seeded the database for the metadata microservice with the `two-videos` database fixture. That database fixture loads test data (you can see it in example-4/fixtures/two-videos/videos.js) into the database with all the details of these two videos.

Now let's run our tests. In the example-4 directory, invoke Playwright like this:

```
npx playwright test
```

In the terminal, we see messages from Playwright showing us the tests in progress and the browser they are running in. If there is a failure, Playwright opens a web page to view the results from the tests.

If you prefer to get all of your results (pass or fail) in the terminal, like me, you can choose to list the test results like this:

```
npx playwright test --reporter=list
```

Getting your results in the terminal is also what we need to run these as part of our CI or CD pipeline, as described in chapter 8.

Just make sure you have the application running before you try to test it! If you haven't done this, you won't have any application to run tests against. Invoke the following:

```
docker compose up --build
```

Running end-to-end tests can take significant time. They are slow because they start a real web browser to run the tests against (even though you don't see it because it's a headless browser, i.e., not displayed). They are even slower because Playwright (by default) is configured to run not just against one browser but against three! If you look near the end of the Playwright configuration file, you'll see that it's configured to run on Chrome, Firefox, and Safari. I don't know about you, but I think it's pretty impressive that these days we can so easily run our automated tests across multiple web browsers.

The test in example-4 should pass (you should actually see three successes, one for each web browser). If you like, now you can try to break it, just like we did earlier with our Jest tests. For example, open the file example-4/gateway/src/views/   video-list.hbs. This is the HTML that is rendered for the FlixTube home page (in the format of a Handlebars template, which we'll discuss in chapter 10). Try changing this HTML so that something different is displayed for each video in the list. Now run the tests again, and you should see that they are broken.

Just be careful that you never run this test against a production database. Loading a database fixture wipes out the related database collections (i.e., resets them to our test data), and we never want to lose production data. We shouldn't be able to do this in production anyway because we would never run the database fixtures REST API in production or connect it to a production database! That is what gives us the ability to load database fixtures, but we only need it for development and testing environments. If you find yourself connecting the database fixtures REST API to a production database someday, be aware that you're on the way to making a seriously damaging mistake (like deleting your customer's data).

> **NOTE** Running the database fixtures REST API in a production environment also gives external access to your database. This is a recipe for disaster, so be careful never to instantiate it in production.

There's so much more we can do with Playwright! This includes clicking buttons, for example, clicking the first video element from listing 9.13 as

```
await firstVideo.click();
```

or, typing values into input fields:

```
anInputElement.type("Hello world");
```

The way to learn more is to read the docs; just follow the Docs link from the Playwright web page: https://playwright.dev/.

Especially interesting is Playwright's visual tracing feature that provides a GUI for us to step through each action of our test visually: https://playwright.dev/docs/trace-viewer-intro. Playwright also has great support for debugging our tests at https://playwright.dev/docs/debug.

We can also mock our backend and REST APIs with Playwright. This is really useful because it allows us to do a kind of unit testing against our frontend. That would mean we aren't really end-to-end testing our whole application anymore, but it can be an extremely valuable technique for testing our frontend in isolation. Read more about it here: https://playwright.dev/docs/mock.

9.8.6 *Invoking Playwright with npm*

Now we can get set up to invoke our Playwright tests with npm just like we did with Jest. Example-4 is a separate project from the other examples for this chapter, and we use a different testing tool (Playwright rather than Jest). Nevertheless, we'd like to be able to run our Playwright tests with the conventional npm test script like this:

```
npm test
```

Listing 9.14 (extract from chapter-9/example-4/package.json) shows the setup in package.json to make this work. We've configured the "test" script to run our Playwright tests.

Listing 9.14   Package.json with npm scripts for running Playwright

```
{
    "name": "example-4",
    "version": "1.0.0",
    "scripts": {
        "test": "playwright test —reporter=list
           ➡ —workers 1"
    },
    "dependencies": {},
    "devDependencies": {
        --snip—
    }
}
```

> Runs our Playwright tests with a single worker. We need it this way because we're sharing a database among all our tests. To run our tests in parallel on multiple workers, we would have to mock our backend or our database.

Unfortunately, as yet, there is no way to run Playwright in watch mode. So we can't implement the npm script `test:watch` like we did with Jest. This will probably change in the future, though, because work on Playwright is still progressing.

9.8.7 *What have we achieved?*

We've almost come to the end of our journey through the testing landscape. We've seen examples of unit testing, integration testing, and now end-to-end testing.

We've discussed the relative performance of tests: integration tests are slower than unit tests, and end-to-end tests are slower than integration tests. We've also seen how each unit test covers only a small amount of isolated code. Integration and end-to-end testing can be very effective because these cover much more code with fewer tests.

The question now is, how many of each type of test should you have? There's no exact answer to this question because it depends on the particulars of each project.

But what I can say is that you can, and probably should, have hundreds or thousands of unit tests. You'll need to have much fewer integration tests and very much fewer end-to-end tests. It's difficult to say how many because it really depends on how long you're willing to wait for a test to run to completion. If you're happy to wait overnight or over a weekend for your test suite to complete, then you probably can afford to have hundreds or thousands of end-to-end tests as well.

As developers, though, we crave fast and comprehensive feedback. For this, we can't beat unit tests. If we can have a huge amount of code coverage through many extremely fast unit tests, then this is what we should be aiming for because fast tests will get used by the development team, and slow tests won't (developers hate waiting for tests). If your tests are slow, developers will tend to avoid them.

At the end of the day, it's not black and white. There isn't even a marked distinction between the different types of tests. Where does unit testing end and integration testing begin? It's not clear. All tests fall on a spectrum, and it's a spectrum with many shades of gray.

9.9   *Automated testing in the CI/CD pipeline*

We have a suite of automated tests. Now we arrive at the real point of automated testing: to put it on automatic! To truly be automatic, our tests need to operate directly on our hosted code repository. When a developer pushes code changes to the code repository, we'd like to automatically run the test suite to check the health of the code. To achieve this, we must run the tests from our CI/CD pipeline, where they can be invoked automatically whenever any developer pushes code to the code repository. Our automated tests are most valuable when used as a checkpoint in front of production deployment, as shown in figure 9.12. If the tests pass, our code goes to production. If they fail, our code won't be deployed to production.

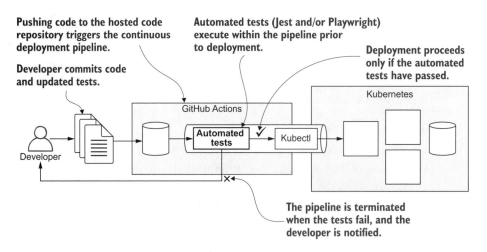

Figure 9.12   Automated testing within the CD pipeline

The reason we spent time earlier discussing the configuration of the npm test script in package.json is because that's how we integrate our automated tests into our CI/CD pipeline. Adding automated testing to our CI/CD pipeline is easy; whatever the project (assuming we configured it correctly), we can invoke this:

```
npm test
```

You might remember that we already made use of this in chapter 8. Review listing 8.3 to see how npm test fits into a GitHub Actions workflow.

9.10 Review of testing

Before finishing the chapter, table 9.2 provides a quick review of Jest and Playwright and how we use these to run tests.

Table 9.2 Review of testing commands

Command	Description
npx jest --init	Initializes the Jest configuration file
npx jest	Runs tests under Jest
npx jest --watch	Runs tests with live reload enabled to rerun tests when code has changed. It uses Git to know which files have changed.
npx jest --watchAll	Same as npx jest --watch, except it monitors all files for changes and not just those that are reported changed by Git
npx playwright test	Runs Playwright tests and opens the test report in our web browser
npx playwright test ⮕ --reporter=list	Runs Playwright tests, but reports results in the terminal
playwright test ⮕ --workers 1	Runs Playwright tests with only a single worker. This disables parallelization, which we can't use if we're sharing a database between our tests.
npm test	The npm script convention for running tests. It runs Jest or Playwright (or even both if correctly configured). This is the command to invoke in our CI/CD pipeline to execute our test suite.
npm run test:watch	This is my personal convention for running tests in live reload mode. You need to configure this script in your package.json file to use it.

9.11 Continue your learning

In this chapter, you learned the basics of automated testing. There's enough here to kick-start your own testing regime, but testing is such a huge subject and is a specialization in its own right. To explore the subject further, refer to the following books:

- *Unit Testing Principles, Practices, and Patterns* by Vladimir Khorikov (Manning, 2020)

- *The Art of Unit Testing*, 3rd ed., by Roy Osherove and Vladimir Khorikov (Manning, est. February 2024)
- *Testing Java Microservices* by Alex Soto Bueno, Andy Gumbrecht, and Jason Porter (Manning, 2018)
- *Testing Microservices with Mountebank* by Brandon Byars (Manning, 2018)

Also see *Exploring JavaScript Testing* by Elyse Kolker Gordon (Manning, 2019), which is a free collection of chapters about testing from other books available from Manning:

- www.manning.com/books/exploring-javascript-testing

To learn more about Jest, see the Jest web page and getting started guide here:

- https://jestjs.io/
- https://jestjs.io/docs/en/getting-started

To learn more about Playwright, please see the Playwright web page and getting started guide:

- https://playwright.dev/
- https://playwright.dev/docs/intro

Summary

- Automated testing is essential for scaling up to large numbers of microservices and being able to know that they are all still working correctly.
- The testing pyramid diagram shows the relationship between unit testing, integration testing, and end-to-end testing and that, generally, you should have more unit tests than integration tests and more integration tests than end-to-end tests.
- Unit testing aims to exercise a small unit of code (say, one function, or one aspect of one function) in isolation from the rest of the code. Testing in isolation means we're only testing the code we care about, and no other code can interfere with the result of that.
- Mocking means creating fake or simulated dependencies to isolate our code.
- Mocking is particularly easy in JavaScript because we can easily create and configure new objects and new functions. This makes testing in JavaScript a very nice experience (at least in my opinion).
- Integration testing exercises a larger portion of code, say, a whole microservice.
- End-to-end testing exercises our whole application or possibly a cut-down or limited configuration of it (e.g., when our microservices application grows too big to run on a single computer or when we'd like to test a specific cross section of it).
- We can run unit and integration tests with the Jest testing framework, a popular JavaScript testing tool.

- We can perform integration tests for a microservice by starting the whole microservice and then triggering its functionality through its normal interface. Our test code can invoke the microservice via HTTP requests or via messages (e.g. RabbitMQ messages).

- We can perform end-to-end tests for a microservices application by starting the application (or some limited part of it) using Docker Compose and then using the Playwright testing framework to interact with the application through the frontend.

- Live reload can be enabled with Jest using the `--watch` and `--watchAll` flags, which automatically rerun our automated tests while we're coding, giving us fast feedback during the development process.

- Our tests can be integrated into our CI or CD pipeline to create an automatic warning system that will notify us when our code has been broken. Typically, JavaScript tests are integrated by implementing the "test" script in the package.json file and then invoking the command `npm test` within the CI/CD pipeline.

Shipping FlixTube

This chapter covers

- Revisiting the tools you've learned so far
- Working with a monorepo for microservices
- Understanding the layout, structure, and main code paths of FlixTube
- Building, running, and testing FlixTube in development
- Building the continuous deployment pipeline for FlixTube

Getting to chapter 10 has been a long road to travel. Along the way, we used numerous tools to build, test, and deploy microservices. In this chapter, we'll see the fruits of our labor come together in the completed version of the FlixTube example application.

You'll learn how FlixTube works as a whole and meet some new microservices. We'll also revise and consolidate our skills in the context of a complete, although still relatively simple, microservices application.

We'll start by building and running FlixTube in development. Next, we'll run our tests from chapter 9 against it. Ultimately, we'll deploy FlixTube to our production Kubernetes cluster and see its continuous deployment (CD) pipeline.

10.1 No new tools!

Congratulations! You've already learned all the main tools you need to start building microservices applications. You can see the list of tools we'll revisit in this chapter in table 10.1.

Table 10.1 The main tools we revisit in chapter 10

Tool	Version	Purpose
Node.js	18.17.1	We use Node.js to run individual microservices (in this chapter, we use the metadata microservice as an example).
Docker	24.0.5	We use Docker to package and publish FlixTube's microservices.
Docker Compose	Included with Docker	We use Docker Compose to run FlixTube for development and testing.
Kubernetes	1.25.12	We deploy FlixTube to a local Kubernetes instance (running on Docker Desktop) and also to a production Kubernetes instance running on the Azure cloud.
Kubectl	1.27.2	We use kubectl to deploy FlixTube to Kubernetes.
GitHub Actions	N/A	We use GitHub Actions to create a continuous integration/continuous deployment (CI/CD) pipeline for FlixTube.
Jest	29.6.4	We use Jest to run tests against the metadata microservice.
Playwright	1.37.1	We use Playwright for testing the FlixTube frontend.

There is, of course, a deeper level of knowledge to be acquired for each of these tools. There are also many other useful tools that you could learn, and new tools will arrive on the scene in the future. But, for the purposes of this book, you've learned the minimum amount of tooling to build products based on microservices. As you dive deeper into ongoing development, you'll find problems that are specific to your project, and you'll need to go further to figure them out. In the future, you'll want to learn more about Docker, Kubernetes, Terraform, and GitHub Actions. For now, though, we have enough tools in our toolbox to complete our first version of FlixTube, so let's get to it.

10.2 Getting the code

To follow along with this chapter, you need to download the code or clone the repository:

- Download a zip file of the code from here: http://mng.bz/p1Ww
- You can clone the code using Git like this:

```
git clone https://github.com/bootstrapping-microservices-2nd-edition/
➥ chapter-10.git
```

For help on installing and using Git, see chapter 2. If you have problems with the code, log an issue in the repository in GitHub.

10.3   *Revisiting essential skills*

As we work through the complete FlixTube example, we'll exercise the essential skills we've learned to build, run, test, and deploy microservices. When you see it in a list like this, you realize just how much ground we've covered!

- Running microservices with Node.js (from chapter 2)
- Packaging and publishing our microservices with Docker (from chapters 3 and 6)
- Building and running our application in development with Docker Compose (from chapters 4 and 5)
- Storing and retrieving data using a database (from chapter 4)
- Storing and retrieving files using external file storage (from chapter 4)
- Communication between microservices with HTTP requests and RabbitMQ messages (from chapter 5)
- Testing individual microservices with Jest (from chapter 9)
- Testing the whole application with Playwright (from chapter 9)
- Deploying the application to a Kubernetes cluster using kubectl (from chapter 6)
- Creating a CD pipeline with GitHub Actions (chapter 8)

Figure 10.1 illustrates the skills we'll revisit and shows their context in the scheme of things. To make the most of this chapter, follow along with the examples. You should get FlixTube running for yourself so you can study it and understand how it works. To test and improve your understanding, you should try making your own changes. Practice is the best way to cement these skills in your mind.

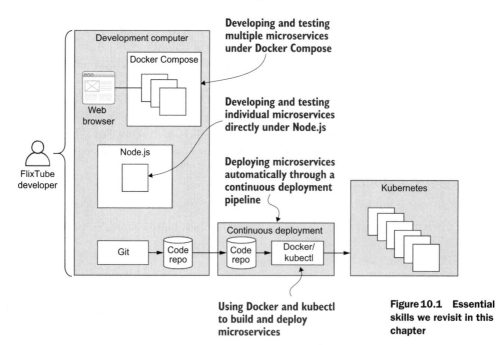

Figure 10.1   Essential skills we revisit in this chapter

10.4 Overview of FlixTube

The code for this chapter only includes a single example: the complete FlixTube project. You can find it in the chapter-10 code repository. Let's start with a bird's-eye view of its structure. Figure 10.2 shows the latest incarnation of FlixTube.

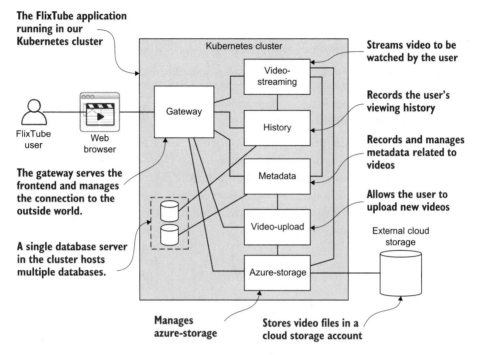

Figure 10.2   Overview of the completed FlixTube example application

10.4.1 FlixTube microservices

You already know some of the microservices shown in figure 10.2, for example:

- Video-streaming (first encountered in chapter 2)
- Azure-storage (from chapter 4)
- History (from chapter 5)
- Metadata (from chapter 9)

There are also some new microservices that you haven't seen yet, for example: gateway and video-upload. Table 10.2 lists the purpose for each of these microservices.

Table 10.2   FlixTube microservices

Microservice	Purpose
Gateway	The entry point to the application that serves the frontend and provides a REST API
Video-streaming	Streams videos from storage to be watched by the user

Table 10.2 FlixTube microservices *(continued)*

Microservice	Purpose
History	Records the user's viewing history
Metadata	Records details and metadata about each video
Video-upload	Orchestrates upload of videos to storage
Azure-storage	Stores and retrieves videos using external cloud storage
Mock-storage	A replacement for the storage microservice that stores videos in the local filesystem. You'll soon see how we use this to make development and testing a bit easier.

10.4.2 *Microservice project structure*

Before we look at the project structure for the entire application, let's first revisit the structure of an individual Node.js microservice. Open the metadata directory under the chapter-10 code repository to follow along.

Using the metadata microservice as an example, figure 10.3 describes the layout of this project. This is a typical Node.js project, and all of FlixTube's microservices have virtually this same structure.

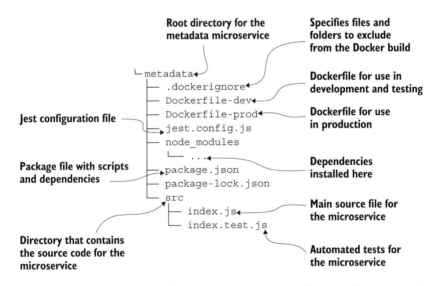

Figure 10.3 The structure of a Node.js microservice project (the metadata microservice)

10.4.3 *The FlixTube monorepo*

Now, let's look at the structure of the FlixTube monorepo. A *monorepo* is a single code repository that contains multiple projects. Instead of each microservice having its own code repository, we combine them all into a single FlixTube monorepo with the layout shown in figure 10.4. Each of FlixTube's microservices has its own subdirectory within the monorepo. Feel free to open the chapter-10 directory to take a look for yourself.

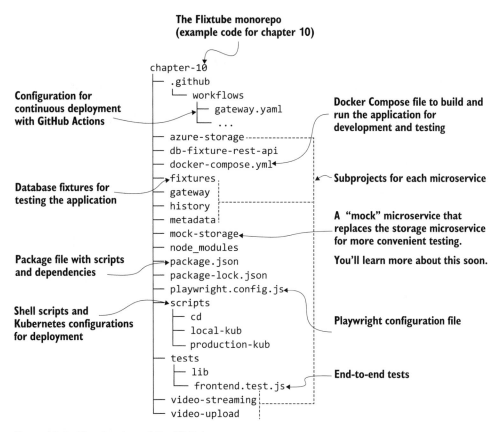

Figure 10.4 The structure of the FlixTube monorepo

For simplicity, FlixTube was built in a single code repository, also known as a monorepo. Starting a microservice project with a monorepo (instead of multiple code repositories) is great for the following reasons:

- It keeps things simple and reduces complexity.
- It makes it easier to get started with microservices.
- It's a perfectly acceptable way to structure a small microservices application.
- It's a convenient way for me to deliver a complete microservices example for you to experiment with.

Having said all that, microservices in production are rarely contained in a single code repository. That's because, at least in the past, using a single repository removed the biggest advantage of using microservices: that they can be independently deployed.

However, with GitHub Actions, which is relatively new on the scene, we can now create separate CD pipelines for subdirectories in our monorepo. We'll see that in action before the end of this chapter. This allows us to enjoy the simplicity and convenience of a monorepo but combined with independently deployable microservices. Good times. But still, if your microservices application grows sufficiently large and unwieldy, you'll probably want to split it out into multiple code repositories. We'll talk more about that in chapter 12.

10.5 *Running FlixTube in development*

Our first step is to have FlixTube running on our development computer. Figure 10.5 shows how it looks in development. Note that we've replaced the azure-storage microservice with a mock-storage microservice. This will be explained soon.

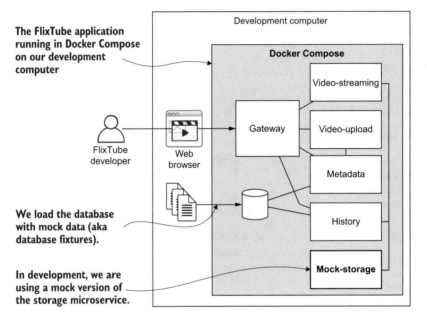

Figure 10.5   FlixTube as it now looks in development

10.5.1 *Booting an individual microservice*

Before booting the whole application, it's worth revisiting how we start an individual microservice. When developing a new microservice or focusing our current work on an existing microservice, we'll frequently need to run that microservice on its own, outside the usual context of the application. Let's run through the commands for starting the metadata microservice. First, change directory into its project under the monorepo:

```
cd chapter-10/metadata
```

We're using Node.js for our microservices, so that means we'll be running our microservices directly under Node.js on our development computer. If you followed along in chapter 2 and chapter 9, you'll already have Node.js installed. If not, return to chapter 2, section 2.5.4, for instructions. Before running a Node.js project, you must first install dependencies like this:

```
npm install
```

To run a Node.js project, use the npm `start` script convention:

```
npm start
```

This invokes a command line that is specified in the project's package.json file. All microservices in FlixTube follow this common Node.js convention. That means you know how to start any microservice in FlixTube to run it standalone in production mode.

On starting the microservice, you'll see error messages indicating the environment variables that must be set for the microservice to commence operation. You should set any required environment variables before trying to start the microservice again.

In the case of the metadata microservice, you'll need to set the following environment variables:

- `PORT`—The port number for the web server to listen on, often set to 3000 for local testing of individual web services.
- `DBHOST`—The connection string for the MongoDB database server. You'll need to have MongoDB installed or, more likely, be running it in a Docker container (see chapter 3 for an example of that).
- `DBNAME`—The name of the database to use for this microservice, for example, `metadata-dev`.
- `RABBIT`—The connection string for the RabbitMQ server.

What's more appropriate during ongoing development is to run the microservice in development mode. This enables live reload (first covered in chapter 2, section 2.6.8), so we can edit our code and have the microservice restart itself automatically to include the changes. We use the script `start:dev` (my personal convention) to run any of the FlixTube microservices in development mode:

```
npm run start:dev
```

To further review production mode, development mode, and live reload, see chapter 2, sections 2.6.7 and 2.6.8.

If you entered all those environment variables a moment ago, it's very obvious that most of the FlixTube microservices, like the metadata microservice, now have dependencies that make them more difficult to start on their own. Most of these either need a database or a RabbitMQ server; some of them require both. We can deal with this in any of the following ways:

- *Install MongoDB and RabbitMQ on your development computer.* This is annoying in the short term, but can be useful in the long term.
- *Instantiate MongoDB and RabbitMQ containers using Docker or Docker Compose.* This is a convenient, effective, and simple way to do this.
- *Mock the libraries for MongoDB, RabbitMQ, and other dependencies.* This is similar to what we did in chapter 9. You'll probably want to do this for your automated testing.

10.5.2 *Booting the entire FlixTube application*

Now let's boot the entire FlixTube application using Docker Compose, the useful tool we first encountered in chapter 4 and have used since. Frequently, during day-to-day product development, we'll build and restart our application, and Docker Compose makes this much simpler. Often, we'll take time out to focus on an individual microservice, but we'll still frequently want to test our larger application as we evolve its constituent microservices.

Listing 10.1 (extract from chapter-10/docker-compose.yaml) reminds us of what a Docker Compose file (docker-compose.yaml) looks like. FlixTube's version of this file is the biggest in this book, so listing 10.1 is just an extract for brevity.

> **Listing 10.1 Docker Compose file: booting FlixTube in development**

```
version: '3'
services:

  db:                              ◁─── Starts the container for the MongoDB database
    image: mongo:5.0.9
    container_name: db
    --snip--

  rabbit:                                        ◁─── Starts the container for the RabbitMQ server
    image: rabbitmq:3.9.21-management
    container_name: rabbit
    --snip--

  db-fixture-rest-api:           ◁─── Starts the REST API for loading database fixtures
    image: db-fixture-rest-api
    build:
      context: ./db-fixture-rest-api
      dockerfile: Dockerfile
    container_name: db-fixture-rest-api
    --snip--

  video-streaming:               ◁─── Builds and starts the video-streaming microservice
    image: video-streaming
    build:
      context: ./video-streaming
      dockerfile: Dockerfile-dev
    container_name: video-streaming
    --snip--

  --snip--           ◁─── All the other FlixTube microservices go here.
```

Most FlixTube microservices have been omitted from listing 10.1, but one you can see is our old friend, the video-streaming microservice. There is also the setup for our database (covered in chapter 4), RabbitMQ (covered in chapter 5), and the database fixtures REST API we'll use in our automated testing (covered in chapter 9).

Now, use Docker Compose to build and start FlixTube:

```
cd chapter-10
docker compose up --build
```

It takes some time to build and start, especially if you haven't done this before. Docker needs to download and cache the base images. You'll need to wait until you see the "online" message printed in the terminal from the gateway microservice.

Now, with the FlixTube application running, open your browser and navigate to http://localhost:4000 to see FlixTube's main page. FlixTube has a shiny new UI! We'll talk more about that soon. For now, take some time to explore FlixTube's UI:

1 Navigate to the upload page.
2 Upload a video (you can find an example video in the videos subdirectory of the chapter-10 repository).
3 Navigate back to the main page to see the uploaded video in the list.
4 Click the video to play it.
5 Navigate to the history page to see the video you played listed in the history.

When you've finished development, don't forget to shut down FlixTube so that it's not continuing to consume resources on your development computer. You can do that by pressing Ctrl-C in the terminal where Docker Compose is running and then invoking the following:

```
docker compose down --volumes
```

10.6 Testing FlixTube in development

Testing is essential to the practice of development. We can and should do manual testing, but nothing beats automated testing for efficiency, reliability, and repeatability.

In chapter 9, we looked at multiple ways of testing using Jest and Playwright. We'll revisit those again here. The various tests that we looked at in that chapter are repeated here in the chapter 10 code repository. We'll run those now against the completed FlixTube example.

Of course, any real application will have many more tests than the few we're running here. This is just a demonstration, and I haven't aimed for anything near complete test coverage. Follow along in the coming sections, and try running these tests for yourself.

10.6.1 Testing a microservice with Jest

The metadata microservice in FlixTube includes the Jest unit tests from chapter 9. Before running the tests, you'll need to install dependencies:

```
cd chapter-10/metadata
npm install
```

Now run the tests using the conventional npm script:

```
npm test
```

This executes the associated command line in the metadata microservice's package.json file that we configured in chapter 9. Figure 10.6 shows the results of a successful test run.

We can also run the tests in live reload mode, which means we can edit our code, and the tests will restart automatically. We do this using another npm script called `test:watch` (my own personal convention):

```
npm run test:watch
```

To review Jest in more detail, return to chapter 9, section 9.5. To revisit the Jest setup for npm and live reload, see chapter 9, section 9.5.8.

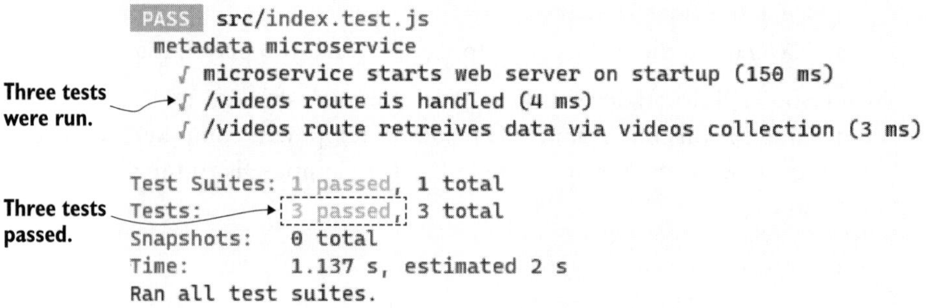

```
                   PASS  src/index.test.js
                     metadata microservice
                       √ microservice starts web server on startup (150 ms)
Three tests      ───►  √ /videos route is handled (4 ms)
were run.              √ /videos route retreives data via videos collection (3 ms)

                   Test Suites: 1 passed, 1 total
Three tests ─────  Tests:    ───► 3 passed, 3 total
passed.            Snapshots:   0 total
                   Time:        1.137 s, estimated 2 s
                   Ran all test suites.
```

Figure 10.6   A successful run of the automated tests for the metadata microservice using Jest

10.6.2   *Testing the application with Playwright*

We can also run the Playwright end-to-end test from chapter 9 against the FlixTube application. In chapter 9, we ran this test against a cut-down version of FlixTube. Here, we run it against the full application. To run this test, you'll need to install dependencies of the FlixTube monorepo:

```
cd chapter-10
npm install
```

Be sure to actually start the whole FlixTube application if you haven't done so already:

```
docker compose up --build
```

Wait for the message telling you the gateway microservice is online (running the tests won't work before that happens).

Now, open a new terminal window, and run the regular npm test script, which, in this case, is configured to invoke Playwright:

```
cd chapter-10
npm test
```

That runs Playwright from the terminal, and you should see results like that shown in figure 10.7. Note how npm test has different meanings in different projects. In the metadata microservice project, this translated to running Jest. In the larger FlixTube monorepo project, it instead translates to running Playwright. This convention means we can run automated tests against our projects without having to remember the details of the particular testing framework that is being used.

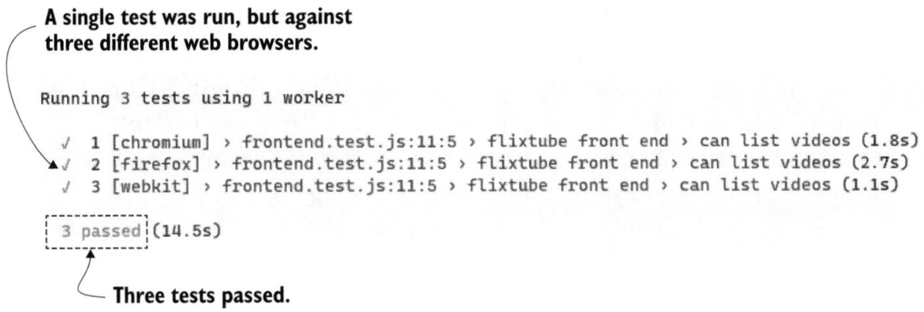

**A single test was run, but against
three different web browsers.**

```
Running 3 tests using 1 worker

  √  1 [chromium] › frontend.test.js:11:5 › flixtube front end › can list videos (1.8s)
  √  2 [firefox]  › frontend.test.js:11:5 › flixtube front end › can list videos (2.7s)
  √  3 [webkit]   › frontend.test.js:11:5 › flixtube front end › can list videos (1.1s)

  3 passed (14.5s)
```

Three tests passed.

Figure 10.7   A successful test run of the automated tests for the FlixTube UI using Playwright

10.7 *FlixTube deep dive*

By now, you should understand FlixTube from a high level. You know the basic purpose of each microservice. You know how to build, run, and test the application on your development computer. Before we deploy FlixTube to production, let's first understand some of its deeper details. Throughout this section, we'll look at the following aspects of FlixTube:

- Database fixtures
- Mocking the storage microservice
- The gateway
- The FlixTube UI
- Video streaming
- Video upload

10.7.1 *Database fixtures*

We first talked about database fixtures in chapter 9, where we used them to load our database with realistic sets of data prior to running automated tests. We saw database fixtures used for automated testing, but they are also useful for manual testing and even for product demonstrations. Being able to boot your application and have it ready to show, complete with realistic data, is extremely useful!

When unit testing with Jest, we didn't need any data fixtures because we mocked the MongoDB database library and were able to replace real data with fake data provided through the mock version of the database library. When integration testing with Jest, we were able to interact with our MongoDB database within our test code by directly using the MongoDB library. This meant we could have test data inline in our test code, and it was convenient not to have to create separate data files for it.

To keep things simple, when doing end-to-end testing with Playwright, we delegated the loading of database fixtures to the database fixtures REST API that I created for testing my own projects. This is a REST API that looks similar to all the other microservices you've seen in this book. We won't look at its code directly, but if you'd like to look at it yourself, you'll find that it's already quite familiar. The code for the REST API is included in the chapter-9 code repository and copied to the chapter-10 code repository so that we can use it when running our tests against FlixTube. Additionally, you can find the original source code for it on GitHub at https://github .com/ashleydavis/db-fixture-rest-api. You can see the setup for the REST API's container in the Docker Compose file earlier in listing 10.1.

For an understanding of what a database fixture looks like, see listing 10.2 (chapter-10/fixtures/two-videos/videos.js). Our database fixtures are stored under the fixtures subdirectory of the chapter-10 repository. FlixTube only has one database fixture in the file videos.js (shown in listing 10.2). The name of the file denotes the database collection that the data will be stored in. The data from this fixture will be loaded into the videos collection.

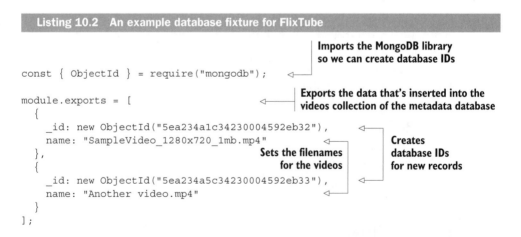

Listing 10.2   An example database fixture for FlixTube

```
const { ObjectId } = require("mongodb");        ◄──┐ Imports the MongoDB library
                                                    │ so we can create database IDs
module.exports = [                              ◄──┐ Exports the data that's inserted into the
  {                                                 │ videos collection of the metadata database
    _id: new ObjectId("5ea234a1c34230004592eb32"),   ◄──┐
    name: "SampleVideo_1280x720_1mb.mp4"                │  Creates
  },                              Sets the filenames    │  database IDs
  {                                   for the videos    │  for new records
    _id: new ObjectId("5ea234a5c34230004592eb33"),   ◄──┘
    name: "Another video.mp4"     ◄──
  }
];
```

The directory that contains the file denotes the name of the fixture. In this case, the name of the directory is two-videos, so the name of the database fixture is two-videos. I've given the fixture this name because its purpose is to load metadata for two videos into our database. This isn't really a great name for the database fixture; normally, we should give meaningful names to our database fixtures so that we can easily remember their purpose.

Each database fixture can consist of many files. Even though here we only have one file for our two-videos fixture, it could have more such files to set the contents of other collections in our database.

If you ran the Playwright test earlier in section 10.6.2, then you've already used this database fixture! Note that the fixture shown in listing 10.2 is actually a JavaScript file. We can use either JSON format or JavaScript for these database fixtures. JSON is appropriate for static data, but JavaScript is a great option for generating dynamic data. That gives us a lot of flexibility for producing test data. In listing 10.2, see how we use the MongoDB library to produce database IDs for our test data.

10.7.2 *Mocking the storage microservice*

For convenience during development, we replaced the Azure version of the video-storage microservice with a mock version. This is similar to the mocking we used in chapter 9, section 9.5.10 except, rather than replacing functions, objects, and libraries with mock versions, we now replace an entire microservice with a fake version. Figure 10.8 shows what FlixTube looks like when azure-storage has been replaced by the mock-storage microservice.

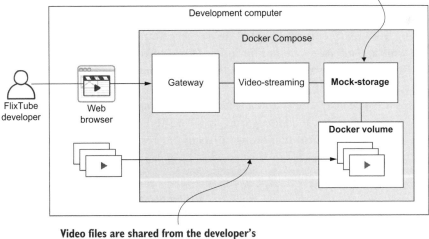

Figure 10.8   Replacing cloud storage with a mock microservice for more convenient and efficient use during development

Our mock-storage microservice isn't a complete fake though! It still does the job of storage, but instead of using cloud storage, it stores videos in the local filesystem. The main reason we do this isn't just for testing; it's for the convenience and performance of being able to limit our entire application to our development computer.

When running in development, we'd prefer to eliminate external dependencies such as connections to cloud storage. In this case, limiting our storage to the local filesystem makes the setup for development easier. Performance is improved because videos are stored locally and not sent out to the cloud. Besides this change, FlixTube works as normal, and the other microservices have no idea that the azure-storage microservice has been kicked out and replaced with a mock version.

Being able to replace complex microservices with simpler mock versions isn't just convenient—it might also be necessary at some point in the future. Right now, FlixTube is a small application, but you can imagine as it grows into the world-dominating streaming service it's destined to be that it will become too big to run on a single computer.

At that point, we need to use every trick in the book to make it fit on our development computer. This includes cutting out microservices that we don't need; for example, we could remove the history microservice from the Docker Compose file if we don't need to test it. The history microservice isn't crucial to the operation of Flix-Tube, so we can remove it without adverse effects if we needed to cut back the size of the application.

> **NOTE** Removing or replacing big complex microservices—possibly even whole groups of microservices—is an important technique for reducing the size of our application so that it can fit on a single computer and be able to run during development.

Listing 10.3 (extract from chapter-10/docker-compose.yaml) shows the setup of our mock-storage microservice in FlixTube's Docker Compose file. It looks similar to the configuration of the azure-storage microservice. One thing that's different is the storage subdirectory that is shared between the host operating system and the container. This is the directory where uploaded videos are stored. Sharing it like this means that we can inspect uploaded videos ourselves on the host operating system (OS) to test that the microservice is functioning correctly.

Listing 10.3   Mock-storage microservice in the Docker Compose file

```
video-storage:                          ◁——    Sets the domain name system (DNS) name as video-storage.
  image: mock-storage                            (The other microservices don't know that the azure-storage
  build:                                          microservice has been replaced with a mock version.)
    context: ./mock-storage      ◁——┐
    dockerfile: Dockerfile-dev          Instead of building the container from the azure-
  container_name: video-storage         storage subdirectory, we build the mock version
  volumes:                              from the mock-storage subdirectory.
    - /tmp/mock-storage/npm-cache:/root/.npm:z
    - ./mock-storage/src:/usr/src/app/src:z
```

```
    - ./mock-storage/storage:/usr/src/app/storage:z
ports:
  - "4005:80"
environment:
  - PORT=80
restart: "no"
```

Shares the video upload directory between the host OS and the container. We can inspect the uploaded videos from the host to ensure the mock-storage microservice works correctly.

It's a great option for development to be able to replace microservices with mocks. It can help make development easier, but there are times when we need to focus on the real version of the microservice; that is, we need to test it rather than the mock version. At those times, we can simply swap the mock version for the real version in the Docker Compose file. If you like, you can try this for yourself.

Listing 10.4 (extract from chapter-10/docker-compose.yaml) shows the commented-out configuration for the real azure-storage microservice. Simply uncomment this and then comment out the configuration for the mock version. You need to set the environment variables STORAGE_ACCOUNT_NAME and STORAGE_ACCESS_KEY in your terminal with the authentication details for your Azure Storage account (see chapter 4, section 4.4.1, to remind yourself how to get these values). Now, rebuild and restart FlixTube, and we can test the real azure-storage microservice in development!

Listing 10.4   The real azure-storage microservice commented out

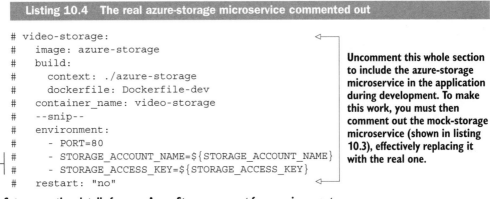

```
# video-storage:
#   image: azure-storage
#   build:
#     context: ./azure-storage
#     dockerfile: Dockerfile-dev
#   container_name: video-storage
#   --snip--
#   environment:
#     - PORT=80
#     - STORAGE_ACCOUNT_NAME=${STORAGE_ACCOUNT_NAME}
#     - STORAGE_ACCESS_KEY=${STORAGE_ACCESS_KEY}
#   restart: "no"
```

Uncomment this whole section to include the azure-storage microservice in the application during development. To make this work, you must then comment out the mock-storage microservice (shown in listing 10.3), effectively replacing it with the real one.

Sets connection details for your Azure Storage account from environment variables (so you don't have to add sensitive details to your code)

Listing 10.5 (extract from chapter-10/mock-storage/src/index.js) shows the code for the mock-storage microservice. The mock version replaces the /video and /upload routes from the real storage microservice with versions that use the local filesystem. The mock microservice is a drop-in replacement because its REST API conforms to the interface of the real azure-storage microservice.

Listing 10.5   The mock-storage microservice

```
--snip--

const storagePath = path.join(__dirname, "../storage");
```

Sets the path for storing videos in the local filesystem

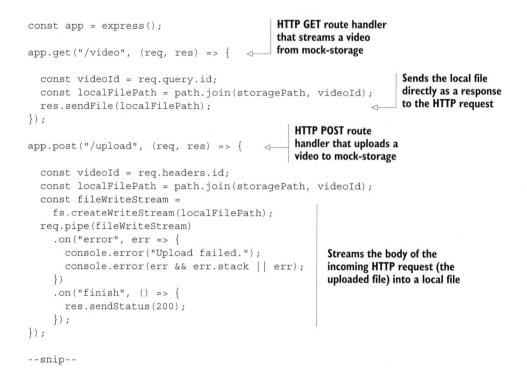

```
const app = express();
```
HTTP GET route handler that streams a video from mock-storage

```
app.get("/video", (req, res) => {
```

```
  const videoId = req.query.id;
  const localFilePath = path.join(storagePath, videoId);
  res.sendFile(localFilePath);
});
```
Sends the local file directly as a response to the HTTP request

```
app.post("/upload", (req, res) => {
```
HTTP POST route handler that uploads a video to mock-storage

```
  const videoId = req.headers.id;
  const localFilePath = path.join(storagePath, videoId);
  const fileWriteStream =
    fs.createWriteStream(localFilePath);
  req.pipe(fileWriteStream)
    .on("error", err => {
      console.error("Upload failed.");
      console.error(err && err.stack || err);
    })
    .on("finish", () => {
      res.sendStatus(200);
    });
});
```
Streams the body of the incoming HTTP request (the uploaded file) into a local file

```
--snip--
```

10.7.3 *The gateway*

FlixTube has a single gateway microservice. It's called a *gateway* because it acts as a gateway into the application for our users. For the current version of FlixTube, this is the single entry point to the whole application. The gateway provides the frontend UI that allows our users to interact with FlixTube in their web browser. It also provides a REST API so the frontend can interact with the backend.

FlixTube doesn't support any kind of authentication yet, but in the future, we'd probably like to upgrade the gateway to authenticate our users. FlixTube users would have to sign in before the gateway allows them to interact with any other microservices in the backend.

Figure 10.9 shows a potential future for FlixTube with more than one gateway. This illustrates a well-known pattern called *backends for frontends*. Each frontend has its own gateway. There is one gateway for access by a web browser, another gateway for access by a mobile app, and another gateway for the FlixTube administrator portal.

If possible, we'd prefer to keep things simple and to support only a single gateway. It's completely okay to share a gateway across multiple types of frontends. But if we find our frontends having different requirements (e.g., different forms of authentication between web and mobile or different security considerations between the web and administrator portals), then backends for frontends is a pattern that can help.

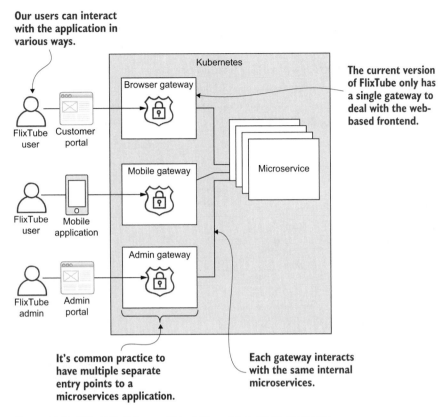

Figure 10.9   What FlixTube would look like with multiple gateways

If we do expand to have multiple gateways, we'd then want to use separate hostnames or subdomains to access them. For example, the main gateway for the browser could use flixtube.com, the mobile gateway could use mobile.flixtube.com, and the administrator portal could use admin.flixtube.com. To assign domain names to your application, you'll need to use a DNS provider to buy domain names and configure each one to point to the IP address of a particular gateway microservice.

Forwarding HTTP requests into the cluster is one of the main jobs of a gateway microservice. We'll see code examples of this in upcoming sections. A more advanced gateway (FlixTube isn't this advanced yet) will have REST API routes that issue requests to multiple internal microservices. Then, it will integrate multiple responses into a single response that is returned to the frontend.

For example, imagine a REST API that retrieves an individual user's history. This might require HTTP requests to a user account microservice (FlixTube doesn't have this yet) and the history microservice before integrating a response and sending it to the frontend. In this theoretical example, the gateway has merged the responses of both HTTP requests.

10.7.4   *The FlixTube UI*

If you haven't had a chance to explore FlixTube's UI, do so now. Build and start the application as discussed in section 10.5.2, and then navigate your web browser to http://localhost:4000. Try uploading a video or two.

Figure 10.10 shows the main page of FlixTube (the video list) after some videos have been uploaded to it. We can click any video in the list to watch it. We can click between Videos, Upload, and History in the navigation bar at the top to switch among the main pages.

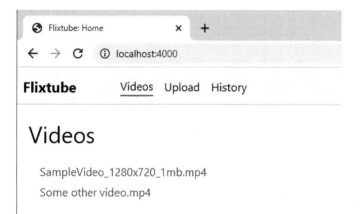

Figure 10.10   The main page of the FlixTube UI shows the list of videos that have been uploaded.

FlixTube is implemented as a traditional server-rendered web page, rather than as a modern single-page application (SPA) rendered in the browser. The FlixTube frontend presented here is a multi-page application (MPA). If this were a real commercial application, I would most likely have coded it as an SPA using React, Angular, or Vue, rather than an MPA. But that's not to say that an SPA is better than an MPA; they both have their tradeoffs, and newer ways of doing things (i.e., building SPAs) aren't necessarily better than older ways of doing things (i.e., building MPAs).

Why not use one of the popular modern SPA frameworks? Well, the simple reason is that it's outside the scope of this book. This book isn't about UIs, and that's why the frontend is as simple as it can be. (Besides that, I didn't want to choose sides and stoke the war between the SPA framework disciples, but all the cool kids use React, right?)

FlixTube uses server-side rendering via Express and the Handlebars template engine with vanilla JavaScript in the frontend. The FlixTube frontend is plain old HTML, CSS, and JavaScript, with no fancy modern frameworks.

Listing 10.6 (extract from chapter-10/gateway/src/index.js) is an extract from the gateway microservice's main code file. It shows the HTTP GET route that renders the main page. The main page shows the list of uploaded videos. This route handler starts by making the HTTP GET request (using Axios) to retrieve data from the metadata microservice. It then renders the web page using the video-list template and passes the list of videos as the template's data.

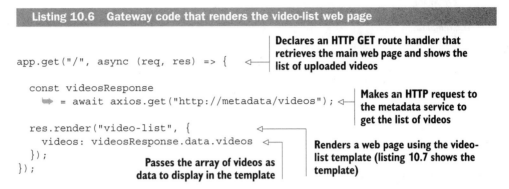

Listing 10.6 Gateway code that renders the video-list web page

```
app.get("/", async (req, res) => {          Declares an HTTP GET route handler that
                                            retrieves the main web page and shows the
                                            list of uploaded videos

  const videosResponse
    = await axios.get("http://metadata/videos");   Makes an HTTP request to
                                                    the metadata service to
                                                    get the list of videos
  res.render("video-list", {
    videos: videosResponse.data.videos              Renders a web page using the video-
  });                                               list template (listing 10.7 shows the
});              Passes the array of videos as      template)
                data to display in the template
```

I didn't use a JavaScript framework for FlixTube, but I did use a CSS framework (Tailwind CSS), so that I could make a nice UI without having to mess around with the nuts and bolts of CSS.

Listing 10.7 (chapter-10/gateway/src/views/video-list.hbs) shows the main page of FlixTube. This is an HTML document contained within a Handlebars template. Handlebars is a simple and powerful template library that we can use to generate web pages based on data. If you look back to listing 10.6, you'll see that the list of videos (retrieved from the metadata microservice) is passed as the template data. The combination of data and template renders the HTML that will be displayed to our user in their web browser.

Listing 10.7 The Handlebars template for the video-list web page

```
<!doctype html>              An HTML5 web page
<html lang="en">
  <head>
    <meta charset="utf-8">

    <title>FlixTube: Home</title>

    --snip--               Various CSS files are included here,
  </head>                  including the Tailwind CSS framework
  <body>
    <div class="flex flex-col">
      <div class="border-b-2 bg-gray-100">     Renders a navigation bar
        --snip--                               at the top of the web page
      </div>

      <div class="m-4">          The main content for the web page
        <h1>Videos</h1>
        <div id="video-list" class="m-4">      Container for the list of videos
```

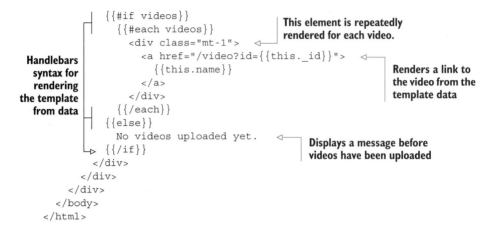

```
{{#if videos}}
   {{#each videos}}
      <div class="mt-1">
         <a href="/video?id={{this._id}}">
            {{this.name}}
         </a>
      </div>
   {{/each}}
{{else}}
   No videos uploaded yet.
{{/if}}
            </div>
         </div>
      </div>
   </body>
</html>
```

Handlebars syntax for rendering the template from data

This element is repeatedly rendered for each video.

Renders a link to the video from the template data

Displays a message before videos have been uploaded

10.7.5 *Video streaming*

At the heart of FlixTube is video streaming. We first looked at this back in chapter 2, and it's been a theme throughout the book. Now, it's time to see how video streaming works in the completed FlixTube example application. Some of this is recapping earlier chapters, but it's important to see how it works in the bigger context now that we have the gateway microservice and the UI.

Figure 10.11 illustrates the path of a streaming video, starting with external cloud storage on the left and ending with display to the user in the web browser on the right. The streaming video passes through three microservices on its journey to the user. Let's now follow that journey through the code.

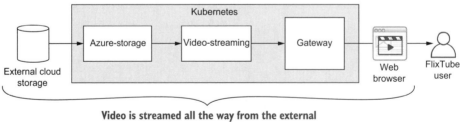

Data is forwarded from one microservice to another by a streaming HTTP request.

Video is streamed all the way from the external storage cloud to the user's web browser.

Figure 10.11 The path of streaming video through FlixTube

Listing 10.8 (extract from chapter-10/azure-storage/src/index.js) is an extract that shows where the streaming video journey starts in the Azure version of the video-storage microservice. The HTTP GET /video route retrieves a video from Azure Storage and streams it to the HTTP response. The details of how this works aren't important at the moment, but if you'd like to remember, return to chapter 4, section 4.4.1.

Listing 10.8 Streaming video from Azure Storage

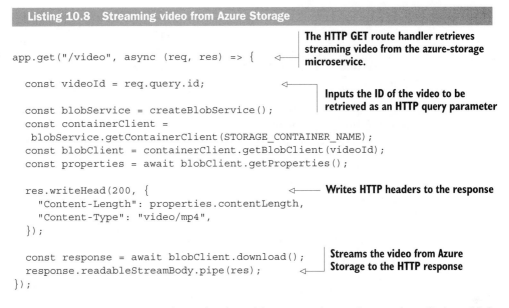

```
app.get("/video", async (req, res) => {
```
← The HTTP GET route handler retrieves streaming video from the azure-storage microservice.

```
  const videoId = req.query.id;
```
← Inputs the ID of the video to be retrieved as an HTTP query parameter

```
  const blobService = createBlobService();
  const containerClient =
   blobService.getContainerClient(STORAGE_CONTAINER_NAME);
  const blobClient = containerClient.getBlobClient(videoId);
  const properties = await blobClient.getProperties();

  res.writeHead(200, {
```
← Writes HTTP headers to the response

```
    "Content-Length": properties.contentLength,
    "Content-Type": "video/mp4",
  });

  const response = await blobClient.download();
  response.readableStreamBody.pipe(res);
});
```
Streams the video from Azure Storage to the HTTP response

Continuing our journey through the video-streaming microservice, listing 10.9 (chapter-10/video-streaming/src/index.js) is an extract showing how the HTTP GET /video route *pipes* the streaming video from azure-storage to its own HTTP response using Node.js streams.

The video-streaming microservice also has another job. It broadcasts the "video viewed" message to other microservices in the application. This kind of *event-driven* programming means that we can later decide to have other microservices respond to the event without us having to update the code for the video-streaming microservice.

As it stands, you might remember from chapter 5, section 5.8, that it's the history microservice that picks up this message and uses it to record the user's viewing history. This use of indirect messaging keeps the video-streaming and history microservices nicely decoupled from each other. It also highlights how applications built on microservices can be flexible and extensible.

Listing 10.9 Forwarding video through the video-streaming microservice

```
app.get("/video", (req, res) => {
```
← Defines an HTTP GET route handler that retrieves streaming video from the video-streaming microservice

```
  const videoId = req.query.id;
  const response = await axios({
    method: "GET",
    url: `http://video-storage/video?id=${videoId}`,
    data: req,
    responseType: "stream",
  });
```
← Forwards the HTTP GET request to the video-storage microservice. Note that the video-streaming microservice isn't aware of whether it's talking to the azure-storage or mock-storage microservice here.

```
response.data.pipe(res);
```
Pipes the response (using Node.js streams) from the video-storage microservice to the response for this request

```
broadcastViewedMessage(messageChannel, videoId);
});
```
Broadcasts the "video viewed" message for other microservices to know that the user is watching a video

Our video-streaming journey continues to the gateway microservice, the last stop before the UI. The HTTP GET /video route in listing 10.10 (extract from chapter-10/gateway/src/index.js) pipes the streaming video from the video-streaming microservice to its own HTTP response. This is where the video leaves the cluster, thus delivering the video to the frontend.

Listing 10.10   Forwarding video through the gateway microservice

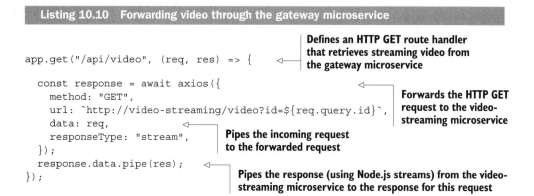

```
app.get("/api/video", (req, res) => {
  const response = await axios({
    method: "GET",
    url: `http://video-streaming/video?id=${req.query.id}`,
    data: req,
    responseType: "stream",
  });
  response.data.pipe(res);
});
```

Defines an HTTP GET route handler that retrieves streaming video from the gateway microservice

Forwards the HTTP GET request to the video-streaming microservice

Pipes the incoming request to the forwarded request

Pipes the response (using Node.js streams) from the video-streaming microservice to the response for this request

Our video-streaming journey concludes in the UI. You can see the HTML video element in listing 10.11 (extract from chapter-10/gateway/src/views/play-video.hbs). The source element and its src field trigger the HTTP GET request to the gateway, which triggers the request to video-streaming, which triggers the request to video-storage. The streaming video is then piped all the way back through azure-storage, through video-streaming, through the gateway, and, finally, to the frontend, displayed to the user through the video element in their web browser.

Listing 10.11   Playing the video in the frontend with the HTML video element

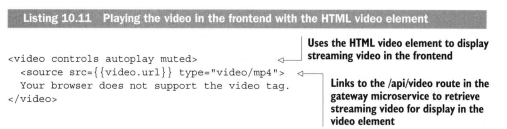

```
<video controls autoplay muted>
  <source src={{video.url}} type="video/mp4">
  Your browser does not support the video tag.
</video>
```

Uses the HTML video element to display streaming video in the frontend

Links to the /api/video route in the gateway microservice to retrieve streaming video for display in the video element

10.7.6 *Video upload*

Video streaming is just one side of the FlixTube equation. The other is video upload, which is how we add videos to FlixTube in the first place. Video upload isn't something we've yet seen in the book, although it's similar to how video streaming works, so you won't have any trouble with it.

Figure 10.12 illustrates the path of video upload through the application. A video file is selected by the user and uploaded from the frontend. The uploaded video arrives in the cluster at the gateway microservice before being forwarded through the video-upload microservice to the azure-storage microservice. There it's safely and securely stored in external cloud storage. Again, we'll follow this journey through the code.

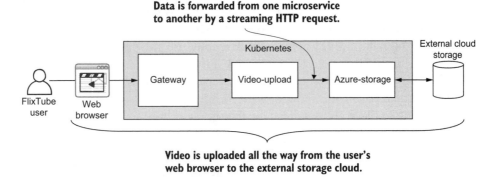

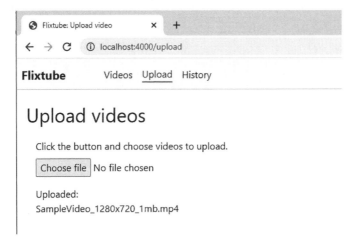

Figure 10.12   The path of an uploaded video through FlixTube

Figure 10.13 is a screenshot of FlixTube's Upload web page. If you followed along in section 10.5.2, you'll have seen this already and tried uploading a video. The user clicks Choose File and selects a file to upload. Once the upload completes, the UI is updated (as shown in figure 10.13) to give some feedback that the upload completed without error. If an error occurs, the error is displayed instead.

Figure 10.13   The FlixTube UI for uploading videos

Listing 10.12 (extract from chapter-10/gateway/public/js/upload.js) is a snippet of the frontend code that uploads the video to the backend. This uses the `fetch` function to upload the video via an HTTP `POST` request. At this point, you might rightly be wondering why we're using yet another HTTP request library. Well, normally, we would use something like the Axios library in the frontend. But, to keep the FlixTube frontend really simple, it's just a vanilla JavaScript web page with no build process. That makes it rather difficult to install an npm package such as Axios and use it in our frontend: because we don't have a build process, we have no way to bundle the Axios code module into our web page. If we did have a build process (most modern web applications do have one), then we would definitely use Axios.

The simplest approach that remains is to use something that comes with the browser to make the HTTP request. We could do this using the good old XMLHttp-Request, but that's kind of complicated. Instead, we'll use the more modern fetch function, which is also significantly simpler to use. Unfortunately, fetch isn't implemented in older versions of web browsers, which may affect our user base. So, we only use it here in place of not being able to use Axios.

Listing 10.12   Using `fetch` to upload videos in the frontend code

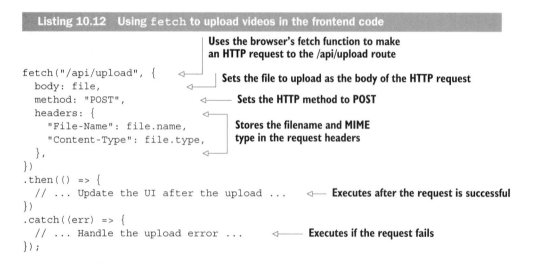

```
                              Uses the browser's fetch function to make
                              an HTTP request to the /api/upload route

fetch("/api/upload", {     ◁
  body: file,                 Sets the file to upload as the body of the HTTP request
  method: "POST",          ◁──── Sets the HTTP method to POST
  headers: {               ◁
    "File-Name": file.name,     Stores the filename and MIME
    "Content-Type": file.type,  type in the request headers
  },                       ◁
})
.then(() => {
  // ... Update the UI after the upload ...   ◁── Executes after the request is successful
})
.catch((err) => {
  // ... Handle the upload error ...   ◁──── Executes if the request fails
});
```

After the upload from the web browser, the HTTP POST request lands in the gateway where it's handled by the /api/upload route shown in the following listing (extract from chapter-10/gateway/src/index.js). Here, we see the request forwarded to the video-upload microservice.

Listing 10.13   The gateway forwarding the HTTP POST to video-upload

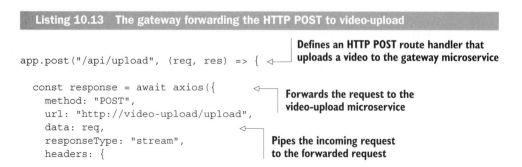

```
                              Defines an HTTP POST route handler that
                              uploads a video to the gateway microservice
app.post("/api/upload", (req, res) => {  ◁

  const response = await axios({     ◁
    method: "POST",                     Forwards the request to the
    url: "http://video-upload/upload",  video-upload microservice
    data: req,                       ◁
    responseType: "stream",             Pipes the incoming request
    headers: {                          to the forwarded request
```

```
      "content-type": req.headers["content-type"],
      "file-name": req.headers["file-name"],
    },
  });
  response.data.pipe(res);
});
```

> Pipes the response (using Node.js streams) from the video-upload microservice to the response for this request

Listing 10.14 (extract from chapter-10/video-upload/src/index.js) shows how the video-upload microservice handles the incoming video. At this point, we create a unique ID for the video by creating an instance of MongoDB's `ObjectId` class. The request is then forwarded to the video-storage microservice.

After the upload is successful, the message "video uploaded" is broadcast to let the other microservice know that a new video is available within the system. The metadata microservice handles this message and records the new video in its database.

Listing 10.14 Handling video upload via HTTP POST

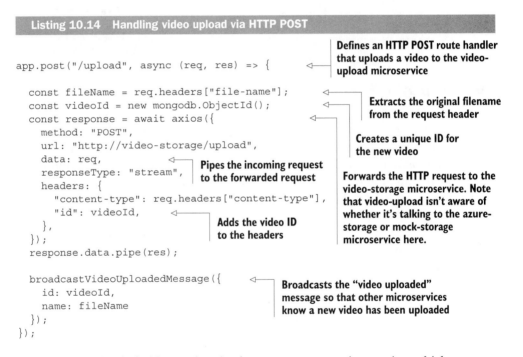

```
app.post("/upload", async (req, res) => {
```
> Defines an HTTP POST route handler that uploads a video to the video-upload microservice

```
  const fileName = req.headers["file-name"];
```
> Extracts the original filename from the request header

```
  const videoId = new mongodb.ObjectId();
```
> Creates a unique ID for the new video

```
  const response = await axios({
    method: "POST",
    url: "http://video-storage/upload",
    data: req,
    responseType: "stream",
```
> Pipes the incoming request to the forwarded request

```
    headers: {
      "content-type": req.headers["content-type"],
      "id": videoId,
```
> Adds the video ID to the headers

> Forwards the HTTP request to the video-storage microservice. Note that video-upload isn't aware of whether it's talking to the azure-storage or mock-storage microservice here.

```
    },
  });
  response.data.pipe(res);

  broadcastVideoUploadedMessage({
    id: videoId,
    name: fileName
  });
});
```
> Broadcasts the "video uploaded" message so that other microservices know a new video has been uploaded

Finally, the uploaded video arrives in the azure-storage microservice, which you can see in listing 10.15 (extract from chapter-10/azure-storage/src/index.js). From here, the video is saved into Azure Storage. Once this whole chain has completed, we've successfully saved a copy of the video the user has uploaded. If you'd like to dive deeper into how a file is added to Azure Storage, load the full index.js for the azure-storage microservice into Visual Studio Code (VS Code).

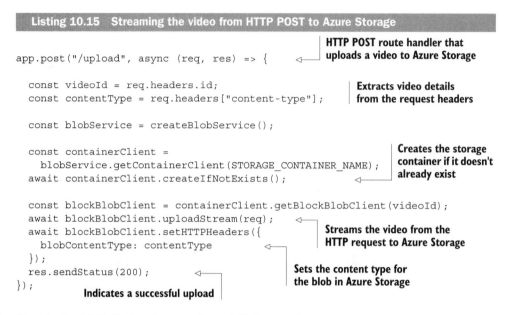

Listing 10.15   Streaming the video from HTTP POST to Azure Storage

```
app.post("/upload", async (req, res) => {          ⟵───┐ HTTP POST route handler that
                                                         uploads a video to Azure Storage

  const videoId = req.headers.id;                       Extracts video details
  const contentType = req.headers["content-type"];      from the request headers

  const blobService = createBlobService();

  const containerClient =                               Creates the storage
    blobService.getContainerClient(STORAGE_CONTAINER_NAME);   container if it doesn't
  await containerClient.createIfNotExists();        ⟵──  already exist

  const blockBlobClient = containerClient.getBlockBlobClient(videoId);
  await blockBlobClient.uploadStream(req);    ⟵─
  await blockBlobClient.setHTTPHeaders({            Streams the video from the
    blobContentType: contentType          ⟵        HTTP request to Azure Storage
  });
  res.sendStatus(200);      ⟵───              Sets the content type for
});                                           the blob in Azure Storage
        Indicates a successful upload
```

10.8   *Deploying FlixTube to our local Kubernetes*

Before we attempt to deploy FlixTube to a production Kubernetes cluster in the cloud, first we should practice deploying it to our local Kubernetes instance that comes with Docker Desktop. Personally, I wouldn't normally run FlixTube this way for development or testing because it's so much easier to boot, restart, and shut down the entire application using Docker Compose than by using Kubernetes. But it's worth using our local Kubernetes instance to practice deployment before we embark on the full production deployment.

If you're just itching to get FlixTube into production, feel free to skip to the next section. But just keep it in mind that deploying to a local Kubernetes instance is a bit easier than deploying to a production Kubernetes cluster in the cloud, so if you have trouble with that, you should return to this section to practice your deployment in a simpler environment.

Figure 10.14 shows what FlixTube will look like running in the local Kubernetes instance. Note that we've replaced the azure-storage microservice with the mock-storage microservice so that we avoid the complication of having to connect FlixTube to the Azure Storage service.

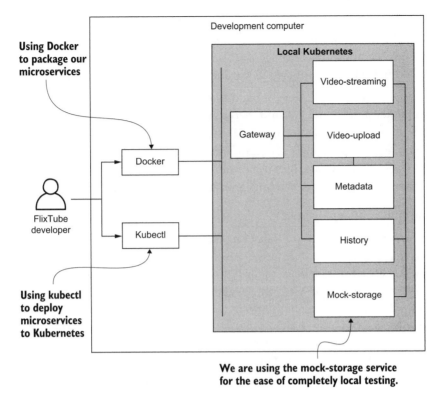

Figure 10.14   Deploying FlixTube to a local Kubernetes instance

10.8.1 Prerequisites for local deployment

Before attempting your local Kubernetes deployment, you need to have Docker Desktop installed with Kubernetes enabled (refer to chapter 6, section 6.5). This should give you the kubectl command-line interface (CLI) tool automatically, but if not, you'll have to install it separately (refer to chapter 6, section 6.6). If you just enabled your local Kubernetes, kubectl should already be connected to your local instance and be ready to go. If you need to check the connection or reconnect kubectl to your local Kubernetes, refer to chapter 6, section 6.8.4. For local deployment, you don't need a container registry.

10.8.2 Local deployment

A shell script is provided in the chapter-10 code repository to do the local Kubernetes deployment. Invoke it like this:

```
cd chapter-10/scripts/local-kub
./deploy.sh
```

Windows users, at this point, you'll need to use your WSL2 Linux terminal because these shell scripts won't work under the regular Windows Terminal.

This shell script is hardcoded to build and deploy all of FlixTube's microservices. There's a lot of duplication here, so it's not the best example, but I wanted to keep it simple so you could easily read the shell script and understand what's happening.

Open the shell script yourself in VS Code to see how it does the following:

- Uses the Docker `build` command to build each microservice (as you learned in chapter 3, section 3.8.2, and revisited in chapter 6, 6.8.1)
- Uses the kubectl `apply` command to deploy each microservice to Kubernetes (as you learned in chapter 6, section 6.8.5)
- Passes various YAML files to kubectl that specify the deployment configuration for each microservice (for an example, open gateway.yaml and take a look)

10.8.3 Testing the local deployment

With FlixTube deployed to our local Kubernetes instance, we should now check that it works. We can use `kubectl get pods`, `kubectl get deploy`, and `kubectl get services` to see that the Kubernetes resources for FlixTube are created and operational.

From the output of `kubectl get services`, you can find the port number (it should be a NodePort at or above port 30000) where you can access the gateway microservice. Open your browser and navigate to the web page on that port number: http://localhost:<the-port-number>. You should now be able to test that the FlixTube front-end is functional. For more details on testing your local deployment, see chapter 6, sections 6.8.5 and 6.8.6.

10.8.4 Deleting the local deployment

When you're done testing, you can delete the deployment using the provided shell script:

```
./delete.sh
```

That shell script invokes `kubectl delete` for each microservice to delete it from Kubernetes. Alternatively, to clean out your local Kubernetes instance, you can simply reset it, as was shown in chapter 6, section 6.5.

Don't forget to disable your local Kubernetes instance when you're finished with it. That will save system resources and battery life if you're using a laptop.

10.9 Manually deploying FlixTube to production

We aren't far from creating a CD pipeline for FlixTube that automatically deploys it to production each time we push code. Before we can automate something, though, we should first be able to do the process manually (otherwise, what are we going to automate?). This next step is more difficult than deploying to your local Kubernetes cluster, so if you have problems here, return to section 10.8 for more practice before continuing.

Figure 10.15 highlights how we'll use Docker to package and publish our images, and then we'll use kubectl to deploy containers to our Kubernetes cluster running on Azure.

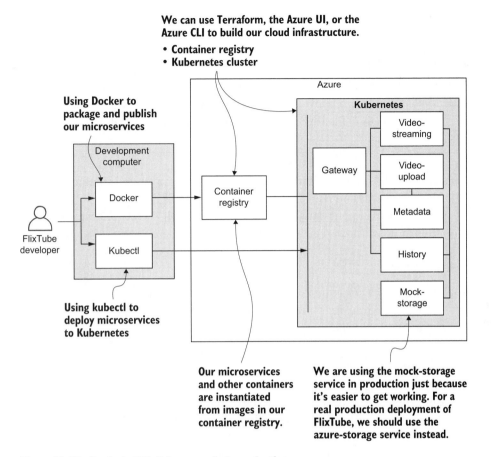

Figure 10.15 Deploying FlixTube manually to production

10.9.1 Prerequisites for production deployment

Before we can deploy FlixTube, we need to have the following in place and ready to be used:

- A container registry where we can publish the Docker images for our microservices. You can create your registry through the Azure portal UI according to the steps in chapter 3, section 3.9.1, or you can create it via Terraform as was shown in chapter 7, section 7.9.2. You need to note down the URL, username, and password for your container registry; see chapter 3, section 3.9.1, to remember how to find those details.

- A Kubernetes cluster where we can deploy our microservices. You can create a cluster through the Azure portal UI like we did in chapter 6, section 6.9, or using Terraform as we did in chapter 7, section 7.11.

- Don't forget to connect your container registry to your Kubernetes cluster like we did in chapter 6, section 6.11.3, or the cluster will fail to pull images from the registry.

- You need kubectl installed as indicated in chapter 6, section 6.6, and authenticated to your Kubernetes cluster as shown in chapter 6, section 6.10.3.

10.9.2 Production deployment

Before publishing images for our microservices to our container registry, we must log in to it and set some environment variables that are used by the deployment shell script.

Open a terminal and set the following environment variable:

```
export CONTAINER_REGISTRY=<url-to-your-container-registry>
```

Again, Windows users will need to use their WSL2 Linux terminal to follow along with these commands and use these shell scripts.

This environment variable is used in the shell script, but we can also use it to authenticate with the registry:

```
docker login $CONTAINER_REGISTRY
```

Now enter the username and password for your registry.

After authenticating with your registry, in the same terminal, you can now run the production deployment scripts:

```
cd chapter-10/scripts/production-kub
./deploy.sh
```

Again, this shell script is hardcoded to build and deploy all the microservices for Flix-Tube. There's still a lot of duplication going on here, but that's to make it simple for you to read. Open the shell script in VS Code, and compare it to the local deployment script (from section 10.8.2) to see the differences.

You'll notice that the production deployment script pushes images to our container registry. It also uses the command envsubst (which we learned about in chapter 8, section 8.9.2) to fill out the template configuration for each microservice, plugging in the CONTAINER_REGISTRY environment variable where it's needed. The expanded template configurations are then piped into kubectl to deploy each microservice to Kubernetes.

10.9.3 Testing the production deployment

With FlixTube deployed to our production Kubernetes cluster, we should now check that it works. Again, we can use kubectl get pods, kubectl get deploy, and kubectl get services to see the Kubernetes resources that have been created for FlixTube. For more on testing the deployed microservice, see chapter 6, sections 6.11.5 and 6.11.6.

From the output of kubectl get services, we can find the IP address of the gateway microservice. Open your browser and navigate to the web page at that IP address: http://<the-ip-address>. You should now be able to test the FlixTube frontend. For more details on testing your local deployment, see chapter 6, sections 6.8.5 and 6.8.6.

10.9.4 *Destroying the production deployment*

When you're done testing and experimenting, delete the deployment using the provided shell script:

```
./delete.sh
```

That shell script invokes `kubectl delete` for each microservice, deleting them all from Kubernetes.

10.10 *Continuous deployment to production*

After testing and practicing manually deploying FlixTube to production, we're now ready to bring the CD pipeline online. You can follow along, but this can be even more challenging than the previous sections. If something goes wrong, you might have to return to local or manual deployments (what we just did in sections 10.8 and 10.9) to figure out the problem.

As we did in chapter 8, we'll create our CD pipeline with GitHub Actions. It should be fairly easy for you to transfer this over to any other CD platform. Like I said in chapter 8, a CD pipeline is really just a glorified way to run a shell script, even when some providers also give you a fancy UI. Figure 10.16 illustrates the structure of FlixTube's CD pipeline.

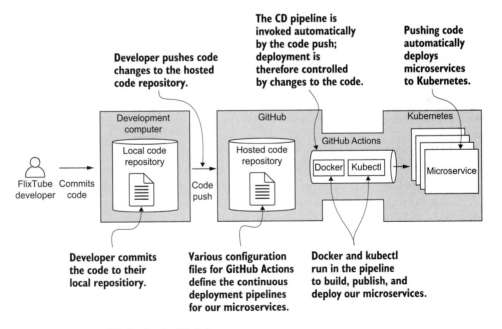

Figure 10.16 The CD pipeline for FlixTube

10.10.1 *Prerequisites for continuous deployment*

To follow along in this section, you need your own GitHub account. You'll already have one if you followed along with chapter 8. Otherwise, sign up for a free account at https://github.com/.

You also need the prerequisites (container registry and Kubernetes cluster) from section 10.9.1. In addition, you need the authentication details for your Kubernetes cluster encoded in Base64; see chapter 8, section 8.9.5, to remember how to do this.

10.10.2 *Setting up your own code repository*

To run the FlixTube CD pipeline for yourself, you must fork the chapter-10 code repository and create secrets per the instructions given in chapter 8, section 8.9.9. You must add the following secrets to your own fork of the code repository:

- `CONTAINER_REGISTRY`—The URL to your container registry
- `REGISTRY_UN`—The username for your registry
- `REGISTRY_PW`—The password for your registry
- `KUBE_CONFIG`—Base64-encoded configuration that authenticates kubectl with your cluster (see chapter 8, section 8.9.5)

10.10.3 *Deploying infrastructure*

Before using CD to deploy FlixTube, we should first deploy the infrastructure the application depends on. This means deploying MongoDB and RabbitMQ to our Kubernetes cluster manually. We don't need to implement CD for these because they won't be changing, so we only need to deploy them once at the start.

There's a shell script in the chapter-10 repository you can use to do this:

```
cd chapter-10
./scripts/cd/infrastructure.sh
```

Take a look at the shell script yourself. It's quite simple, invoking `kubectl apply` for MongoDB and RabbitMQ configurations to deploy them to your cluster.

Way back in chapter 4, I advocated for making our Kubernetes cluster stateless—that is, removing our persistent MongoDB database from the cluster and storing our data in an external (and managed) database. The reason I'm saying to add MongoDB directly to your cluster here is purely for your own convenience. It's probably easier for you to deploy MongoDB to your cluster than to create an external database and connect that to your cluster. For a real production application, though, I would recommend that you extract your database to a managed MongoDB database running outside your cluster (search for "managed MongoDB," and you'll find plenty of options). Return to chapter 4, sections 4.4.5 and 4.5.3, for my full argument on why you should do this.

10.10.4 One CD pipeline per microservice

Under the chapter-10 code repository, look in the directory .github/workflows, and you'll see separate GitHub Actions workflow files (YAML files) for each microservice.

For one example, open the CD pipeline configuration for the gateway microservice; the full workflow is shown in listing 10.16 (chapter-10/.github/workflows/gateway.yaml). Notice that most of the work is delegated to shell scripts that are configured by the environment variables defined in this listing.

Listing 10.16   Enabling a separate CD pipeline for the gateway

```
name: Deploy gateway          ◁──── Names the CD pipeline

                              Runs the workflow on push to the main branch
on:
  push:
    branches:                 Scopes the CD pipeline to the gateway subdirectory. This workflow will
                              only run when the gateway microservice has changed. This is what
      - main    ◁             allows for independent CD pipelines for our microservices within the
    paths:                    monorepo.
      - gateway/**  ◁

  workflow_dispatch:     ◁    Allows the CD pipeline to be triggered
                              from the GitHub Actions UI
jobs:
  deploy:
    runs-on: ubuntu-latest

    env:
      VERSION: ${{ github.sha }}                              ◁
      CONTAINER_REGISTRY: ${{ secrets.CONTAINER_REGISTRY }}       Sets environment
      REGISTRY_UN: ${{ secrets.REGISTRY_UN }}                     variables used in
      REGISTRY_PW: ${{ secrets.REGISTRY_PW }}                     the shell scripts
      NAME: gateway                                               and deployment
      DIRECTORY: gateway                                     ◁   configurations

    steps:

      - uses: actions/checkout@v3

      - name: Build                               Builds the Docker image
        run: ./scripts/cd/build-image.sh  ◁

      - name: Publish                             Publishes the Docker image
        run: ./scripts/cd/push-image.sh  ◁       to the container registry

      - uses: tale/kubectl-action@v1       ◁──── Installs and configures kubectl
        with:
          base64-kube-config: ${{ secrets.KUBE_CONFIG }}
          kubectl-version: v1.24.2

      - name: Deploy                             Expands the configuration template
        run: ./scripts/cd/deploy.sh   ◁         and deploys the microservice
```

The most interesting thing in listing 10.16 is how the CD pipeline is scoped to the gateway subdirectory. This is what connects this CD pipeline to just the gateway microservice (the code for which is contained under that subdirectory). This workflow is invoked only when code for the gateway microservice has changed.

This "scoping" feature means we can focus each workflow to an individual microservice, allowing each microservice to have an independent deployment schedule. This gives us the true power of microservices (that they are independent) even though, for convenience, we've collocated all the FlixTube microservices in a single code repository (the FlixTube monorepo).

If you'd like to see each of the shell scripts, open the chapter-10 code repository in VS Code and explore them for yourself. You'll see what I hope are by now familiar commands: using Docker to build and publish images, with envsubst (from chapter 8, section 8.9.2) for expanding templated configuration and kubectl to deploy our microservices.

10.10.5 Testing the CD pipeline

Now we're ready to test our CD pipeline. Don't forget, you must fork the chapter-10 code repository into your own GitHub account and configure GitHub secrets mentioned in section 10.10.2 for this to work.

You can trigger the CD pipeline in one of two ways. First, try making a code change to the main branch. Try something simple like adding console.log("Hello world"); to the gateway microservice. Pushing your code change should trigger the CD pipeline: the microservice will be built, published, and deployed to Kubernetes. You can also trigger the CD pipeline manually through the GitHub Actions UI, as we've seen earlier in chapter 8, section 8.7.10.

If all is going well, you can trigger the CD pipeline for each microservice and deploy the entire FlixTube application. With the deployment of FlixTube done, you can again use the kubectl commands from section 10.9.3 to check that FlixTube is operational and find the IP address to connect to the frontend.

Deployment for FlixTube has now been put on automatic. As we move forward, adding features and editing the code for FlixTube, the microservices are automatically deployed to production, ready to be used by our customers, without us having to think much about it. This frees us to focus on customer-facing features, and, hopefully, the hassle of infrastructure and deployment starts fading away into the background.

10.11 FlixTube in the future

Congratulations! If you've followed along in this chapter, you now have FlixTube running in production, and you're all set up to continue developing and evolving it. You can make code changes, test them in development, and then deploy your updates to production.

Where to now for FlixTube? That's for you to imagine! In chapter 12, we'll discuss the technical aspects of FlixTube's future:

- How do we scale up to cater to our growing user base?
- How do we scale up our development and deployment processes as the application grows and the size of the development team increases?

For now, just imagine the types of microservices you'd like to add to FlixTube in the future. Figure 10.17 gives you some inspiration as to what it might look like as it grows.

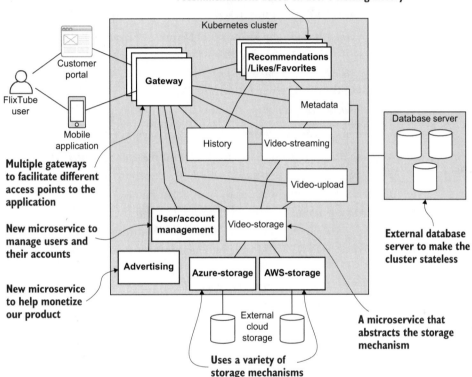

Figure 10.17 What FlixTube could look like in the future

10.12 Continue your learning

In this chapter, we studied the structure and layout of the FlixTube example application. We built, ran, and tested it in development. Then, we deployed it to production through its CD pipeline.

You have FlixTube running, so what now? Reading any book will only take you so far. The key to you retaining these skills is to practice, practice, and then practice some more. Experiment with the code. Try to add features. Try to add new microservices. Try to break FlixTube just to see what happens. Practicing the art of development is what takes you to the next level.

Development isn't without challenges. In fact, it's a never-ending roller coaster of problems and solutions. When you hit problems with any tool or technology, go back and review the appropriate chapter in this book. You might find the answer you need. Otherwise, you'll need to go deeper and explore other resources.

The final chapters in this book contain guidance that will help you navigate your future development path with microservices. The references at the end of each chapter (including this one) will help you continue your learning journey. But just remember that your key to success and retaining these skills is consistent practice.

To learn about UI development, see the following books:

- *React Quickly*, 2nd ed., by Morten Barklund and Azat Mardan (Manning, 2023)
- *Angular in Action* by Jeremy Wilken (Manning, 2018)
- *Getting MEAN with Mongo, Express, Angular, and Node*, 2nd ed., by Simon D. Holmes and Clive Harber (Manning, 2019)
- *Micro Frontends in Action* by Michael Geers (Manning, 2020)

To learn more about development with microservices, see these books:

- *Designing Microservices* by S. Ramesh (Manning, est. Spring, 2024)
- *Microservices: A Practical Guide*, 2nd ed., by Eberhard Wolff (Manning, 2019)
- *Microservices in Action* by Morgan Bruce and Paulo A. Pereira (Manning, 2018)
- *Microservices Patterns* by Chris Richardson (Manning, 2018)
- *The Tao of Microservices* by Richard Rodger (Manning, 2017)
- *Microservices in .NET*, 2nd ed., by Christian Horsdal Gammelgaard (Manning, 2021)
- *Microservice APIs: Using Python, Flask, FastAPI, OpenAPI and More* by José Haro Peralta (Manning, 2022)

Summary

- We can develop, run, and test individual microservices using Node.js.
- We can develop, run, and test an entire microservices application on our development computer using Docker Compose.
- Testing frameworks such as Jest and Playwright can be used to run automated tests against our code libraries, microservices, and even the entire microservices application.
- The main features of FlixTube are uploading and streaming videos. Multiple microservices play a part in providing these features.
- Database fixtures can be used to load sets of test data into our database. This is useful not just for automated testing but also for manual testing and conducting product demonstrations.
- To reduce the size of our microservices application for local development and testing, or even just to isolate parts of it, we can replace entire microservices or groups of microservices with mock versions of them. For example, in this chapter,

for convenience of testing and deployment, we used the mock-storage microservice in place of the real azure-storage microservice.

- The gateway microservice is the entry point to the FlixTube application for our customers. It provides the frontend that our customers can use to interact with FlixTube.
- FlixTube is deployed to Kubernetes by a continuous deployment (CD) pipeline built on GitHub Actions. It delegates the work to several shell scripts that build, publish, and deploy the microservices.
- Expansion of templated configuration is done using the command `envsubst`, which takes values from environment variables and substitutes those values into the Kubernetes deployment configuration files.

Healthy microservices

This chapter covers

- Techniques to ensure our microservices remain healthy
- Using observability to understand the behavior of our microservices
- Debugging microservices and Kubernetes
- Patterns for reliability and fault tolerance

Errors happen. Code has bugs. Hardware, software, and networks are unreliable. Failures happen regularly for all types of applications, not just for microservices. But microservices applications are more complex, and so problems can become considerably more difficult to debug as we grow our application. The more microservices we maintain, the greater the chance at any given time that some of those microservices are misbehaving!

We can't avoid problems entirely. It doesn't matter if they are caused by human error or unreliable infrastructure. It's a certainty—problems happen. But just because problems can't always be avoided, doesn't mean we shouldn't try to mitigate against them. A well-engineered application expects problems, even when the specific nature of some problems can't be anticipated.

As our application evolves to be more complex, we'll need techniques to combat problems and keep our microservices healthy. Our industry has developed many best practices and patterns for dealing with problems. We'll cover some of the most useful ones in this chapter. Following this guidance will make our application run more smoothly and be more reliable, resulting in less stress and easier recovery from problems when they do happen.

This chapter isn't immediately practical; there's no example code in GitHub, so there's no code to follow along with. Think of this as a toolbox of techniques for you to try out in the future as you move forward and continue to develop your own microservices application.

11.1   Maintaining healthy microservices

A healthy microservices application is composed of healthy microservices. A healthy microservice is one that isn't experiencing problems such as crashing, bugs, CPU overload, or memory exhaustion. To understand the health of our application, we need to do the following:

- Observe the behavior of our microservices to understand their past and current states.
- Take action when problems occur to protect our customers.
- Triage problems so the worst ones are addressed first.
- Debug problems and apply fixes as needed.

Using FlixTube's metadata microservice as an example, figure 11.1 gives you an idea of the infrastructure for a healthy microservice in production. Notice that there are multiple replicas of the microservice and that requests are evenly balanced between instances of the microservice using a load balancer. Should any single microservice go out of commission, one of the replicas can stand in while the failing instance is restarted.

This redundancy ensures the ongoing reliability of the microservice and the application. In this chapter, you'll learn about replicating microservices on Kubernetes and other techniques to facilitate fault tolerance and recovery from errors.

A microservice can suffer problems even without the dramatic effect of going out of commission. How do we know what's going on inside a microservice? It doesn't have to be a black box. We often need some kind of telemetry service (shown in figure 11.1) to record events reported from various microservices so that we can visualize the aggregated data in a way that we can understand.

What can we do to ensure that our microservices remain healthy? Similar to a real medical professional, we must know how to *take the temperature* of our patient. We have numerous techniques at our disposal to help us diagnose the state and behavior of our microservices.

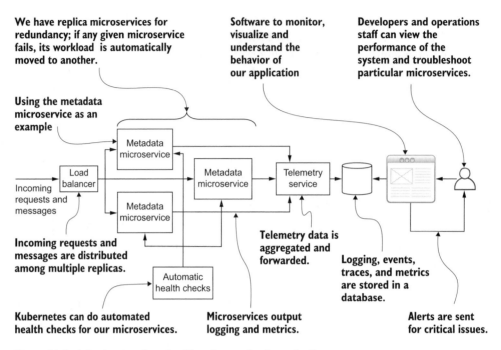

We have replica microservices for redundancy; if any given microservice fails, its workload is automatically moved to another.

Software to monitor, visualize and understand the behavior of our application

Developers and operations staff can view the performance of the system and troubleshoot particular microservices.

Using the metadata microservice as an example

Incoming requests and messages are distributed among multiple replicas.

Telemetry data is aggregated and forwarded.

Logging, events, traces, and metrics are stored in a database.

Kubernetes can do automated health checks for our microservices.

Microservices output logging and metrics.

Alerts are sent for critical issues.

Figure 11.1   Infrastructure for a healthy microservice in production

Table 11.1 lists the main techniques you'll learn in this chapter to take the temperature of our microservices.

Table 11.1   Techniques for understanding the behavior of microservices

Technique	Description
Logging	Outputting information about the behavior of our microservices to show what is happening as it's happening
Error handling	Having a strategy for managing and recovering from errors
Automatic health checks	Configuring Kubernetes to automatically detect problems in our microservices
Observability	Outputting and recording telemetry that we can use to understand the interactions between our microservices

What happens when something has gone wrong? How do we fix it? Coping with problems that have occurred requires investigation and debugging. In this chapter, you'll learn the strategies to find the cause of a problem so you can fix it.

11.2 *Monitoring and managing microservices*

Getting our application into production is just the first step. After that, we need to continually know if our application is functioning or not, especially as new updates to the code are rolled out.

We must have transparency regarding what our application is doing; otherwise, we have no idea what's going on in there, and we can't fix problems unless we know about them. In this section, we'll look at some techniques for monitoring the behavior of our microservices:

- Logging
- Error handling
- Automatic health checks
- Observability

11.2.1   *Logging in development*

Logging to the console is our most basic tool for understanding the ongoing behavior of our microservices. Through logging, we output a text stream showing the important events, activities, and actions that have taken place within our application.

The stream of logs coming from an application can be thought of as the history of the application, showing every pertinent thing that has happened over its lifetime. We can use console logging in both development and production. Figure 11.2 illustrates how it works for the metadata microservice in development.

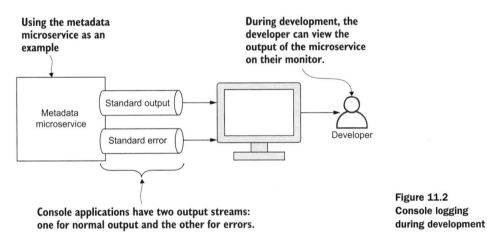

Figure 11.2
Console logging
during development

Every microservice, like every process, has two output streams for logging:

- Standard output
- Standard error

In JavaScript, we output logging to the standard output channel like this:

```
console.log("Useful information goes here");
```

We output errors to the standard error channel like this:

```
console.error("Useful information goes here");
```

NOTE   If you're using a language other than JavaScript, then it will have its own functions for outputting to standard output and standard error.

That's all we need to output to the console. Many developers adopt a sophisticated logging system for outputting logs from their microservices, but we don't really need that to be effective—direct console logging is simple and works well.

What should be logged?

Given that logging has to be added explicitly by the developer and is always optional, how do you choose what to log? Here are a few examples:

- What to log:
  –Pertinent events in your application and their details
  –Success/failure of important operations
- What not to log:
  –Things that can easily be ascertained from other sources
  –Anything that's secret or sensitive
  –Any personal details about your users

If you find yourself drowning in details from too much logging, feel free to go in and remove logging that isn't useful. For every console log, you just have to ask the question, can I live without this detail? If you don't need it, delete it.

Generally speaking, though, more logs are better than fewer logs. When it comes to debugging in production, you need all the help you can get to understand why a problem occurred. Tracing back through the log is an important step in understanding the sequence of events that resulted in the problem.

You won't be able to add more logging after the problem has occurred! Well, you can if you isolate and reproduce the problem, but that in itself can be difficult. More logging is better because when you do hit a problem, you want to have as much information as possible to help you solve it.

11.2.2   *Error handling*

Errors happen. Our users suffer. It's like a fundamental law of computer programming! Here are some examples of errors:

- Runtime errors (an exception is thrown that crashes our microservice)
- Bad data being input (from faulty sensors or human error in data entry)
- Code being used in unexpected combinations or ways
- Third-party dependencies failing (e.g., RabbitMQ)
- External dependencies failing (e.g., Azure Storage)

How we deal with errors matters. We must plan to handle and recover from errors gracefully to minimize the harm caused to our users and our business. What happens when errors occur? How will our application deal with these? We must think through these questions and develop an error-handling strategy for our application.

Often in our JavaScript code, we'll anticipate errors and handle these in our code using exceptions, callbacks, or promises. In those cases, we usually know what to do. We can retry the failed operation, or, if possible, we might correct the problem and restart the operation if there isn't any automatic corrective action that's obvious. We might even have to report the error to the user or notify our operations staff.

Sometimes we can anticipate errors, but other times not. We might fail to catch a particular type of error because we didn't know it could occur or because certain types of error (e.g., a hard drive failure) happen so infrequently that it's not worth specifically handling them. But to be safe, we must account for errors that we can't even imagine!

What we need is a general strategy for how we handle unexpected errors. For any process, including individual microservices, this boils down to two main options: *abort and restart* or *resume operation*. You can see these error-handling strategies illustrated in figure 11.3.

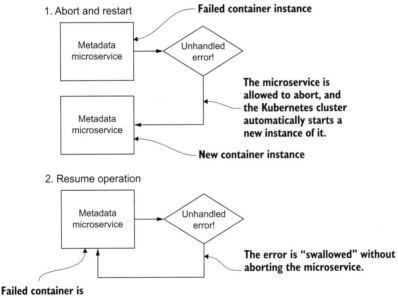

Figure 11.3 Strategies for handling unexpected errors

ABORT AND RESTART

The abort and restart strategy intercepts unexpected errors and responds by restarting the process. The simplest way to use this strategy is to just ignore any errors we don't care about. Any exception that we don't explicitly handle with a try/catch statement in our code results in the process being aborted.

This is the simplest error-handling strategy because it literally means *doing nothing*. Just allow unexpected errors to occur and let Node.js abort our program in response.

When a production microservice is aborted, we'll rely on Kubernetes to automatically restart it for us, which it does by default. (This behavior in Kubernetes is configurable as well.)

RESUME OPERATION

The resume operation strategy intercepts unexpected errors and responds by allowing the process to continue. We can implement this in Node.js by handling the uncaught-Exception event on the process object like this:

```
process.on("uncaughtException", err => {
    console.error("Uncaught exception:");
    console.error(err && err.stack || err);
});
```

If we handle the uncaughtException event like this, we take explicit control over unexpected errors. In that case, Node.js won't take its default action of aborting the process. The process is simply left to continue as best it can, and we have to hope that the error hasn't left the process in a bad state.

Printing the error to the standard error channel means that it can be picked up by our production logging system, which we'll discuss soon. This error can then be reported to our operations team, and it doesn't have to go unnoticed.

ABORT AND RESTART: VERSION 2

Now that we understand how to handle uncaught exceptions in Node.js, we can implement a better version of the abort and restart strategy:

```
process.on("uncaughtException", err => {
    console.error("Uncaught exception:");
    console.error(err && err.stack || err);
    process.exit(1);
});
```

In this code, we take explicit control of the handler for unexpected errors. As before, we print the error so that it can be noticed by our operations team. Next, we explicitly terminate the program with a call to process.exit.

We pass a nonzero exit code to the exit function. This is a standard convention that indicates the process was terminated by an error. We can use different nonzero error codes here (any positive number) to indicate different types of errors.

WHICH ERROR HANDLING STRATEGY SHOULD WE USE?

To restart or not to restart, that is the question. Many developers swear by abort and restart, and in most situations, it's a good idea to simply let our processes be aborted because trying to recover a microservice after a crash can leave it limping along in a damaged state.

With abort and restart, we can monitor for crashes to know which microservices have had problems that need to be resolved. If you couple this with good error reporting, it's a good general strategy that you can apply by default.

Sometimes, though, we might need to use the resume operation strategy. For some microservices (e.g., microservices that deal with customer data), we must think through the implications of aborting the process.

As an example, let's consider FlixTube's video-upload microservice. Is it okay for this microservice to be aborted at any time? At any given moment, it might be accepting multiple video uploads from multiple users. Is it acceptable to abort this microservice, potentially losing user uploads? I would say no, but if this is your microservice, you might have a different opinion and that's okay. There's no one right way to do this.

> **NOTE**   When deciding which strategy to use, it's probably best to default to abort and restart, but occasionally resume operation will be more appropriate.

11.2.3   *Logging with Docker Compose*

When using Docker Compose in development, we can see the logging from all of our microservices in a single stream in our terminal window. Docker automatically collects the logging and aggregates it into a single stream, as indicated in figure 11.4. Obviously, this is useful (during development) to get a broad overview of what our application is doing at any given time.

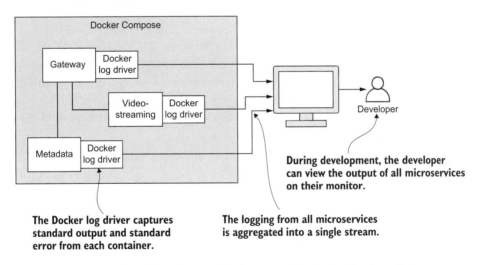

Figure 11.4   When using Docker Compose, Docker aggregates the logging from all of our microservices into a single stream.

Redirecting logging to a file

Here's a trick that I find very useful. When we run Docker Compose, we can redirect its output and capture it to a log file. The `tee` command means we can both display output in the terminal and save it to a file.

(continued)

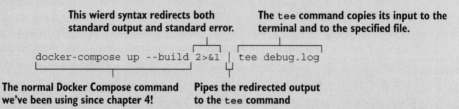

This wierd syntax redirects both standard output and standard error.

The `tee` command copies its input to the terminal and to the specified file.

```
docker-compose up --build 2>&1 | tee debug.log
```

The normal Docker Compose command we've been using since chapter 4!

Pipes the redirected output to the `tee` command

Now we can load the log file (in this example, debug.log) in Visual Studio Code (VS Code) and browse it at our leisure. We can search for particular strings of text. For example, if we're trying to find a problem with the database, we might search for logs that contain the word "database."

I even like to put special codes (character sequences) in my logging to distinguish the logs for particular subsystems or particular microservices. This makes it easier to search or filter for the types of logs we're interested in.

11.2.4 Basic logging with Kubernetes

When running microservices in development under Docker Compose, we run the application locally on our development computer. That makes it easy to see the logging from our application and understand what's happening in our code.

We can also retrieve logging from our production microservices running remotely on Kubernetes, but it's slightly more difficult. To see the logging, we must be able to extract it from the cluster and pull it back to our development computer for analysis.

KUBECTL

We first met kubectl in chapter 6, but we'll use it again now to get logs from a particular microservice running on Kubernetes. Let's say we're running FlixTube as it was at the end of chapter 10 (you can spin it up if you like and follow along). Imagine that we'd like to get logging from an instance of our metadata microservice.

Given that we could have multiple instances of the metadata microservice (we don't yet, but we'll talk about creating replicas later in this chapter), we need to determine the unique name that Kubernetes has assigned to the particular microservice that we're interested in. What we're actually looking for here is the name of the pod. You might remember from chapter 6 that a Kubernetes pod is the thing that contains our containers. A pod can actually run multiple containers, even though, for Flix-Tube, as yet, we're only running a single container in each pod. Revisit chapter 6, section 6.10.3, to remind yourself how to authenticate kubectl with your cluster. After authenticating kubectl, we can use the `get pods` command to see the full list of pods in our cluster as shown here:

```
> kubectl get pods
NAME                                    READY   STATUS    RESTARTS   AGE
azure-storage-57bd889b85-sf985          1/1     Running   0          33m
database-7d565d7488-2v7ks               1/1     Running   0          33m
gateway-585cc67b67-9cxvh                1/1     Running   0          33m
history-dbf77b7d5-qw529                 1/1     Running   0          33m
metadata-55bb6bdf58-7pjn2               1/1     Running   0          33m
rabbit-f4854787f-nt2ht                  1/1     Running   0          33m
video-streaming-68bfcd94bc-wvp2v        1/1     Running   0          33m
video-upload-86957d9c47-vs9lz           1/1     Running   0          33m
```

The unique name for the pod that contains the single instance of our metadata microservice

Scan down the list to pick out the name of the pod for our metadata microservice and find its unique name. In this case, the name is `metadata-55bb6bdf58-7pjn2`. Now we can use the `logs` command to retrieve the logging for the metadata microservice. In this instance, there isn't much to see, but it's helpful that we know how to do this.

```
> kubectl logs metadata-55bb6bdf58-7pjn2
Waiting for rabbit:5672.
Connected!

> metadata@1.0.0 start /usr/src/app
> node ./src/index.js

Microservice online.
```

The unique name of the pod for which we are retrieving logs

The console logging retrieved from the microservice

Just remember to replace the name of the pod with the name of an actual microservice from your cluster. The unique name is generated by Kubernetes, so the name for your metadata microservice won't be the same as the name that is generated for my version of it. Here's the general template for the command:

```
kubectl logs <pod-name>
```

Just insert the particular name of the pod from which you'd like to retrieve the logs.

STERN

Using the command `kubectl logs` is a great starting point for getting logs for a microservice on Kubernetes. It's included with kubectl, which is convenient, but it's kind of a hassle having to look up the unique name of the microservice when you want to retrieve its logs.

A better option is to use a tool called Stern to retrieve logs. Then, you don't have to specify the full name—a partial name will work just as well. For example, getting the logs for the metadata microservice looks like this:

```
stern metadata
```

In this case, Stern will match all pods that start with the name *metadata*. That means if we have multiple replicas of the metadata microservice, we'll get the logs for all of them, which is useful and much more convenient than using `kubectl logs`. Stern also continues to output ongoing logs until you terminate it (with Ctrl-C). Stern is so good for finding logs across microservices that it's part of my essential toolkit for working with Kubernetes. See Stern's code repository for installation and usage instructions: https://github.com/stern/stern.

KUBERNETES DASHBOARD

Another useful way to view logging (and other information) for your pods (and other resources) is to use the Kubernetes dashboard. This is a visual way to inspect and explore your cluster, and you can even make modifications to your cluster through it (although I don't recommend manually tweaking a production cluster!).

We haven't seen the Kubernetes dashboard yet in this book. The dashboard doesn't come by default with a Kubernetes installation. On Azure, for example, you won't have a dashboard unless you install it. If you're using Kubernetes elsewhere, you might find the dashboard does come preinstalled. Installing and accessing the dashboard isn't difficult, and you can find the official instructions on the Kubernetes website at http://mng.bz/OPKa.

With the dashboard, we can quickly drill down to inspect the state of any pod. Figures 11.5, 11.6, and 11.7 show how we do this. Note in these screenshots, there's also other useful information (e.g., CPU and memory usage) that can help us understand the state of our microservices.

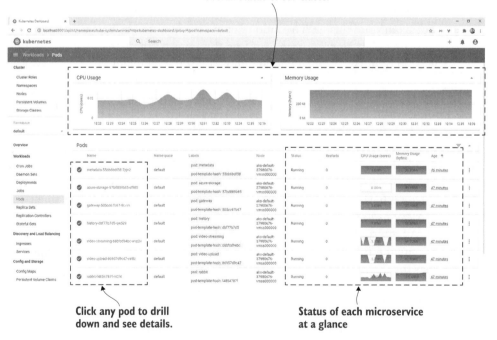

Figure 11.5   The Kubernetes dashboard showing all the pods in our cluster

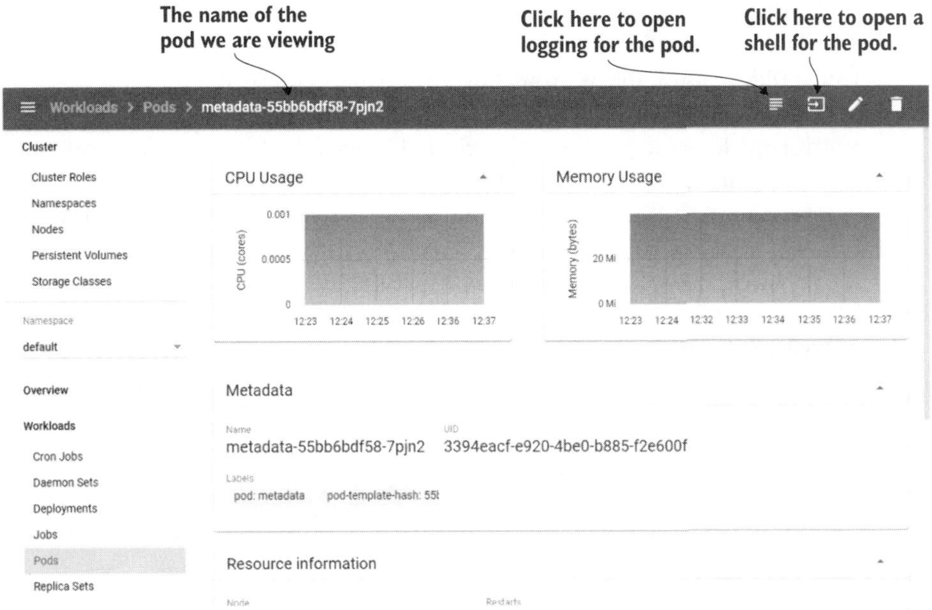

The name of the pod we are viewing

Click here to open logging for the pod.

Click here to open a shell for the pod.

Figure 11.6 Viewing the details of the pod that contains our metadata microservice

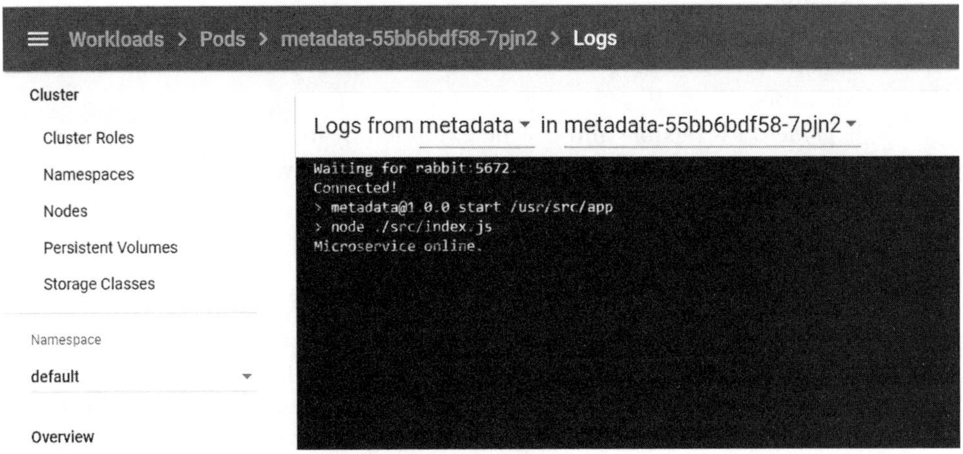

Figure 11.7 Viewing the log for the metadata microservice

11.2.5 Kubernetes log aggregation

Many who are trying to debug a production Kubernetes installation would like to have aggregated logging, that is, a way to see the combined logging produced by all microservices in our cluster. You'll start to want something like this as your application grows larger because tracking down logs individually from each microservice can be quite tedious and time consuming.

Unfortunately, Kubernetes doesn't have any kind of log aggregation built in (it's not like I haven't asked for it, though). So, we need to find a separate solution for this. You could, if you want to go way down this particularly deep rabbit hole, implement your own custom logging aggregation service and install it in your cluster to capture and record logs for your microservices. However, I don't recommend it because it's quite difficult to get working and to maintain. It's best to save your time and use third-party enterprise logging or observability software. But just in case you're interested to see what it takes to make your own logging aggregation service for Kubernetes, check out my blog post at www.codecapers.com.au/kubernetes-log-aggregation.

11.2.6 *Enterprise logging, monitoring, and alerts*

A common solution for large-scale enterprise monitoring of microservices is the combination of Fluentd, Elasticsearch, and Kibana. Other options specifically for monitoring metrics are Prometheus and Grafana. These are professional, enterprise-scalable solutions for monitoring and alerting. But they are heavyweight, resource-intensive, and not so easy to get working anyway, so don't rush into integrating these into your application.

We won't dive into any details on these technologies here because it would be beyond the scope of this book. It's enough for now to have a brief overview of each of these technologies.

FLUENTD

Fluentd is an open source logging and data collection service written in Ruby. You can instantiate a Fluentd container within your cluster to forward your logs to external log collectors.

Fluentd is flexible and can be extended by its many plugins. One such plugin is what allows us to forward our logging to Elasticsearch. Learn more about Fluentd by visiting the following web sites:

- www.fluentd.org/
- https://docs.fluentd.org/

ELASTICSEARCH

Elasticsearch is an open source search engine written in Java. You can use Elasticsearch to store and retrieve logging, metrics, and other useful data. Learn more about Elasticsearch at their website: www.elastic.co/elasticsearch/.

KIBANA

Kibana is an open source visualization dashboard built on top of Elasticsearch. It allows us to view, search, and visualize our logs and other metrics. You can create fantastic custom dashboards with Kibana.

The great thing about Kibana, and it can be a real lifesaver, is that you can configure it to automatically alert you when there are problems in your cluster. You specify the conditions under which the alert is raised and the action that is taken.

The paid version of Kibana also has support for email notifications and some other options, including triggering of webhooks to invoke whatever custom response you need. Learn more about Kibana in general at www.elastic.co/kibana.

You can find Kibana demo dashboards at www.elastic.co/demos and browse the supported notifications at http://mng.bz/YRda.

PROMETHEUS

Prometheus is an open source monitoring system and time series database. Alongside Kubernetes, Prometheus is a graduated project of the Cloud Native Computing Foundation (CNCF), which puts it with some very esteemed company.

We can configure Prometheus to scrape metrics from our microservices at regular intervals and automatically alert us when things are going wrong. Learn more about Prometheus here: https://prometheus.io/.

GRAFANA

While Prometheus is great for data collection, queries, and alerts, it's not so good at visualization. We can create simple graphs with Prometheus, but it's limited.

It's fortunate then that Grafana, which allows us to create visual and interactive dashboards, is so easy to connect to Prometheus. Learn more about Grafana here: https://grafana.com/.

11.2.7 Observability for microservices

Observability is a technique for surfacing rich and interesting details about the behavior of our distributed application. As any fan will tell you, this is more than just aggregated logging and monitoring. To implement observability, we preemptively output detailed telemetry from our application. The latest standard for this is the OpenTelemetry protocol. We capture this telemetry in software such as that provided by Honeycomb, Datadog, New Relic, Sumo Logic, or others, and this allows us to observe the interactions of our microservices.

Observability, being able to see the totality of what our system is doing, is a great aid to our investigation of problems and figuring out which microservice is causing problems. It allows us to query and visualize the telemetry data from our application. We can ask questions (Is this problem related to a particular user? Is this problem related to a particular region?) and drill down into the behavior of our application to figure out what's going on. Observability software such as Honeycomb, shown in figure 11.8, helps us connect the dots between microservices, correlating requests and messages between microservices and helping us pinpoint the location of errors.

To learn more about implementing OpenTelemetry and Honeycomb into your microservices, see my intro video and example code:

- http://learn.codecapers.com.au/v/alkBpw2U7rA
- http://mng.bz/G9gJ

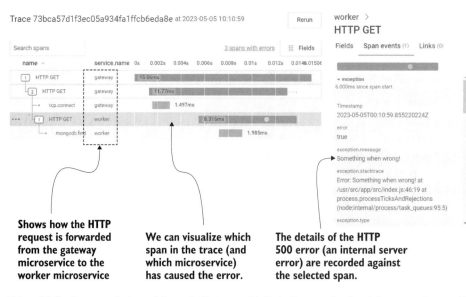

Shows how the HTTP request is forwarded from the gateway microservice to the worker microservice

We can visualize which span in the trace (and which microservice) has caused the error.

The details of the HTTP 500 error (an internal server error) are recorded against the selected span.

Figure 11.8   An example trace (shown in Honeycomb) that allows us to pinpoint an error in a multi-microservice request

11.2.8 *Automatic restarts with Kubernetes health checks*

Kubernetes has a great feature for automated health checks that allows us to automatically detect and restart unhealthy microservices. You may not need this particular feature because Kubernetes already defines an unhealthy pod as one that has crashed or exited. By default, Kubernetes automatically restarts misbehaving pods.

If we aren't happy with the default, Kubernetes lets us create our own definition of "unhealthy" on a case-by-case basis. We can define a readiness probe and a liveness probe for a microservice so that Kubernetes can query the health of it. The *readiness probe* advertises that the microservice has started and is ready to start accepting requests. The *liveness probe* then advertises that the microservice is still alive and is still accepting requests. Both are illustrated in figure 11.9.

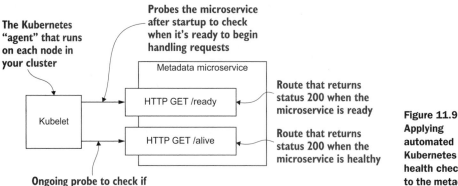

The Kubernetes "agent" that runs on each node in your cluster

Probes the microservice after startup to check when it's ready to begin handling requests

Route that returns status 200 when the microservice is ready

Route that returns status 200 when the microservice is healthy

Ongoing probe to check if the microservice is healthy

Figure 11.9 Applying automated Kubernetes health checks to the metadata microservice

We can use these two Kubernetes features to elegantly solve the problem we discovered in chapter 5 when we first connected the history microservice to our RabbitMQ server (section 5.8.5). The problem was that the history microservice (or any other microservice that connects to an upstream dependency) must wait for its dependency (in this case, RabbitMQ) to boot up before it can connect and make use of it.

If the microservice tries to connect too early, it's simply going to throw an exception that could abort the process. It would be better if we could simply make the history microservice wait quietly until RabbitMQ becomes available. That is why we used the `wait-port` npm module in chapter 5, but that was an awkward workaround. However, using Kubernetes, we now have the tools for an elegant fix.

The problem as just described only really happens when a microservices application is first booted up. Once your production application is running and your RabbitMQ server is already started, you can easily and safely introduce new microservices that depend on RabbitMQ without them having to wait. But don't start to think that it's not a problem because there is another side to this:

- What happens when RabbitMQ crashes and is then automatically restarted by Kubernetes?
- What happens if we'd like to take RabbitMQ down temporarily to upgrade or maintain it?

In both circumstances, RabbitMQ will go offline, and this breaks the connection for all the microservices that depend on it. The default for those microservices (unless we specifically handle it) is to throw an unhandled exception that most likely aborts the microservice. Now any microservices that depend on RabbitMQ will constantly crash and restart while RabbitMQ is down.

This is also true of any system dependencies besides RabbitMQ. Generally speaking, we'd like to be able to take any service offline and have the downstream services wait quietly for that service to become available again. When the service comes back online, the downstream services can resume normal operation.

We can now use the readiness and liveness probes to solve these problems. Listing 11.1 (an addition to chapter-10/scripts/cd/gateway.yaml) shows an update to the Kubernetes deployment YAML file for the gateway microservice from chapter 10. It defines readiness and liveness probes for our gateway microservice.

Listing 11.1 Adding Kubernetes probes for the gateway microservice

```
apiVersion: apps/v1
kind: Deployment
metadata:
  name: gateway
spec:
  replicas: 1
  selector:
    matchLabels:
      app: gateway
```

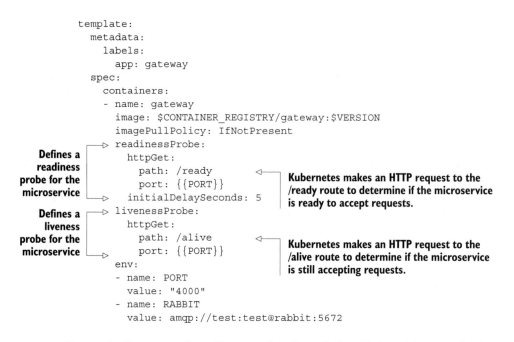

Defines a readiness probe for the microservice

Defines a liveness probe for the microservice

```
template:
  metadata:
    labels:
      app: gateway
  spec:
    containers:
    - name: gateway
      image: $CONTAINER_REGISTRY/gateway:$VERSION
      imagePullPolicy: IfNotPresent
      readinessProbe:
        httpGet:
          path: /ready
          port: {{PORT}}
        initialDelaySeconds: 5
      livenessProbe:
        httpGet:
          path: /alive
          port: {{PORT}}
      env:
      - name: PORT
        value: "4000"
      - name: RABBIT
        value: amqp://test:test@rabbit:5672
```

Kubernetes makes an HTTP request to the /ready route to determine if the microservice is ready to accept requests.

Kubernetes makes an HTTP request to the /alive route to determine if the microservice is still accepting requests.

To get the liveness and readiness probes from listing 11.1 working, we also have to add HTTP GET route handlers for /ready and /alive to our gateway microservice. But what should these routes do?

In the simplest cases, we just have to return an HTTP status code of 200 to indicate success. That's enough to pass both probes, and it lets Kubernetes know that a microservice is both ready and live. In certain situations (e.g., with the history microservice), we can then add additional code to customize the definition of what it means to be ready and live. For example, in any microservice that depends on RabbitMQ, we would add code for the following:

- *A* /ready *route that returns status 200 only once RabbitMQ becomes available*—This tells Kubernetes that the microservice has entered its ready state.
- *An* /alive *route that returns an error code when RabbitMQ becomes unavailable*—This causes the microservice to be restarted, but the new microservice (due to the /ready route) won't be placed in a ready state until RabbitMQ comes back online.

A strategy like this solves two problems. First, if we don't use readiness and liveness probes, our history microservice will constantly start up, crash, and restart while RabbitMQ is down. This constant restarting isn't an efficient use of our resources, and it's going to generate a ton of error logging that we'd have to analyze (in case there's a real problem buried in there!).

Second, we could handle this explicitly in the microservice by detecting when RabbitMQ disconnects and then polling constantly to see if we can reconnect. This would save the microservice from constantly crashing and restarting, but it requires significantly more sophisticated code in our microservice to handle the disconnection and reconnection to RabbitMQ. We don't need to write such sophisticated code because that's what the probes are doing for us. To learn more about the pod lifecycle and the different kinds of probes, see the Kubernetes documentation: http://mng.bz/z0PA.

11.3 Debugging microservices

With some form of monitoring or observability in place, we can visualize the behavior for our application. We use this to understand its current state and historical behavior. It's useful to have this kind of information in hand when problems occur.

Once a problem has become apparent, we must now put on our detective hats. We need to analyze the information we have to understand what went wrong. We can ask questions of our data and track the clues back to the root cause to find out why it happened. Along the way, we'll run experiments to further hone in on the culprit.

Usually, we can't fix a problem until we've identified the cause. Of course, sometimes we can randomly stumble on a solution without knowing the cause. But it's always sensible to be able to ascertain the root cause anyway. That way, we can be sure that the supposed fix has actually fixed the problem and not just hidden or changed it.

Debugging is the process of tracking down the source of a problem and subsequently applying an appropriate fix. Debugging microservices is similar to debugging any other kind of application; it's a form of troubleshooting that is part art and part science. We need to ask questions that lead to hypotheses about the problem. We need to run experiments to test those hypotheses and hope to find an answer to the problem. It should be noted that, often, figuring out the right questions to ask can be the most difficult part of this process!

Debugging is normally quite difficult, but debugging microservices is more so because our application is distributed across multiple microservices. Locating a problem in a single process can be difficult on its own, but finding a problem in an application composed of many small interacting processes—that's a whole lot more trouble.

As you might already know, searching for the source of a problem is actually the most difficult part of debugging. It's like searching for the proverbial needle in the haystack. If you have any inkling of where to look for the problem, you stand a much greater chance of finding it quickly. That's why developers who are experienced with a particular codebase can often find bugs in it much more quickly than those who are less familiar.

After finding the source of the problem, we must now fix it. Fortunately, it's often (but not always) much quicker to fix a bug than it was to find it in the first place.

11.3.1 The debugging process

In an ideal world, you'd find and fix all problems during development and testing. Indeed, if you have a thorough testing practice and/or comprehensive automated test suite, you'll find many of your bugs before production. If possible, that's the best way because debugging is much easier on your development computer.

To debug any code, we can follow this process:

1   Triage problems.
2   Gather evidence.
3   Mitigate the effect on customers.
4   Isolate the problem.
5   Reproduce the problem.
6   Fix the problem.
7   Reflect on how to prevent the problem in the future.

As with anything that's part art and part science, this isn't a strictly defined process. Sometimes, we must trace an iterative path through these steps in an unpredictable way. For the purposes of explanation, though, let's pretend that we can solve our problem by going through these steps in a straightforward, linear manner.

TRIAGING PROBLEMS

Usually, it's not just one problem that's affecting us and our customers. Often, we'll have many problems, so we must prioritize these by their severity—that is, how badly they affect our customers and our business.

The *triage* process comes from the medical world, where medical professionals rank patients for treatment based on how urgently they need attention. We can do a similar thing: rank problems by how bad they are so that we can focus on debugging the worst ones first.

GATHERING EVIDENCE

After triaging problems and selecting the highest-priority problem to solve, our next step is to gather as much evidence as we can. This is anything that can help direct us more quickly to the real location of the bug. If we start debugging close to where the problem actually is, we can narrow in on it much more quickly. We need to learn as much as we can about the problem as quickly as possible. The evidence includes things like these:

- Logging and error reports
- Traces for relevant request paths through the system (like the one shown earlier in figure 11.8)
- Bug reports from users
- Information from Stern, kubectl, the Kubernetes dashboard, or from our observability software
- Call stacks for any crash that might have occurred
- The implicated versions, branches, or tags of our code
- Recently deployed code or microservices

We must compile this information immediately because, often, the next thing we must do for the benefit of our customers is make the problem just disappear as quickly as possible.

MITIGATING THE EFFECT ON CUSTOMERS

Before attempting to solve or find the cause of the problem, we must ensure that it's not adversely affecting our customers. If our customers are negatively affected, then we must take immediate action to rectify the situation.

At this point, we don't care what caused the problem or what the real long-term fix for it might be. We simply need the fastest possible way to restore the functionality that our customers depend on. They'll appreciate our immediate action to find a workaround that allows them to continue using our application. There are multiple ways we can do this:

- If the problem comes from a recent code update, revert that update and redeploy the code to production. This is often easier with microservices because if we know that the microservice that was updated caused the problem, we can easily revert that single microservice and restore it to the previously working version, say, an earlier image in the container registry.
- If the problem comes from a new or updated feature that isn't urgently needed by the customer, we can disable that single feature to restore the application to a working state.
- If the problem comes from a microservice that isn't urgently needed, we can temporarily take that microservice out of commission.

I can't overstate the importance of this step! It could take hours or days (maybe even weeks at worst) to solve a problem. We can't know ahead of time how long it will take, and we can't expect our customers to stand by and wait for that to happen. It's more likely that they'll change allegiance to one of our competitors instead.

What's worse is that solving a problem under pressure (because our customers are waiting on us) is extremely stressful and results in poor decision making. Any fix we apply under stress is likely to add more bugs, which only compounds the problem.

For the sake of our customers and ourselves, we must temporarily ignore the problem and find the fastest way to restore our application to a working state (as depicted in figure 11.10). This takes away the pressure, allows our customers to continue without interruption, and buys us the time we need to solve this problem.

REPRODUCING THE PROBLEM

After making sure that the application is working again for our customers, we can now move on to locating the cause of the problem and solving it. To do this, we must be able to reproduce the problem. Unless we can definitely and consistently repeat the problem, we can never be certain that we've fixed it. What we're aiming to do is create a *test case* that demonstrates the bug. That is a documented sequence of steps that we can follow to reliably cause the bug to show itself.

Ideally, we'd like to reproduce the bug on our development computer. That makes it easier to run experiments to track down the bug. Some problems, though, are so complex that we can't easily reproduce them in development, especially when our application has grown so big (e.g., it has many microservices) that it no longer fits in its entirety on a single computer.

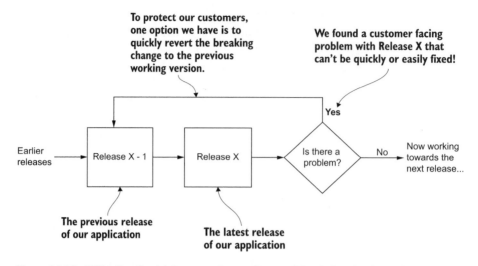

Figure 11.10   Mitigating the risk to our customer after a problem is found by immediately rolling back to a previous working version

In this situation, we must reproduce the problem in a *test environment*. This is a production-like environment that is purely for testing (it's not customer facing). Debugging in the test environment, which is similar to debugging in production, can still be very difficult, though, and ultimately, we'd still like to reproduce the problem in development.

In the test environment, we can run experiments to further understand which components of the application are involved in the problem and then safely remove any that aren't contributing to it. Through a process of elimination, we can cut back our application to a point where it's small enough to run in development. At this point, we can transfer from the test environment to our development computer. We'll talk more about creating test environments in chapter 12.

If we're doing automated testing, this is the point where we should write an automated test that checks that the bug is fixed. Of course, this test fails initially—that's the point of it. We'll use it later as a reliable way to know that the problem has been fixed. Writing an automated test also ensures that we can repeatedly reproduce the problem. Each and every time we run this test, it should fail, confirming that we've indeed found a reliable way to reproduce the bug.

ISOLATING THE PROBLEM

Once we've reproduced the problem in development, we now start the process of isolating it. We repeatedly run experiments and chip away at the application until we've narrowed down the scope and pinpointed the exact source of the bug.

We're effectively cutting away the space in which the problem can hide, progressively reducing the problem domain until the cause becomes obvious. We're using a *divide and conquer*–style of process, as illustrated in figure 11.11.

We start with a large problem space. At this stage, finding the cause of the problem is like trying to find a needle in a haystack.

Each step down this diagram represents cutting the problem space in half. This is a binary search for the cause of the problem.

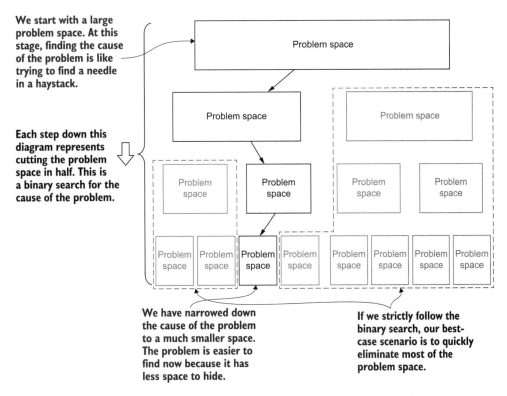

We have narrowed down the cause of the problem to a much smaller space. The problem is easier to find now because it has less space to hide.

If we strictly follow the binary search, our best-case scenario is to quickly eliminate most of the problem space.

Figure 11.11 Cutting away the problem space until we isolate the exact source of the bug

By the way, microservices are great for this. Our application is already nicely factored into easily separable components. This makes it much easier to pull our application into pieces. In general, it's pretty easy to just drop an individual microservice out of the application (just comment it out of your Docker Compose file!). As you drop each microservice, ask the following question: Can you still reproduce the problem?

- *Yes.* That's great. You've just reduced the problem domain by one microservice.
- *No.* That's great. You've possibly just implicated that microservice in the problem.

Either way, you're iterating your way toward the cause of the problem.

Sometimes, we'll quickly identify the source of a problem. At other times, debugging can be a painfully slow, time-consuming, and frustrating process. It depends on our general level of experience, our familiarity with the codebase, whether we have seen this kind of problem before, and the complexity of the particular problem itself.

NOTE Debugging at its worst requires persistence, patience, and commitment. Don't be afraid to reach out for help. There's nothing worse than being stuck on a problem that you can't solve.

If you know where to start looking for a problem, then you already have a massive head start. You might also be able to take an educated guess at what is causing the problem. If that works out, you're quite right to skip much of this process and immediately focus your attention on the cause of the bug. However, if you don't know where to look, or if your guess turns out to be wrong, you'll have to be more scientific about debugging and apply this full process.

FIXING THE PROBLEM

You've identified the root cause of the problem. Now you just have to fix it! Fortunately, fixing problems is much easier than finding them in the first place. Usually, identifying the broken code is enough to make you imagine what the solution would be. Sometimes, it's more difficult, and you'll have to invest some creative thinking to come up with a solution. The hardest part is definitely over though. You've found the needle in the haystack, and now you can work out the best way to remove it.

If you're doing automated testing, and you've already written the failing test that reproduces the problem, then you have a convenient and reliable yardstick to show you when the bug has been fixed. Even if the fix turns out to be difficult, at least you have a way to know for sure that the problem is solved. That's a useful thing to have as you iterate and experiment your way towards a fix.

REFLECTING ON PREVENTING THE PROBLEM IN THE FUTURE

Every time we solve a problem, we should pause for a moment to reflect on what can be done to prevent the problem from happening again in the future, or what could have been done to find and fix the problem more quickly. Reflection is important for us as individuals and as teams to continuously refine and improve our development process.

We might have written an automated test that will prevent this specific problem again in the future. But still, we need something more than that. We should seek practices and habits to help us eliminate not just this specific problem, but all of this class or kind of problem.

The amount of time that we spend reflecting and then the amount of time we invest in upgrading our development and testing process depends a lot on the problem itself and the severity of it.

We should ask questions like these:

- Is this kind of problem likely to happen in the future such that we should proactively mitigate against it?
- Are the effects of this problem severe enough that we should proactively mitigate against it?

Answering these questions helps us understand how much effort to expend preemptively combatting this type of problem in the future.

11.3.2 *Debugging production microservices*

Sometimes we can't get away from it; we literally have to debug our microservices in production. If we can't reproduce the problem in test or development, then our only option is to conduct experiments in production to further understand the problem.

CHECKING PODS FOR ERRORS

The first step in debugging any microservice is to check its logs for relevant error messages. We've covered this already, but here's a reminder of the ways you can do this:

```
kubectl logs <pod-name>
```

Or, if you have Stern installed, do this:

```
stern <pod-name>
```

It's useful to be able to get the logs for the previous instance like this:

```
kubectl logs --previous <pod-name>
```

That last command allows us to retrieve the logging for a crashed microservice. Inspecting those logs for errors or warnings can usually give us some idea as to why it crashed.

Listing all pods can show us if any of the pods are currently in error or suffering from repeated restarts:

```
kubectl get pods
```

For example, at one point, when I was trying to get the video-streaming microservice working in my cluster, I was seeing the following errors:

```
NAME                         READY STATUS               RESTARTS AGE
video-streaming-57f4-trng4 0/1   ErrImagePull        0  6s
video-streaming-5d6f-dljr5 0/1   ImagePullBackOff 0     5m19s
```

Those errors (`ErrImagePull` and `ImagePullBackOff`) are telling me that the Kubernetes cluster is failing to pull the image from the container registry. This is a very common problem, and it means I've probably misconfigured the connection from the cluster to the container registry (see chapter 6, section 6.11.3, if you need to remember how to do that with Azure).

We can get a wealth of information about a particular pod and any errors it might be suffering, say, for the metadata microservice, using the following commands:

```
kubectl get pod metadata-55bb6bdf58-7pjn2 -o yaml
kubectl describe pod metadata-55bb6bdf58-7pjn2
```

Just remember to plug in the name of the particular pod you're interested in:

```
kubectl get pod <pod-name> -o yaml
kubectl describe pod <pod-name>
```

In fact, you can find detailed information about deployments, services, and other Kubernetes resources using the general syntax of these commands:

```
kubectl get <resource-type> <resource-name> -o yaml
kubectl describe <resource-type> <resource-name>
```

Don't forget, you can also use the Kubernetes dashboard (from section 11.2.4) to visually find any of this same information.

SHELLING IN

To make a deeper inspection than logging can give us, we can use kubectl to open a shell into (open a terminal into) any pod (at least any that has a shell installed). Once we know the name of the pod (invoking `kubectl get pods` to see their names), such as the pod that contains the metadata microservice, we can open a shell to it like this:

```
kubectl exec --stdin --tty metadata-55bb6bdf58-7pjn2 -- bash
```

We can actually use this to invoke any command within a pod. Here's the general format:

```
kubectl exec --stdin --tty <pod-name> -- <command>
```

Typically, I use the shorter version of the command to save typing:

```
kubectl exec -it <pod-name> -- <command>
```

As you might be able to sense, we're in extremely dangerous territory here. When you're inside a microservice like this, there is the potential for much damage, and any mistakes could easily make the problem much worse! Don't shell into a production microservice on a whim, and if you do, don't change anything because you can easily break it.

Of course, this only matters if it affects your customers. If you're instead debugging microservices in your own private cluster or in a test environment, then you aren't affecting any customers, so feel free to push, prod, and poke your microservices however you like—it's a great learning experience to do this! Just be very careful if you're inspecting a microservice in a customer-facing system.

PROXYING IN

By default, for better security, most of our microservices will only be accessible from within our Kubernetes cluster. But sometimes, we'd like a way to access such microservices for testing purposes or diagnosing problems. To expose an internal microservice so that we can test it from our development computer without exposing it to the outside world, for example, we can't make requests directly to our metadata microservice from outside the cluster, but we can make it accessible just for ourselves using port forwarding. For example, here we expose the metadata microservice locally on port 6000:

```
kubectl port-forward metadata-55bb6bdf58-7pjn2 6000:80
```

While the `port-forward` command is running, we can make requests to http://localhost :6000, and those requests are forwarded to port 80 on the metadata microservice in our cluster.

This is an invaluable technique for remotely testing our microservices to check that they are responding correctly to requests. We can also use this technique to connect to third-party services, such as the RabbitMQ dashboard, that we might have running our cluster. Here's the general format:

```
kubectl port-forward <pod-name> [<local-port>:]<pod-port>
```

CHECKING POD ENVIRONMENT VARIABLES

A common mistake when deploying microservices is to forget to add or to misconfigure environment variables. I suffer from this with annoying regularity.

The first defense against this is that your microservice should throw an error if a required environment variable is missing; we covered this way back in chapter 2, section 2.6.6. It means you can check the log for a microservice, and it will tell you which environment variable is missing.

You can check for badly configured environment variables by seeing all the values that are actually set for a microservice:

```
kubectl describe pod metadata-55bb6bdf58-7pjn2
```

That gives you a wall of information relating to the microservice, but you can quickly scan through it to pick out the names and values of the environment variables.

TIP I often use the `grep` command to pluck a particular environment variable from the full, detailed output.

Just remember to plug in the name of the pod you're interested in:

```
kubectl describe pod <pod-name>
```

CHECKING SERVICE NAMES AND PORT NUMBERS

Another common mistake is to try to make microservices communicate with each other using misconfigured service names and port numbers. For example, if the gateway microservice is making requests to the metadata microservice, and those requests are failing, you should check that the name and port number are correct on either side of the request.

First, check the code or environment variables for the calling microservice (in this example, the gateway microservice) to be sure that it's using the correct name (e.g., "metadata") and the right port number (e.g., 80) for the callee (the metadata microservice). Second, check the details of the Kubernetes service for the callee to ensure that the actual name and port for it are what you think they are!

You can bring up details for all services like this:

```
kubectl get services
```

For full details on a particular service, use this:

```
kubectl get services <service-name> -o yaml
kubectl describe service <service-name>
```

11.4   Reliability and recovery

We can't avoid problems, but there are many ways that we can deal with these in our application to maintain service in the face of failures. With our application in production, we have an expectation that it will perform with a certain level of reliability, and there are many tactics we can employ to architect robust and reliable systems. This section overviews a small selection of practices and techniques to help us build fault-tolerant systems that can quickly bounce back from failure.

11.4.1   Practicing defensive programming

A first step is to code with the mindset of *defensive programming*. When working this way, we have the expectation that errors will occur, even if we can't anticipate what those might be. We should always expect the following:

- We'll get bad inputs to our code.
- Our code contains bugs that haven't manifested yet.
- Our code will have bugs added to it at some point in the future.
- Things we depend on (e.g., RabbitMQ) aren't 100% reliable and, occasionally, have their own problems.

When we adopt the defensive mindset, we'll automatically start looking for ways to make our code behave more gracefully in the presence of unexpected situations. Fault tolerance starts at the coding level. It starts within each microservice.

11.4.2   Practicing defensive testing

As you're probably aware, testing plays a huge role in building resilient and reliable systems. We covered testing in chapter 9, so all I'd like to say here is simply that testing the "normal" code paths isn't enough. We should also be testing that the software we create can handle errors. This is the next step up from defensive programming.

We should be practicing *defensive testing* and writing tests that actively attack our code. This helps us identify fragile code that could do with some more attention. We need to make sure our code can recover gracefully, reporting errors, and handling unusual situations.

11.4.3   Protecting our data

All applications deal with user data, and we must take necessary steps to protect our data in the event of failures. When unexpected failures occur, we need to be confident that our most important data isn't damaged or lost. Bugs happen; losing our data should not.

Not all data is equal. Data that is generated within our system (and can hence be regenerated) is less important than data that is captured from our customer. Although all data is important, it's the source data that we must invest the most in protecting.

The first step to protecting data, obviously, is to have a backup, which should be automated. Most cloud vendors provide facilities for this that you can enable.

NOTE Don't forget to practice restoring from your backup! Backups are completely useless if we're unable to restore them.

At least now, should the worst happen, we can restore lost or damaged data from the backup. In the industry, we have a saying: *our data doesn't exist unless it exists in at least three places.* Here are some other guidelines we can follow to protect our data:

- Safely record data as soon as it's captured.
- Never have code that overwrites source data.
- Never have code that deletes source data.

The code that captures our data is some of the most important code in our application, and we should treat it with an appropriate level of respect. It should be extremely well tested. It should also be minimal and as simple as possible because simple code leaves less space where bugs and security problems can hide.

The reason we should never overwrite or delete our source data is that a bug in that code can easily damage or destroy the data. We know bugs happen, right? We're in the defensive mindset, so we're expecting unforeseen problems to happen. To learn more about working with and protecting your data, see my book, *Data Wrangling with JavaScript* (Manning, 2018).

11.4.4 *Replication and redundancy*

The best way to tackle the failure of a microservice is by having *redundancy*. We do that by having multiple (usually at least three) instances of each microservice sitting behind a load balancer, which you can see in figure 11.12. The load balancer is a service that shares incoming requests across multiple microservices so that the "load" is distributed evenly among them.

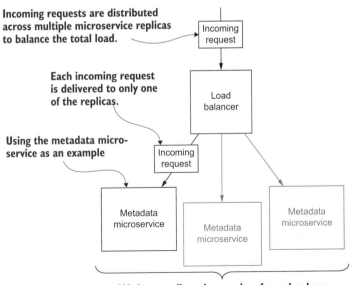

Figure 11.12   A load balancer distributes incoming requests across multiple redundant instances of a microservice.

If any microservice happens to fail, the load balancer immediately redirects incoming requests to the other instances. In the meantime, the failed instance is restarted by Kubernetes. This redundancy means that we can maintain a continuous level of service even in the face of intermittent failures. Redundancy is implemented by *replication*. We also use replication for increased performance, but we'll save that until chapter 12.

Just because our system can handle failures doesn't mean we should tolerate these. All failures should be logged and later investigated. We can use the debugging process from section 11.3 to find and fix the cause of the failure.

IMPLEMENTING REPLICATION IN KUBERNETES

Each of the microservices that we've deployed for FlixTube so far only had a single instance. This is perfectly okay when creating an application for learning (like we did with FlixTube) or when we're in the starting phase of developing our own microservices application. It's just not going to be as fault tolerant as it could be.

This is easily fixed, though, because Kubernetes makes it easy for us to create replicas. The amazing thing is that it's just as simple as changing the value of a field in the Kubernetes deployment YAML code that we've already written—that's part of the power of *infrastructure as code.*

We can easily change the number of replicas by setting the value of the `replicas` property for any microservice in our Kubernetes deployment. You can see an example of this for the gateway microservice in listing 11.2 (an addition to chapter-10/scripts/cd/gateway.yaml), which is an update to the YAML code from chapter 10.

The number of replicas has been updated from one to three. We can apply this change by invoking `kubectl apply`. Once completed, our gateway microservice will have three redundant instances handling requests instead of just one. With this small change, we've massively improved the reliability and fault tolerance of our application!

Listing 11.2   Adding replicas to our gateway microservice

```
apiVersion: apps/v1
kind: Deployment
metadata:
  name: gateway
spec:
  replicas: 3          ◁─┐   Sets the replica count to 3. Applying this
  selector:                  deployment creates three replicas of our
    matchLabels:             gateway microservice.
      app: gateway
  template:
    metadata:
      labels:
        app: gateway
    spec:
      --snip--
```

11.4.5   *Fault isolation and graceful degradation*

One thing that microservices are really good at is fault isolation. We do have to take some care, however, when using this. What we're aiming for is that problems within our cluster are isolated so that they have minimal effect on the user.

With appropriate mechanisms in place, our application can gracefully handle faults and prevent these from manifesting as problems in the frontend. The tools we need for this are timeouts, retries, circuit breakers, and bulkheads, which are described in the following sections.

As an example, let's consider the video-upload microservice. Just imagine that something has gone wrong with it, and it's no longer functional. At this moment, we're working hard to rectify the situation and quickly restore it to a working state. In the meantime, our customers would like to continue using our product. If we didn't have mechanisms to prevent it, errors might go all the way to the frontend, bringing our service down, and badly disrupting our customers.

Instead, we should implement safeguards that stop this wholesale disruption of our user base. This is illustrated in figure 11.13. The top part of the figure shows the error propagating all the way to the user and causing problems for them. The bottom part of figure 11.13 shows how it should work: the gateway stopping the error in its tracks, thus containing the fault within the cluster.

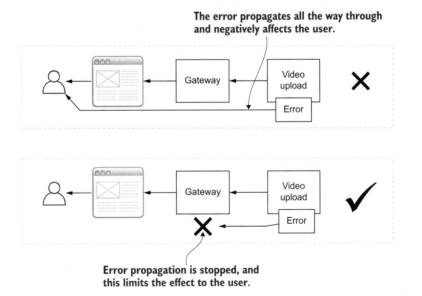

Figure 11.13   Isolating faults within the cluster from the user

We can then handle the situation by showing the user an error message saying that the video-upload feature is currently not available. Video upload might be broken, but our users can continue using the rest of the application.

This is a huge benefit that microservices brings to the table. If we were using a monolith, and one of its components (e.g., the video-upload component) was broken, that usually takes down the entire monolith, leaving our customers with nothing. With microservices, however, the fault can be isolated, and the application as a whole can continue to function, albeit in a degraded state.

This idea of fault isolation is often called the *bulkhead pattern*, so named because it's conceptually similar to the actual bulkheads that are used in large ships. When a leak occurs in a ship, it's the bulkheads that prevent the leak from escaping to other compartments and eventually sinking the ship. This is fault isolation in the real world, and you can see how it's similar to fault isolation in a microservices application.

11.4.6 *Simple techniques for fault tolerance*

Here are some simple techniques you can start using immediately to implement fault tolerance and fault isolation in your own microservices application.

TIMEOUTS

In this book, we used the built-in Node.js `http.request` function and the Axios code library to make HTTP requests internally between microservices. We control our own microservices, and, most of the time, we know those will respond quickly to requests that are internal to the cluster. There are times, however, when a problem manifests itself and an internal microservice stops responding.

In the future, we'd also like to make requests to external services. Just imagine that we've integrated FlixTube with Dropbox as a means to import new videos. When making requests to an external service such as Dropbox, we don't have any control over how quickly these external services respond to our requests. Such external services will go down for maintenance occasionally, so it's entirely likely that an external service such as Dropbox will intermittently stop responding to our requests.

We must consider how to handle requests to a service that doesn't respond. If a request isn't going to complete anytime soon, we'd like to have it aborted after some maximum amount of time. If we didn't do that, it could take a long time (if ever) for the request to complete. We can't very well have our customer waiting so long! We'd prefer to abort the request quickly and tell the customer something has gone wrong, rather than have them waiting indefinitely on it.

We can deal with this using *timeouts*. A timeout is the maximum amount of time that can elapse before a request is automatically aborted with an error code. Setting timeouts for our requests allows us to control how quickly our application responds to failure. Failing quickly is what we want here because the alternative is to fail slowly, and if something is going to fail, we'd like to deal with it as quickly as possible so as not to waste our customer's time.

SETTING A TIMEOUT WITH AXIOS

Reading the Axios documentation tells me that the default timeout is infinity! That means, by default, an Axios request can literally go forever without being aborted. We definitely need to set the timeout for any requests we make with Axios.

You can set the timeout for each request, but that requires repeated effort. Fortunately, with Axios, we can set a default timeout for *all* requests.

Listing 11.3   Setting a default timeout for HTTP requests with Axios

```
const axios = require("axios");

axios.defaults.timeout = 2500;
```
⟵ **Sets the default timeout for requests to 2,500 milliseconds or 2.5 seconds**

RETRIES

We know that HTTP requests sometimes fail. We don't control external services, and we can't see their code, so it's difficult for us to determine how reliable they are—and, even the most reliable services can have intermittent failures.

One simple way to deal with this is to retry the operation a number of times and hope that it succeeds on one of the subsequent attempts. This is illustrated in figure 11.14. In this example, you can imagine FlixTube's video-storage microservice requesting a video to be retrieved from Azure Storage. Occasionally, such requests fail for indeterminable reasons. In figure 11.14, two successive requests have failed due to an intermittent connection error, but the third request succeeds.

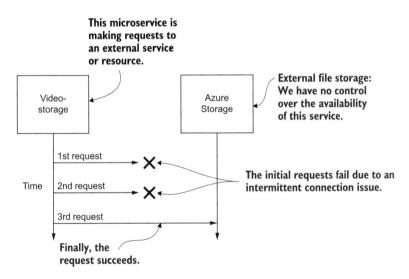

Figure 11.14   Retrying an HTTP request until it succeeds

Assuming that the network is reliable is one of the fallacies of distributed computing, and we must take steps to mitigate against request failures. Implementation in JavaScript isn't particularly difficult. In listing 11.4, you can see an implementation of a `retry` function that I've used across a number of projects. The `retry` function wraps other asynchronous operations, such as HTTP requests, so these can be attempted multiple times.

Listing 11.4 also includes a helpful `sleep` function used to make pauses between attempts. There's no point immediately trying to make a request again. If we do it too quickly, it's probably just going to fail again. In this case, we give it some time before making another attempt.

Listing 11.5 is an example of how to call the `retry` function, showing how it can wrap an HTTP `GET` request. In this example, we allow the request to be retried three times with a pause of 5 milliseconds between each request.

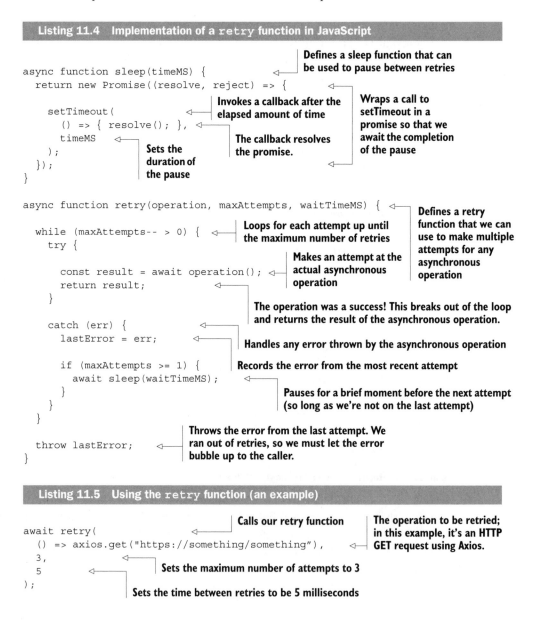

Listing 11.4 Implementation of a `retry` function in JavaScript

```
async function sleep(timeMS) {
  return new Promise((resolve, reject) => {

    setTimeout(
      () => { resolve(); },
      timeMS
    );
  });
}
```

- Defines a sleep function that can be used to pause between retries
- Invokes a callback after the elapsed amount of time
- The callback resolves the promise.
- Sets the duration of the pause
- Wraps a call to setTimeout in a promise so that we await the completion of the pause

```
async function retry(operation, maxAttempts, waitTimeMS) {

  while (maxAttempts-- > 0) {
    try {

      const result = await operation();
      return result;
    }

    catch (err) {
      lastError = err;

      if (maxAttempts >= 1) {
        await sleep(waitTimeMS);
      }
    }
  }

  throw lastError;
}
```

- Defines a retry function that we can use to make multiple attempts for any asynchronous operation
- Loops for each attempt up until the maximum number of retries
- Makes an attempt at the actual asynchronous operation
- The operation was a success! This breaks out of the loop and returns the result of the asynchronous operation.
- Handles any error thrown by the asynchronous operation
- Records the error from the most recent attempt
- Pauses for a brief moment before the next attempt (so long as we're not on the last attempt)
- Throws the error from the last attempt. We ran out of retries, so we must let the error bubble up to the caller.

Listing 11.5 Using the `retry` function (an example)

```
await retry(
  () => axios.get("https://something/something"),
  3,
  5
);
```

- Calls our retry function
- The operation to be retried; in this example, it's an HTTP GET request using Axios.
- Sets the maximum number of attempts to 3
- Sets the time between retries to be 5 milliseconds

11.4.7 Advanced techniques for fault tolerance

We've seen some simple techniques for improving the reliability and resilience of our application. Of course, there are many other, more advanced techniques we could deploy for improved fault tolerance and recovery from failures.

We're almost beyond the scope of the book, but I'd still like to share with you a brief overview of some more advanced techniques. These will be useful in the future as you evolve a more robust architecture for your application.

JOB QUEUE

The *job queue* is a type of microservice found in many application architectures. This is different from the message queue we saw in RabbitMQ. It's similar, but it's a level of sophistication above that.

We use a job queue to manage heavyweight processing tasks. Let's imagine how this could work for a future version of FlixTube. We can say that each video requires a lot of processing after it's uploaded. For example, we'd like to extract a thumbnail from videos or convert videos to a lower resolution for better performance playback on mobile devices. These are the kinds of CPU- and storage-intensive tasks that should happen after a video is uploaded, but that don't have to happen straight away.

Now imagine that 1,000 users have each uploaded a video, all roughly at the same time. We don't have any kind of elastic scaling yet (we'll talk about that in chapter 12). So, how can we manage the huge processing workload resulting from so many videos landing in FlixTube at the same time? This is what the job queue does. You can see an illustration of how it works in figure 11.15.

The job queue records the sequence of jobs that need to be performed to the database. This makes it resilient against failure. The entire application could crash and restart, but so long as the database survives, we can reload the job queue and continue processing where it left off. Individual jobs can also fail; for example, the microservice doing the processing crashes, but because failed jobs aren't marked as complete, they will naturally be attempted again later.

The job queue also allows for control over the performance of this processing. Instead of maxing out our application to process the 1,000 uploaded videos all at once, we can spread out the load so that processing is scheduled over a longer time period. It can also be scheduled across off-peak hours. This means we won't have to pay for the extra compute that might otherwise be required if we wanted to do the processing all at once in a massive burst.

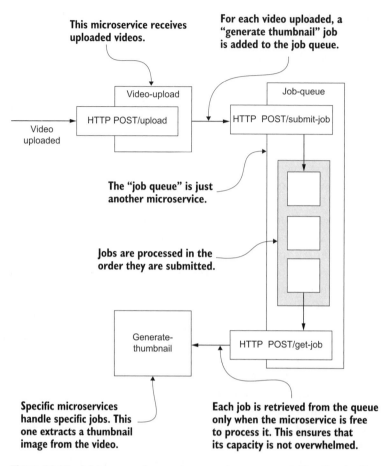

Figure 11.15   A job-queue microservice manages a queue of video thumbnail-generation jobs.

CIRCUIT BREAKER

The *circuit breaker* is like a more advanced version of a timeout. It has some built-in smarts to understand when problems are occurring, so that it can deal with these more intelligently. Figure 11.16 illustrates how a circuit breaker works.

In normal situations, the status of the circuit breaker is set to the On state, and it allows HTTP requests to go through as usual (1). If at some point a request to a particular resource fails (2), the circuit breaker flips to the Off state (3). While in the Off state, the circuit breaker always fails new requests immediately.

You can think of this as a "super" timeout. The circuit breaker knows the upstream system is failing at the moment, so it doesn't even bother checking. It immediately fails the incoming request!

This failing quickly is why we used timeouts. It's better to fail quickly than to fail slowly. The circuit breaker works by already knowing that we're failing; so, instead of just failing more quickly, it can fail immediately.

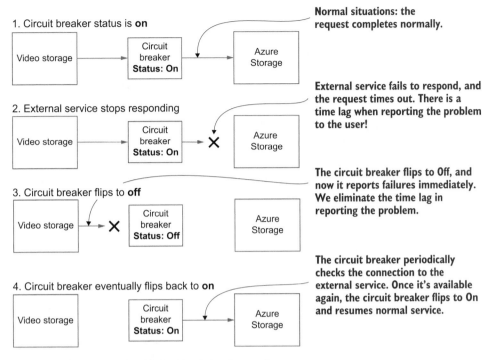

Figure 11.16   Illustrating how the circuit breaker works

Periodically, on its own time (with a delay that you can configure), the circuit breaker checks the upstream service to see if it has resumed normal operation. When that happens, the circuit breaker flips back to the On state (4). Future incoming requests are now allowed through as normal. Implementing a circuit breaker is much more difficult than implementing a timeout or a retry, but it's worth keeping in mind for future use, especially if you find yourself needing a more sophisticated technique.

11.5   Continue your learning

You now have many techniques in your toolkit for keeping your microservices healthy and reliable! To learn more about observability, logging, and monitoring in production, read these books:

- *Cloud Observability in Action* by Michael Hausenblas (Manning, 2023)
- *Observability Engineering* by Charity Majors, Liz Fong-Jones, George Miranda (O'Reilly 2022)
- *Software Telemetry* by Jamie Riedesel (Manning, 2021)
- *Logging in Action* by Phil Wilkins (Manning, 2022)
- *Elasticsearch in Action*, 2nd ed., by Madhusudhan Konda (Manning, 2023)

There's also a great book about *crash testing* your application:

- *Chaos Engineering* by Mikolaj Pawlikowski (Manning, 2021)

Summary

- Microservices applications are typically more complex than traditional monolithic applications, and this additional complexity means it can be more difficult to find and fix the ongoing problems that are a part of life for any developer.
- To maintain a healthy application, we must do the following:
  - Observe its behavior to understand its history and current state.
  - Take action when problems occur to protect our customers.
  - Triage problems so the worst ones are addressed first.
  - Debug problems and apply fixes as needed.
- We can monitor and manage the health of our microservices through the following:
  - Logging
  - Error handling
  - Automated health checks
  - Observability techniques
- We can view logs from pods in Kubernetes using kubectl, Stern, or the Kubernetes dashboard.
- Observability is a technique for surfacing rich and interesting details about the behavior of our distributed application and allows us to do the following:
  - Dig down into the behavior of our application to ask questions and find answers regarding problems that are occurring.
  - Connect the dots between microservices, correlating chains of requests and messages to really understand what's going on in there.
- A microservices application can be made more fault tolerant than a monolithic application. Crashes within individual microservices can be contained within the cluster, shielding our customers from their effects.
- The are many techniques for fault tolerance; here's a handful:
  - Automatically restarting failed microservices using Kubernetes health checks.
  - Redundancy for managing crashes, which means if we have multiple instances of a microservice available, when one of them crashes, there is always another ready to step in and resume its workload
  - Timeouts to ensure that hung network requests are aborted in a timely manner
  - Automatic retries for failed network requests
  - Using a job queue to ensure that essential jobs are handled, even if the microservice crashes while handling a job
  - Using a circuit breaker, which is an advanced combination of timeouts and retries

Pathways to scalability 12

This chapter covers

- Scaling microservices to bigger development teams
- Scaling microservices to meet growing demand
- Mitigating problems caused by changes
- Understanding basic security concerns
- Converting a monolith to microservices
- Spectrum of possibilities and hybrid approach
- Building with microservices on a budget

We've spent the whole book working toward a production microservices application, so where to now? It's time to see what microservices can offer us in the future.

Throughout this book, we've taken many shortcuts that helped us get started quickly and cheaply with microservices. These shortcuts make it simpler to learn microservices and to bootstrap our fledgling application. Even though FlixTube is a simple application built with a relatively simple process, we're still using microservices, and this is an architecture that provides us many pathways to future scalability.

In this chapter, we discuss how to manage a growing microservices application. How do we scale up to a bigger development team? How do we scale up to meet the demands of a growing customer base? We also need to talk about basic security concerns and how they relate to microservices. Then, we'll briefly touch on what it takes to convert an existing monolith to microservices.

We'll finish the book by reiterating the techniques that can make bootstrapping a microservices application simpler, easier, and cheaper. This is practical advice that can help a small team, a startup, or a solo developer kick-start their own microservices application while still having a future full of possibilities for scalability!

12.1   *Our future is scalable*

Microservices offer us numerous pathways to scaling up our application. In this chapter, we'll look at the kinds of things we must do moving forward to scale our application and workflow so that we can grow our development team around our growing application. We'll follow up by looking at how to scale the performance of our application for greater capacity and throughput.

You probably don't need any of these techniques yet; you'll only need these when your application has grown big enough to expand your development team or when your customer base has increased so much that you need to scale up for better performance.

We're moving into very advanced territory here, and this chapter mostly gives you a taste of the ways in which you can scale your application in the future. This is really just the tip of the iceberg, but it's enough to give you an awareness of the path ahead.

The problems we'll address in this chapter are good problems to have. If you come to the point where you must scale up, that's a good thing. It means your business is successful. It means you have a growing customer base. At this point, you can be really happy you chose a microservices architecture because it makes scaling up much more straightforward.

This chapter isn't intended to be hands-on. Think of it as some insight as to where your microservices journey might go in the future. That said, many of these techniques are fairly easy to try, but in doing so, you might make a mistake and inadvertently break your application cluster.

So, don't try any of this on your production infrastructure that existing staff or customers depend on. But do feel free to go back to chapter 10, and follow the instructions there to boot a new production instance of FlixTube. You can use that for experimentation as a risk-free way to try out anything in this chapter that sounds interesting.

12.2   *Scaling the development process*

First, let's tackle scaling our development process. In this book, so far, we've experienced the development process and production workflow from the point of view of a single developer working on a small microservices application. Ultimately, in chapter 10, we had our entire application in a monorepo (all microservices in a single code repository). We'll now raise our focus up from the single developer to the level of the team.

The simple process we've used so far can work really well for a small team while our product is still small:

- Developers working on a single codebase (our monorepo), writing and testing code on their development computer
- Developers pushing code changes to the hosted code repository, which triggers continuous deployment (CD) pipelines to deploy updated microservices to production

This simple process is a great way to get started and move quickly when building a new application. But we can only take it so far. Our fledgling development process suffers from the following problems:

- *We don't want code going directly from developers to customers.* We'd like our developers to be able to test their code in a production-like environment, but we want that "work in progress" to be buffered from customers to ensure that it works well before inflicting it on them.
- *We don't want developers interfering with each other.* As we grow our development team, developers working in a single codebase will be treading on each other's toes more frequently (e.g., causing merge conflicts and breaking the build).
- *Our single code repository isn't scalable.* To manage the complexity of our growing application, at some point, we might have to break apart our monorepo. This ensures that, even though the application might grow extremely complex, the code for each individual microservice can remain small, simple, and manageable.

To build a scalable development process, expand to multiple teams, and make the most of microservices, we must do some restructuring.

12.2.1 *Multiple teams*

As we evolve our application, we'll be adding more microservices to the mix to implement features and expand our application's capabilities. As the workload grows, we'll also have to grow the team to handle it. At some point, when our single team grows too large, we'll need to split it into multiple teams. This keeps our teams small and allows us to benefit from the communication and organizational advantages that come from small teams.

Applications based on microservices provide natural seams that can be used to carve up the applications for development by multiple teams. Figure 12.1 shows what our team structure looks like in the early stages of development, when we're using our simple development process.

Figure 12.2 shows what our structure might look like after we've grown and split into separate teams. We've carved up the

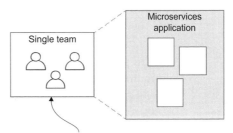

In the early stages of a new microservices application, we'll likely have a single team working across the whole application.

Figure 12.1   When starting a new application, it should be small enough that one team can manage all microservices by themselves.

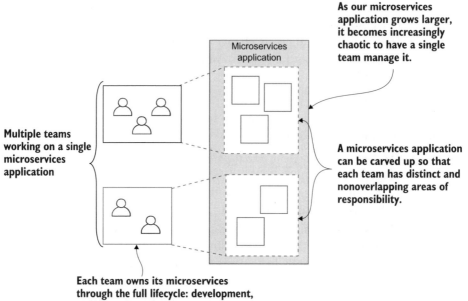

Microservices
application

As our microservices
application grows larger,
it becomes increasingly
chaotic to have a single
team manage it.

Multiple teams
working on a single
microservices
application

A microservices application
can be carved up so that
each team has distinct and
nonoverlapping areas of
responsibility.

Each team owns its microservices
through the full lifecycle: development,
testing, and production.

Figure 12.2   As we grow our application, the development can be split so that separate teams are
managing independent microservices or groups of microservices.

application so that each team is responsible for a different set of microservices with
zero overlaps. This helps prevent the teams from interfering with each other. Now, we
can grow our team of teams to any size we like by dividing our application up along
microservices boundaries.

Each team owns one or more microservices, and, typically, they are responsible for
their own microservices—all the way from coding, through testing, and then into production. The team is often responsible for the operational needs of their microservices, keeping them functional, healthy, and performant.

Of course, there are many ways to implement this, and the team structure and development process for any two companies will differ in the details. However, this method
of organizing self-reliant teams is scalable, which means we can grow a huge company
around a huge application and still maintain an effective development process.

12.2.2 *Independent code repositories*

To this point, the FlixTube application we've developed lives in a single code repository (our monorepo). You can see in figure 12.3 how this looks.

Using a monorepo makes things easier at the start of our project—there's less complexity and less development infrastructure (the infrastructure that supports our
development process) to create and manage. Given that we can have independent CD
pipelines for our microservices in a single code repository, we can actually go quite a

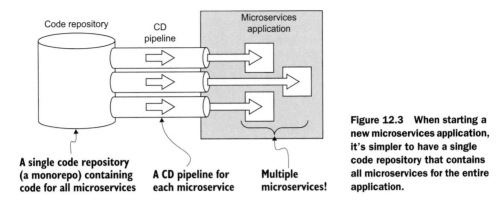

Figure 12.3 When starting a new microservices application, it's simpler to have a single code repository that contains all microservices for the entire application.

A single code repository (a monorepo) containing code for all microservices

A CD pipeline for each microservice

Multiple microservices!

long way into our microservices journey using only a monorepo (see chapter 10, section 10.10.4, for a reminder of how to do this).

This is important, because making the most of microservices means they need to have independent deployment schedules (if you can recall, this is how we defined a microservice way back in chapter 1, section 1.5). If we can only have a single CD pipeline for our code repository, it will become very annoying because doing a deployment means rebuilding and redeploying all of our microservices (very time consuming and about as risky as deploying an entire monolith), even when only one microservice has changed. Fortunately, we're using GitHub Actions, which allows us to have as many CD pipelines as we need in a single repo, so we can create independently runnable CD pipelines for each microservice. This means that code changes for one microservice will rebuild and redeploy only that one microservice.

You should push your monorepo as far as it can go. You want to keep things simple for as long as possible. To a point, this approach works very well. However, when scaling up your team and your application, there will come a time when the monorepo starts to feel like it's restricting your flexibility and your growth. When you feel this pain, it's time to start extracting your microservices to separate code repositories (shown in figure 12.4)

Wait until we feel the pain, though—we should only split our monorepo when it's growing out of control. At this stage, by splitting the monorepo into multiple pieces, we bring back simplicity. Yes, the whole microservices application is still going to be complex, but each separate code repository that we split out, each microservice, will be simple, and its interactions with other microservices should also be simple. Thus, we come back to what was explained in chapter 1, section 1.4: the microservices architectural pattern is meant to split up a complex whole into simple pieces. The whole is always going to be complex, but we can zoom in on any of the cleanly separate pieces (the microservices) and easily understand each of them.

If restructuring to multiple code repos seems like a huge amount of work and too much additional complexity, I completely sympathize with you! In fact, I'd argue that this one aspect is responsible for much of the perceived complexity normally attributed to microservices.

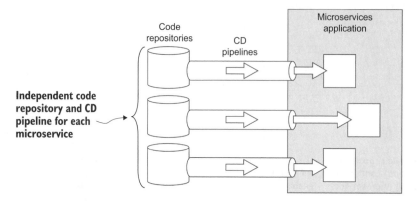

Figure 12.4   **As we grow our application, we'll need to split our microservices out to separate code repositories so that the code for each one is simple and independent.**

Even though our application as a whole will ultimately become incredibly complex (this is inevitable for modern enterprise applications), if we can switch our perspective down to a single microservice, the picture looks very different. Things suddenly seem a lot simpler. Because the complexity gets added slowly, it's more manageable. And when we focus on individual microservices, which are simple, rather than focusing on the whole application, which is bound to be complex, the overall complexity of the application has much less of an effect.

This is what actually saves the day for complexity in microservices applications. An individual microservice is a tiny and easily understood application with a small codebase. It has a relatively simple deployment process. Each microservice is simple and easy to manage, even though they can work together to build powerful and complex applications. This change of perspective from complex application to simple microservice is important for managing complexity.

Splitting our development process into microservice-sized chunks adds some additional complexity, but this pales in comparison to how complex our application may eventually become. By redirecting our focus from whole application complexity to individual microservices, we've essentially freed our application to scale to truly enormous proportions, even when each and every microservice remains just as simple to work with as it ever was.

But don't be too enthusiastic about making the change to separate code repositories for your microservices. If you make this change too early, you might find that you're paying for the cost of the transition at a time when it's still too early to gain benefit from it. You don't want to pay the cost before you can make use of the benefit.

Good software development is all about making good tradeoffs. Stick with a monorepo for as long as that makes sense for you. But be aware that it's not supposed to be this way. As your application grows more complex and as you grow your team, this simple approach eventually breaks down. There comes a point when splitting your code repositories might be necessary to manage complexity on a larger scale, while maintaining a productive development process.

12.2.3   Splitting the code repository

Our first task is to split our monorepo into multiple code repositories so that we have a distinct and separate repository for every microservice. Each new repository will contain the code for a single microservice and the code for deploying it to production.

We also need a separate code repository for the Terraform code that creates our infrastructure (the code we developed in chapter 7). This is the code that creates our container registry and Kubernetes cluster. This code doesn't belong to any particular microservice, so it needs its own code repository.

Figure 12.5 illustrates how we can take our FlixTube project from chapter 10 and break it up into multiple code repositories. To build each new repository, we invoke `git init` to create a blank repository, and then copy the code into the new repository and commit it. Otherwise, we might want to take the extra steps required to preserve our existing version history (see the following sidebar).

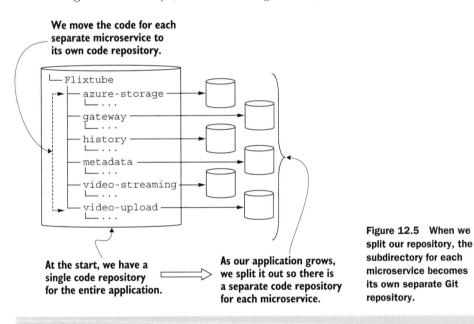

We move the code for each separate microservice to its own code repository.

At the start, we have a single code repository for the entire application.

As our application grows, we split it out so there is a separate code repository for each microservice.

Figure 12.5   When we split our repository, the subdirectory for each microservice becomes its own separate Git repository.

> ### Preserving the version history
>
> When creating new code repositories from old ones, we can use the command `git filter-branch` with the `--subdirectory-filter` argument to save our existing version history. To do this, see the Git documentation for details: https://git-scm.com/docs/git-filter-branch.
>
> You can also search the web for examples of "filter-branch"—there are many!

12.2.4 *The meta-repo*

Is using separate code repositories getting you down? Do you miss your monorepo and crave those simpler days of a single code repository? Well, here's some good news.

We can create a *meta-repo* that ties together all of our separate repositories into a single aggregate code repository. You can think of the meta-repo as a kind of virtual code repository. This means we can claw back some of the simplicity and convenience of the monorepo without sacrificing the flexibility and independence of having separate repositories. To create a meta-repo, we need the meta tool, available here: https://github .com/mateodelnorte/meta.

A meta-repo is configured by creating a .meta configuration file that lists a collection of separate repositories. See figure 12.6 for an example of where a .meta file would live in relation to the FlixTube project. Listing 12.1 shows the structure of this file.

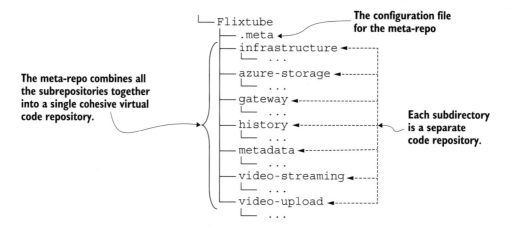

Figure 12.6   The .meta configuration file ties together separate repositories into a meta-repo.

Listing 12.1   Configuring FlixTube's meta code repository (.meta)

```
{
  "projects": {
    "gateway": "git@github.com:bmdk/gateway.git",
    "azure-storage":
      ➥ "git@github.com:bmdk/azure-storage.git",
    "video-streaming":
      ➥ "git@github.com:bmdk/video-streaming.git",
    "video-upload":
      ➥ "git@github.com:bmdk/video-upload.git",
    "history": "git@github.com:bmdk/history.git"
    "metadata": git@github.com:bmdk/metadata.git",
  }
}
```

Lists the separate code repositories that comprise this meta-repo

References the microservice's code on GitHub (just for illustration—these code repositories don't actually exist)

Using the meta tool allows us to run single Git commands that affect the entire collection of repositories. For example, let's say we'd like to pull code changes for all the microservices under the FlixTube project at once. We can use meta to do that with a single command:

```
meta git pull
```

We're still working with separate code repositories, but meta allows us to invoke commands simultaneously against multiple code repositories at once, so that it feels very much like we're back to working with a monorepo.

Meta gives you a lot of additional flexibility. You can use it to create our own custom sets of microservices. As a developer on a big team, you can create a meta-repo just for the set of microservices that you normally work on. Other developers can have their own separate meta-repos. You might even like to create multiple meta-repos so that you can easily switch between different sets of microservices, depending on what you're currently working on.

As a team leader, you can create separate meta-repos for different configurations of your application, each with its own Docker Compose file. This makes it easy for your team members to clone the code for a complete set of microservices. Then they can use Docker Compose to boot that application configuration. This is a great way to provide an "instant" and manageable development environment for your team.

12.2.5 *Creating multiple environments*

As we gain customers for our application, it becomes important that we buffer them against problems from ongoing "work in progress" or protect them from new features that are partially completed or only partially tested. The development team needs a production-like environment in which to test their code before putting it in front of customers.

Each developer must test their code on their development computer, but that's not enough. They must also test their code once it's integrated with changes from other developers. To make it as "real" as possible, this testing should be done in a production-like environment—just not the one that our customer is using!

We need a workflow for our developers to take their changes on a journey from their development computer, through an integration environment, into a test environment, and finally, once all the tests have passed, on to the customer-facing environment. Although no two companies will have exactly the same workflow, you can see what a typical workflow looks like in figure 12.7.

Setting up multiple environments is actually fairly simple, and we already have most of what we need in our existing Terraform code that was presented in chapter 7. We have already parameterized our code with an `app_name` variable that we used to create separate application resources based on the name we assigned to it (revisit chapter 7, section 7.10.2, where we first added this variable).

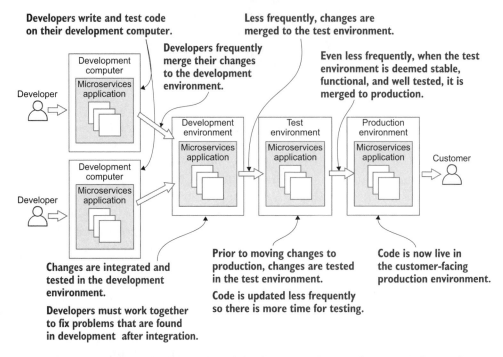

Figure 12.7   Progressing code changes through development and test environments before getting to production

We could now use `app_name` (set from the command line) when invoking Terraform to create different instances of FlixTube for testing and production. We just need to provide different names for each instance. For example, we could set `app_name` to `flixtube-development`, `flixtube-test`, or `flixtube-production` to create our separate environments.

We can improve on this, though, like in listing 12.2 (an update to chapter-9/example-1/scripts/variables.tf), by introducing a new variable called `environment`. We then convert `app_name` to a computed local variable that depends on the value of the `environment` variable.

Listing 12.2   Deriving `app_name` from `environment` in Terraform

```
variable "environment" {}            ◁──┐  Adds a new Terraform variable that specifies the current
                                         │  environment. We need to provide this when running
                                         │  Terraform via the command line, setting it to development,
locals {                                 │  test, or production, for example.
  app_name = "flixtube-${var.environment}"  ◁──┐  Creates a local variable for app_name
}                                                │  that builds separate versions of the
                                                 │  application for each environment (e.g.,
                                                 │  flixtube-development, flixtube-test, or
                                                 │  flixtube-production)
```

Introducing this new variable (`environment`) allows us to set the current environment from the command line. Listing 12.3 shows how we input values to our Terraform variables, including the new variable `environment`, from the command line.

We can reuse the same Terraform project to create as many separate environments as we like, all hosted in the same cloud account but differentiated by name (e.g., flixtube-development, flixtube-test, or flixtube-production). We can use this to create a workflow like that in figure 12.7 or something even more sophisticated, depending on what we need.

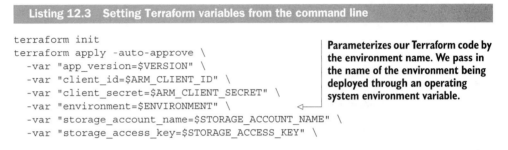

> **Listing 12.3 Setting Terraform variables from the command line**

```
terraform init
terraform apply -auto-approve \
  -var "app_version=$VERSION" \
  -var "client_id=$ARM_CLIENT_ID" \
  -var "client_secret=$ARM_CLIENT_SECRET" \
  -var "environment=$ENVIRONMENT" \
  -var "storage_account_name=$STORAGE_ACCOUNT_NAME" \
  -var "storage_access_key=$STORAGE_ACCESS_KEY" \
```

Parameterizes our Terraform code by the environment name. We pass in the name of the environment being deployed through an operating system environment variable.

12.2.6 Production workflow

We can now create multiple environments and use them to stitch together a testing workflow to protect our customers against broken code. The remaining question is, how do we trigger the deployment for any particular environment? This is simpler than you might think.

We can use separate branches in our code repository to target deployments to different environments. Figure 12.8 shows an example setup for this. It's a fairly simple branching strategy, but there are more sophisticated versions in the wild.

Our development team works in the development (or main) branch. When they push code to that branch, it triggers a CI pipeline that runs tests and a CD pipeline that deploys to the development environment. This allows our whole team to integrate and test their changes frequently together in a production-like environment.

How frequently should the developers push code changes? As often as possible! Once per day, if not multiple times per day, is best. The less time we have between code merges, the less often we'll see errors caused by conflicting changes and bad integrations. This is the main idea behind *continuous integration* (CI), an important practice that underpins continuous deployment (CD).

Less frequently (say, once per week), we'll merge from the development branch to the test branch. This triggers the deployment to the test environment. Code merges from development to test are less frequent, and this gives us time to test, fix problems, and stabilize the code before we hand it over to our customers.

Finally, when the code in the test branch is good to go (say, every one to two weeks), we then merge it to the production branch. This deploys updated microservices to production so that our customers can get their hands on whatever awesome new features and bug fixes we've added.

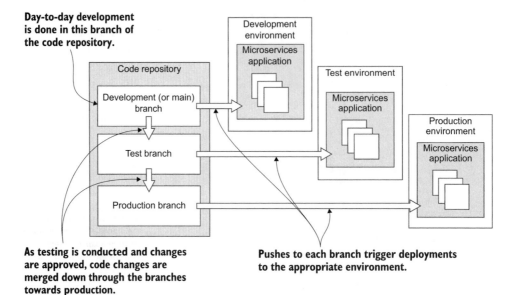

Figure 12.8   Code from development, test, and production branches is automatically deployed to the appropriate environment.

This workflow of moving code through branches can be applied with or without automated testing. It gives plenty of room for manual and exploratory testing and allows managers to make a conscious decision to deploy to production. Of course, automated testing makes this so much better and much more scalable! If an automated test fails at any point in the workflow, the deployment is automatically not allowed. The addition of fast and reliable automated testing means we can safely ramp up our deployment frequency, to the point where many modern companies deploy to production on a daily basis.

Using GitHub Actions, we can easily configure separate CD pipelines for each branch, as indicated in listing 12.4. This particular workflow for the gateway microservice targets the main branch (or development branch), but we can just as easily make additional separate workflows for our other branches (test and production) that deploy this microservice to the different environments.

Listing 12.4   Configuring the branch for a CI/CD pipeline

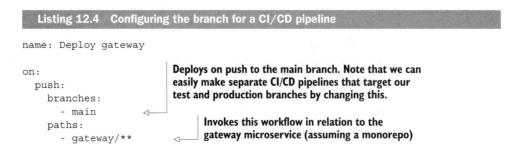

```
workflow_dispatch:
                              ◁――┐  Allows deployment to be invoked manually
jobs:                            │  through the GitHub Actions UI
    --snip—
```

One thing to pay attention to when we implement this multibranch/multi-environment strategy is that each environment needs its own separate Terraform state so that updates to our infrastructure can remember the state of each separate environment. That's tricky, but with a bit of figuring out, we can store our Terraform state in cloud storage (e.g., Azure Storage) and access it by name based on the environment (development, test, or production). That way, we can persist our Terraform state and run Terraform itself in our CI/CD pipeline (updating our infrastructure as we push changes to our Terraform code repository).

12.2.7 *Separating application configuration from microservices configuration*

In this book, we've followed the practice of keeping the configuration for our microservices and our application colocated in the same code repository. By this, I mean that when we push code for a microservice, its CD pipeline will not only build and publish that microservice but also deploy it to our cluster. The configuration of the entire application is spread out across the different code repositories of its microservices. This is a simple and convenient way to work, and it makes deployments easy. But when we try to scale up, we might find this approach too limiting.

An alternative and quite common approach is to create a code repository separate from the code repositories for our microservices that contains the configuration of the application. This *application config* code repository is where we set the version numbers of the microservices currently deployed and the configuration for their environment variables. You can see what this looks like in figure 12.9.

After we make this kind of change, our deployments must now be separated into two phases:

1 The first phase is the CD pipeline for each microservice, which now only builds and publishes that particular microservice.
2 The second phase involves updating the version number of the microservice in the application configuration code repository, and pushing that change invokes its CD pipeline deploying the updated microservices to our cluster.

As you can see, separating our application configuration into another code repository makes our deployment process more complicated. It can also be more error prone—think of what might happen when you update the version number for a microservice but accidently type in an older version instead of the new version number. So don't be too eager to make this change because it can bite you (it will make things more difficult for you) if you don't really need it.

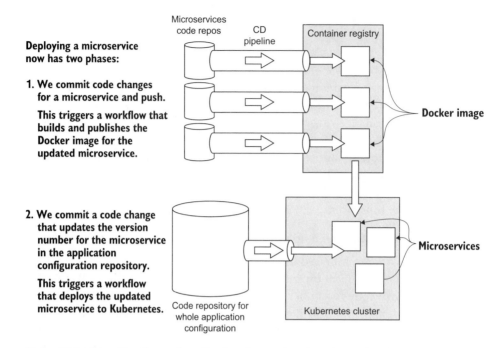

Deploying a microservice
now has two phases:

1. We commit code changes
   for a microservice and push.

   This triggers a workflow that
   builds and publishes the
   Docker image for the
   updated microservice.

2. We commit a code change
   that updates the version
   number for the microservice
   in the application
   configuration repository.

   This triggers a workflow
   that deploys the updated
   microservice to Kubernetes.

Figure 12.9   Separating the configuration for microservices from the application configuration using separate code repositories

But splitting out our application configuration can be useful for a number of reasons:

- Having our application configuration in one place so it's easy to locate
- Seeing the history of application updates in one place
- Having multiple, but separately configured, instances of our application
- Promoting particular versions of microservices from one environment to another (without rebuilding and retesting them)
- Restricting access to the application configuration code repository while still allowing all the developers in our company to access the code (for security and auditing purposes)

12.3 Scaling performance

Not only can we scale microservices applications to larger development teams, we can also scale these up for better performance, giving our application a higher capacity to handle a larger workload.

Using microservices gives us granular control over the performance of our application. We can easily measure the performance of our microservices (e.g., see figure 12.10) to find the ones that are performing poorly, overworked, or overloaded at times of peak demand.

On the other hand, if we were using a monolith instead of microservices, we would have limited control over performance. We could vertically scale the monolith, but

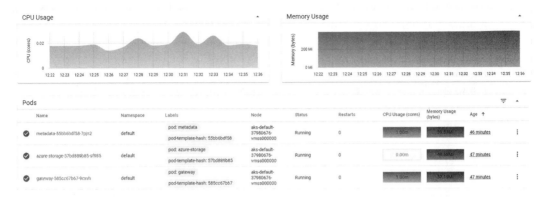

Figure 12.10   Viewing CPU and memory usage for microservices in the Kubernetes dashboard

that's basically it. Horizontally scaling a monolith is much more difficult. And we simply can't independently scale any of the "parts" of a monolith. This is a bad situation because it might only be a small part of the monolith that causes the performance problem. Yet, we would have to vertically scale the entire monolith to fix it! Vertically scaling a large monolith can be an expensive proposition.

Instead, with microservices, we have numerous options for scaling. We can independently fine-tune the performance of small parts of our system to eliminate bottlenecks and to get the right mix of performance outcomes. There are many advanced ways we could tackle performance problems, but in this section, we'll overview the following "easy" techniques for scaling our microservices application:

- Vertically scaling the entire cluster
- Horizontally scaling the entire cluster
- Horizontally scaling individual microservices
- Elastically scaling the entire cluster
- Elastically scaling individual microservices
- Scaling the database

NOTE   I say "easy" but that's only after we took 11 chapters to get to this point!

Scaling often requires risky configuration changes to our cluster. Don't try to make any of these changes directly to a production cluster that your customers or staff are depending on. Later, we'll briefly look at *blue-green deployments*, a technique that helps us manage large infrastructure changes with much less risk.

12.3.1   Vertically scaling the cluster

As we grow our application, we might come to a point where our cluster generally doesn't have enough compute, memory, or storage to run our application. As we add new microservices (or replicate existing microservices for redundancy), we'll eventually max out the nodes in our cluster. (We can monitor this in the Azure Portal or the

Kubernetes dashboard.) At this point, we must increase the total amount of resources available to our cluster. When scaling microservices on a Kubernetes cluster, we can just as easily make use of either vertical or horizontal scaling.

Figure 12.11 shows what vertical scaling looks like for Kubernetes. We scale up our cluster by increasing the size of the virtual machines (VMs) in the node pool. We might start with three small-sized VMs and then increase their size so that we now have three large-sized VMs. We haven't changed the number of VMs; we've just increased their size.

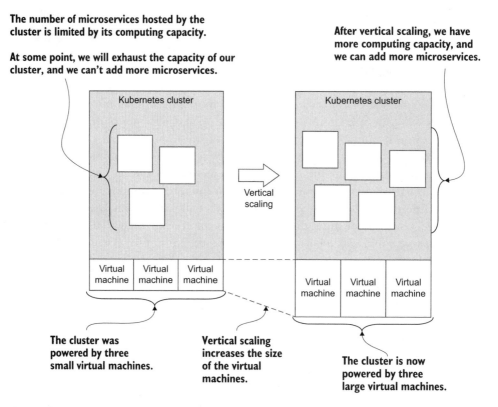

Figure 12.11   Vertically scaling your cluster by increasing the size of the VMs

Using Terraform, shown in listing 12.5, we change the `vm_size` field from `Standard_B2s` to `Standard_B4ms` (see chapter 7, section 7.11.1, for the original setup). This upgrades the size of each VM in our Kubernetes node pool. Instead of two virtual CPUs, we now have four. Memory and hard drive are also increased. You can compare Azure VM sizes for yourself here: http://mng.bz/0lxv.

We still only have a single VM in our cluster, but we've increased the size of it. Scaling our cluster is as simple as a code change. Again, we see the power of infrastructure as code, the technique where we store our infrastructure configuration as code and make changes to our infrastructure through that code. Take care, though: you'll pay for the amount of computing power you use, so a bigger VM will cost you more.

Listing 12.5 Vertically scaling the cluster with Terraform

```
default_node_pool {
  name = "default"
  node_count = 1
  vm_size = "Standard_B4ms"
}
```
Sets a bigger VM for each of the nodes in the cluster

12.3.2 *Horizontally scaling the cluster*

In addition to vertically scaling our cluster, we can also scale it horizontally. Our VMs can remain the same size, but we simply add more of them. By adding more VMs to our cluster, we spread the load of our application across more computers.

Figure 12.12 illustrates how we can take our cluster from three VMs up to six. The size of each VM remains the same, but we gain more computing power by having more VMs.

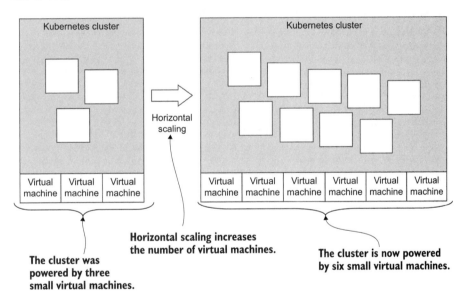

Figure 12.12 Horizontally scaling your cluster by increasing the number of VMs

Listing 12.6 shows the code change to add more VMs to our node pool. Back in listing 12.6, we had `node_count` set to 1, but here we've changed it to 6! Note that we've reverted the `vm_size` field to the smaller size of `Standard_B2ms`.

In this example, we increase the number of VMs, but we keep the same small size for each, although, there is nothing stopping us from increasing both the number and the size of our VMs. Generally, though, we might prefer horizontal scaling because it's less expensive than vertical scaling. That's because using many smaller VMs is usually cheaper than using fewer but bigger and higher-priced VMs. Stay tuned until the end for some tips on how to keep costs down for your microservices application.

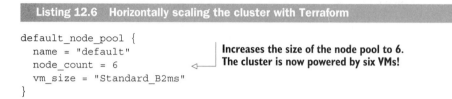

Listing 12.6   Horizontally scaling the cluster with Terraform

```
default_node_pool {
  name = "default"
  node_count = 6
  vm_size = "Standard_B2ms"
}
```

Increases the size of the node pool to 6. The cluster is now powered by six VMs!

12.3.3 *Horizontally scaling an individual microservice*

Assuming our cluster is scaled to an adequate size to host all the microservices with good performance, what do we do when individual microservices become overloaded? The answer is that for any microservice that becomes a performance bottleneck, we can horizontally scale it to distribute its load over multiple instances, as shown in figure 12.13. We're effectively giving more compute, memory, and storage to this particular microservice so that it can handle a bigger workload.

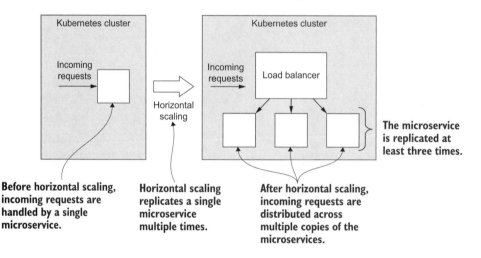

Figure 12.13   Horizontally scaling a microservice by replicating it

Again, we can make this change using code. In fact, we already did this in listing 11.2 from chapter 11. A snippet of the Kubernetes deployment YAML code is repeated again here in listing 12.7.

Here, we set the `replicas` field to 3. In chapter 11, we made this change for redundancy. Having multiple instances means that when any single instance fails, the others can temporarily pick up its load while it restarts. Here, we make the same change to the `replicas` field, but this time for performance reasons. Often, we need to make this change for both reasons. We'd like to have redundancy and good performance, and this is solved by creating replicas of our microservices where necessary.

Listing 12.7 Horizontally scaling a microservice

```
apiVersion: apps/v1
kind: Deployment
metadata:
  name: gateway
spec:
  replicas: 3
  selector:
    matchLabels:
      app: gateway
  template:
    metadata:
      labels:
        app: gateway
    spec:
      --snip--
```

Sets the number of replicas for the microservice to 3. We can now spread the load evenly among three instances of this microservice.

12.3.4 *Elastic scaling for the cluster*

Moving into even more advanced territory, we can now think about *elastic scaling*, where we automatically and dynamically scale our cluster to meet varying levels of demand. At periods of low demand, Kubernetes can automatically deallocate resources that aren't needed. At periods of high demand, it can allocate new resources to meet the increased load. This makes for substantial cost savings because, at any given moment, we only pay for the resources that we need to handle the load on our application at that time.

We can use elastic scaling at the cluster level to automatically grow our cluster when it's nearing its resource limits. Yet again, this is just a code change. Listing 12.8 shows an update to our Terraform code from chapter 7 to enable the Kubernetes autoscaler and set the minimum and maximum size of our node pool. This horizontal scaling works by default, but there are many ways we can customize it. Search for "auto_scaler_profile" in the Terraform documentation to learn more: http://mng.bz/K9YO.

Listing 12.8 Enabling elastic scaling for the cluster with Terraform

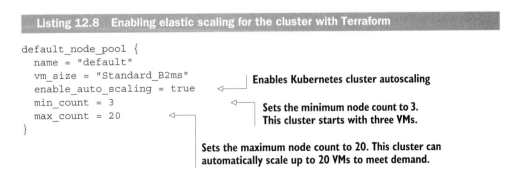

```
default_node_pool {
  name = "default"
  vm_size = "Standard_B2ms"
  enable_auto_scaling = true
  min_count = 3
  max_count = 20
}
```

Enables Kubernetes cluster autoscaling

Sets the minimum node count to 3. This cluster starts with three VMs.

Sets the maximum node count to 20. This cluster can automatically scale up to 20 VMs to meet demand.

12.3.5 *Elastic scaling for an individual microservice*

We can also enable elastic scaling at the individual microservice level. Listing 12.9 is a sample of a Kubernetes resource you can deploy to your cluster to give the gateway microservice a "burstable" capability. The number of replicas for the microservice is expanded and contracted dynamically to meet the varying workload for the microservice (bursts of activity). To learn more about pod autoscaling in Kubernetes, see the Kubernetes docs at http://mng.bz/9Q2r.

Listing 12.9   Enabling elastic scaling for a microservice

```
apiVersion: autoscaling/v2
kind: HorizontalPodAutoscaler
metadata:
  name: gateway
spec:
  scaleTargetRef:
    apiVersion: apps/v1
    kind: Deployment          Sets the range of instances for this microservice.
    name: gateway             It starts at 3 instances and can scale up to 20 to
  minReplicas: 3              meet variable levels of demand.
  maxReplicas: 20
--snip--
```

12.3.6 *Scaling the database*

The last kind of scaling we'll look at is scaling our database. Back in chapter 4, you might remember we talked about the rule that each microservice should have its own database (see section 4.5.4).

There are multiple problems in sharing databases between microservices; one is that it severely limits our scalability. Consider the situation depicted in figure 12.14. We have multiple microservices sharing one database. This is a future scalability nightmare!

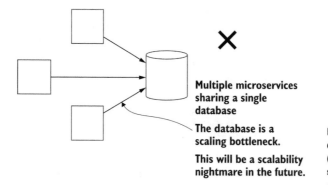

Multiple microservices sharing a single database

The database is a scaling bottleneck.

This will be a scalability nightmare in the future.

Figure 12.14   Why we don't share databases between microservices (except possibly for replicas of the same microservice)

These microservices aren't independent. The shared database is a fixed integration point among these, and it can become a serious performance bottleneck. If microservices share data, they will be tightly coupled. This severely limits our ability to restructure and refactor in the future. By sharing databases, we're hampering our own future ability to address performance problems.

This scenario can completely destroy the "easy" scaling that we've worked so hard to achieve. If we want to structure our application like this, we might as well not be using microservices at all!

Instead, our application should look like figure 12.15. Every microservice has its own separate database. These microservices are independent, which means we can easily apply horizontal scaling if necessary.

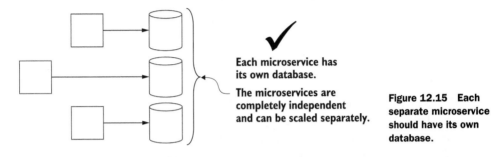

Each microservice has its own database.

The microservices are completely independent and can be scaled separately.

Figure 12.15   Each separate microservice should have its own database.

At this point, I'd like to make it clear that just because we must have separate databases doesn't mean we also require separate database servers. There is a cost to managing database servers, and we usually like to keep that cost down. It's perfectly okay to have a single database server that contains our separate databases, as figure 12.16 illustrates. Having just one database server for your whole application makes it simpler and cheaper to get started with microservices.

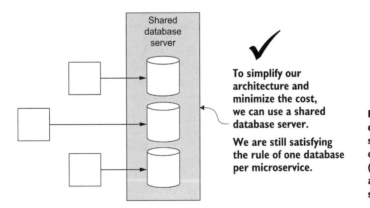

To simplify our architecture and minimize the cost, we can use a shared database server.

We are still satisfying the rule of one database per microservice.

Figure 12.16   It's completely okay to have separate databases running on a shared database server (this is often the simplest and cheapest way to get started).

In the future, if we find that the workload for any particular database has grown too large, we can easily create a new database server and move that database to it, as figure 12.17 shows. When needed, we can create dedicated servers for whichever of our databases need the extra compute, memory, or storage.

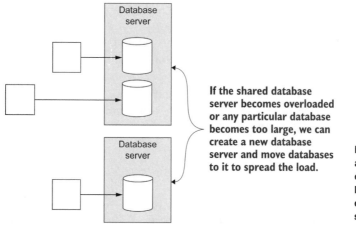

If the shared database server becomes overloaded or any particular database becomes too large, we can create a new database server and move databases to it to spread the load.

Figure 12.17   As our application grows larger, we can scale it by splitting out large databases into their own independent database servers.

Need an even more scalable database? We used MongoDB in this book, and it offers a database-sharding feature (see figure 12.18). This allows us to distribute a single large database over multiple VMs. You might never need this level of scalability. It's only required for extremely large databases, but it's good to know we have this option if we ever need it.

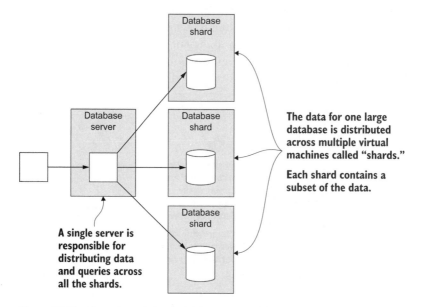

The data for one large database is distributed across multiple virtual machines called "shards."

Each shard contains a subset of the data.

A single server is responsible for distributing data and queries across all the shards.

Figure 12.18   For extremely large databases, we might need MongoDB's sharding feature to distribute a single large database across multiple VMs.

12.3.7 *Don't scale too early*

It's difficult to plan for scaling. We can't easily predict how we might need to scale in the future. The usual outcome in trying to future-proof our application is that we succeed only in the much-maligned overengineering of it. By that, I mean complicating the design and architecture of our application to deal with future possibilities that haven't arrived yet. Usually, we'll get that very wrong and end up making it unnecessarily complicated and more difficult to work with.

This makes it more difficult to add features to our application (slowing down our development velocity) and even makes it harder to scale when later we come to a point where we actually do need to scale—just not in the way we predicted.

So don't be tempted to scale too early because you might actually impede your future scalability rather than accommodate it. It's difficult to predict what's coming in the future: what features we'll need, how our application will be used, and in what ways we'll need to scale it. In the meantime, don't try to scale it; keep it as simple as you can. Having simple code and a simple architecture is the best way to respond to the future when it finally arrives.

12.4 Mitigating problems caused by changes

Part of the reason we're using microservices in the first place is for fault isolation. In the previous chapter, in section 11.4, we talked about various techniques for finding and fixing problems that might show up in our application. Any problem can go unnoticed in our system until conditions align so that the problem manifests itself.

But how do these problems get there in the first place? And can we mitigate against them earlier in the development process (where they are cheaper to deal with and before they cause problems for our customers)?

There are some problems we can't do anything about. There's no predicting when our hardware, network, or cloud provider is going to be unreliable. But many problems happen because our developers push broken code to production. We can aim to catch these problems early, when the code is pushed. Following are some techniques to help you do that.

12.4.1 Automated testing and deployment

Getting frequent application updates safely into the hands of customers is the reason we've automated deployments. With robust CD pipelines in place for our microservices, reliable deployment is something we'll come to take for granted. It will fade into the background as the magic pipeline to our customers, and, if we're lucky, we might even start to forget how it works.

Automated deployment is essential for scaling up with microservices. Automated testing is also very important. As we scale up with microservices, it becomes more difficult to keep up with testing, unless, of course, our testing is automated.

Having automated tests in our CD pipeline provides a gateway to production that can automatically be slammed shut to stop broken code from being deployed to production. If the code doesn't compile or if automated tests fail for a particular microservice, the latest code for that microservice won't be deployed. This is an important protection that can halt bad code in its tracks.

12.4.2 *Branch protection*

One way to stop developers from pushing breaking code changes directly to production is to enable *branch protection* on the production branch of our code repository.

GitHub, for example, can be configured to prevent pushing directly to particular branches. Instead, our developers must submit a pull request that must pass automated tests and be reviewed by one or more other developers before the code change is allowed to be merged into that branch. This creates a useful checkpoint before production where code can be checked for problems before it's foisted on our customers.

You can read more about branch protection for GitHub here: http://mng.bz/j1Ge.

12.4.3 *Deploying to our test environment*

If our developers can't push directly to production, how do they test their code? Of course, they need a testing environment like we discussed in section 12.2.5. Part of our development workflow must include a thorough shakedown of new code in the testing environment before it gets anywhere near production. If we don't have a testing environment, then we simply won't catch the many bugs that only seem to manifest themselves in a production-like environment.

12.4.4 *Rolling updates*

When deploying an update to Kubernetes, we can make use of its *rolling update* feature to tentatively and incrementally deploy new versions of microservices. For example, imagine we have three replicas of our gateway microservice (see chapter 11, section 11.4.4). We want to roll out an updated version of this microservice. First, we replace the first replica with the new version. If that goes well, we move on and replace the second replica. All going well, we eventually replace the third and final replica. We take it slowly and make sure that each new replica works before moving onto the next one. This is a successful rollout.

However, if at any point a problem occurs—say, we notice after replacing the first replica that it starts failing—we can then undo that change (hopefully) without adversely affecting our customers (see chapter 11, section 11.3.1).

Kubernetes can manage this automatically for us, and you can see a simple configuration for the FlixTube gateway microservice in listing 12.10. Using this configuration, new deployments of the gateway microservice will roll out one replica at a time, but only proceeding as each new instance passes its readiness probe (see chapter 11, section 11.2.8). If a new instance fails to become ready, that deployment will halt, and we'll need to debug it and possibly roll back the change (see debugging in chapter 11, section 11.3).

Listing 12.10 Enabling rolling updates for the gateway microservice

```
apiVersion: apps/v1
kind: Deployment
metadata:
```

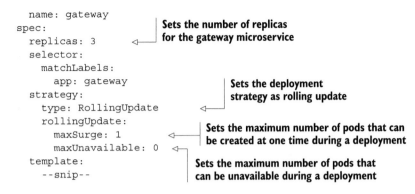

You can read more about rolling updates in the Kubernetes documentation; it's a long read though. Search for "rolling update" in the page to find the relevant parts: http://mng.bz/W1lW.

12.4.5 Blue-green deployments

Making changes to infrastructure is a risky business, and it needs to be well managed. Make a mistake with any of the scaling techniques you've read about in this chapter, and you can bring down your entire cluster. It's best that we don't make these kinds of changes to customer-facing infrastructure, so I'll now present a technique for keeping risky changes like that at arm's length from our customers.

The technique is called *blue-green deployments*. We create two production environments and label them as *blue* and *green* (these labels don't really matter; call them whatever you want). We can easily do this if we parameterize our Terraform code to create different environments distinguished by name (we talked about this in section 12.2.5).

The first environment we create is labeled the *blue* environment. Our customers are using our application via our domain name (e.g., www.company.com). We route them via DNS record to the blue environment. Now, to protect our customers, we'd prefer not to make any risky changes to the blue environment (regular and frequent updates to individual microservices are okay, however, because that doesn't risk any effect on the infrastructure).

To make any risky or experimental changes (e.g., experimenting with scaling), we create a whole new production infrastructure that we label as the *green* environment. Our developers now work in the green environment, so any work they do is separated from the blue environment that our customers use, as shown in figure 12.19.

Once work on the green environment is completed, it's tested, and if it's known to be working well, we can simply switch the domain name system (DNS) record from blue to green.

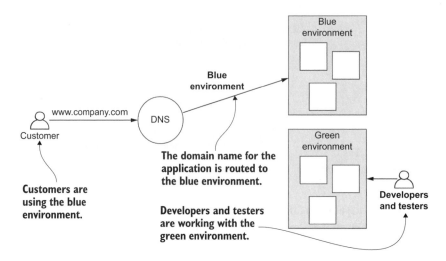

Figure 12.19   Customers use the blue environment, while developers and testers work with the green environment.

Our customers can now use the green environment, and our developers and testers can change over to working with the blue environment, as shown in figure 12.20.

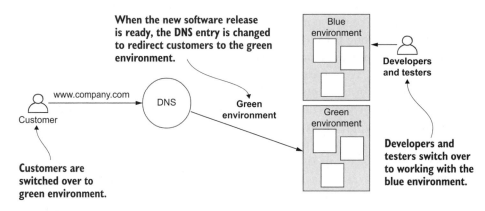

Figure 12.20   When the green environment is ready and tested, customers are switched over to it. Developers and testers then switch to the blue environment and continue working. When the blue environment is ready and tested, customers switch again, and the cycle continues.

Should any problem be discovered with the new green environment, we can simply flip the DNS switch back to the blue environment and restore working functionality for our customers. In the future, we can continue to flip between blue and green environments, thus keeping our customers protected from potentially risky changes to our infrastructure.

This kind of blue-green deployment only really works if we keep our cluster stateless, which I advocated for back in chapter 4 (section 4.4.5). When we keep our data outside our cluster, it means we can seamlessly switch our customers back and forth between different clusters without having to move their data. Keeping our data in a managed database outside the cluster and keeping our customer assets and files in cloud storage is also much safer. If we were copying customer data from cluster to cluster (e.g., when changing from blue to green environments), we would have to be very careful not to lose or corrupt that data. But when the data isn't even in the cluster to begin with, then there's nothing to copy and so no risk to our customer data.

12.5 Basic security

We've briefly talked about security at various points throughout the book. We haven't done it any justice, though, because security is very important—even at the early stages of development—so much so that security really deserves its own book. Well, thankfully, there is a great book on security specifically for microservices: *Microservices Security in Action* by Prabath Siriwardena and Nuwan Dias (Manning, 2020). For now, though, let's understand some of the basics.

Every application needs some level of security. Even if your data isn't sensitive, you don't want anyone to be able to fraudulently modify it. Even if your systems aren't critical, you don't want an attacker to disrupt your system and processes.

We must make effective use of security techniques such as authentication, authorization, and encryption to mitigate against malicious use of our application or data. We might also have to structure our data to protect the privacy and anonymity of our customers according to the regulations in our particular region. FlixTube doesn't have any of this yet, although we've taken some care already with the following:

- *The only microservice exposed to the outside world (and, therefore, exposed to attack) is the gateway microservice.* This is by design! Our internal microservices aren't directly accessible from outside our cluster.

- *Although, initially, we exposed our RabbitMQ server and MongoDB database to the world for early experimentation, we quickly closed those off.* We did this to prevent direct external access to these crucial resources. This is important! Don't expose such critical resources to the outside world unless you're 100% sure they are protected against attack.

In the future, we'd like to upgrade FlixTube with at least the following security features:

- An authentication system at the gateway.
- HTTPS for the connection with our customers. This will encrypt their communications, and using an external service such as Cloudflare means you can get this online quickly.

Of course, the level of security needed by any given application is only as important as the systems and data we're trying to protect. The amount of security we add to FlixTube is going to be much less than the security that's needed by a banking application or government website.

Security has to come from both ends of the organization. Your company should have security policies and a strategy that meets the requirements of the domain and your customers. Then, you and every other developer have a role to play in thinking about and implementing security according to the standards of your company. You should be writing simple, yet secure code. And as with defensive programming (see chapter 11, section 11.4.1), you should adopt a defensive mindset when it comes to security.

First and foremost, when writing code and building microservices, we should ask the following: How would someone attack this system? This primes our mind to proactively address security problems at the time when it can make the most difference: before we're attacked.

12.5.1 *Trust models*

FlixTube's needs are simple enough that we can adopt a security model of *internal trust*, also known as *trust the network* (depicted in figure 12.21). In this model, we do all the authentication at the entry point to the system (the gateway microservice). The microservices within the cluster all trust each other implicitly and rely on the security of the underlying network to protect them from external attack.

The internal trust model is a simple way to get started with microservices. Simple is often better than complicated when it comes to security because simple offers fewer places for security problems to hide. We must be careful when introducing more complex security because any kind of added complexity can actually introduce security loopholes. Ironically, sometimes adding more security makes the security worse, not to mention that it can also degrade the user experience for our customers.

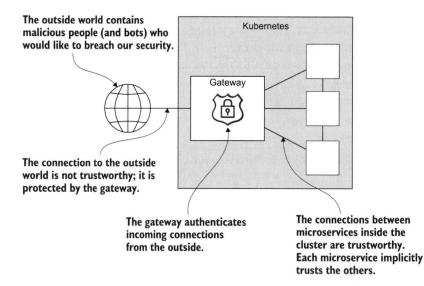

The outside world contains malicious people (and bots) who would like to breach our security.

Kubernetes

Gateway

The connection to the outside world is not trustworthy; it is protected by the gateway.

The gateway authenticates incoming connections from the outside.

The connections between microservices inside the cluster are trustworthy. Each microservice implicitly trusts the others.

Figure 12.21   An internal trust model. Authentication is applied to external requests at the gateway. Internal microservices trust each other and communicate without authentication.

If your security needs are higher than FlixTube's, then the internal trust model might not be enough. This will also be the case if you have multiple clusters and you have microservices that need to communicate across clusters.

A more secure model that you should consider is called *trust nothing* or *zero trust* (depicted in figure 12.22). In the zero trust model, all connections between microservices—both internal and external—are authenticated. Microservices don't automatically trust each other. We're making the assumption that any particular microservice could be hijacked or compromised, especially if the microservice is hosted externally in some other cluster.

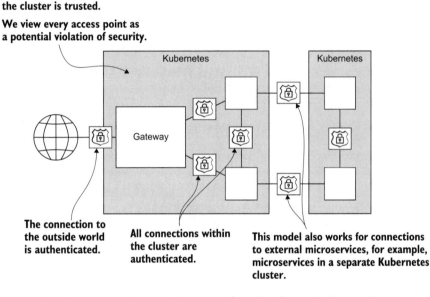

Figure 12.22 A trust-nothing model. All connections, both internal and external, are authenticated. This model supports connections to external microservices.

12.5.2 *Sensitive configuration*

Any application has sensitive configuration data that needs to be protected. You might remember from chapter 8 that we stored various private details (container registry password and Kubernetes authentication) in GitHub secrets alongside our code repository on GitHub (see chapter 8, section 8.9.9).

As we build our application, there will be other passwords, tokens, and API keys that we'll need to store securely. We could store any of this sensitive information in our code, and that would certainly be convenient. But it means that anyone who has or can get access to our code will also have access to operational information that can easily be used to subvert or take down our application.

GitHub secrets (or similar, depending on your CD provider) are a good way to store this information. You might, however, prefer to have a solution that's independent of your source control or CD provider. For that scenario, Kubernetes has its own storage solution for secret configuration. You can read about it here: http://mng.bz/84xD.

If that doesn't suit your needs, there are various other products that can help. As an example, you might like to learn more about Vault, another open source product from HashiCorp (the developers of Terraform). Find out more at www.vaultproject.io/.

12.6 *Refactoring to microservices*

Way back in chapter 1 (section 1.1), I promised that after learning how to build a microservices application from scratch, we'd eventually come back and discuss more on how to refactor an existing monolith to microservices. How we go about converting a monolith will be different in the details for any given monolith. There are so many ways we could go about this, but in this section, I'll leave you with some basic strategies and tactics for conversion that anyone can use.

The basic idea is the same as any development process. As was introduced in chapter 2, section 2.4, it's all about iteration, small and simple changes, and keeping the code working as you go (illustrated in figure 12.23).

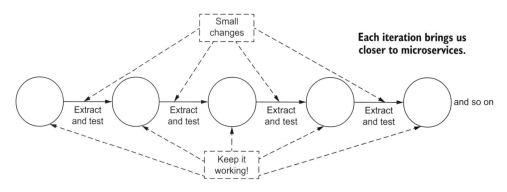

Figure 12.23   Refactoring a monolith to microservices can only be done in an iterative sequence of small and well-tested steps.

Conversion of a monolith is a huge job (depending on the size and complexity of the monolith), and a *big bang* conversion is unlikely to be successful. The only safe way to get to the other side is through small and manageable chunks of work, with extremely thorough testing along the way.

We can't just stop working on the product either. We still have a responsibility to add the features and fix the bugs that are requested by the business. It's also essential that we keep the product working; we can't let problems pile up while we restructure it.

12.6.1 *Do you really need microservices?*

Before you start converting your monolith to microservices, you really need to ask this question: Are microservices really necessary? The conversion to microservices is likely to be long and difficult. It will introduce significant complexity and test the patience and resolve of your development team. Here are a few more questions to consider:

- Is it really worth the cost of doing the conversion?
- Do you really need to scale?
- Do you really need the flexibility of microservices?

These are important questions. Make sure you have good answers.

12.6.2 *Plan your conversion and involve everyone*

You can't simply strike out toward microservices in the dark! To stand the best chance of success, you need a documented vision about what your product will look like when you arrive.

Use domain-driven design to model your business as microservices (see the end of this chapter for a book reference). Aim for a simple architecture. Plan for the immediate future and not for the far-off, uncertain future. Work backward from your architectural vision to what you have now. This is the sequence of changes you must make to convert to microservices. This doesn't have to be planned in detail, but you do need a general idea of where you're going.

We need a plan for what we're building and an idea of how we're going to get there. It has been said that a battle plan never survives contact with the enemy (paraphrased from Helmuth von Moltke, the Elder). Plans always change, but that doesn't mean we don't need a plan. Instead, we should be planning to allow change to occur naturally during the process as we learn more about how our application should be structured. As we move forward, we must revisit and revise and update our plan so that it remains relevant for as long as we're following it.

The conversion plan should be created together with the team (or a subset of representatives) because implementing this conversion will be a shared and difficult exercise. We need to have everyone invested in it.

It's not enough just to have made a plan. Now you must communicate it to the wider company. Make sure the developers know what's expected of them. Communicate with other business departments, describing it in a language that's meaningful to them, so they know why this is taking place and the value it brings. Everyone, absolutely everyone, must understand the high stakes of this operation!

12.6.3 *Know your legacy code*

Before and during the conversion, you should invest significant time getting to know your monolith. Create test plans. Conduct experiments. Understand its failure modes. Develop an idea of what parts of it are going to break through each step of the conversion.

12.6.4 *Improve your automation*

Good automation is crucial to any microservice project. Before and during the conversion, you should be constantly investing in and improving your automation. If you aren't already on top of your infrastructure and automation, you need to start working on it right away (even before starting the conversion!). You might find that changing your company's mindset around automation is actually the most difficult part of this process.

You need reliable and fast automated deployment (see chapter 8). Any features that you convert should either have automated testing already, or you should implement automated testing with good coverage while you're converting the feature to microservices (see chapter 9).

With microservices, you can't get away from automation. If you can't afford to invest in automation, you probably can't afford to convert to microservices.

12.6.5   *Build your microservices platform*

Before the conversion starts, you need a platform on which you can host newly created microservices. You need a production environment to host microservices as these are incrementally extracted from your monolith (see figure 12.24).

In this book, you have the recipe to build one such platform. Create a private container registry, and create your Kubernetes cluster according to either chapter 6 or 7. After creating your first microservice, now create a shared template for your team: a blank microservice that can be the starting point for every other microservice. If you have different types of microservices, create multiple templates, one for each type.

Create your automated testing pipeline, and make it easy for developers to use. Create documentation, examples, and tutorials so your developers can quickly understand how to create and deploy new microservices to your platform.

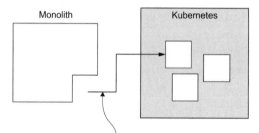

As you extract chunks of functionality from your monolith, instantiate them as microservices in your Kubernetes cluster.

Figure 12.24   Small chunks of your monolith can be incrementally extracted and moved into your Kubernetes cluster.

12.6.6   *Carve along natural seams*

Now look for existing components in your monolith that align with microservices in your architectural vision. These present great opportunities for chunk-by-chunk extraction of components from your monolith to microservices, as figure 12.25 illustrates.

If you struggle to find natural seams, your job will be much more difficult. If your monolith is a *giant ball of mud* or full of *spaghetti code*, you may have to refactor first or refactor during extraction. Either way, it's going to be tricky. To be safe, your refactoring should be supported by automated testing (if necessary, build automated testing along the way). It will get messy—be prepared.

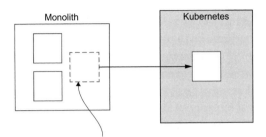

Your monolith will contain components that represent natural seams.

Look for components that are easy to carve out to be separate microservices.

Figure 12.25 A monolith will usually have natural seams. Use these to identify individual components that can be incrementally extracted to microservices.

12.6.7 *Prioritize the extraction*

When deciding the order to convert components to microservices, prioritize those components that would benefit the most from being moved to microservices. It might be because that code is changing more frequently or because there are performance or scalability benefits from extracting that component.

Having these important parts of the monolith extracted early to microservices brings immediate and practical benefits, and you'll start to feel the effect straightaway. This early bang for the buck should make a measurable improvement to your development pace. It will reduce your deployment risk, and it can help you convince others that the conversion is going well.

12.6.8 *And repeat . . .*

By repeatedly extracting small chunks to microservices and testing as you go, you'll safely convert your monolith to a microservices-based application (figure 12.26). It's not going to be easy. It will probably take a long time (multiple years, depending on the size and complexity of your monolith). But it's doable! You just have to keep chipping away at it, one small piece by one small piece, until the job is done.

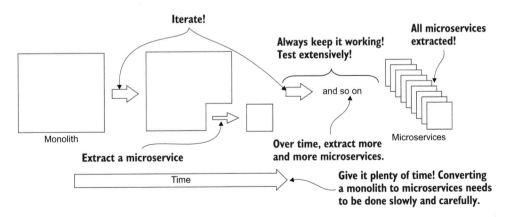

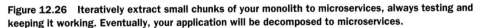

Figure 12.26 Iteratively extract small chunks of your monolith to microservices, always testing and keeping it working. Eventually, your application will be decomposed to microservices.

12.7   *The spectrum of possibilities*

Are you struggling to achieve the high ideals that have been set up around microservices? Usually, when we establish our architectural vision for microservices, we're aiming for what I like to call the *developer's utopia of microservices.* This is the place where we all want to live—if only we could. The only problem is, this isn't always achievable in the real world where the demands from the business and the baggage of the legacy codebase often stomp all over our dreams of a beautiful and elegant architecture. And then, there's the argument raging in the industry about which way is better: monolith or microservices?

Sometimes, I wonder why we bother to argue about it. There's really no such thing as monolith versus microservices. In reality, there is a spectrum of possibilities between monolith and microservices. There is no reason to suppose that any one point on this spectrum is better than any other.

As visualized in figure 12.27, there is a range of options between the monolith and microservices (and continuing on to functions as a service). Who can say which position on this continuum is best for you? Certainly not me. Only you can decide that.

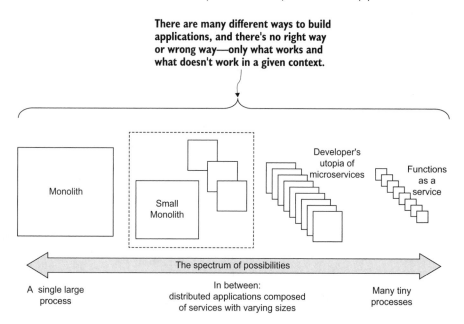

Figure 12.27   **There's no such thing as monolith versus microservices. In reality, there is a spectrum of possibilities.**

12.7.1   *It doesn't have to be perfect*

Don't struggle trying to achieve someone else's idea of perfection. The notion of perfection doesn't even exist—it's just a concept in your mind and you'll find that everyone has a slightly different perception of it. This makes it almost impossible to align a team around perfection. My advice: forget about perfection and just focus on the real, practical needs of the business and your customers.

Of course, we should be trying to move toward a better vision of our application (wherever on the spectrum that might be), but we don't necessarily need to ever reach that end point. It's just something to aim for. But every step along that journey to a better system should be selected to positively affect the team, business, or customers. If, at any time, we find that continuing to press forward isn't delivering the value we expect (or worse, that it's becoming counterproductive), we should stop and reassess what we're doing and why we're doing it.

12.7.2 The diminishing return on investment

You might be surprised to learn that we don't have to push all the way from monolith to microservices to start reaping the rewards on offer from using a distributed architecture. Pushing toward "perfect microservices" has a diminishing return on investment (ROI). You can see the journey illustrated in figure 12.28. At the start, there will be some big wins, but the further along we get in our conversion, the less value we'll get. As we get closer and closer to microservices, the wins will get smaller and smaller. As our services become *too small*, the costs will start to outweigh the benefits.

At some point, it's okay to decide that the big wins are over, that you're happy with the outcome, and you can stop the conversion. You might end up with a smaller monolith and a bunch of microservices—or some other combination along the spectrum—but if that works for you, that's okay. Maybe you decide that you can now leave the system as it is—adding new code either to new microservices or to the smaller monolith as you continue adding features to your application.

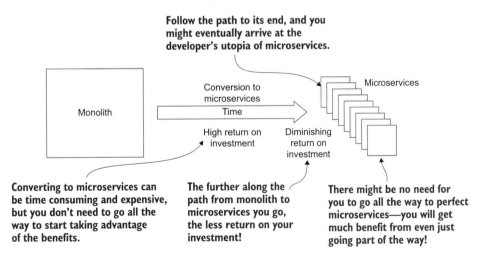

Figure 12.28 A timeline of conversion to microservices. In the early days, you get a high ROI. As you proceed, however, you'll get diminishing ROI, and it might not make sense to go all the way to the developer's utopia of microservices.

We're all aiming for good outcomes for our business and customers, and we shouldn't feel embarrassed at all about what it actually takes to achieve that, however it might look. If it does the job, it does the job. End of story.

12.7.3   *The hybrid approach*

If pushing all the way to a perfect microservices system offers a diminishing ROI, why bother with microservices? Maintaining a microservices architecture in the real world is far from easy. You might think you've architected the perfect system, but as you scale up, it will be touched by the hands of many developers, and you'll probably find it's actually very difficult to keep your architecture conforming to the idealistic vision you had for it.

My advice now, after building many different applications (both monolithic and microservices), is simply to aim for somewhere in the middle of the spectrum. The *hybrid approach* of using a monolith surrounded by a "constellation" of microservices is by far a much easier architecture to achieve and to maintain over time (see figure 12.29).

The hybrid approach is now my default position for new projects when I'm not sure if they will benefit from microservices. A setup like this means that we can move features to microservices when it makes sense to do so, all while keeping the convenience and ease of the monolith for the main body of the code.

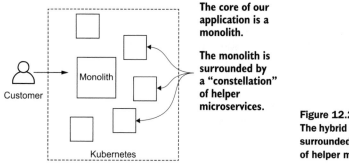

The core of our application is a monolith.

The monolith is surrounded by a "constellation" of helper microservices.

**Figure 12.29
The hybrid approach: a monolith surrounded by a "constellation" of helper microservices**

This architectural model means we can have the best of both worlds. For simplicity, most of our code is in the monolith. But when we want the performance, scalability, flexibility, or fault tolerance of microservices, we can satisfy those needs. Best of all, we don't have to continually beat ourselves up when the reality of our system fails to conform to the developer's utopia of microservices. We can stop worrying about microservices and instead focus on meeting the needs of our customers.

How would I have used this model for FlixTube? I would have put most of the code in the monolith and delegated certain jobs to microservices. Jobs like "compute a thumbnail for a video" or "use machine learning to decide the subject of a video" are a perfect fit for delegation to microservices—those are the kinds of jobs that are sensitive to performance and scalability requirements and it makes a lot of sense to keep them at arm's length from our customers.

12.8 Microservices on a budget

Distributed architectures have always been a useful and powerful way to create complex applications. Microservices are popular now because of the current confluence of cloud technologies, modern tools, and automation. Advances in tooling and technology have made building with microservices simpler and more cost effective than ever before.

But a microservices application is still a complex thing to build. Even though each individual microservice is simple, you might struggle with the complexities of the application as a whole, especially if you're a small team, a solo developer, or a lean startup.

Throughout this book, you've learned various tips and techniques that make it easier to learn and get started with microservices. These will continue to help you in the future, should you need them. I present these insights here, again, in a more concise form:

- *Educate yourself to use modern tools, and make the best use of them!* Rolling your own tools is time consuming, difficult, and a distraction from what you should be doing: delivering features to your customers.
- *Start with a single code repository (a monorepo) with multiple CD pipelines (one for each microservice).* Later, when you've separated out multiple code repositories, create one or more meta-repos to bring these back together (as outlined earlier in section 12.2.4).
- *Use a single database server that hosts one database per microservice.* You can still satisfy the rule of one database per microservice, but hosting those databases on a single server makes it easier for you to manage and cheaper to run.
- *Create a Kubernetes cluster with a single VM.* Create only a single instance for each microservice (no replicas). In the beginning, you probably don't need redundancy or performance. This helps keep costs down.
- *Make a simple CD pipeline for each microservice that deploys it directly to your cluster.* Use separate production and testing branches if you need to deploy to a testing environment before deploying to your customer-facing environment.
- *There is no need to have a code repository for your application configuration that is separate from the code repositories for your microservices unless you really need the flexibility of that approach.* When you separate your application configuration from the configuration of your microservices, it makes your deployment process much more complicated (refer to section 12.2.7).
- *Use external file storage and an external database server, making your cluster effectively stateless.* This lowers the risk for experimenting with your cluster. You might break your clusters, but you won't lose your data. It also supports blue-green deployments, presented earlier (refer to section 12.4.5).
- *Use Docker Compose to simulate your application on your development computer for development and testing.* Employ live reload for fast development iterations.
- *In the early days, you might not need automated testing, but it's essential for building a large, maintainable microservices application.* When building a minimal viable product

(MVP) for a startup, however, you don't need it. It's too early in the product's life-cycle to make such a big commitment to infrastructure. We must prove our product before we can invest in the more advanced infrastructure!

- *You might not have automated testing, but you still need to test!* Set up for efficient and reliable manual testing. You need a script to quickly start your application on a development computer, from nothing to a testable state, in a short period of time. You can use Docker Compose and database fixtures to achieve this.

- *Docker makes it easy to deploy third-party images to containers running in your cluster.* That's how we deployed RabbitMQ in chapter 5. You can find many other useful images on DockerHub: https://hub.docker.com/.

- *Invest early in your automation, especially automated deployment.* You'll rely on this every working day, so make sure it works well.

12.9   *From simple beginnings . . .*

Just look at how far we've come together! Figure 12.30 shows the journey we have taken. We started by creating a single microservice. Then, you learned how to package and publish it using Docker. You learned how to develop and test multiple microservices on your development computer using Docker Compose. Ultimately, you created a production environment in the cloud on Kubernetes and deployed your microservices application to it. Complexity management is at the heart of modern development. That's why we invest time learning advanced architectural patterns like microservices.

What a great journey this has been! But I'm sad to say that our time together has come to an end. Your journey will continue, of course, and I wish you all the best in building your own complex applications with microservices.

Please join the mailing list at www.bootstrapping-microservices.com for future news about this book and related content.

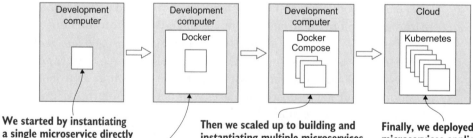

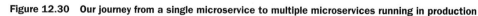

Figure 12.30   Our journey from a single microservice to multiple microservices running in production

12.10 *Continue your learning*

For one final time, let's finish the chapter with some references to books that will help you learn more and carry your understanding and knowledge forward. To learn more about domain-driven design, read the original book on it:

- *Domain-Driven Design* by Eric Evans (Addison-Wesley, 2003)

If you don't have much time, you can find a good summary in the free e-book, *Domain Driven Design Quickly* by Abel Avram and Floyd Marinescu (InfoQ, 2018), available here: http://mng.bz/E9pR

To better understand security for microservices, read this book:

- *Microservices Security in Action* by Prabath Siriwardena and Nuwan Dias (Manning, 2020)

To learn more details on theory, design, and development with microservices, pick any of these books:

- *Designing Microservices* by S. Ramesh (Manning, est. Spring 2024)
- *The Tao of Microservices*, 2nd ed., by Richard Rodger (Manning, est. Spring 2024)
- *Microservices Patterns* by Chris Richardson (Manning, 2018)
- *Microservices in Action* by Morgan Bruce and Paulo A. Pereira (Manning, 2018)
- *Microservices in .NET Core*, 2nd ed., by Christian Horsdal Gammelgaard (Manning, 2021)
- *Spring Microservices in Action*, 2nd ed., by John Carnell and Illary Huaylupo Sánchez (Manning, 2021)
- *Microservice APIs with Python* by José Haro Peralta (Manning, 2022)

Summary

- Microservices can be scaled up to larger and multiple development teams by
  - Putting each microservice in its own code repository
  - Ensuring that each microservice has a separate CD pipeline for an independent deployment schedule
- We can create a meta-repo (a composite repository constructed from separate code repositories) to bring separate code repositories into a convenient and cohesive whole.
- Through a small refactor of our Terraform infrastructure code, we use it to easily create separate environments, or instances of our application, so that we can have a production environment for our customers that is separate from the environment we use for testing new code changes.
- We can control deployments to production by creating a workflow where developers must merge their code changes through one or more branches. These merge points are opportunities to review and test the code before it's inflicted on our customers.

- We can configure our CD pipeline to automatically deploy to particular environments; for example, we discussed a strategy where when we push to the *test* branch of our code, it deploys to the *test* environment, and when we push to the *production* branch, it deploys to the *production* environment.
- There are multiple ways we can scale up with microservices to meet the demands of a growing customer base:
  - *Vertically scaling the cluster*—We can increase the size of each VM in the cluster.
  - *Horizontally scaling the cluster*—We can increase the number of VMs that power our cluster.
  - *Horizontally scaling a microservice*—We can increase the number of instances (replicas) for microservices that need more CPU power or more throughput.
  - *Elastically scaling the cluster*—We can configure our cluster to automatically scale up and down the number of VMs that power it depending on the demand currently placed on it.
  - *Elastically scaling a microservice*—We can configure each microservice to automatically scale up and down its number of instances depending on the demand currently placed on it.
  - *Scaling the database*—Keeping to the rule "one database per microservice" is the key to scaling our database in the future. If we need extra performance from our database, we can scale it vertically or horizontally.
- There are various strategies that can help prevent problems from affecting our customers:
  - Making use of reliable automated testing and deployments
  - Enabling branch protection to put a review and testing checkpoint in front of developers pushing changes to the production branch
  - Testing in the test environment before merging changes to production
  - Using Kubernetes' rolling updates feature to safely roll out changes to microservices
  - Using blue-green deployments to more safely make risky changes and restructuring to our application and its infrastructure
- Security for microservices is as important as for any application, if not more so, given that a microservice application might have more than one publicly accessible gateway.
- We can employ security techniques such as authentication and authorization to protect access to our system.
- Refactoring from a monolith to microservices can only be accomplished through a series of small and well-tested steps.
- There's no such thing as monolith versus microservices; in reality, we have a spectrum of possibilities to choose from.
- A good default position is to be somewhere in the middle of the spectrum—what I like to call the *hybrid approach*: a monolith for most of the codebase that is

surrounded by a constellation of microservices. This gives us the best of both worlds: the convenience and simplicity of the monolith most of the time, and the flexibility and scalability of microservices when we need those.

- There are many ways we can make microservices more affordable and less complex when we're starting out. This makes microservices an effective and efficient starting point for startups, small teams, and solo developers.

index

Kubernetes in Action, Second Edition
by Marko Lukša and Kevin Conner

ISBN 9781617297618
1017 pages *(estimated)*, $69.99
Fall 2024 *(estimated)*

Terraform in Action
by Scott Winkler

ISBN 9781617296895
408 pages, $49.99
May 2021

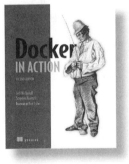

Docker in Action, Second Edition
by Jeff Nickoloff and Stephen Kuenzli
Foreword by Bret Fisher

ISBN 9781617294761
336 pages, $49.99
October 2019

Microservices Patterns
by Chris Richardson

ISBN 9781617294549
520 pages, $49.99
October 2018

For ordering information, go to www.manning.com

MANNING

A new online reading experience

liveBook, our online reading platform, adds a new dimension to your Manning books, with features that make reading, learning, and sharing easier than ever. A liveBook version of your book is included FREE with every Manning book.

This next generation book platform is more than an online reader. It's packed with unique features to upgrade and enhance your learning experience.

- Add your own notes and bookmarks
- One-click code copy
- Learn from other readers in the discussion forum
- Audio recordings and interactive exercises
- Read all your purchased Manning content in any browser, anytime, anywhere

As an added bonus, you can search every Manning book and video in liveBook—even ones you don't yet own. Open any liveBook, and you'll be able to browse the content and read anything you like.*

Find out more at www.manning.com/livebook-program.

*Open reading is limited to 10 minutes per book daily